Law's Promise, Law's Expression

Law's Promise, Law's Expression

Visions of Power in the Politics of
Race, Gender, and Religion

Kenneth L. Karst

Yale University Press
New Haven and London

Designed by Jill Breitbarth and set in Palatino type by
Keystone Typesetting, Inc., Orwigsburg, Pennsylvania.
Printed in the United States of America by Vail-Ballou
Press, Binghamton, New York.

Library of Congress Cataloging-in-Publication Data

Karst, Kenneth L.
Law's promise, law's expression : visions of power in the
politics of race, gender, and religion / Kenneth L. Karst.
p.   cm.
Includes bibliographical references and index.
ISBN 0-300-05760-1 (cloth)
        0-300-06507-8 (pbk.)
1. Civil rights—United States.   2. Equality before the
law—United States.   3. Social movements—United
States.   4. Law and politics.   I. Title.
KF4750.K37   1994
342.73'085—dc20   [347.30285]   93–36591   CIP

A catalogue record for this book is available from the
British Library.

The paper in this book meets the guidelines for
permanence and durability of the Committee on
Production Guidelines for Book Longevity of the Council
on Library Resources.

10   9   8   7   6   5   4   3   2

To Glinda/Peter Pan/Cinderella
and
all the members of her supporting cast

Contents

Preface

The power of law was a notable preoccupation of the "social issues agenda" of Presidents Ronald Reagan and George Bush. Given the agenda's apparent effectiveness in presidential campaigns through 1988, there was little surprise in 1992 when some politicians turned the volume even louder: "We are America. These other people are not America."[1] That strategy proved counterproductive, but even now parts of the social issues agenda retain power. From its earliest uses, antedating President Reagan's election by some two decades, the agenda has promoted a politics centered on the status of social groups. The target audiences have been voters who have felt left out, even threatened, by various social changes following the upheavals of the 1960s and 1970s: the secularization of the state and the successes of the civil rights movement, the women's movement, and the gay rights movement. In seeking to weld these voters into a nationwide constituency, the promoters of the social issues agenda have promised to use the power of government, and particularly the power of law, to restore major parts of an earlier day's social order.

A considerable literature explores the clash of cultures and the role of the social issues in national politics.[2] Here I offer an extended essay on these themes, placing law in the foreground of discussion. Most of the social issues agenda has been an agenda for law reform—or, in some instances, for a more vigorous enforcement of existing law. For the agenda's intended audiences, much of the promise of law lies in its perceived potential for governing the expression of public values—not just the power of law to regulate expression, but the expressive power of law itself.

In this book I do not offer an explanation of the rise of the political right, or a model of American politics in the 1980s; my aim is interpretive, not scientific. Nor do I offer a generalized theory about American political culture. My focus is narrower: on the social issues agenda as a set of promises to deploy law in the service of cultural counterrevolution. The promises were addressed to social groups that were seen— accurately—to include many potential swing voters. It is these groups that I shall call the constituency for cultural counterrevolution.

The heart of the book considers the social issues agenda for law, particularly constitutional law, in the fields of race, gender, and religion. Our main focus in these chapters (3 through 6) will be the interaction of law with that political agenda. One persistent theme is an ideology of masculinity. Not all of the social issues agenda evokes the anxieties of manhood; schoolhouse religion, for example, is an exception. Still, those anxieties are a principal target of the agenda, not only as it touches issues of gender (the status of women, or the status of gay men and lesbians) but also as it touches issues of race. Bracketing the four central chapters are two of introduction and one of conclusion. We begin by looking at the role of law in the genesis of the social issues agenda and at some of the techniques for using the symbols of law and government to mobilize a national political constituency around the social issues. The final chapter centers on the responses of the courts to the social issues agenda's legislative products.

The most important developments in our constitutional law in the last generation, including those dealing with issues of race and gender, have accompanied larger transformations in American society and in the politics generated by those transformations. Admitting all that, it remains true that changes in our constitutional law—and specifically the Supreme Court's decisions in such celebrated cases as *Brown v. Board of Education* and *Roe v. Wade*—have had their own acculturating effects. This book highlights the important role our courts can play in making and preserving a national community in a society of many cultures.

The main doctrinal foundation for analysis of constitutional issues throughout the book is the principle of equal citizenship. That principle presumptively insists that every individual is entitled to be treated by the organized society as a respected and responsible participant. Stated negatively, the principle presumptively forbids the organized society to stigmatize an individual as a member of an inferior or dependent caste, or as a nonparticipant. I traced the origins of the equal citizenship principle, and its partial vindication in modern constitutional law, in my book *Belonging to America: Equal Citizenship and the Constitution* (1989). I shall not repeat that analysis here, but will take the principle as a doctrinal starting point. In chapter 7 I argue that judicial review of governmental action in the social-issues contexts of race, gender, sexuality, and religion should focus not so much on "procedural" questions (such as the representative or deliberative qualities of the legislative process) as on substantive concerns—specifically, concerns for the full inclusion of all Americans as equal citizens.

I am grateful for the invitations that allowed me to present some of these ideas in lectures at the law schools of the University of Illinois, the University of California, Davis, and UCLA. Longer versions of these lectures have appeared as articles, parts of which are scattered throughout this book.[3] For their careful readings of a draft and for their perceptive comments, I am indebted to Alex Aleinikoff, Akhil Amar, Alison Grey Anderson, Julian Eule, Catherine Hancock, Joel Handler, Lynne Henderson, Leonard Levy, Greg Tanaka, and Jon Varat. John Covell of Yale University Press has encouraged this project from the beginning and provided crucial help in making it a reality. Harry Haskell, my amiable and skillful editor at the Press, made our collaboration a pleasure. For research assistance, I thank the UCLA Law Library's incomparable research librarians and Genie Gifford, Lorien Kranen, Judith London, and Charlotte Robinson Maya. My thanks also to Dean Susan Westerberg Prager and the UCLA School of Law for the sabbatical leave that allowed me to complete much of the manuscript. I had the great good fortune to spend that semester in residence at the Department of Political Science of the University of Hawaii at Hilo; I am grateful to Prof. A. Didrick Castberg and his colleagues for making my stay so rewarding, both professionally and personally. The book's dedication also expresses thanks, and more than thanks.

When I began this project in the late 1980s, I was prepared to take the long view. High on the list of political priorities of the Justice Department and the White House staff had been the appointment of federal judges, including Justices, who were thought to be "safe" on the social issues. It strained even my considerable capacity for optimism[4] to expect the federal judiciary in its late-1980s incarnation to give the Constitution's guarantee of equal citizenship a generous reception. Yet even then this book did not seem an exercise in fantasy. I could remember my own law school days, when the Vinson Court was in flower. In 1951 few observers would have predicted the result in *Brown*, and even fewer would have anticipated that the Court would recognize a constitutional right to control such intimate decisions as contraception or abortion.

Looking at demographic trends in American society, and looking at trends in the political uses of issues such as abortion, it seemed plain even in the late 1980s that America's historic cultural dynamism had not abated. True, the 1992 presidential election seemed to be influenced only marginally by the social issues, and more centrally by the anemia of the national economy. Yet, as I suggest in chapter 7, even before the election the nation seemed to be turning some corners, not only in the politics of the social issues but in our constitutional jurisprudence.

As long as America is culturally divided, American politics will continue to reflect those divisions. So the story of "social issues" will never end. Even as I am "closing the book" in the summer of 1993, two clusters of gay rights issues are stirring the waters of politics: the treatment of gay and lesbian members of the armed services, and proposed ballot initiatives to disable various state and local governments from prohibiting discrimination on the basis of sexual orientation. Both of these subjects have already reached the courts. As this book goes to press, however, neither set of issues has been definitively resolved—nor is it certain that either will be resolved in court. Any resolution, legislative or judicial, lasting or temporary, will gratify some Americans and leave others discontented. For people on all sides of these and other social issues, I offer this remark attributed to Orson Welles: "If you want a happy ending, that depends, of course, on where you stop your story."

1

Imposing Order: Law and the Origins of the Social Issues Agenda

Imagine James Madison's reaction if someone had predicted in 1789 that one day presidential candidates would make special efforts to communicate their views on the enforcement of state and local criminal law, the power of a state to forbid a woman to have an abortion, and the lawfulness of officially sponsored prayer in local public schools. In raising these issues in the 1988 and 1992 campaigns, President Bush renewed his support for the "social issues agenda" of President Reagan's administration.[1] That agenda looked toward a return to an earlier era's dominant attitudes about the place of religion in public life and about "family values," a cluster of traditional beliefs concerning marriage and family, the roles of men and women, and sexuality. Two complementary themes, dating from President Nixon's "Southern strategy" two decades earlier, rounded out the social issues agenda: distance from the civil rights movement and toughness toward crime. From the beginning the agenda's most publicized aims have included nullifying some Supreme Court decisions of the 1960s and 1970s, and by the 1990s the agenda remained largely addressed to the state of American law. But the political appeal of these policies lies deeper than any specific concerns about the state of the law concerning official religion, family values, race, or crime. The subtext of the social issues agenda was—and is—cultural counterrevolution.

The agenda was designed to create a political constituency out of identifiable groups of voters, and all the social issues are strongly associated with the status of social groups. That association may be positive or negative. In the language of political managers, a "target group" is the intended audience for a message, but the metaphor of targeting reminds us that the messages of status politics also serve purposes that are more sinister. Because they touch the emotions, the social issues lend themselves to the sort of imagery, especially the vivid imagery of

1

television, that gladdens the heart of a political media consultant. To its
intended audience, the imagery typically has pictured the candidate as
one of Us, and—more to the point—has depicted enemies who threat-
en the group, and suggested that the candidate will use the powers of
law to save Us from Them.

THE PROMISE OF ORDER
AND THE POWER OF EXPRESSION

All four themes of the social issues agenda have been attuned to
a profound disquiet felt by a number of Americans in the face of cultural
changes that took on high visibility during the two decades that preceded President Reagan's election in 1980. To mobilize these citizens the
agenda has offered a politics of nostalgia, a promise to impose Order on
a society that the members of particular constituencies believe to be
riven by Disorder.[2]

The Order to be imposed is not the absence of conflict; it is the old
social Order, the traditional rank-ordering of groups in society. This sort
of Order is imposed, in two senses. Most obviously, people in positions
of power maintain their version of Order by imposing it, through law
and by other means, on those who occupy positions of lesser status.
More generally, as I emphasize by capitalizing the word, the status
Order exists as a construct that human minds impose on the raw stuff of
society.

In this latter sense, of course, even our understanding of the natural
order is something we impose on our experience of an environment that
would otherwise seem chaotic.[3] Failure in this effort leads to—indeed,
is—madness. In infancy we learn how the symbols that order our experience are connected to our ability to maintain our places in the world.
When the one-year-old points at a round object and says, "ball"—a
label adults have imposed on her understanding of what she sees—she
is, in turn, asserting a kind of control over the object. She is learning
that expression is power.

In imposing Order on society, too, expression is power. Expression
draws the boundaries that divide us into groups, with momentous
effects on our individual identities. If you doubt the power of expression, ask yourself what meanings come to mind when someone you
don't know is identified as black, or gay, or a woman—and then ask
yourself where those meanings came from. The answer is easy: Any

social group's status finds its definition in expression, both private and public. In defining meanings in our public life, no form of expression is more powerful than the law.

Cultural counterrevolution, then, is primarily a contest for influence among social groups over dominance of expression in public, a contest over the meanings attributed to behavior.[4] When a political candidate promises to use the power of government to restore Order in the area of "family values," he is not just advocating particular changes in the law, or endorsing the traditional morals of the white middle class. He is also consciously taking a position in a series of group status conflicts. The Order he promises exists mainly in the minds of his audience; it is the renewed predominance of a series of traditional images: of marriage and family, of the roles of men and women, and of sexual morality.

Let us begin with a snapshot dated 1952. In the background stands a little house, one of a row of little houses in a suburb. In the foreground is the white family that lives in the house: the father, who earns the family's living; the mother, who tends the house and the children; and the two children who will soon go to school. Add the dog and the car, and imagine the redwood picnic table and the barbecue in the backyard, and you have the picture. If you are over the age of thirty and white, and your parents were of the middle class, you have your own picture of the house's interior; the chances are good that you used to live there.

Nevertheless, this picture in the "family values" album obscures much of the reality of American life, even in 1952. First, many millions of Americans are missing: rural white families; nonwhite families, both rural and urban; gay and lesbian couples; two–wage-earner families; single mothers; the poor. It is an understatement to say that the politics of nostalgia in recent years has not been designed to appeal to people of these descriptions. In the Order promised by the social issues agenda, outsiders have been expected to adjust their lives to approximate the image in the snapshot. Some outsiders simply lack the wherewithal to make any such adjustment. Others, who might be able to adjust, choose not to do so; instead, they claim the right of inclusion as equal citizens even as they retain their identities.

Our 1952 snapshot may be misleading even as to the people in the picture. Was there sex outside marriage, for example? Consider the couple in the snapshot. They had been high school sweethearts, but during the war, before they were married, he was overseas and she was in college. Were they celibate during that long separation? How would we ever know? Sex, either inside or outside marriage, was largely invisible.[5] We do know that if the young woman became pregnant, and the option of abortion was unavailable, her parents would help her to hide her pregnancy. She would go away, on what was explained as a "visit," to have the baby and place the child with an adoption agency. Her husband-to-be, of course, was expected by his service mates to demonstrate his manhood in a variety of ways, some of which were nothing to write home about. In public, however, America's traditional images of "family values" had little visible competition.

The generation that came to adulthood during the Great Depression had emerged from World War II in search of security. With the aid of the GI Bill, many of them had bought houses like the one in our snapshot, and many had gone to college. Among the people missing from the snapshot, however, fewer could take advantage of those benefits. The war had looked as though it might work a major transformation of American society. Women, both married and single, had been working in factories. New job opportunities had produced a second great migration of black people from the rural South to the cities of the North and West. White generals, under pressure from Washington, had finally pronounced black soldiers to be fit for combat duty. Gay and lesbian Americans by the hundreds of thousands had discovered each other in the services and in the cities where service personnel gathered. At war's end, however, women were told that their duty was to leave the factories and make room for men; black Americans—veterans or not—learned, the hard way, about the durability of racial discrimination; and lesbians and gay men mostly stayed in the closet. The legal underpinnings of the old status Order remained largely unchanged, and on the surface of American society the war's transformative power seemed to have dissipated.

Under the surface, though, important social changes were building. The Supreme Court's 1954 decision in *Brown v. Board of Education*[6] both symbolized and accelerated the changes.[7] During the next decade, as black Americans pressed their claims to equal citizenship, others joined their cause, including many young white college students from the North and West who went south to help mobilize black voters. When these students returned home, they formed the nuclei for a "new politics" that burst into high visibility in the mid-1960s. By the end of the decade, with the civil rights experience as the most prominent model, the modern women's movement and the gay liberation movement had begun.

The wider social convulsion that came to be called "the movement" of the 1960s was not a political party, not even a coherent ideology, but an aggregate of diverse critical beliefs and heterodox behavior centered in the youth culture of America's postwar generation. Above all, the movement was a variegated collection of insurgent messages. Some of the messages were pure protest: opposition to the Vietnam War and the military draft. Other messages combined protest and affirmation: racial justice, equality for women, sexual freedom. Still other messages were harder to classify, but unmistakably rejected the dominant world view among the white Americans who had found their security in corporate suburbia. In part, the movement was a mutiny against reigning moral and legal codes that the challengers saw as hypocritical and repressive. Even in its overtly political manifestations, the movement "took root primarily at the level of sensibility in a largely personal revolt against postwar American society and culture."[8]

The active participants in this upheaval, from the "heads and seekers"[9] to the practitioners of the new politics, looked forward to an emancipation of their own identities and to a more inclusive, more cohesive community. They saw these individual and social goals as intertwined: "The personal is political." Some young people sought to return to Nature, expressing their search for a new authenticity in long hair, overalls, or the blues. Others, hoping to escape the shackles of linear Reason, sought a new and higher consciousness in chemicals, Eastern mysticism, or acid rock. Observing the scene, Daniel Bell perceived a shift "from the Protestant ethic to the psychedelic bazaar."[10] Nearly all the flower children were searching for a spiritual communion they had missed in their parents' world. For some, even the claim to sexual freedom was not merely self-indulgence, but part of an alternative morality associated with the quest for authenticity and awareness. In the eyes of sympathizers and skeptics alike, the movement's varied messages seemed an eruption of Nature from below the crust of Reason.

The members of some social groups—notably the vanguard of the women's movement and members of minorities identified by race, ethnicity, religion, or sexual orientation—heard these messages as the voice of liberation. For some other listeners, however, the same messages tapped into deep-seated anxieties. In the dominant cultural view, women and black people had long been associated with Nature, as opposed to Culture; with wildness, as opposed to civilization. Uncivilized Nature must be controlled, not only in the unreasoning Other, but in oneself.[11] The idea of sexual liberation, of course, could be seen to threaten self-control at the very center of the self. The suburbs looked at the flower children with the special loathing engendered by desire.

A culture is a community of meaning and morality, the matrix of the sense of self. Many citizens, viewing the challenge to dominant cultural patterns as "an attack on reason itself,"[12] feared the imminent degeneration of the only communities and the only identities they had. The insurgent messages implied not just a preference for modern over traditional views of society, but a cultural challenge that promised to revise the nation's public morality—and, not incidentally, to change the status ordering of groups in America.[13] If the existing Order should collapse, what rough beast might rise from the rubble?[14]

When the Vietnam War ended, the political and cultural tides turned, and by the mid-1970s the main interest of the movement was historical. Yet, a notable egalitarian reordering of American society was well under way. Given the historic role of law in maintaining the subordination of groups, the reshaping of that law had been a necessary and prominent part of the transition. The "color line," long fundamental to most Americans' conception of social status, had been eradicated in some arenas of public life and blurred in most of the others. The gender line, fundamental to a conception of family and society that many believed to be ordained by God, had become blurred in two ways. First, with the aid of new laws and court decisions, women by the millions were entering territories previously reserved to men. Second—and not unrelated to the success of the women's movement—sexual freedom had broadened considerably. The gay rights movement had acquired a visibility that would have been unimaginable a generation earlier. The older moral propriety had kept sex out of sight; now, in public, it was a constant presence. Once, religion's place in the nation's public life had been accurately portrayed by Justice David Brewer's 1904 lecture series "The United States a Christian Nation." Now the Supreme Court had accepted the argument of religious outsiders that officially sponsored prayer and Bible reading in the public schools were unconstitutional.

In political and legal terms, these changes augured the inclusion of a number of new groups of Americans as full participants. In cultural terms, the changes marked a new tolerance, a widening of the range of acceptable beliefs and behavior. In all, it was a cultural revolution, and the revolutionaries had seized the transmitters.

Cultural difference alone does not make a clash of cultures. Much that was represented by the 1960s movement recalled earlier critical vocabularies. Pacifism, free love, derision for the striving middle class—all were familiar to the generations that had read H. L. Mencken, Sinclair Lewis, and Jack Kerouac, with little umbrage taken. In America's "segmented society," one time-tested response of the dominant culture to cultural difference has been avoidance: if you don't see it, it won't vex you.[15] The perspective of the earlier social critics could be summed up in a turn-of-the-century English aphorism: Do anything you like, "as long as you don't do it in the street and frighten the horses."[16] But now large numbers of young people—glaringly including sons and daughters of the white middle class—were doing their thing in the streets, dramatically rejecting cultural patterns that were part of their parents' self-definition. The equation is a familiar one: deep cultural challenge + high visibility = conflict. A clash of cultures is a struggle over expressive dominance.

For some people, notably working-class white men, the egalitarian changes wrought by the civil rights movement and the women's movement have seemed to threaten economic interests. But the target audiences for the social issues agenda have also included substantial numbers of Americans, including middle-class Christian conservatives, whose jobs were secure and whose incomes were rising. Many of these citizens have felt little or no status anxiety, but have supported part or all of the social issues agenda for reasons mainly located in religious belief.[17] Although the constituency for cultural counterrevolution has not been sharply confined by the boundaries of race or religion or geography or social class, undoubtedly the constituency's largest numbers have been found among evangelical or fundamentalist Protestants[18] and practicing Catholics; among people of middle age or older; among people with limited formal education; among people with lower income in both white-collar and blue-collar occupations; and in the South.[19] The other side of this coin is the charge that the rising tide of secularism in the 1960s and the early abortion rights movement expressed elite biases.[20]

In any case, the electoral appeal of Presidents Reagan and Bush extended well beyond the concerns identified in the social issues agenda. In the aggregate, the voters who elected those two Presidents expressed not only their repudiation of "the values of the sixties" but also their interests, such as preferences for limited government and reduced taxes. Even in the area of "values," the issues were not focused solely on race, gender, or religion. For example, many voters were concerned about what they saw as a decline of national military power and national pride in the aftermath of the Vietnam War.[21] Finally, interests and values came together for many voters in their skepticism about the governing capacity of "liberals" whom they saw as "out of touch"—particularly including the practitioners of behavioral science.[22]

And yet, one important reason why this cluster of disparate groups could be welded into a political alliance was that the groups' members shared concerns that were not merely economic but cultural. The nation's identity—who "we" were as a nation—seemed to be moving under their feet, and the tremors called into question not just the authority of traditional values but the individual identities bound up with those values. In offering to discipline what these Americans saw as moral chaos, the social issues agenda also offered them the hope that they could maintain their traditional places in the pecking orders of American society. For two decades the authors of the agenda sought to exploit these anxieties, promising to impose Order by invoking the power of government and the authority of law.[23] Because the political aspect of a clash of cultures is a contest over public meanings, the law is a natural focus of contention, as the community's definitive expression of those meanings. It is this function that makes law, in Thurman Arnold's words, "a great reservoir of emotionally important social symbols."[24]

LAW, EXPRESSION, AND THE STATUS OF GROUPS

Some of the most important cultural redefinitions of the 1960s and 1970s were accelerated by decisions of the Supreme Court. Here is a list of leading subjects of the conservative social issues agenda. Enter any of these political arenas, and you will find that the Court has left its imprint: race relations; crime control; men's and women's social roles; marriage and divorce; contraception and abortion; illegitimacy; religion in the public schools; financial aid to religious schools. If the Court has become a focus for political energies generated by emotion, the reason is that the Constitution's applications to these subjects are seen to symbolize aspects of our self-identification.

The politics of cultural counterrevolution began well before 1970, as politicians mobilized voters by attacking the decisions of the Warren Court on school desegregation, criminal justice, and school prayers.[25] The Burger Court's 1973 abortion rights decision may or may not have increased the counterrevolutionaries' numbers, but surely it added intensity to a growing cultural antagonism.[26] If the 1960s movement saw the Warren Court as its pillar of strength and the early supporters of cultural counterrevolution saw the Court as demon in chief, in the 1980s their successor constituencies looked upon a reconstituted Court and saw images that had traded places. All these pictures are caricatures, minimizing countercurrents within the Court. No doubt, too, the pictures magnify the Court's role in American life, and sometimes even overestimate its role in American law. Yet it would be fatuous to deny that the Warren Court was a strong contributor to the process that redrew the nation's cultural map, or that the Court in the 1980s was far more responsive to the social issues agenda.

In some areas of cultural redefinition the Supreme Court of the 1960s and early 1970s seemed to play a crucial catalytic role—as with its decisions on racial equality. In other areas the Court seemed, in the main, to be moving with the social current—as with its decisions on women's equality and on issues touching sexuality and its expression. Sometimes the Court justified its decisions by offering expansive interpretations to acts of Congress, particularly the civil rights acts.[27] More often, it struck down laws and other governmental action in the name of the Constitution's guarantees of equality, liberty, or religious freedom. But if the Court's legal explanations ranged over a wide field, in another perspective its behavior had a sharper focus. In case after case the Court's rulings validated the claims of historically subordinated social groups who were insisting on their rights to equal citizenship. Given the entrenchment of existing inequalities, the idea of status equality for social groups was not neutral; it threatened those who stood to lose their status advantages. Equal citizenship is a general principle, but validation of the principle meant that, in the conflict of cultures, the Court had taken sides.

Considering the breadth of the cultural and political changes that burst into high visibility in the 1960s, it is impossible to isolate the details of the social mechanisms by which the Court's decisions might have influenced those changes, let alone to measure that influence. At a more abstract level, though, we can identify some of the ways in which the Court lent its support to egalitarian changes in the social Order— and so helped set the stage for the cultural counterrevolution.

To speak of the status of a social group is to use a deceptively simple term to encapsulate millions of diverse states of mind. A group's status in American society, like any other cultural creation, is an amalgam of the meanings that Americans assign to membership in the group. The Supreme Court's contributions to cultural redefinition in the 1960s and early 1970s took two main forms. First, the Court held that some attributions of meaning to group membership—for example, assumptions about white supremacy[28] or about women's natural dependency[29]— were out of bounds for government. To fill the void thus created, the Court offered its own substitute meanings. In the name of the Constitution the Justices authoritatively declared that women and the members of racial, ethnic, and religious minorities were entitled to the rights of equal citizenship. Second, the Court's decisions effectively destroyed some of the instruments of group subordination: laws and other governmental practices that had kept black Americans (or women, or other groups) "in their place" and out of public life. With the restrictions removed, many of those citizens became active and visible participants in their communities, and that behavior, in turn, contributed new meanings to our civic culture. When official racial segregation came to an end, the sight of black citizens exercising their rights of access was a lesson for all of us, reinforcing the ideal that American citizenship comes in only one class.

Recognizing the power of expression, the Supreme Court also promoted the values of equal citizenship by two indirect means, both centered on the expression that shapes the definition of group status. First, the Court dealt with government's own expression, holding, for example, that official prayers in the public schools violated the First Amendment's prohibition against an establishment of religion.[30] Given that expression is power, it is not surprising that a politics targeted on status anxiety has featured the display of cultural icons, the affirmation of traditional values, and the portrayal of enemies. Labeling and silencing are indispensable means of group domination, and often are accomplished with the aid of law. Just as surely, however, freedom of expression is crucial to a group's liberation from subordinate status. The Supreme Court's second indirect contribution to group status equality was embodied in a series of decisions expanding the freedom of expression, safeguarding the self-liberating speech of historically subordinated groups.

America has always been a nation of many peoples, and throughout our history the most insistent demands for legal suppression of speech typically have arisen out of conflicts at our cultural boundaries. When the expression of a subordinated group challenges a dominant community of meaning, passions are bound to be inflamed. Consider the civil rights movement in the 1960s. Not only were its messages disturbing to the South's established Order of racial status, but its distinctive expressive methods—its provocative sit-ins and freedom rides, its clamorous demonstrations, its agitating marches—were foreign to the vision of freedom of expression then prevailing in First Amendment doctrine. In that vision, citizens sat around a table, deliberating and exchanging views with the utmost civility, reasoning together toward the civic truth that would decide public issues.[31]

A freedom of expression centered on civic deliberation and the speech of Reason might be apt for a polity in which nearly all major values were shared and disagreements mainly concerned ways and means. If this vision retains plausibility today as a picture of the First Amendment's core, surely the explanation is that American society has always included communities of this kind, and nearly all of us have witnessed civic discussions in the deliberative mode. But we have also witnessed public debate of quite a different kind. If yesterday's television images showed us the freedom marchers in Selma and the angry crowds who shouted at black students entering Little Rock's Central High School, today's images include the young women who enter family planning clinics and the anti-abortion demonstrators who shout at them. Political expression at the cultural boundaries typically is not deliberative, and often is not civil.

If you assume that freedom of speech is designed for civic discussion in the speech of Reason, you may find it easy to conclude that Unreason should be controlled or silenced by law.[32] And what kinds of expression do we consign to the category of Unreason? Of course: (i) speech that rejects the common sense of what "we all know," where "we" are those who share the conventional wisdom and morality;[33] and (ii) modes of expression—from silent sit-ins to noisy demonstrations—that go against the dominant cultural grain. Ignoring that our own perspectives *are* perspectives,[34] "we" simply think of them as neutral and abstract Reason. I have capitalized Reason and Unreason to emphasize that I am referring to constructs of the mind, mostly maintained by insiders, mostly with the effects of preserving a community's existing boundaries and continuing the exclusion of those currently defined as outsiders.

An interpretation limiting the First Amendment's protection to the speech of Reason and the mode of civic deliberation would poorly serve the needs of a multicultural society.

The civic speech of Reason is a thin layer that has crystallized atop the vast pool of a dominant culture's "cultural unconscious"[35]—the very condition that causes us to treat deviations from "normal discourse"[36] as irresponsible, perverse, irrational. Mostly, we use the speech of Reason to announce and defend choices we have made in a process in which Reason has played a minor role. Mostly, too, we apprehend our culture in ways that have little to do with articulated Reason.[37] Because our definitions of Reason, like our definitions of Order, are culturally based, they, too, are subject to the stresses of status anxiety. Members of the groups that resort to law for the purpose of maintaining Order—that is, preserving their favored status positions—do not see the clash of cultures as a competition between different brands of Reason. After all, their dominance has allowed them to define what counts as a reason, and thus to say who will be regarded as reasonable and deserving of a voice.[38] They see their cultural challengers not only as the authors of Disorder but as the embodiment of an Unreason that must be suppressed. So, an officially defined Reason not only grows out of the prevailing Order of status dominance but reinforces it as well.

As we shall see in chapter 3 when we inquire into the expressive aspects of law in relation to gender and sexuality, and in chapter 4 when we look at race relations from a similar perspective, the suppression of Unreason is rooted in the same anxieties about self-definition that generate efforts at group domination: men's fear of the feminine, whites' fear of "the blackness within,"[39] heterosexuals' anxieties about sexual orientation. Historically, all these fears have been associated with the fear of sexuality. It is no accident that the 1960s, a period of sexual "revolution," also saw the acceleration of movements of political and cultural challenge that sought major redefinitions of America's social boundaries. Nor, considering that culture is the matrix for individual identity, is it any accident that today both the law and the politics of cultural counterrevolution not only resist compromise but resist resolution.

The recent history of abortion regulation, for example, illustrates what Isaac Newton might have called the Third Law of Cultural Politics: Every legal change perceived to affect the status ordering of groups provokes an opposite legal reaction, a resort to legislation and litigation aimed at harnessing the law and turning it in a different direction. The hopes and fears evoked by the social issues agenda tend to polarize both citizens and the politicians who mobilize constituencies. Although the social issues often do implicate interests in the classical sense—the distribution of money or of jobs—their emotional centers lie in cultural symbols. To the extent that law and government officially endorse the values of a cultural group as the "true" American values, the members of that group can feel justified in claiming the status of "true" Americans. Those who seek to alter these symbolic uses of law and government cannot realistically expect to secure a position of status dominance, simply trading places with the groups that have subordinated them in the past. Their main status goal is more modest: to establish themselves as full members of the community, as equal citizens. Yet, every important step they take toward that goal encounters resistance. This is an old story in America, typified by the active opposition of many Southern whites, well into the 1970s, to the legal changes that were dismantling the Jim Crow system of subordination. This generation's cultural counterrevolutionaries have behaved in much the same way as their predecessors in earlier times: those who once resisted the integration of Catholics, for example, or those who have opposed successive waves of the movement for women's equality. In such a political environment a contest over the symbolic uses of law and government—either to maintain the existing Order of status dominance or to undermine it—will be a zero-sum game, in which every status gain for one side implies a status loss for the other.

This setting is ripe for what James Madison called the tyranny of "faction." Madison recognized the likelihood that particular factions might achieve dominance in state and local governments. He believed, however, that the framers of the proposed Constitution had devised structures that would minimize the risk of factional dominance in the national government. In the Congress, for example, the presence of many factions would require the formation of coalitions, with the composition of the majority shifting from one issue to the next.[40] Chapter 2 shows how cultural politics since 1980 has produced not only the nationalization of "factions" centered on the social issues but an increasingly polarized alignment on those issues. Madison's hopes for the national government have become harder and harder to realize. At the state and local levels, however, his fears of factional domination have been amply justified, with the polarizing effects of the social issues playing a leading role.

It may be true, as a general proposition about the social issues, that "public discourse is more polarized than the American public itself."[41] The example often cited is the abortion issue, about which Americans typically have mixed feelings, supporting women's right of choice but believing it is all right for government to place some obstacles in the path of "abortion on demand." It is possible for government to translate those mixed feelings into law, with the courts' constitutional blessing.[42] Nonetheless, there is no escaping polarization when an issue is seen as part of a contest over status dominance. Examples abound; here I merely list a few questions about law that have tended to polarize state and local politics, reserving fuller discussion of all these issues for later chapters.

Local proposals to offer same-sex couples a formal legal status approximating marriage are both supported and opposed primarily because of their expressive aspects as symbols of governmental acceptance of gay and lesbian relationships. There is no middle ground in this status conflict; it presents an either/or choice. A similar expressive, community-defining function is served by official display of the symbols of religion. Similarly, although a state law restricting access to abortion touches gravely important material interests of individual women, such a law also has its expressive, community-defining aspects and its uses in ordering the status of social groups. Symbol and substance are intertwined in all these issues, and any views government may express are likely to offend someone's deeply held values.

For all the state and local issues in this sampling, parallel issues can be found at the level of the national government. The polarizing influence of these legislative issues is not just a side-effect of the centralization of power in Washington, but the product of a political strategy. The entire social issues agenda promotes a large-scale zero-sum game of status dominance, centered on the expressive apparatus of government. The agenda is not just a response to the passions of cultural division; it is designed to keep those passions inflamed, to assure that a struggle over factional dominance and subordination will be a central and long-lasting feature of national politics. During President Nixon's administration, Vice President Spiro Agnew urged a strategy of "positive polarization" that would "divide on authentic lines," and the young Patrick Buchanan's advice to the President was, "Cut . . . the country in half; my view is that we would have far the larger half."[43] The strategy was famously successful for two decades—and seemed to backfire only in 1992, when the same Patrick Buchanan made the same message of division the centerpiece of an inflammatory speech to the Republican national convention. In the next chapter, as we explore the social issues agenda's uses and techniques in further detail, we strike a rich vein of irony: The authors of the agenda are the same people who regularly exhort us to be true to the vision of the framers of the Constitution.

2

Law and Status Politics
in the Theater State

Although the constituents of cultural counterrevolution and the managers of the social issues agenda respond to each other, they are not identical, any more than a horse is identical with its rider. Where the constituents have looked to reestablish a traditional social Order and the dominance of traditional cultural norms, the managers have looked to maintain the dominance of a political faction. Where the constituents have envisioned the end of status anxiety in a successful conclusion to a cultural struggle, the managers have been content to prolong the struggle—and the anxiety that can produce votes and contributions—indefinitely. In these ways the social issues follow the time-tested pattern of American politics: conditions are defined as "problems" for politics by operatives who seek the spoils of power.[1] One striking feature of the politics of cultural counterrevolution is the degree to which constituents and political managers alike have concentrated on gaining control over the means of public expression.[2]

THE SOCIAL ISSUES AND THE
SYMBOLS OF GOVERNMENT

We have seen how the social issues agenda for law and government is designed to appeal to Americans who feel displaced, or left out. Some of the disaffected groups are large. Evangelical and fundamentalist Christians, for example, are anything but a splinter group. In the early 1980s weekly broadcasts by television evangelists were said to reach 40 percent of the nation's households.[3] True, that estimate was made before some of those spiritual leaders became famous for more fleshly pursuits, but even in 1988 white evangelicals were estimated to comprise nearly 20 percent of the voters in the presidential election.[4] Despite their numbers, these citizens see themselves as a minority that

16

a secularized polity has belittled—or, worse, ignored. One reason is that they are underrepresented in the "mainstream" expressive apparatus that plays so important a part in defining public meanings: the public schools, the large daily newspapers, the broadcast networks, the most prominent universities.[5] Not only are these institutions centers of communications; many of them are centers for the allocation of prestige. If a main focus of the politics of cultural status is expression itself, the explanation is that many of the constituents of cultural counterrevolution see expression as one of the main prizes of political victory. Undoubtedly, the promoters of the social issues agenda, like all political managers, have their eyes on the capture of government's distributive and coercive powers. When those managers translate impulses toward cultural counterrevolution into a set of "problems" for politics, however, they are mobilizing voters around the capture of government's expressive capacity, including the expression embodied in law.

One definition of culture is the assignment of meaning to behavior.[6] Because we articulate the meanings that define and redefine our culture not only through speaking and writing but also through our day-to-day conduct in public, every social situation provides the makings of diverse explanations, diverse meanings.[7] These choices among potential meanings are especially obvious in our political life. Candidates for office turn to the social issues not only to reach particular constituencies, but also because other kinds of legislative issues are more complex—not just harder to explain, but harder to understand and resolve. Should we reconsider the deregulation of the airlines? severely limit the emission of "greenhouse" gases into the air? restrict imports of foreign-made automobiles? commence a new assault on poverty? Questions like these mostly lead not to quick answers but to hosts of other questions. They are not "hot-button" issues, for they lack drama. In part, an electoral strategy emphasizing the social issues commends itself because the medium dictates the message. You can't transmit any coherent position on the imbalance in foreign trade in a thirty-second television announcement, but you can send a powerful message about crime—and its political correlative, race—by showing a picture of Willie Horton. In the age of television, group-status politics is not just emotion-laden; it is also cost-efficient.

The habits of political image making take on a life of their own. In the era of the "permanent campaign," what begins as a style of electioneering becomes a style of governing.[8] Posturing about values, after all, is easier than asking your constituents to make the sacrifices necessary if we are ever going to face up to the trade imbalance or the budget deficit. (Perhaps it was not entirely accidental that the 1980s were not just the decade of the social issues but also a decade of debt.) Some elected officials promote the values of cultural counterrevolution not by getting laws enacted but by using their offices as platforms for expressing those values. Their supporters are not naive; they know, in the context of cultural redefinition, that lip service really serves.

More generally, capturing government is prized because government itself is an all-pervading medium of public communication. Government uses the power of the purse to subsidize some messages and withhold support from others,[9] and every day not just public schools but innumerable public agencies at all levels engage in instruction and advocacy, both explicit and implicit. The main purpose of conducting official prayers in public school classrooms would not be to give children a chance to pray. As Justice John Paul Stevens remarked when the Supreme Court struck down an Alabama law requiring a "moment of silence for meditation or voluntary prayer" in public schools, a child who is inclined to pray has plenty of opportunity to do so during the school day.[10] Rather, the point of the law is the state's official stamp of approval—of one Christian sect, of Christianity in general, of monotheism, or of prayer or religion in general.

If government in modern America often appears to be a theater state,[11] the reason is that myth and ritual and symbol are crucially important instruments in the definition and redefinition of a culture.[12] The media consultants who design political ads for television understand the importance of imagery in capturing the viewers' attention and obtaining the emotional response that will imprint a message on their minds. But words, too, have their mythical, "magical" uses, not just the word-imagery of metaphor but the narratives that create word-pictures.[13] The symbolic messages of status politics are readily conveyed by the oldest medium of all, the political speech, for they are easily reduced to caricatures that will fit into the listeners' accumulated store of myths and devils.

Here is an excerpt from a speech by Sen. Jesse Helms during his 1990 reelection campaign in North Carolina: "Think about it. Homosexuals and lesbians, disgusting people marching in our streets demanding all sorts of things, including the right to marry each other. How do you like them apples? Isn't our obligation, yours and mine, to get up and do some demanding of our own? What about the rights of human beings, born and unborn? What about the rights of women who want to stay in the home doing the most important job there is—raising our children?"[14] Notice all the references to "rights." The senator understands that the state of the law on these subjects is of great concern to his supporters. They may not articulate their sense that the law expresses something important about the meanings of America—and thus about their own place in the world—but Senator Helms understands those feelings and plays on them. His words carry an emotional punch for at least two reasons. In several rapid-fire references to legal rights, the senator evokes the fear that the traditional gender line is being eroded. At the same time he reinforces the listeners' sense of identity, inviting them to define themselves by contrast with an abstract and threatening image of Otherness. The lines are clearly drawn, with a faceless group as the enemy: It is "our" obligation to stand up to "disgusting people," to deny their assertions of rights and to claim rights of our own. Good and Evil; Us and Them; as the senator says, think about it.

The construction of enemies is an old technique, with roots deep in the dirt of political history.[15] The most effective modes of today's status politics feed on the same fear and greed that powered yesterday's less sophisticated politics of anti-Catholicism, anti-Semitism, nativism, and racism. A vague, abstract symbol, either of "our" group or of the Other, can stand for a wide range of referents, and for a correspondingly wide range of possible political actions—indeed, it can stand for a whole world view and a whole sense of self. One result is that a particular legislative proposal may be supported or opposed because it is seen as a symbol of those larger identity-defining values.

An example is the bill, adopted by Congress in 1989 but vetoed by President Bush, to provide federal funding for abortions to indigent women who are the victims of rape or incest.[16] Standing alone, this proposal had appeal for a considerable number of Americans who otherwise described themselves as "pro-life," including President Bush himself.[17] But arguments about slippery slopes are as common among politicians as they are among lawyers, and the opponents of this funding proposal successfully linked it to the more general question of the President's identification with the pro-life cause. Status politics has a way of doing just that: influencing people to dig in, to resist compromise, to treat each of the social issues as a zero-sum game: Good or Evil; Us or Them.

The most vivid image in the quoted excerpt from Senator Helms's speech was the picture of lesbians and gay men marching in the streets. What particularly disgusted the senator, apparently, was not that some Americans might have homosexual identities, but that they should openly declare them and yet insist on legal rights that would legitimize those identities. The contest between the senator and the gay rights marchers is, more than anything else, a struggle for the power that inheres in expression. The issue of the "right to marry," more carefully stated, is the question whether gay or lesbian couples should be allowed to create domestic partnerships, formal unions with marriage-like contractual and property consequences. Important material concerns would be implicated by the establishment of such a status; one example among many is health insurance for an employee's partner. Yet even without this status the gay couple can make a contract, or hold property in joint tenancy. And if the law should be passed, a citizen (for example, Senator Helms) who finds a marriage-like status for gay couples "disgusting" need not enter one. As we shall see in chapter 3, what matters most, on both sides of the issue, is the state's official expression, recognizing the couple as a couple.

The struggle over expressive dominance can also take the form of efforts to use law to limit or silence someone else's expression. In the debates over legislation restricting pornography and racist speech, all sides invoke the rhetoric of "silencing."[18] But another method of controlling expression is to regulate behavior that has little to do with "speech" in its traditional definitions. Jim Crow laws and the social practices they regulated were, among other things, a system of expression. A major part of the abortion rights controversy is a contest over public symbols about sexuality. If the managers of electoral campaigns see the social issues largely as political theater, the reason is that the clash of cultures is a clash of symbols.

THE SOCIAL ISSUES AND THE NATIONALIZATION OF "FACTIONS"

The program offered by the social issues agenda can be used by politicians at all levels of American government. What is striking— what would perhaps surprise James Madison most of all—is the way political issues focused on sex and gender, long assumed to be the province of local communities, have become national. The change has two dimensions. First, the social issues are present in every region of the country. Second, the same issues regularly present themselves to the Congress, to the executive branch, and to the federal courts. The first development is part of a more general nationalizing of communications, and thus of American culture; increasingly, locally dominant cultures have had to confront national cultural norms. The second development is part of the centralization of governmental power; increasingly, national legal and political norms have been imposed on those who dominate local politics. Together, these two trends have produced what we now recognize as a fact of American life: intensified cultural conflict, pursued in a national political arena and creating national constituencies.

There is something new in seeing so many of these morality plays performed on a national stage, but the center of gravity of American politics had moved to Washington well before today's social issues arrived.[19] In the nation's early days, a considerable proportion of political power was decentralized—as John Jay attested in 1795 by resigning as Chief Justice of the United States to become governor of New York. With the centralization of government came the centralization of power.[20] By the middle of the twentieth century most major political issues had become, irreversibly, issues for the national government. In 1953, when Earl Warren resigned as governor of California to become Chief Justice of the United States, his move reflected not only a nationalizing trend but a new importance for the Supreme Court. We have seen how the cultural counterrevolution got its start in the politics of resistance to the decisions of the Warren and Burger Courts on school segregation, criminal justice, school prayers, and abortion.

Although the social issues agenda is closely attuned to the importance of the white South in presidential politics,[21] the agenda has also been addressed to working-class whites, many of them Catholics, who identify themselves as members of ethnic groups of eastern and southern European origin. These voters are to be found all over the country, but their political importance as swing voters has been centered in the cities of the Northeast, from Chicago to Newark.[22] The political rise of Christian fundamentalism is also a nationwide development, with a significance in keeping with the fundamentalists' numbers. In the 1970s evangelists who were broadcasting on national television discovered a way to make their medium interactive, allowing viewers who phoned the studios not just to pledge money but to pray with the people who took their calls[23]—an innovation that sharply increased the evangelists' audiences.[24] Although the nationally prominent preachers rarely use their broadcasts to endorse candidates, their messages have been more overtly political when they have turned to legal issues such as school prayer or gay rights.[25] Where the "mainline" Protestant denominations[26] tend to lack cohesiveness on issues concerning sexuality and the roles of women, the positions of the conservative Protestant sects and of the hierarchy of the Catholic church have been more clearly defined.[27] That relative clarity has aided political operatives seeking to mobilize scattered voters into national political factions.

Huge numbers of Americans, no doubt including most readers of this book, have their names on nationwide mailing lists of groups whose reason for being is status politics. Direct-mail advertising, carefully targeted to recipients already identified as supporters of particular causes, grew spectacularly from the 1970s on, and played an especially important role in the nationwide mobilization of the new Christian right.[28] This newer version of cultural politics alters the emphasis of political expression. Typically, the recipient of a message about sex education in the schools, or about abortion funding, is invited not only to do something (support a cause, vote for a candidate) but also to be someone—to make a commitment, an acknowledgment of self-identification. The appeal of this invitation lies in the awareness of the importance of law as an expression of the values of a community. Nothing is better calculated to persuade the letter's recipient to identify with a political group than a request for aid in reforming the law to express his or her own values.

As liberal groups such as Common Cause also know, computerized direct-mail techniques do, indeed, permit the rapid nationwide mobilization of letter writing to legislative representatives; on some issues (school prayer, abortion, the Equal Rights Amendment), it is possible to get mailings of this kind into the hands of millions of Americans.[29] The interactive technique works here, too. Even solicitations of money frequently are cast as invitations to "send a message" to Washington. Indeed, the new technology of mailgrams and phone banks permits the overnight mobilization of thousands of "personal" messages from constituents to officeholders.[30] For many of the constituents who respond by telephoning or writing to their representatives, or by "voting" in straw polls, or by contributing money, expression is not just an instrument for achieving some policy goal; it is also an end in itself. Whether or not their preferred candidates or measures succeed, their participation allows the constituents to believe that their values count for something in the polity's decisional process.[31] For people who feel that their values have been ignored—by a males-only Senate Judiciary Committee, or by a secularized "cultural elite"—participation may be its own reward.

Early in the heyday of the new right, Richard Viguerie said, "[Liberals] think of direct mail as fundraising. They miss the whole boat if they think that. It is a form of advertising. . . . It's a way of mobilizing our people; it's a way of communicating with our people; and it marshals our people."[32] On their television screens and in their mailboxes, these voters find regular reminders that they are a nationwide constituency whose voices are being heard. This group political consciousness, and the substantive preferences it represents, have for some time been identifiable as aspects of "a major cultural movement," a counterrevolution of national scope.[33]

Increasingly, the messages of this social issues populism have come to flow from the constituents to the specialists in constituent mobilization. As a result, each passing year has found political operatives on all sides better able to fashion nationwide political appeals, tailored to their audiences' established preferences. In the realms of religion and sex and gender, the appeals have made heavy use of emotion-laden symbols. When the intended audience consists of conservative Protestants, the Bible is an especially powerful symbol, but it is by no means the only one; Senator Helms's word-cartoon of the gay rights marchers is another such symbol. The basic tactic of direct-mail political advertising—not just by the new right, but across the whole political spectrum—is an appeal to fear.[34]

Today many a candidate's main goal is to project a personality, and in seeking to do so many turn naturally to social issues focused on the community-defining functions of law.[35] Sidney Blumenthal's comment about the new media-centered politics is of special pertinence when we think of the politics of religion, sex, and gender, or the politics of race and crime:

The [political] consultant must stimulate the public's wish fulfillment for the candidate through manipulation of symbols and images, enticing voters to believe that the candidate can satisfy their needs. The relationship of dreams to reality is analogous to the relationship between advertising and politics. Ads are condensed images of wish fulfillment. Political commercials are sometimes made to be deliberately irrational in order to reach voters on other than a conscious plane. Image-making, no matter how manipulative, doesn't replace reality; it becomes part of it. Images are not unreal simply because they are manufactured. Comprehending this new image-making is essential to understanding modern politics.[36]

As the media specialists know, nightmares about impending doom are every bit as effective as dreams of wish-fulfillment. Whatever else they may do, today's practitioners of a nationwide cultural politics traffic in manufactured images of enemies who are scary.

THE SOCIAL ISSUES, THE CONGRESS, AND THE PRESIDENT

Each time the Supreme Court strikes down a state law on constitutional grounds, it substitutes a uniform national principle of law for a diversity of state rules.[37] Any item on the social issues agenda that responds to the Court's decisions is necessarily a national issue, to be pressed not only in the courts but in the executive and legislative branches of the federal government. Apart from the making of judicial appointments, both the President and members of Congress are regularly called upon to stand up and be counted on the social issues. In the theater of politics, of course, standing up and being counted have importance, whether or not the gestures will have any direct effect on anyone's behavior.

The issue of abortion rights, for example, repeatedly gives the President and Congress occasion to take a stand. The attempt to overturn the Supreme Court's 1973 decision in *Roe v. Wade*[38] by constitutional amendment was doomed from the beginning; yet President Reagan and some members of Congress correctly saw the various amendment proposals as a series of opportunities to associate themselves with the pro-life movement. Senator Helms's "human life" bill,[39] declaring that human life begins at conception—assuming it were enacted and then interpreted to have some effect beyond expressing Congress's opinion—almost certainly would have been unconstitutional; yet it provided media exposure for the issue and for the bill's sponsor.

The posturing of politicians is by no means the whole story. There are material consequences of some of the action Congress takes in the field of abortion rights, and even graver consequences of what Congress chooses not to do. Particularly important are its decisions on federal funding, not just for abortion procedures for poor women, but for family planning counseling, overseas aid to health and population control programs, and domestic medical research. In any of these contests in Congress the pro-life forces have had one major advantage in the inertial drag of the legislative process: it is generally easier to block legislation than to pass it.

That rule of thumb took on new force in the congressional politics of the 1980s. As particularistic interest groups of all kinds rapidly increased in number and effectiveness, they were joined by religious groups. Between 1950 and 1985 the number of major religious lobbies in Washington grew from sixteen to at least eighty.[40] The lobbyists are in the national capital not merely because they seek to influence Congress and the executive departments, but also because Washington gives them a platform from which they can project their messages to a constituency that stretches across the nation.[41]

At the same time the political parties, especially the national parties, have declined in popular appeal and in political muscle.[42] Election finance is mainly in the hands of the candidates, not the parties, and political action committees (PACs) have come to play an increasing role in congressional campaign fundraising.[43] In the Congress, where power used to be centralized in the hands of a small group of senior members, power has been dispersed. This dispersal, combined with the multiplicity and influence of interest groups, allows for many more access points to political power—an "advocacy explosion" that further weakens party discipline.[44] Newer voters have been less inclined than their parents to have strong party loyalties; among voters of all ages, ticket splitting has grown. The candidate is more important than the party; indeed, in a political world increasingly populated by media specialists, the candidate's projected image is more important than the issues: "The issues in a campaign are the candidates, not the things they refer to as the issues. The question [for the consumer/voter] is which candidate will *feel* more like you do in relation to an issue."[45] For this form of marketing, social issues are perfect. Focusing on the law's expression of values that define both communities and individual identities, they provide an opportunity to tap voters' feelings about themselves and the candidates. It is no wonder that presidential candidates regularly take positions on social issues that center on state law and are only marginally concerned with the President's direct responsibilities.

Some influential national PACs and interest groups are focused on single social issues such as abortion or crime. The groups focus their resources—particularly their electoral mobilization—on support for incumbents in congressional districts in which the swing of relatively few votes can change electoral outcomes. As a result, these nationwide groups can have considerable influence on particular representatives' floor voting on legislation, including appropriations of money—and even more influence on the representatives' behavior in the pre-vote legislative process.[46] In such a district a group may be able to exercise something approximating a veto power, strongly inhibiting the district's representative from voting for bills that it opposes.[47]

The President, of course, has something more than influence that effectively amounts to a veto; he has the veto power itself. Once the President vetoes a bill, it takes a two-thirds vote in each house for Congress to override and enact the bill into law. It is extremely difficult to enact civil rights legislation, for example, over the opposition of a President who wants to maintain the legislative status quo. And when an executive department issues regulations embodying new interpretations of existing laws—as the secretary of health and human services did in a 1988 rule forbidding abortion counseling in federally funded family planning clinics[48]—it creates a new "status quo" that Congress itself is powerless to change unless it can override a presidential veto.[49]

One of the meanings of group subordination is that the members of the group find it hard to secure the changes in law they need in order to escape from their subordinate status. Historically, a group's escape typically has been accomplished in a process that is locally variable and discontinuous, with intense bursts of status improvement punctuating longer periods of stagnation. One recent example is the legislative success of gay and lesbian Americans in some regions during the past two decades. They have secured the repeal of sodomy laws—a major symbol of stigma—in about half the states, and in scores of local communities they have secured the cooperation of public officials in anti-discrimination efforts ranging from redirection of police behavior to enactment of AIDS discrimination ordinances.

One response to gay bashing, then, might be to move away from a hostile community to one that is more accepting—as, presumably, black people in Louisiana in the 1890s were "free" to move north to avoid racial discrimination in railroad cars. But until 1993 the single most important governmental expression stigmatizing gay Americans had a nationwide reach that no one could escape by moving: the Defense Department's policy purporting to exclude lesbians and gay men from the armed services. The policy (examined closely in chapter 5) had been refurbished early in the Reagan years, and it kept its importance for Republican presidents right through the 1992 election because the South continued to be seen as the key to the "realignment" the party's candidates had sought for more than twenty years.

Until the mid-twentieth century, the base of the Democratic party in national politics was "the Solid South." After President Lyndon Johnson signed the Civil Rights Act of 1964 into law, he said to an aide, "I think we just delivered the South to the Republican Party for a long time."[50] As to presidential elections, Johnson's prediction came true as early as 1968. In that year Richard Nixon carried most of the South[51] on the basis of a "southern strategy" that foreshadowed two features of the 1980s social issues: distance from the civil rights movement and toughness toward crime.[52] The Nixon campaign emphasized the dual themes of opposition to busing remedies for school desegregation and support for "law and order"—the latter term expressing resistance to the Warren Court's decisions restricting law enforcement in the name of the Bill of Rights.

A generation has passed since 1968, and much has changed in the law and politics of race relations, in the South as elsewhere in the nation. But not everything changed. Race continued up to 1990 to be an effective "wedge issue," attracting significant numbers of working-class whites away from their post–New Deal attachments to the Democratic party.[53] Although this change was evident in varying degrees throughout the country, for two decades it was central to a strategy for bringing a newly aligned "Solid South" solidly behind Republican presidential candidates. The South's special role has been apparent across the whole range of subjects on the social issues agenda. Large numbers of southern whites are active fundamentalist Protestants,[54] and most of these are blue-collar or lower white-collar voters.[55] More than any other region of the country, the South has been influenced by "culture-Protestantism."[56] Laws enacted by southern legislatures have reflected religious orthodoxy on questions of "sex, divorce, abortion, equal rights for women, pornography, drugs, alcohol, education, child-rearing, parental authority, dress, and general behavior."[57] So, for a generation religion and "family values" were wedge issues, too, joining race in cracking party loyalties throughout the white South, converting Democrats into Republicans.[58]

A President who identified the white South as his electoral base might be expected to support a legislative agenda attuned to cultural counterrevolution. He would be cool to the civil rights movement, and would express that coolness in the language of opposition to "quotas." He would favor officially sponsored prayer in the public schools and federal funding for religious organizations' counseling of pregnant women, but would oppose federal funding for abortion counseling—and, of course, he would oppose funding for any sort of abortion procedure, even when the woman has become pregnant through rape or incest. In proposing new social issues legislation, he would win some battles and lose others. In opposing legislation—for example, legislation promoting equality for racial and ethnic minorities, for women, or for gay Americans—he had an excellent chance to win if he should choose to dig in his heels.[59]

In this scene—a vignette of presidential positions on the social issues up to 1992—we are hip-deep in paradox. Even before the Civil War the white South had seen itself as a culture under siege. From the occupation by Union troops to the modern Supreme Court's enforcement of the Fourteenth Amendment, this defensive attitude and its underlying sense of "frustration, failure, and defeat"[60] were reinforced by application of the nation's power, prominently including national law. Culturally speaking, some upper-class white southerners used to think of themselves as peripheral to the centers of the Northeast; if Thomas Wolfe could not go home again, the reason was that his novels had touched an exposed nerve in his old community. In 1942 Gunnar Myrdal wrote that the South was becoming "Americanized."[61] From 1969 to the 1992 the South—especially the white Protestant South—had a major influence on the social issues agenda of the President, and thus on the policies of the national government. As a result, through the community-defining functions of political expression, for a generation America became significantly more "southernized" in our law and in the culture of our public life.

The social issues of religion and "family values" were prominent in the South in early 1992, when Patrick Buchanan contested President Bush's candidacy for reelection, challenging from the right. Buchanan attracted about one-third of the votes in some of the early primaries, including those in the South. Partly for the purpose of bringing Buchanan's supporters back into the fold, the President's strategists did not oppose the effort of religious conservatives to play a major role in the Republican party's national convention. As a result, the party's platform, and the general tone of the convention, offered clear evidence that the Christian right, which some analysts had given up for dead,[62] was not only alive but thriving. During the spring of 1992 Vice President Dan Quayle's attack on a "cultural elite" gained national publicity, but he had begun that effort a year earlier in a speech to the Christian Coalition.[63] The coalition, under the national leadership of Rev. Pat Robertson, was established in the wake of Robertson's failed bid for the 1988 presidential nomination; its main purpose until 1992 was to capture state and local Republican organizations.[64] About 20 percent of the delegates to the 1992 Republican convention were religious conservatives, including large numbers in ten state delegations and the platform committee.[65] The platform adopted wholesale the program of the religious right, and Robertson himself was a prominent speaker at the Republican convention. So was Buchanan, who occupied a prime-time television slot better than Ronald Reagan's. In contrasting the Republican candidates with the Democratic team, Buchanan gave what was, in function if not in form, the convention's keynote address. Again, notice the prominence of questions about legal rights:

George Bush is a defender of right-to-life, and a champion of the Judeo-Christian values and beliefs upon which America was founded. (Applause/cheers) Mr. Clinton, however, has a different agenda. At its top is unrestricted abortion on demand. When the Irish-Catholic governor of Pennsylvania, Robert Casey, asked to say a few words on behalf of the 25 million unborn children destroyed since Roe v. Wade, Bob Casey was told there was no room for him at the podium of Bill Clinton's convention, and no room at the inn. (Boos)

Yet a militant leader of the homosexual rights movement could rise at that same convention and say, "Bill Clinton and Al Gore represent the most pro-lesbian and pro-gay ticket in history." And so they do. (Boos)

. . . Elect me, and you get two for one, Mr. Clinton says of his lawyer-spouse. (Boos) And what does Hillary believe? Well, Hillary

believes that 12-year-olds should have a right to sue their parents.
(Boos) And Hillary has compared marriage and the family as institutions to slavery and life on an Indian reservation. (Boos) Well,
speak for yourself, Hillary. (Applause/cheers/chants of "Go, Pat,
go.")

This, my friends—this is radical feminism. The agenda that Clinton & Clinton would impose on America—abortion on demand, a
litmus test for the Supreme Court, homosexual rights, discrimination against religious schools, women in combat units—that's
change, all right. But it is not the kind of change America wants. . . .
And it is not the kind of change we can abide in a nation we still call
God's country. (Applause/cheers/chants of "Go, Pat, go.")[66]

"There is a religious war going on in this country for the soul of
America," Buchanan said later. The 1992 version of the social issues
agenda for "family values," like the agenda of the Reagan years, promised cultural counterrevolution and focused on the law. From the beginning that agenda had offered to defend the gender line against assaults
on the traditional Order. Now, however, the principal enemy was given
a new name: radical feminism.

3

"Family Values": Policing the Gender Line

In 1992 Rev. Pat Robertson had this to say about a proposed Equal Rights Amendment to the Iowa state constitution: "It is about a socialist, anti-family political movement that encourages women to leave their husbands, kill their children, practice witchcraft, destroy capitalism and become lesbians."[1] More typically, the politics of "family values" has taken a softer line, inviting Americans to look back to an imaginary age of innocence. Yet Robertson's harsher language did capture an important feature of the "family values" theme: its capacity to mobilize constituents by persuading them to look to the future with apprehension. The basic message, sometimes inexplicit but never far from the surface, is that the gender line is under attack and must be defended by law. From abortion to gay rights, the social issues agenda for family values is designed to arouse fear for the erosion of the sexual Order, the traditional patterns of group status dominance.

A DEFERRED PROLOGUE: THE ANXIETIES OF MANHOOD AND THE EXPRESSION OF POWER

To refer to any form of dominance is to strike a masculine chord—and an ideology of masculinity is conspicuous in the social issues agenda for law and government. A surprisingly large portion of the political expression aimed at the constituents of cultural counter-revolution has carried a single message, either explicitly or by unmistakable implication: A vote for the candidate is a vote for a government that will use its powers to keep the traditional gender line bright and clear, so that women can be women and men—white men, especially—can be men. From the politics of motherhood to the politics of sexual orientation to the politics of race and crime, the social issues agenda speaks to the anxieties of manhood. The discussion that follows is a prologue to

31

the substantive issues that lie immediately before us. (If any lawyer/ reader's first reaction is one of doubt that this discussion has anything to do with law, be assured that it does; a trial lawyer might call it "laying a foundation.")

Historically, the ideal of manhood, like the word *manhood* itself, has expressed at least two meanings: masculinity and eligibility for equal citizenship.[2] For most of our national history these meanings have been intertwined; a competence identified with masculinity has seemed a condition of full citizenship, and active participation in the community's public life has offered males reassurance of their masculinity. Because it is an abstract ideal, a construct of the mind, manhood in the sense of masculinity is in some measure unattainable; it can be pursued, but never wholly achieved. On the other hand, the achievement of manhood is seen by most males as essential to their identities. In combination, these elements are a recipe for anxiety.

Manhood, then, is not just an ideal; it is also a problem. The problem begins early, when a little boy must seek his gender identity by separating himself from his mother and from the softness and domesticity and nurturance she represents.[3] (I use the term *represents* advisedly; gender, unlike sex, is not found in nature but created and understood through representation, the playing of roles labeled "masculine" or "feminine.") Thus, masculinity begins in escape—the perceived need to separate from a feminine identity. The main demands for positive achievement of masculinity arise outside the home, and those demands reinforce the boy's need to express—and so to be—what his mother is not. In the hierarchical and rigorously competitive society of other boys, one categorical imperative outranks all the others: Don't be a girl. Femininity is a "negative identity," a part of the self that must be repressed.[4]

The manhood pursued through male rivalry is more than maturity, more than adulthood; it also includes a set of qualities customarily defined as masculine. Although masculinity is defined against its polar opposite, the identification with competence and power in a male-dominated world has made it seem to be society's norm for being fully human. Femininity has been seen as deviance from the norm, as a fundamental flaw—a failure, at the deepest level, to qualify. Pondering this reality, Simone de Beauvoir called the traditional form of femininity "mutilation."[5]

We are all consumers of images of manhood.[6] According to these images a man is supposed to be: active; assertive; confident; decisive;

ready to lead; strong; courageous; morally capable of violence; independent; competitive; practical; successful in achieving goals; emotionally detached; cool in the face of danger or crisis; blunt in expression; sexually aggressive and yet protective toward women. "Proving yourself" as a man can take many forms, but all of them are expressive, and all are variations on the theme of power.

When Henry Kissinger said, "Power is the ultimate aphrodisiac," perhaps the wish was father to the thought.[7] Surely his pronouncement on the causal link between power and sex is only part of the story. If power is sexy, sex is also power. When men fear women and seek to dominate them, one reason is that they have learned to identify male sexuality with conquest.[8] In another perspective, however, the subordination of women must be understood as part of men's nervous efforts to repress the "feminine" in themselves, to keep their manhood visible to other men—in short, to carry on a continuous campaign focused on the expression of power.[9] The deepest fear of all, embedded in a never-ending drama of male rivalry, is the fear of being dominated by other men, humiliated for not measuring up to the manly ideal. The dreaded humiliation can take many forms—from loss of status or class to physical domination to the display of fear—and all of them are varieties of powerlessness.[10]

Although the problem of manhood begins in the challenges posed for individual boys and men, it translates directly into a problem for the whole society. The personal is political; the pursuit of manhood reinforces an ideology of masculinity, a formula for ordering power relationships among social groups.[11] The ideology's most obvious effects are felt in the relations between men and women, especially between men as a group and women as a group. To the extent that manhood is equated with the capacity for citizenship, the exclusion of women from full membership is easily rationalized.[12] In ways that are less conspicuous but equally pernicious, the ideology of masculinity has long played a crucial part in the subordination of racial and ethnic minorities, and in the subordination of lesbians and gay men.

The heart of the ideology of masculinity is the belief that power rightfully belongs to the masculine—that is, to those who display the traits traditionally called masculine. This belief has two corollaries. The first is that the gender line must be clearly drawn, and the second is that power is rightfully distributed among the masculine in proportion to their masculinity—as determined not merely by their physical stature or aggressiveness, but more generally by their ability to dominate and to avoid being dominated. Both parts of the ideology contribute to the subordination of groups. This function is easy to see in efforts to express the gender line in sharp definition; the ideology of masculinity will be effective in assigning power only if those who are masculine are clearly identified. The second corollary of the ideology highlights the centrality of male rivalry. By making anxiety into an everyday fact of life, it leads nervous men to seek reassurance of their masculinity through group rituals that express their status dominance over other groups. In combination these two beliefs purport to justify power by tautology, to ground the legitimacy of domination in domination itself.

At least since the mid-nineteenth century the main path to manhood for American males has been the competitive pursuit of individual achievement in work and in other sectors of public life. But changes in modes of work—especially the rise of large-scale industry and increased bureaucratization—have reduced many men's individual opportunities to exercise independence, take risks, seek to master other men, and otherwise behave in ways traditionally seen as manly.[13] The same changes have also reduced individual men's sense of control over their own fates. As playwrights and novelists remind us, a man's apprehensions about failure and his anxiety about masculine identity are two perspectives on the same fear. Obviously, anxiety is part of the human condition, and women have no special immunity; here I focus on the anxieties of manhood because they are central to the ideology of masculinity.

A man who finds the path of individual achievement to be rough going may try to express his power in ways officially defined as antisocial, such as rape or wife beating.[14] Alternatively, he may attach himself to a group that pursues power and status through domination of members of other groups. An ugly example from overseas is instructive. In Germany between the wars, the Nazi movement found its greatest acceptance among men who saw themselves falling out of the middle class and who were searching in desperation for ways to reassert their worth as men and their status as citizens.[15] Today's analogues in thuggery, from British football hooligans to American skinheads, are also searching for symbols of power. As individuals they seek to avoid the sense of humiliation by joining in groups to act out their squalid little dramas of domination.

It is easy to scorn the losers who seek to express their manhood by wearing swastikas or stomping their victims *du jour* with metal-toed boots. It is less convenient for us—and here I mean men who are more fortunate—to recognize that the losers' fears are our fears in exaggerated form; that their behavior expresses feelings akin to those lurking in the shadows of our minds; that our own behavior, though by more genteel means, often contributes to group subordination. One standard mode of repression of our negative identities is to project them on other people, and especially on members of groups that have been subordinated. The process works so well that it becomes second nature to see those people not as persons but as the abstractions we have projected upon them. Each abstraction is a mask, and it bears a label: blackness, for example, or femininity, or homosexuality.[16] To a great many men, these masks of the Other are, at some level, frightening; when we police the color line and the gender line in the world around us, we are policing the same line in our own minds, defending our senses of self.[17] The fear of members of subordinated groups is more than a fear of competition, or even retaliation. No specter is more terrifying than our own negative identity.

To say that a negative identity must be repressed is not to say that a white man fears becoming female or gay or black. The fear is that he will be perceived as being effeminate or gay or socially black. (By "socially black" I mean representing in his own behavior the negative images that white Americans commonly project upon black people.[18]) Much of the pressure to express power, and thus masculinity, is created by those fears. Joel Williamson ends his study of race relations in the South with this comment: "White America, in its stubborn and residual racial egotism, resists the realization of how very deeply and irreversibly black it is, and has been. The struggle against that awareness, the rage against the realization of their blackness and its legitimacy is the struggle of white people in race relations. To recognize and respect the blackness that is already within themselves would be to recognize and respect the blackness that is within the nation, and, functionally, to surrender the uses, physical and psychological, that they have learned to make of blacks as a separate people."[19] This thoughtful passage would also make good sense if we were to substitute "male" or "heterosexual" for "white," and substitute "feminine" or "gay" for "black."

The importance of gender as a marker of individual identity and social status creates powerful incentives for keeping the gender line clearly defined—not just in our individual self-definitions but in our social interactions. Under the regime of the ideology of masculinity, men must be seen to be traditionally masculine and women must be seen to be traditionally feminine. Because the social meaning of gender is so strongly associated with sexuality, the ideology demands that both men and women be seen as unambiguously heterosexual. And, because the gender line is as unstable as any other social construct, it requires reinforcement by social controls, notably including the law.

The law's importance in maintaining the gender line lies only secondarily in its material uses—for example, as an instrument for excluding women or gay men and lesbians from participating in enterprises both public and private. Primarily, the law has maintained the gender line by officially expressing it, legitimizing it as a social Great Divide. Law, like all government, is an "omnipresent teacher," even when it teaches the lessons of subordination and exclusion.[20]

The material and expressive uses of law feed on each other. The material successes of the women's movement during the last generation have had major expressive effects, blurring the gender line and so weakening the grip of the ideology of masculinity. This change in the ideological climate, in turn, has relaxed some of the material exclusions traditionally imposed on lesbians and gay men. It is not just coincidence that the Americans most disturbed about the liberalization of society's response to same-sex orientation are also the most concerned to see that women return to "the family"—by which is meant a life of domesticity. If today's cultural counterrevolutionaries have focused their political attention on the law, especially constitutional law, surely one reason is that they are aware of the law's expressive function in defining the gender line.

In this perspective the maintenance of Order implies using law to express and preserve the prevailing ordering of group status relationships: men over women, whites over blacks, heterosexuals over gays. But the use of law to express inequality and exclusion is inconsistent with the central ideals of the American civic culture, and so "we," the dominant, have always felt pressed to find rationalizations for subordinating the members of any social group.[21] "We construct a stigma-theory, an ideology to explain [their] inferiority and account for the danger [they represent]."[22] The theory that has served to rationalize the exclusion of women and gay and lesbian Americans from equal citizenship is, of course, the ideology of masculinity itself. There are differences in the stigma-theory that has rationalized the exclusion and segregation of black people, but, as chapters 4 and 5 verify, among the notions expressed by white superiority are the anxieties of male rivalry.

RELIGION, SEX, AND POLITICS

During the 1980 presidential election the head of the National Christian Action Coalition issued a "Family Issues Voting Index." To illustrate the nation's drift into moral bankruptcy, the index listed these evils: "planned parenthood, the pill, no-fault divorce, open marriages, gay rights, palimony, test-tube babies, women's liberation, children's liberation, unisex, day care centers, child advocates, and abortion on demand. A man is no longer responsible for his family; a woman need not honor and obey her husband. God has been kicked out and humanism enthroned."[23] This catalogue was not just a lament; it was a political shopping list.

The list's two unifying themes are the importance of maintaining a clearly defined gender line and the dangers of sexual freedom, notably the freedom of women to control their sexual behavior and maternity. These themes reinforce each other. In the view of the index's author, a woman who chooses not to center her life on domestic service—on the roles of dependent, obedient wife and nurturing mother—is defying not only tradition but the will of God. He urges his readers to vote for candidates who will direct the powers of law and government toward restoring the Order of the traditional family.

Religion, sex, and politics: in my younger days, these were the subjects you weren't supposed to discuss at the dinner table. Today religion's involvement with the politics of sex and gender is an everyday fact of American life. But even in earlier times, when polite conversation excluded these subjects, religion and sex and politics were tightly intertwined. The linkage usually remained tacit rather than explicit, but when articulation seemed necessary, someone—typically a man— could be counted on to do the job. The idea of a clearly marked gender line, with domesticity every woman's divinely ordained role, was expressed directly in 1873 by a Supreme Court Justice. Illinois limited the practice of law to men, and so excluded Myra Bradwell, an unusually well qualified applicant who had been running a legal newspaper. The Supreme Court rejected her claim that Illinois had violated her rights under the privileges and immunities clause of the Fourteenth Amendment.[24] Justice Joseph Bradley added a separate concurring opinion, anticipating by a century the National Christian Action Coalition's view of the interconnections of religion, sex, and politics:

> Man is, or should be, woman's protector and defender. The natural and proper timidity and delicacy which belongs to the female sex evidently unfits it for many of the occupations of civil life. The constitution of the family organization, which is founded on the divine ordinance, as well as in the nature of things, indicates the domestic sphere as that which properly belongs to the domain and functions of womanhood. The harmony, not to say identity, of interests and views which belong, or should belong, to the family institution is repugnant to the idea of a woman adopting a distinct and independent career from that of her husband. . . . The paramount destiny and mission of woman are to fulfill the noble and benign offices of wife and mother. This is the law of the Creator.[25]

In the more secularized society of our own day, religious conservatives have invoked the same "law of the Creator" in making their own appeals to the Constitution. A decade ago a group of parents challenged mandatory reading assignments in public schools in a district in Tennessee. A first-grade reading textbook, for example, showed boys cooking and girls reading. One of the plaintiff parents, writing to the Kingsport *Times News*, said that this sort of text "preached" secular humanism by suggesting to children "that there are no God-given roles for the different sexes."[26]

Women have not always been cast in the maternal, domestic role. An old Christian tradition contrasts Mary, Mother of God, with Mary Magdalene, daughter of Eve.[27] If Justice Bradley equated "woman" with the abstraction of motherhood, other men with even greater influence have identified "woman" with the abstraction of temptation. All of us—from the fundamentalist who finds truth in a literal reading of the Bible to the atheist who professes a nonreligion—inhabit a social system infused with the longstanding Christian tradition that has placed sexual desire at the core of original sin, regarded sex as a wildness that can be tamed only by severe external discipline, and viewed women as that wildness incarnate.

This tradition was not the doctrine of the earliest Christian church, but crystallized in the writings of Saint Augustine of Hippo (354–430). In an exceptionally illuminating work, Elaine Pagels has spelled out Augustine's crucial contribution to this Christian tradition.[28] He argued forcefully that sexual desire was not only the proof of humankind's original sin, but the penalty for that sin, sexually transmitted to every succeeding generation. For Augustine, the forbidden fruit symbolized personal control over the will. (The view that sexual repression is the price of civilization was also Sigmund Freud's. There is irony here, but only in small deposits; in attending to the concerns of women, Freud was only a slight improvement on Augustine.) In the sin of reaching for the forbidden fruit, Augustine argued, humanity lost the capacity for self-government. The necessary result was that government by other humans—masters over slaves, husbands over wives, tyrants over their subjects—must be endured if we are to defend against the wild forces unleashed by sin in our nature. It seems no accident that these doctrines of total obedience to authority served the purposes of the Roman emperors who had made Christianity their established church.

From Saint Augustine to Justice Bradley to the "Family Issues Voting Index," the interaction of religion, sex, and politics has tended not only to objectify women as mothers or temptresses but to legitimize a social Order that excluded them from equal citizenship. As sexual objects, women in public life would only distract men from the serious pursuits of governance.[29] As maternal objects, women are delicate and need protection. In either of these perspectives women must be kept away from power, out of public life, under control. The ideology of masculinity and the anxieties of manhood are close to the surface here. Some years before the sex scandals of the 1980s touched the world of television evangelism, a leader of the new Christian right epitomized the resort to hypermasculinity as a way of coping with anxiety. His exclamation, "Christ was not a lamb, but a ram!"[30] said more than he intended to say.

One who views sex as subversive and women as a threat of Disorder will, logically enough, want to impose controls on women's sexual behavior and maternity, and to forbid the expression of sexual intimacy between members of the same sex. Historically, all manner of social controls, prominently including the law, have been deployed to these ends. During the 1960s and 1970s, however, the legal controls over sex and its expression declined in vigor. For many Americans this weakening was centrally in mind when they said, "Things are out of control." What bothered them most was the extent to which the law—so long a set of basic controls over women's sexual conduct and maternity, and a set of public symbols of a sexual morality proclaiming traditional "family values"—had been refashioned into an instrument and symbol of what many women were calling liberation. In 1965, in *Griswold v. Connecticut*,[31] the Supreme Court recognized a married couple's constitutional right to practice contraception, and in 1973 the Court decided *Roe v. Wade*,[32] recognizing a woman's right to choose whether to have an abortion. In the eight years between *Griswold* and *Roe* the Court also brought the Constitution to bear in libertarian and egalitarian ways on such matters as the right to marry, access to the divorce courts, the "illegitimacy" of children, and the private possession of obscene material in one's home.[33] Legislatures, too, joined in: making divorce easier almost everywhere; repealing sodomy laws in about half the states; and providing government funding for birth control services—in some large states, even for abortion.

For the political operatives who promote the social issues agenda, these changes in the law have been interesting chiefly because they have offered a rich store of political imagery laden with emotion. For them the central point of the "family values" part of the agenda is not to achieve a cultural counterrevolution but to play on status anxieties, and so to mobilize a constituency.

WOMEN AS UNREASON

Women have worn the label of Unreason ever since the idea of Reason made its appearance in Western thought. Indeed, from the earliest human societies to our own times, Nature has been seen as female, and women have represented Nature, the disorderly earth spirit that men must tame if civilization is to flourish.[34] Men's fear of women[35] has centered on women's sexual behavior and maternity, which must be controlled, lest they engulf Reason and all its works.[36] One explanation for this need is that men have wanted the assurance of offspring: not only assurance that they would have children, but assurance that the children were their own.[37] But that explanation is just one illustration of a larger concern. Men are worried not only about their identity as fathers but about their identity as men.

When a boy finds his gender identity in separation from his mother, she is seen not as a person but as an object, a nurturing part of Nature to be used and controlled.[38] For this reason among others, boys and men as a group tend to be strongly aware of the boundaries of the self, to emphasize differences and discontinuities, to explain their experience by fitting it into categories that are bipolar.[39] Men define femininity as what they must not be: nurturant, domesticated, dependent, passive/receptive/compliant, delicate, timid. This construct of woman is an abstraction, an image of the negative identity a man must repress. The view of women as dangerous, as needing control, is directly connected to men's need to hold fast to the masculine, to control the "woman" in themselves.

This rocky path to male self-identification produces what Dorothy Dinnerstein called the "under-personification" of real women: the tendency among men to see individual women as objects through which they can seek one or another kind of fulfillment.[40] Sexuality and maternity are the focal points for this objectification. Only one feature of humans serves unambiguously to separate them into categories defined by the social constructs of "man" and "woman": the difference in sexual and reproductive function. Male control over women's maternity and sexual behavior has always been central in the subordination of women.

The labeling that equates women with unreasoning Nature has, of course, taken the form of express written argumentation.[41] But far more important contributions to the labeling of women as sexual and maternal objects have been made by other expressive means that are not so explicit. Thus, for many generations American law effectively placed women outside the boundaries of the community of equal citizens. For the most part they could not vote or hold public offices or even serve on juries or practice law. If a woman was married, the law placed her children, her property, even her person largely in her husband's control. These legal disabilities not only hindered women from speaking with authority;[42] they also communicated a powerful message, implicitly affixing the label of Unreason on every woman.

In the traditional view, women were not allowed to be active sexual agents, but must leave that sort of self-expression to men. Women could control their own sexual behavior and maternity only through a strategy of denial—and for a married woman even that strategy depended on her husband's consent. Morals legislation, too, was designed to keep women in their place. Not only did the law criminalize abortion; in addition, obscenity laws characterized contraceptive devices as "articles designed for indecent and immoral use," and banned their distribution and use.[43] Candid treatment of sexual expression and behavior, in fiction or in other literature, regularly fell afoul of the obscenity laws.[44]

Nongovernmental controls were at least as effective as the law in communicating the message that women were out of their element when they left the domestic sphere. These controls at once labeled a woman as incompetent and denied her all manner of expressive opportunities. Employers severely restricted the jobs that she could fill. "Women's work" was paid less than other jobs were paid, and even when women and men were hired for the same job, the women were paid less than their male coworkers. The sexual harassment of women on the job[45] communicated to women and men alike the view of "woman" as object. This systematic subordination in the workplace was not even seen by men (or by many women) as discrimination; men were assumed to be the family breadwinners, and a woman was expected to find her security under male protection. On the same assumptions, women were educated for a domestic life and usually for nothing else. Private etiquette, too, informally limited women's expression. Men, but not women, were socially permitted to use earthy language,[46] and "Shall we join the ladies?" signaled not only the extinguishment of cigars but the end of what men called serious talk.

Even before the twentieth century, this picture had changed in some particulars. In the past two decades the pace of change has accelerated. Today most of the restrictive laws are gone—with the flagrant exception, in a number of states, of laws excepting marital rape from criminality.[47] Today civil rights laws forbid many of the private practices that have restricted women's opportunities, especially in the world of work. Not everything has changed, however. In the economic sphere, women's average pay remains significantly lower than men's, and "the feminization of poverty" has steadily increased. These conditions are easily measured. But if we had to identify the one condition of women that has proved most resistant to change, surely it would be a condition that is not measurable on any commonly accepted scale, yet is incontestably a part of virtually every woman's daily life: the objectification of women.

In the next two sections of this chapter we examine, through the prisms of law and status politics, two clusters of issues intertwined with the views of women as sexual and maternal objects: the legal regulation of pornography, and legal restrictions on birth control services and abortion. The chapter concludes with a look at another set of disputes centered on the gender line: the gay rights issues raised by the remaining sodomy laws and by proposals for official recognition of same-sex unions. All these issues have grave consequences for the material conditions of people's lives, but much of what is at stake centers on expression, both governmental and private. In regulating expression, and in providing their own authoritative statements of the meanings of behavior, law and government are seen as drawing the gender line more clearly or making it more indistinct. The main thread of our story, then, is the centrality of expression in the politics of the gender line, and the linkage between law and that expression. The bearing of the First Amendment is visible on the surface of these issues. Yet, as we shall see, interpretations of other parts of the Constitution also affect expression—and are themselves expressive—in this zone where religion, sex, and politics intersect.

PORNOGRAPHY AND LAW AS IMAGES OF POWER

During the century-long political struggle over Temperance, the Drys always understood that, whatever the state of the law, any Wet would be able to find a drink. What the Drys wanted most—even after Prohibition imposed its costs of crime and official corruption and death by the glassful—was the image of Order embodied in a formal public acknowledgement of the dominance of their values. A similar process is visible in today's conflicts over the control of sexual behavior and expression.

Over the last half-century efforts to restrict indecent expression—that is, to keep sex and sexuality secret—have illustrated this perennial feature of American cultural politics. In 1957 the Warren Court reaffirmed an earlier dictum[48] that obscenity was no part of the "expression of ideas" and so was not "protected speech."[49] Nonetheless, in the 1960s, with the sexual revolution in full flower, the Court narrowed its definition of what was obscene and limited the occasions for permissible government regulation.[50] "Obscenity" remained outside the First Amendment's protection, but a lot of sexually explicit material circulated freely. As part of his "southern strategy" for election, Richard Nixon criticized this libertarian trend, and in the 1970s, after President Nixon had appointed four Justices, the Burger Court's decisions eased the way for local prosecutors to go after obscenity.[51] These decisions were significant mainly as symbols of Order, of officially defined cultural values. Obscenity was again branded as Unreason, but the post-1970s constitutional doctrine seems to have had little practical effect except in smaller communities and in some cities, mainly in the South.

Annual sales of sexually explicit books, magazines, films, and video-
tapes are estimated in the billions of dollars.[52] Comparing this traffic
with existing constitutional doctrine, we hear the echo of the old saw
about Prohibition: "The Wets have their liquor and the Drys have their
law."

Public expression about sexuality remains a theme of political controversy. In these cultural contests the rhetoric of "family values" has
served both PACs in search of money and politicians in search of votes.
Recent examples are the late-1980s skirmishes over Federal Communications Commission regulations of "indecent" broadcasting and the
conflicts over federal funding of sexually explicit art that reached a
climax of sorts in President Bush's 1992 firing of the head of the National
Endowment for the Arts.[53] In fighting these battles, and as members of
the Attorney General's Commission on Pornography, adherents of the
religious right have had some limited success in claiming the roles of
guardians of public morality.[54]

During the same period some feminists, who have nothing else in
common with the constituency for cultural counterrevolution,[55] have
attacked the distribution of sexual imagery from a different direction.
They have argued that the harm of pornography—which they define as
the sexually explicit portrayal of women as sexual objects for domination—is not that it undermines public morals, but that it is a central cause of the subordination of women. A model ordinance drafted
by Catharine MacKinnon and Andrea Dworkin would authorize any
woman to sue for damages or for an injunction against the production
and distribution of pornography, the coercion of actors or models into
performing for the producers of pornography, and the forcing of pornography on unwilling viewers. A modified version of this ordinance
was adopted in Indianapolis. The lower federal courts promptly held
the ordinance unconstitutional, and the Supreme Court affirmed that
decision summarily, without opinion.[56]

The proponents of the model ordinance see pornography not as a
side effect of the sexualization of women's subordination but as "the
central link in the cycle of abuse" that sexualizes the domination of
women by men, including domination by violence.[57] They argue that
pornography falls outside the First Amendment's protection because it
is not an idea but a practice of subordination, "the essence of a sexist
social order, its quintessential social act." For the proponents, the regulation of pornography is "not a moral issue" but an issue of power.[58]

Although I believe this argument fails as a constitutional justification for censorship, it is a grand failure, one that illuminates a large and vitally important area of human interaction. Several of the argument's insights are indispensable to any serious effort to end the subordination of women: (i) that sexuality is a social construct; (ii) that our society's construct of sexuality, largely the creation of men, sexualizes men's domination and women's subordination, and so affects relations of power; (iii) that the construct is formed by the interaction of speech and other expressive conduct; (iv) that the construct is maintained by the combined application of governmental and "private" (that is, non-governmental) power; (v) that this form of stigma—the association of women's sexuality with subordination—is a group harm deserving both recognition and remedy; and (vi) that women's control over their maternity and their sexual behavior and expression is crucial to their liberation from subordination.[59] The debate over pornography regulation has had little success in changing the law, but it has transformed discussions of women's status. From now on, no one can pretend to think seriously about this subject without inquiring into the contributions of the social construct of sexuality to the process of subordination.

The most troublesome point in the argument of the antipornography feminists is its fundamental premise: that pornography is a central cause of the stereotypical construct of "woman." The assumption seems belied by history. In nineteenth-century America, when pornography consisted mostly of the printed word and was rarely distributed beyond the well-to-do, the status of women was far worse than it is today. Indeed, the women's movement has achieved its greatest gains simultaneously with the greatest growth in the distribution of pornography. Ironically, too, a careful state-by-state study has shown a positive correlation between the volume of sex magazines in circulation and a composite of social indicators of equality between men and women.[60] One possible explanation for both of these correlations is that the open expression of sexuality—for adults, the *real* sexual revolution[61]—and the improvement in women's status both derive from the same sources: the sudden appearance of safe birth control methods widely available to women, and the concomitant emergence of women as visible sexual actors.

No one can dispute that pornography reinforces attitudes that sexualize women's subordination; but so do movies, romance novels, billboards, television (both the programming and the advertising), newspapers, song lyrics, magazines, rock videos, clothes fashions, the art on gallery walls, and the cosmetics on drug store shelves. My point is not just that this list shows how the argument for suppression of pornography by injunction "proves too much" as a matter of First Amendment doctrine.[62] More fundamentally, the list undermines the argument's main factual premise. America has spawned a huge culture industry, and its center of gravity is profoundly sexist. In view of that industry's pervasive influence, and in view of the long history of women's subordination and the relatively recent appearance of pornography in full flood, it seems a major exaggeration to say that pornography is central in constructing our society's view of women's sexuality.[63]

On the other hand, it is possible to exaggerate in the opposite direction. Two feminist critics, arguing that the movement against pornography diverts political resources away from more pressing concerns in the struggle for women's equality, encapsulated that argument in an unfortunate title: "Pornography is about Images, not Power."[64] The (perhaps unintended) implication—that images and power are separate—seems quite wrong. The world of images and the world of power are mutually interactive, even interdependent. Much of modern government's allocation of power is accomplished by influencing or controlling expression, including the government's own expression. Surely, too, power— specifically, the power of men over women—is pornography's principal theme.[65] But pornography is at once a literature of male domination and a literature of male fear. Recognizing the relevance of fear offers another perspective on the question whether pornography is a central cause of the sexualization of women's subordination.

The men who consume pornography do not think of themselves as powerful. Indeed, when they resort to pornography's illusions of domination they are responding to the anxieties of masculinity—not just the fear of women but the fear of male rivalry.[66] Pornography does not make those anxieties go away, but neither has it created them. Consider Lucinda Finley's affecting account of a showing of a pornographic film at Yale. The audience, mostly college-age males, was augmented by a group of women who stood in silent protest. In response to the protesters, the sponsors of the showing had agreed to a preliminary screening of an antipornography film called *Raw Images*, consisting mainly of a montage of pornographic images of escalating violence. During this film, Finley reports, young men in the audience hooted and yelped, laughing loudly and shouting encouragement to men in the film who were committing increasingly ghastly acts of sexual violence. She describes her own feelings of sickened revulsion—a natural reaction to a sickening, revolting scene—and she concludes, "If these 'perfectly normal,' Ivy League educated men hold these attitudes, who doesn't?"[67]

In labeling the young men's performance as sophomoric, I do not excuse it. Yet, to fathom their conduct, we must recognize that it *was* a performance, a drama of domination akin to those enacted in other venues by the neo-Nazis, the skinheads, and the "defense intellectuals" who use sexual imagery to describe nuclear war.[68] In this perspective the main "attitude" revealed by the yelping Yalies is anxiety about their own standing among their male peers. Imagine that each of the young men had watched *Raw Images* with one of the young women—the two of them alone. In such a setting, we can suppose, his expressed response would have been markedly different. Finley was there, and I wasn't—but I can recall a similar scene from my own college days, when I wanted to leave but suppressed that impulse to avoid humiliation.[69] My guess is that each of the shouting males that Finley describes was performing for the other males, seeking to demonstrate a form of manhood that he thought they would recognize.

Whether or not I have guessed correctly about the sources of these young men's obnoxious behavior, it is clear that men in our society are trained to believe that their masculinity is something to be proved. Especially for a young man with this anxious perspective, many an encounter with a woman is an identity test, and so is every occasion when a group of men jointly confront the general issue of man/woman relations. The workers who whistle when a woman walks by a construction site are not just sending a message of sexual challenge to the woman. Each of them is assuring the others—and his own uncertain self—that he has what it takes to be sexually assertive, that he is a real man.[70]

A man who sees his relations with women as one test after another is bound to fail the course, and he can never look forward to graduation. His uses of sexual aggressiveness to shore up an unsteady ego are self-perpetuating. The women who must deal with these assertions are aware that they are being objectified, and they are schooled in the culture's traditional inclination to sort women into categories labeled "good" and "bad." This dual awareness guarantees a high failure rate for the man who "comes on" as a matter of routine. Even an occasional triumph gives him little reassurance; on the Groucho Marx principle, the woman who responds favorably to his advances must be worth little as a conquest.[71] Usually, though, his come-ons are rejected, reconfirming his sense of inadequacy and giving him more and more to prove. Projecting these feelings on the objectified Other, he sees every woman as a taunt and a threat, at once the object of desire and hostility. In a popular song of the 1940s the singer said he would prefer a paper doll to a "real-life girl." The real-life women who are most directly and immediately hurt by pornography—in particular, the women who are coerced into performing as actors and models[72]—are not made of paper. Here, though, we are looking at the male consumer. For him pornography's paper dolls, like aspirin tablets, offer temporary relief from the symptoms of anxiety. If his consumption of pornography should be thwarted by law, he will find substitute symbols of sexual objectification, not just in magazine ads or on television, but in every woman he sees.

Another, quite different objection to using suits for damages and injunctions as a means of suppressing pornography can be approached through one of the legal arguments used to defend such a law's constitutionality. The argument is that because pornography is "noncognitive" expression, it can be regulated on a lesser showing of justification than would be required for regulating speech at the First Amendment's "core." The argument grows out of a vision of the First Amendment centered on "deliberative processes" and excluding communication "on a subconscious level."[73] On this view sexual imagery can be consigned to the category of "low value speech" because it "bypasses the process of public consideration and debate that underlies the concept of the marketplace of ideas."[74] Besides, it is said, pornography "has little or nothing to do with public affairs."[75] In other words, sexual imagery can be treated as a First Amendment stepchild because it is not the civic speech of Reason.

I argued in chapter 1 that a First Amendment model centered on civic deliberation was bad news for the members of subordinated groups. This effort to apply the model to the regulation of pornography illustrates my point. Calling sexual imagery low-value speech is perfectly attuned to two goals of the cultural counterrevolutionaries: to deny women's active sexual agency, and to get women out of the public world of work and back into their "God-given roles" as wives and mothers— that is, back under male protection. The politicians who invented the social issues agenda have no trouble making this connection. At both national and local levels of government, they have trained their impressive weaponry against the dissemination of information about birth control and abortion, sex education in the schools, pregnancy counseling for teenagers, and candid discussions of sexuality in the media. In 1920 Margaret Sanger said, "Birth control is woman's problem."[76] Women needed frankness about sex in Sanger's day—not just individually, but in public, for reasons relating to the power of women as a group. Women still need that candor, and for the same reasons.[77]

Imagine for a moment that the courts had upheld the constitutionality of the Indianapolis antipornography ordinance. Similar ordinances would be most likely to be enacted in places where their feminist sponsors could find powerful allies among the constituents of the cultural counterrevolution. In these communities that same constituency would exercise considerable influence over the election of prosecutors and state judges. As antipornography laws proliferated, some of the primary targets for censorship by injunction surely would be feminist sexual imagery: writing and films created by women artists, offering new and egalitarian visions of sexuality, and aimed at ending the "social context of ignorance and shame" that male pornography needs if it is to thrive.[78] Some of these forms of expression would be called pornographic, not just by the new right or by antipornography feminists, but by the feminist writers and filmmakers who produce them. Imagine a lawsuit seeking to enjoin the showing of a film containing such feminist sexual imagery, and then multiply this case by a number representing the cultural counterrevolution's myriad local organizations.[79]

Carefully examining the statements of feminist artists who employ strong imagery of sexuality, Robin West has made the unassailable point that this expression—she calls it "good pornography"—seeks to transform our understanding of sexual difference and sexual relations.[80] By challenging traditional views, these artists aim to break the stranglehold of institutions that deny or confine women's sexual expression and behavior—notably, those that would force "the family" into the new right's restrictive definition. A transformation of this kind would give candid recognition to what Ann Snitow has called "the frightening malleability of gender," and would recognize women as sexual actors, not passive victims.[81] Furthermore, as West points out, these artists can count on the female half of their audience to see their work from a perspective that is not male-centered: "Women who consume pornography see (and seek) *ideas* in pornography, even if men do not."[82] This line of argument, which more fully expounds a view expressed in the Indianapolis case by the Feminist Anti-Censorship Task Force,[83] reduces to rubble the notion that pornography is "noncognitive." It also illustrates how the bounds of Reason—initially defined, as always, by the conventional wisdom of dominant groups—can be expanded when an "outsider" gets to offer her own meanings, to create her own definitions of reality.

With strikingly divergent long-range purposes in view, the defenders of "decency" and the antipornography feminists seek new laws regulating the distribution of sexual imagery.[84] Yet the moralists must surely understand, deep down, that our culture's definitions of women's sexuality have passed a point of no return. Women in large numbers are in the public world to stay—and to that purpose they need control over their own maternity and their sexual behavior and expression. It is inconceivable that women will be persuaded, in the name of "family values," to return to a world in which their sexual behavior is locked within the walls of male authority. Surely, too, feminists of all persuasions know that an end to pornography would leave largely unscathed a popular culture that bombards women from all directions with symbols of sexual objectification. Even so, for both the moralists and the antipornography feminists, the enactment of new legislation appears to have a value of its own as a cultural totem. Here, as in the long cultural conflict over Temperance, law is seen as an official statement of the meanings of behavior, an authoritative pronouncement of public values—in short, as an image of Order and power.

MATERNAL IMAGES: ABORTION AND THE EXPRESSION OF WOMEN'S STATUS

In the mid-1950s, when abortion was largely illegal in the United States, it was practiced nonetheless. One group estimated the annual number of abortions somewhere between 200,000 and 1.2 million, saying it had "no objective basis" for selecting any particular figure within that range.[85] Estimates for the 1960s cluster around an annual rate of one million[86]—but "the abortion issue" in national electoral politics did not materialize until after the Supreme Court's 1973 decision in *Roe v. Wade*.[87] The number of abortions did rise after 1973, but the increase was less dramatic than one might have supposed, and in the 1980s, even as the Supreme Court was relaxing the constitutional limits on state restrictions, the number of abortions held steady at about 1.5 million per year.[88] Although the Court upheld a Reagan administration regulation forbidding employees of federally funded family planning agencies to give advice concerning abortion,[89] it seemed clear that the agencies' doctors and staff members would be imaginative enough to find ways to go on letting patients know that abortion is one of their options.[90] The 1992 election guaranteed that the order would be overturned. On the twentieth anniversary of *Roe v. Wade*, just two days after President Clinton was inaugurated, he rescinded the gag order.[91]

Four months before the 1992 election, a majority of the Supreme Court declined to follow the trajectory of recent decisions to the point of overruling *Roe*. Instead the majority reaffirmed *Roe*'s central holding that, up to the point of fetal viability, a pregnant woman has a constitutional right to choose whether to have an abortion.[92] Chapter 7 examines some of the opinions in this case, along with other manifestations of a new center of gravity of the politics of abortion rights. Although the abortion issue surely will continue to polarize politics in some states, almost certainly its importance in presidential politics will recede.

Imagine, though, what might have happened if the Court had overruled *Roe*. Undoubtedly there would have been a sharp decline in the number of abortions reported in official statistics, but no one could have predicted with confidence the degree of decline in abortions actually performed. The Supreme Court's pre-1992 decisions upholding state restrictions on abortion had given new vigor to the abortion rights movement, and—even with *Roe* gone—politics in a number of states would have preserved a woman's right of choice. Furthermore, any states that severely restricted the right would find their law enforcement capacities strained, for women's groups had already organized to assure women access to safe abortions, legal or not.[93] The prospect, in a post-*Roe* world, would have been one of massive disobedience of law, recalling the levels of disobedience of liquor laws during the Prohibition era, and Northern defiance of the Fugitive Slave Act in the years preceding the Civil War. When law is seen as an instrument of status dominance in a conflict of cultures, no one should be surprised when the losers of the legislative battle refuse to accept the law's legitimacy. Today's demonstrators and counterdemonstrators at birth control clinics have this much in common with yesterday's civil rights marchers and their catcalling antagonists.

In sum, the *Roe* decision seems not to have been an independent cause of any dramatic increase in the number of abortions performed, and even *Roe*'s demise as a precedent likely would not have reduced that number in anything like the degree that the average viewer of television talk shows might expect. To many partisans in the continuing controversy over abortion, however, comments such as these are almost irrelevant. Since the late 1960s, when feminists first called for repeal of restrictive abortion laws, "the abortion issue" has moved to the symbolic center of a cultural conflict, with one side seeking to maintain the traditional gender line against the other side's assault. If the anti-abortion theme has served as a political rallying point for cultural counterrevolution, one important reason is that it can be used to evoke a generalized fear of the idea of women as active sexual agents.

The sexual Order represented by the traditional gender line is patriarchal. Within this Order, in theory, both men and women are supposed to confine their sexual behavior to marriage, but penalties for transgressions are mostly imposed on women. Within this Order, sex for women is supposed to be passive/receptive, with its affirmative—and self-affirming—content limited to the possibility of motherhood. Within this Order, in short, the idea of motherhood plays a central role in shaping the identities of all women, mothers or not: "Through motherhood, every woman has been defined from outside herself: mother, matriarch, matron, spinster, barren, old maid—listen to the history of emotional timbre that hangs about each of these words."[94] This list of labels, by itself, says much about the role of controls over women's sexual behavior and maternity in maintaining a social system that subordinates women.

Just to state the terms of the traditional sexual Order is to recognize how much it has weakened. In the generation since the birth control pill became widely available, an alternative model increasingly has reflected social reality: women actively express their sexuality; sex is not tied to marriage, or to motherhood; within marriage, motherhood can be delayed or avoided altogether; motherhood does not necessarily imply marriage. In short, the alternative model claims for women a measure of control over their sexual conduct and maternity that was unimaginable in the 1950s.[95] (Choice means responsibility, including anguish over the decision to end a potential life; the new freedom is not a bed of roses.)

Many "pro-life" women see other women's exercise of this control as "selfish," or even as an instrument of hedonism.[96] Opponents of the constitutional right of choice contribute to this perception when they refer to women's control over their sexuality and maternity as raising "life-style issues."[97] But the reason abortion rights are a women's issue is not that motherhood inconveniences a woman's pursuit of a particular life-style. Nor is the point a "sex discrimination" argument that a law forbidding abortion denies sexual freedom only to women and not to men.[98] The right of choice is a women's issue because a woman's control over her sexual behavior and her maternity is essential to her right to full participation in the public life of the community.[99] The *Griswold* and *Roe* decisions are most satisfactorily defended as effectuating the principle of equal citizenship.[100]

Some of these recent offenses against the traditional sexual Order are grudgingly tolerated by those who would prefer to preserve that Order, but only so long as the transgressions remain veiled. What evokes the greatest fear—and makes possible a politics of fear—is public expression, the heightened visibility of an active sexuality among women. The *Griswold* and *Roe* decisions, of course, typify the power of law to assist women in claiming their new degree of control and their new capacity for expression. But the same decisions also illustrate the expressive quality of law itself. In liberating women from the traditional sexual Order, constitutional law has contributed not just its power but its moral force.

In the years since the legality of abortion became a major public issue, activist women on both sides have tended to see the issue's resolution as a symbol of their own personal worth. "Pro-life" activists have defended the value of the traditional role of homemaker, and "pro-choice" activists have defended the value of participation in public spheres previously reserved for men.[101] If the abortion issue represents a conflict over the status of cultural groups, not far below the surface of this conflict lies an awareness of the close connections between women's sexual freedom and other aspects of women's autonomy. The legalization of abortion has brought the expression of a particular kind of active sexuality—one that did scare the horses—out of the shadows and into the clinic on Main Street: "Abortion—organized legal abortion—is associated with sex because it is seen to reveal sex; it is a signifier that makes sex *visible* . . . . Above all, it helps identify and categorize a new sexual subject [that is, actor]: the 'promiscuous' white teenage girl."[102] For middle-class adult women with economic independence, the right of "choice" has been, for some time and for all practical purposes, irrevocably here. For them—unlike the poorer women whose very lack of independence and choice has kept them out of the political arena—issues about abortion and birth control have been, more than anything else, conflicts about public symbols.

And so it has been for the men and women who are the target audience for the social issues agenda. They, too, have seen the right of "choice" as embodying not only the changes that have been labeled a sexual revolution but also the changes adding up to a new status for women in American society. Randall Terry, the founder of Operation Rescue, agrees with the feminists who make a connection between abortion and women's new opportunities. He assures women that "in most of Middle America, people can make it on one income" (the husband's), and says the program of the National Organization of Women evidences a "put-your-kids-in-day-care-and-go-out-and-pursue-a-career, proabortion mentality." The abortion issue, as he sees it, is one major battlefield in "a cultural civil war" pitting "Satan's agenda" against God's "moral absolutes."[103] For many cultural counterrevolutionaries, both the changes in mores governing women's sexuality and the changes in women's expectations outside the home are threatening. Rolled into a package labeled "abortion," these changes were, right through the 1980s, a political manager's dream. They still offer endless prospects for emotion-laden imagery, at once evoking the objectifications of woman-as-mother and woman-as-temptress. What turned the politics of abortion choice in another direction was the growing sense that *Roe* might be overruled.

The "benign office" of mother, said Justice Bradley in 1873, is part of the "paramount destiny . . . of woman." In this view, central to the traditional sexual Order, motherhood is not something a woman chooses, but something that happens to her. It happens, of course, within the other part of her divinely ordered destiny: the benign office of wife. This image of "mother" is not an image of a real woman with real children, or of a real woman active in the public world of work—let alone of a real woman who controls her own sexual behavior. It is, instead, an objectified image of "woman" as a disembodied vessel of domestic nurturance.

The demonstrators shouting outside the birth control clinic illustrate this objectification. Every frightened young woman before them has her own history and her own (typically dismaying) prospects, but what the demonstrators see is a projected image of one or another negative identity they believe they must suppress: actively sexual single woman, or destroyer of life. The one part of the young woman's life story they can easily imagine is a scene that objectifies her in the role of temptress: "She brought it on herself." In the traditional sexual Order, it is immoral to allow a woman to separate sex from its consequences; an unwanted pregnancy is the penalty for an unmarried woman's sexual behavior— and here, standing before them, is this woman who wants to avoid paying the price.[104]

Chiefly, though, the demonstrators objectify the young woman as a fetus-container, an abstract symbol of motherhood. Implicit in this picture is the constructed image of the fetus-as-person, an image applied not only to late-term fetuses but to prenatal life immediately after conception. (The imagery of child killing has informed even the right-to-life movement's impassioned opposition to the testing or importation of RU-486, the French "abortion pill" that, combined with a prostaglandin, induces menses.) The demonstrator who shouts, "Don't kill your baby!" is first metaphorically separating the fetus from the pregnant woman, and then investing the fetus with a will to live and an individual personality—all this in the absence of a neural system sufficient for even the rudiments of will or personality.[105] This image of fetus-as-person is "a metaphor for 'man' in space, floating free, attached only by the umbilical cord to the spaceship," while the particular woman who stands before the demonstrators "has become empty space."[106]

In the abstract, then, the young women entering the clinic serve as threatening symbols of active female sexuality or as equally threatening symbols of denial of woman's nurturing destiny. For the actual young women, however—especially the teenagers—the right to decide about abortion touches a question of identity. At least since the invention of "childhood," the passage from childhood to adulthood has seldom been easy, either for boys or for girls.[107] For today's female teenager, the passage has taken on new complications, mainly in the area of sexuality. She is flooded with messages about who she is and who she ought to be—and the messages are contradictory. One main theme is that she has a considerable measure of sexual freedom. The theoretical availability of contraception gives credibility to that message, and so do the activities and attitudes of her peers.[108] The commercial sexualization of young women pervades the popular culture. The effect of all this communication, however, is anything but liberating, for the underlying message "is not one of female self-assertion or sexual autonomy but one of availability to fantasized male desire."[109]

The counterpoint to this commercialized sexuality is a persistent theme of female dependence. Most teenagers live with their parents and remain, in many respects, dependent on them. In moving to a new relationship with her parents, one that involves both connection and separate identity, the young woman may see her sexual behavior and expression as a central ground on which that passage can be negotiated, the one place in her life where she wields real power. Contraception (or, as a last resort, abortion) is only one means available to the young woman;[110] as she tests the meanings of adulthood, "pregnancy itself may become a kind of resource."[111] One major risk here is that sexual behavior will prove to be the medium through which the young woman simply moves from dependence on her parents to dependence on her boyfriend. Even in the movies and magazines and advertisements that promote her sense of sexuality, the young woman is mainly treated as a passive object, and is repeatedly told that her personal worth, her happiness, her true identity are to be found only in connection with a man.

This cycle of female passivity and dependence on men is not universal among white teenagers.[112] It is not even the norm for black teenagers, who more typically see themselves as actively exercising their powers of choice, not only concerning sexual behavior, but also concerning pregnancy and motherhood and their attachment to men.[113] These experiences remind us that the traditional—and still prevailing—pattern of dependence is not given in Nature, but is socially constructed. If alternative models are to come to the fore, they will do so primarily through women's own expression. Some of the expression will take the form of consciousness raising and other, more public, forms of speech. One of the secondary effects of "the pill" is that women who really do take control over their maternity and their sexual behavior and expression are freed to find a new voice as well.[114] Some of the most important expression, however, is contained in the behavior that bespeaks a woman's active choices in shaping her self.

The average ages at which women marry or have children have increased significantly in the last generation, in response to increased opportunities for education and employment. Many of the young women, including teenagers, who add to current statistics on "premarital sex" would, in an earlier era, have been married. Today they may be in college or self-supporting or both—precisely because the availability of contraception and abortion affords them a greater measure of control over their sexual behavior and maternity than their mothers once had.[115] The exercise of these controls is undoubtedly expressive, but the activities are not "speech" in its First Amendment definition. Even when the expression of a new form of sexuality does take the form of speech, it fits poorly into a model of the First Amendment centered on civic deliberation. Yet the traffic in and out of birth control clinics conveys its messages every day, just as the legal restrictions on contraception and abortion once conveyed their messages of subordination. And if, in the nineteenth century, the exclusion of women from the practice of law had an effect equivalent to symbolic speech, so today does the presence of women as upwards of 40 percent of many law school student bodies—not to mention the presence on our Supreme Court of Justices Sandra Day O'Connor and Ruth Bader Ginsburg.

Let us pause here, to note once more the marked difference between the cultural counterrevolution and the social issues agenda. Even in 1980 it was clear to most observers that large numbers of women were in the work force to stay; more recently, economic recession has reminded most families that they need more than one breadwinner if they are to avoid deep cuts in their standard of living. To take their places in the public world of work and governance, women need to control their own maternity; even in 1980 most women were ready to insist on that control. But the futility of this part of the social issues agenda matters not a bit to the political managers who are selling cultural counterrevolution. Just as anglers know that some fish respond only to live bait, the managers know that the ideal deplorable condition is one their candidate can go on deploring indefinitely.

If the politics of women's status is a waning politics of nostalgia, still the anxieties of manhood give the same politicians another chance at a politics of fear.[116] They can promise to police the gender line in a different way: using the power of government to silence the expression of gay identity. The problem for American law, including constitutional law, is that the fulfillment of this part of the social issues agenda, too, takes the form of group subordination.

THE "FAMILY," THE GENDER LINE, AND THE EXPRESSION OF GAY IDENTITY

When Senator Helms scored points off "homosexuals and lesbians, disgusting people, marching in the streets demanding the right to marry each other," he captured in a few words his audience's presumed abhorrence of the twin abstractions of "homosexuals" and "homosexuality."[117] When a cause has carried the banner of gay rights, the main promoters of the social issues agenda have been delighted to express their opposition. This field offers a near-perfect example of how political issues involving religion and sex and gender tend to focus on government expression, to implicate the status ordering of cultural groups, and to confront decision makers with zero-sum choices that resist compromise. These tendencies are observable across the whole range of lesbian and gay rights issues, from employment discrimination to child custody.[118] Here, however, we concentrate on two recent points of contention: laws criminalizing homosexual sodomy, and the question whether government should offer same-sex couples a status approximating marriage. (In chapter 5 we consider the Defense Department's policy that, until 1993, purported to exclude gay men and lesbians from the armed services.) Both the sodomy laws and the same-sex "marriage" issue take their primary importance from the messages conveyed by government about the status of lesbians and gay men in American society.

The sodomy laws are still on the books in about half the states, but they are enforced only rarely. Their main function today is symbolic, representing not only the organized community's disapproval of people of homosexual orientation[119] but the community's devotion to a sharply defined gender line.[120] The laws' defenders have argued explicitly that a repeal might be taken as official endorsement of a gay or lesbian identity or of homosexual conduct,[121] and that even an unenforced sodomy law will help maintain the community's "moral climate" by expressing its formal condemnation of homosexual orientation.[122] True enough: official expressions of this kind are effective—as the Jim Crow laws were effective for generations in defining the status of black Americans. The moral climate maintained by the unenforced sodomy laws brings acid rain into millions of lives. One person's community-defining moral condemnation is another's community-denying stigma.

Viewed from either angle, it is hard to see a workable compromise. Either the sodomy law stays on the books or it is repealed (or held unconstitutional).[123] If the law remains, it stands as a symbol of moral condemnation, stigmatizing gay and lesbian citizens; if the law is repealed or held invalid, many citizens will see that act as one more example of a secularized society's dismissal of their values. Arguably, a compromise of sorts is achieved by maintaining a law criminalizing sodomy but leaving it unenforced. Similarly, one who wanted to "split the difference" on the issue of gay rights might favor repeal of the sodomy laws but resist the proposal of a marriage-like status for gay or lesbian couples.[124] But such efforts at compromise will not make the cultural conflicts disappear. If the main antagonists in these confrontations resist half-way solutions, the reason is not intransigence but realism about what is at stake: one group's status dominance, and the subordinate status of another group. Unavoidably, dominance is a zero-sum game.

In Boston in 1991 four Roman Catholic bishops attacked a proposed domestic partnership ordinance on the ground that "the extension of the title *family* to gay and lesbian couples . . . on an equal plane with true families" would mean "undermining the family in our society today." They went on: "If family life is ignored or despised or undermined, there is no natural foundation for social and civil life."[125] Surely, however, the proponents of the ordinance did not despise family life. To the contrary, they cherished its values—society, caring, commitment, intimacy, security, self-identification—and wanted to make those blessings fully available to all of Boston's citizens.[126] Legal recognition of a domestic partnership could, for example, afford visitation rights when a partner is in the hospital, or the right to give a message to a partner's child at school, or even health insurance for the partner of a public employee. These are important benefits, available to married couples;[127] denying them to gay couples raises serious problems under the equal protection clause, and I believe one day the courts will vindicate those claims.

The bishops were not trying to deny anyone hospital visitation rights or health insurance. Their concern is expressed by their reference to "true families." They were asking for the political and cultural equivalent of a copyright or a trademark—that is, for the city to conclude that familial relationships founded on heterosexual marriage had an exclusive entitlement to be considered families. The proposed ordinance, however, spoke neither of "marriage" nor of "family" but of "domestic partnership." So it was not even the name, but the general *idea* of "the family" that the bishops wanted to limit to heterosexual married couples, along with their children. (A note for readers who are not lawyers: Even in copyright law, you can't copyright such an abstract idea—for excellent reasons closely related to the values underlying the freedoms of speech and the press.) Anyone who thinks the "copyright" analogy is overdrawn should be prepared to answer this question: How else should we read the bishops' unsupported assertion that "the family" would be undermined if government were to recognize gay or lesbian couples as domestic partners?

The Boston proposal failed on a 7–6 vote, but in 1993 New York joined some twenty-five other cities in adopting such a proposal.[128] Whatever the city of Boston may do about one or another proposed ordinance, a great many Bostonians will go on living in domestic relationships that do not fit the pattern of traditional marriage. Many of these people are parents, and many of their unions, including gay and lesbian unions, are more stable than the average union in the category labeled "true families" by the bishops.[129] This stability challenges a widespread assumption, outside the gay community, that a "gay life-style" implies sexual promiscuity.[130] By definition, after all, it is couples in committed relationships who seek the law's formal recognition. In other words, the bishops correctly assume that the main points of contention raised by the proposed ordinance are not the ways people actually live their lives, but the symbols of government as indicators of legitimacy.[131]

If the central issue for the bishops is the meaning of "the family," the same issue is central for Boston's gay and lesbian couples. This agreement illustrates a larger point about cultural conflicts focused on law: The opposing parties tend to invest the conflicts with similar symbolic meanings, at the same level of importance. The good news here is that although the antagonists may see each other as moral lepers, at some level of abstraction they share "the same moral universe."[132] The bad news is that much of the explanation for this agreement lies in the connections linking both the legal issues and their symbolic value to the zero-sum game of status dominance.

Beneath the imagery, then, lies another kind of substantive reality. When the promoters of the social issues agenda appeal to "family values," and when the Massachusetts bishops speak of preserving "true families," they are talking about maintaining the dominance of the traditional sexual Order. That Order is, indeed, threatened when public expression lends legitimacy to violations of the Order's prescriptions for a distinctly gendered, patriarchal society.[133] Senator Helms would have no trouble in recognizing the proposed Boston ordinance as a splendid opportunity for the politics of fear. Because a gay identity blurs the gender line, its public display can be counted on to evoke the anxieties of manhood. For the man who considers himself heterosexual, the public expression of a gay identity by others—especially other men—

readily becomes a projected image of his own negative identity, a part of himself he must suppress if he is to be a real man in the eyes of others.[134] If he should support a politician who portrays gay and lesbian Americans as domestic enemies, and who promises to mute their public expression, no one should be surprised.

By the same token, for lesbians and gay men the visibility of their sexual identity has always been a matter of central importance.[135] In an earlier time, most saw their homosexual orientation as something they must keep hidden; the costs of disclosure were likely to be enormous. Over the last two decades this strategy of denial has been replaced, for millions of acknowledged gay men and lesbians, by the call to their brothers and sisters—also numbering in the millions—to "come out of the closet," affirming their sexual orientation. Coming out, which is both a choice of personal identity and a public act, perfectly illustrates how the personal is political.

Until the middle years of this century, a major problem for gay and lesbian Americans lay in their lack of awareness of each other's existence.[136] Imagine yourself in the position of someone who is gay or lesbian in the years before World War II. The only model of intimate relationship you know at first hand is the male/female couple, and virtually nothing in your daily experience suggests the possibility of any alternative. If you do not live in a good-sized city, you may not know anyone else who shares your sexual orientation. Even if you see reflections of your own sexual identity in the press, they are images of depravity and scandal, of people who are alienated from their families, hounded by the authorities, and shunned by the larger society.[137] Probably you will conceal your sexual orientation even from those who are closest to you, and the reasons for that concealment will partake of both shame and guilt. You will fear the consequences of disclosure, and a part of you will have accepted the larger society's characterization of homosexuality as an inclination toward sin. Much of your demoralization owes to your sense of isolation. You lack the support of others who share your feelings—not because those people do not exist, but because they, too, have been unwilling to bear the costs of open expression of their true selves. In all, this experience is a dreary illustration of the vicious circle of labeling and silencing.

The first important breaks in the circle came during World War II, when American society was subjected to some major dislocations. Large numbers of people shifted from small communities to a more anonymous life in urban centers of defense production. In addition, millions of men (and smaller numbers of women) were called into the armed services.[138] Military service typically took people to new places; gay and lesbian service members who previously had lived in isolation came upon homosexual communities in New York, San Francisco, and Los Angeles. By war's end a great many gay men and lesbians not only had discovered each other but had found a new freedom to express their true identities.

Expression and self-discovery were part of the same process, and much of the expression took the form of action. In acting out their sexual identities, gay men and lesbians not only communicated to each other but came to see themselves in a new light. One of the major staging grounds for self-discovery and mutual support turned out to be the gay bar. Political expression of the traditional kind was—and still is—to be found in some of the bars, but the most important expression that happened there was simply the presence of the patrons. In the years before the gay liberation movement gathered momentum, the bars allowed gays to drop the masks most of them wore when they were on the job or with their families. Despite the risks of arrest and other forms of official harassment,[139] the gay bar offered the kind of security that comes from being surrounded by accepting people—people who will value you for your true self.

The act of attending a gay bar, the act of two men dancing, or the wearing of clothes or haircuts in the styles prevailing in the gay community does not fit the model of the civic speech of Reason. Yet all these self-expressive acts have served distinctly political purposes, helping to mobilize individuals to identify themselves in a group and to join in group actions. Community organization anywhere is founded on emotion. To tap the emotions of others, you must show your own emotions—and here actions do speak louder than words. Feelings are communicated most effectively by acts that are expressive. "The natural expression of wanting is trying to get."[140] The gay bars provided a public arena in which gays could act out their hopes and their fears in expressive conduct. When a gay man dresses in drag, for example, he not only mocks the gender line but does so in a way that plays on the tensions associated with gender, invoking emotions that help cement a community.[141] California's Supreme Court—in 1959, a decade before the gay liberation movement crystallized—effectively recognized a right to congregate in gay bars.[142] That decision was not based on the First Amendment, but it did promote the freedom of association. The gay bar served as precursor for a host of other gay and lesbian institutions and meeting grounds, including "churches, health clinics, counseling services, social centers, professional associations, and amateur sports leagues."[143] Central to the gay bar's contributions to community development was its function as a focus for expressive action.

If consciousness raising within the group is an essential first step in a group's liberation from subordinate status, the next requirement is the education of the society outside the group. What differentiates gay men and lesbians from other historically subordinated groups is that a fundamental part of their communication to the larger society consists of the open avowal of the very characteristic that so many people in that society stigmatize: their homosexual orientation. This is a message that cannot be conveyed by the group as a whole, as a civil rights organization might seek public support by placing an advertisement in the *New York Times*. Coming out is something only an individual can do.[144] Viewed in political context, however, the decision of a single person to come out serves a function that converts his or her affirmation into a singular form of symbolic speech.

Ironically, this result flows out of the tendency we all have to objectify those who are different. If your own orientation is heterosexual, when a friend tells you of her homosexual orientation, at least part of you is likely to see her as embodying homosexuality itself. Inevitably, you will redefine your view of homosexuality to make room for the richness of your friend's qualities. Her whole life story, matched against her sexual orientation, becomes an enacted narrative of inclusion. When a famous professional football player comes out, the reader of the sports pages confronts the inadequacy of the stereotypical model of the gay man. This athlete is a person—not an abstract projection of heterosexual men's anxieties about their own masculine identities, but a live embodiment of one traditional set of masculine virtues, who also turns out to be gay. The political importance of his avowal of homosexual orientation lies not so much in his statement as in the expressive qualities of all his actions on the field. Once he comes out, his life as an athlete translates into the enactment of another narrative. When your friend comes out, when the athlete comes out, the *person* is political.

Today these liberating uses of free expression are shadowed by the cloud that hangs over all gay men. Not only has the AIDS calamity taken thousands of lives; it has also had major political side-effects.

Initially, the epidemic seriously retarded the movement toward full inclusion of gay men and lesbians in the community of equal citizens. This
effect was centered in the system of expression within which the meanings of homosexual identities are constructed; they are new versions of
the old story of labeling and silencing. For many Americans who considered themselves heterosexual, the threat of AIDS heightened their
sense of distance, not only from gay men[145] but from lesbians, whose
incidence of AIDS was (and remains) among the lowest in the nation.
As always, this sense of distance increases the tendency to let an abstraction obscure the real person.[146] The federal government's slowness
in acting to combat the epidemic clearly was linked to a widely shared
perception of AIDS in the 1980s as "the homosexuals' disease."[147] On
the other hand, the crisis has brought a new sense of mutual responsibility within the gay community, and has, in the words of a journalist,
"exposed our humanity to the rest of the world."[148]

A concern about the political impact of the AIDS epidemic seems to
have been one influence that led Justice Lewis Powell to shift his vote,
changing the Supreme Court's decision in the 1986 case of *Bowers v.
Hardwick*.[149] With his vote, a 5–4 majority upheld the constitutionality of
a Georgia law that generally prohibited sodomy—but in an opinion
explicitly limiting the Court's ruling to cases of homosexual sodomy.[150]
This appalling decision has been heaped with criticism—even, belat-
edly, by Justice Powell himself, after he left the Court[151]—and I need not
add to the pile of scorn here.[152] Suffice it to say that the case offers a
textbook example of the law's expressive uses in maintaining the traditional gender line. Both the Georgia statute and the *Hardwick* case are
important, not for any coercive application of law, but for their expressive qualities. The main significance of both the law and the Court's
decision is that they reinforce a system of group status dominance and
subordination.

In his oral argument to the Court in the *Hardwick* case, Georgia's
assistant attorney general commented that the decision of the federal
court of appeals, holding the law invalid, had created the danger of a
"reshuffling" or "reordering" of society.[153] In 1991 the bishops of Massachusetts were saying much the same thing, in a more genteel way,
when they argued that a domestic partnership ordinance would undermine "true families." In predicting some social reordering, the Georgia
lawyer was right, and the bishops were right. Recognizing the equal
citizenship of members of a historically subordinated group does re-

shuffle the society to a degree, and the reshuffling may be especially noticeable by those who are asked to move over and make room at the table of equal citizens. A similar remark would have been equally apt in 1953, at the oral argument in *Brown v. Board of Education*.

With status politics principally in mind, Murray Edelman wrote, "Every term and every entity in the environment is a signifier, and signifiers evoke a range of meanings that continue to widen endlessly."[154] Every one of the "family values" legal issues reviewed in this chapter is a complex signifier, presenting a range of opportunities for assigning alternative meanings. The "official" meanings so selected are widely seen to affect group status relationships. In the area of pornography, for example, one major issue goes to the likely effect of regulation: Will it improve or harm the status of women? When government regulates the expression of nongovernmental actors, the freedom of expression comes into play not only because the First Amendment is law but also because that freedom is seen by most Americans as an important part of our civic culture. Surely some such understanding influenced the jury that acquitted a Cincinnati museum director of an obscenity charge based on the display of seven homoerotic photographs as part of an exhibit of 175 works of Robert Mapplethorpe, a distinguished photographer.[155] To recognize the role of the First Amendment in cases like these is to introduce another element into the discussion of law as power and control: Because the power of law is dispersed among a great many governmental actors, some uses of law have the effect of releasing people from the control of other forms of law.

Both the cultural counterrevolutionaries and their adversaries, when they look to law for control of behavior, are thinking beyond the immediate effects of the law on the conduct so governed. Both proponents and opponents of the sodomy laws are less concerned with the actual practice or prohibition of homosexual sex than they are with the law's acculturating effects. One who sponsors a law prohibiting the sale of contraceptive devices to minors, for example, may hope that its enforcement will affect minors' attitudes concerning the use of contraceptives. Such a hope seems vain,[156] but other enactments plainly do demonstrate the acculturating influence of law's regulation of behavior. Consider, for example, the prohibition of sex discrimination in employment, enacted as part of the Civil Rights Act of 1964. Enforcement of this provision has its most immediate effects on the behavior of employers and unions and workers, both men and women. But the behavior resulting from the law's enforcement also has indirect long-term effects on attitudes. As women become more visible in crews of electricians, not just electricians (male and female) but all of us are becoming acculturated to new perceptions of women's capacities and new attitudes toward the social roles women may appropriately occupy.

In the area of "family values," where religion and sex come together, the whole system of legal regulation stands as a code of authoritative pronouncements about good and evil. The law, especially the criminal law, speaks to everyone, shaping the moral order and defining the community itself.[157] Legislation regulating sexual morality, in other words, specifies not only what conduct is permissible but also who really belongs. In the cultural counterrevolution, one of the main purposes of capturing government is to define and stigmatize "deviance," excluding people from respectable membership in the community: for example, the young unmarried woman who is pregnant, and thus visibly sexually active; or lesbians and gay men who "flaunt"—that is, openly avow—their sexual orientation.[158] This exclusionary function of law is understood not only by those who are stigmatized but also by those who are using the law to draw the community's boundaries.

Some expressive uses of law, in other words, are radically at odds with the ideal of equal citizenship—indeed, are presumptively unconstitutional when they stigmatize a social group. An example in the family values area is the 1992 amendment to the Colorado constitution that explicitly forbade state and local governments to adopt laws prohibiting discrimination on the basis of sexual orientation. In chapter 7, when we consider the relation of judicial review to the politics of exclusion, we shall see that this effort to shore up the gender line and the traditional status Order violates not just the ideal of a community that embraces all Americans, but the constitutional principle of equal citizenship.

4

Representations of Race

Long before any Europeans arrived, North America was multicultural; when Europeans came to stay, the continent became multiracial as well. Even during the colonial era, racial subordination was not a simple matter of white people's dominance over people of African origin or ancestry, and certainly it is not so simple today.[1] Nonetheless, in dealing with race this book focuses on the relations between black and white Americans, making only fleeting references to discrimination against Americans whose origin or ancestry is Native American, or Latin American, or Asian/Pacific. Racial and ethnic patterns are changing rapidly in California and all along the southern border. As a result, tensions have already matured into private violence, and nativism again bids to distort our politics as it has in earlier generations.[2] But this book's focus is the role of law in the recent politics of cultural counterrevolution, and in that politics typically it is black Americans who have been held up as objects on which white voters are invited to project various kinds of anxieties. Furthermore, to the extent that voting has become racially polarized in various states and cities, the polarization is a black/white split.[3]

How shall we think about race? Should we make race an explicit focus of our public policy? Or should we do our best to ignore race, and get on about the business of securing the equal citizenship of each one of us? Americans both black and white—not just as groups, but individual Americans—are conflicted about their answers to this question. The way we think about race is no side issue, but the central problem of our race relations.[4] In this country as elsewhere, the importance of race as a social marker derives from the meanings all of us assign to race. With only a small exaggeration, we can say that race *is* the sum of its representations. Among the myriad forms of expression that shape the meanings of race, none have been more influential than the messages communicated by politics, government, and law.

IMAGES OF DISORDER

The political era personified by the media campaign consultant is still young, but two television advertisements are already legendary. The first ad, repeatedly televised during President Bush's 1988 campaign, featured the glowering black face of Willie Horton, a convicted murderer. After his conviction he had been given a furlough from a Massachusetts prison, during which he had broken into a white couple's home, tied up the man, and raped the woman. The ad's effectiveness was not a matter of luck; it resulted from careful research—not just into the governorship of Bush's opponent, Michael Dukakis, but into the hopes and fears of the ad's intended consumers.[5]

The second modern media classic, broadcast in 1990 to North Carolina voters, succeeded in invigorating Sen. Jesse Helms's faltering campaign for reelection. The video image was simple: a white man's hands, first holding and then crumpling a letter. An announcer's voice made the setting clear: the man had been rejected for a job because an employer's affirmative action program gave preference to a minority applicant. Every white viewer could feel the ad's dramatic force, not just as a message opposing "quotas" but as a symbol of the status changes that had permitted Harvey Gantt, a black man, to offer a serious challenge to Senator Helms.[6]

No doubt some North Carolinians who viewed the "white hands" ad were among the cultural counterrevolution's earliest recruits, a generation earlier. Many southerners, black and white, had seen the Supreme Court's 1954 decision invalidating school segregation as a threat to the traditional Order of white supremacy, placing in question millions of individual identities. Within a decade, Congress had intensified the challenge by enacting the Civil Rights Act of 1964, which broadly prohibited racial discrimination not only by the institutions of government but by private employers and by the operators of hotels, restaurants, and other places of public accommodation. In the meanwhile the Warren Court, pursuing other doctrinal paths, had seemed to undermine the prevailing social Order in two additional ways: by holding official prayers in public schools unconstitutional, and by imposing increasingly strict federal constitutional limits on local law enforcement.[7] In the aggregate, these changes in constitutional and statutory law gave politi-cians an ideal opportunity for mobilizing voters to repel the menace of Disorder. Especially in the South, attacks on the Court made good politics long before the term *social issues agenda* was coined—and in those attacks the issue labeled Crime went hand in hand with the issue labeled Race.

Even in those early days, the inclination of white people to associate the movement for racial equality with the threat of Disorder was not limited to the South. As civil rights litigation worked its way north and west, the Supreme Court in the 1970s extended the integration remedy of school busing to cities such as Denver and Columbus, Ohio. During the same years both the Supreme Court and the lower federal courts were giving real bite to the employment discrimination provisions of the 1964 Civil Rights Act. In this particular challenge to the old status Order, many working-class whites both north and south saw a threat of competition they could take personally.[8]

Every integration implies a disintegration. The civil rights gains that brought middle-class and working-class black people new opportuni-ties in employment and housing and higher education also gave them avenues out of the central cities. As a result those areas lost most of the leaders and the institutions (churches, businesses, clubs, PTA groups) that had played indispensable roles in making the urban black popula-tion into a community. Some working-class residents remained, along with nearly all of the most impoverished, now even more concentrated and more disheartened. Ironically, the central city's despair was all the greater now that its residents were hearing, all around them, the mes-sages of equality and opportunity.[9] In the 1960s young men in the poorer black neighborhoods of Los Angeles and Detroit and Wash-ington, D.C., exploded in riot, and in succeeding years those young men's counterparts have found violence to be a persistent part of their everyday lives. When Los Angeles and other cities were convulsed again in 1992, few ghetto residents expressed surprise. Many of those residents have seen the "war on drugs," for example, as a program targeted on young black men,[10] and they have similar views about the origins of racial disparities in the frequency of arrest, prosecution, and conviction, and in the severity of sentencing.[11] Today everyone in urban America—and, given television's pervasive reach, everyone else—has a set of stock images of "crime," prominently featuring the faces of young black men.

Commenting on racial politics, Andrew Hacker asks, "What, precisely, is the threat? After all, the United States is not South Africa,
where whites are heavily outnumbered by indigenous blacks, who
might mobilize their strength to dominate the society. Of course, there
is fear of crime. It crops up in every poll, and has become a conversa-
tional staple. Still, most white Americans do not live in or near areas
where violence stalks the streets." Hacker goes on to suggest that
whites are afraid of black political power, dreading "that blacks will
treat whites as whites have treated blacks," and here he does draw the
South African analogy.[12] There is something to be said for this view, but
to understand the depth of white fears of violence by young black men
we need to go beyond any perceived threat to whites' dominance of
political (or even economic) institutions; we must also take another look
at the anxieties of manhood.

At the heart of those anxieties lies the fear of being dominated by
other men, humiliated for not being "man enough." Physical domination is something males learn early; by the time a boy becomes a man,
almost certainly he will have experienced both sides of the dominance/
submission game, both as an individual and in team efforts. When
plantation overseers whipped slaves, especially male slaves, a major
point of the punishment was humiliation. Many a slave experienced
severe beating as a demonstration of his powerlessness, a deprivation
of his self-respect, a denial of his title to manhood.[13] And back of the
white hand that wielded the lash was the fear—the night-and-day,
never-ending fear—of a slave rebellion that would be all the bloodier for
what had gone before. After Emancipation, when some 90 percent of
America's black population lived in the South under the Jim Crow
system, black violence against whites was markedly overmatched by
white racial violence, including lynching as the ultimate enforcer of the
caste system.[14]

Today most violent crime involves attackers and victims of the same
race. When violent crime is interracial, however, black-on-white crime
far outdistances white-on-black crime.[15] Surely, one of the contributing
causes of violence by young black men, against either white or black
victims, is the assumption—by no means limited to black men—that
physical aggression is one indicator of manhood that is within their
reach. The chilling rhetoric that permeates the gang culture reflects and
reinforces this assumption.[16] The recent vogue for the "takeover" bank
robbery, in which the gang terrorizes both employees and customers,

reminds us that the violence is in part a performance, designed to impress the victims and bolster the actors' self-images.[17] Interracial crime adds a dimension to the assertion implicit in the act; if a white male can be humiliated in the process, so much the better for the young male aggressor's temporary ego enhancement.

First and foremost law represents power, control, authority. Most Americans, on hearing generalized references to "law," surely think first of the criminal law and the police. These have been the connotations of the "law and order" theme in the social issues agenda. "Permissive" judges and candidates serve as lightning rods for the discharge of white constituents' fears of young black men who are out of control. When a rock singer uses the imagery of a war between young black men and the police, with pointed suggestions for killing officers, it is not enough for the true-blue cultural counterrevolutionary to join the multitudes who are appalled by the viciousness of the message[18] and the cynicism of those who profited from distributing it.[19] The counterrevolutionary must go on to insist that distribution of the lyric should be punished as criminal conduct "violating state sedition, anti-anarchy, anti–civil disorder and anti–incitement-to-riot statutes."[20] In these tense settings, where the possibility of interracial violence becomes the center of attention, the promise of law is first and foremost a promise of restraint and power, of order and Order.

By an overwhelming preponderance, residents of the black ghettos and the barrios of the Southwest are convinced that the crime statistics do not tell the whole story of interracial violence. The statistics, say the residents, systematically omit a form of interracial physical aggression that deserves to be recognized: rousting, pushing, chokeholding, and beating of young black and Latino men by (typically white) police officers—informal punishments inflicting not only physical pain but the pain of humiliation.[21] When an individual police officer is accused of this sort of abuse of authority, the facts are almost sure to be disputed. When all these disputes are aggregated, no pretense of "science" can definitively settle the questions raised by the more generalized charge of systematic harassment. Yet, now as during Jim Crow, it is a good bet that most white people do have some sense, deep down, that there is more than a little substance to that charge.[22]

Most Americans can still recall two video images from 1992: a group of white Los Angeles police officers beating Rodney King, and a group of young black men attacking Reginald Denny during the riots that followed the acquittal of three of the four officers prosecuted in a state court for the King beating. It is hard for most Americans, black or white, to excuse either of these attacks, but it behooves us to try to understand them.[23] The anger in these beatings is obvious enough; what needs emphasis is the fear—not the victims' fear, but the fear inside the attackers. To the men who administered each of these beatings, surely the victim must have seemed not so much a person as a dehumanized and scary projection of their own fears. When Rodney King was lying on the ground, he was no longer a threat to the officers; but surely they saw him as an abstract figure representing a group they had learned to fear: violent black men. When Reginald Denny was lying on the ground, he was no threat to his attackers; but surely they saw him as an abstraction, a representative of a larger and threatening group of white men who, in their view, had been "keeping the black man down."[24] To call the beatings "mindless" is exactly right; what was engaged was not so much minds as glands. I do not imagine for a moment that any white viewer could feel what a black viewer felt while watching those images, or that any black viewer could feel what a white viewer felt. But this white male viewer saw in both beatings the purpose not only to inflict pain but also to assert the sort of dominance that boys learn to express as they grope in the dark toward some image of manhood.

In any case, the 1991 report of the Christopher Commission supports the views that ghetto and barrio residents of Los Angeles express about police attitudes and police behavior toward minority citizens,[25] and so do the reports of other investigators in other cities.[26] As the 1992 Los Angeles riots unfolded, they became much more than a simple release of pent-up black rage against whites,[27] but the riots *started* with that impulse.[28] Behind many white males' attitudes toward black male aggression lies not just the fear of black political power but the more personalized fear of being the object of that rage, being physically dominated and humiliated by black men.

The "white hands" and Willie Horton advertisements exemplify the uses of television in the construction of political enemies. The images roused strong emotional responses, in part because their visual messages were inexplicit, yet unmistakable. "Symbols should always be unambiguous to the senses while remaining slightly beyond the reach of reason."[29] In one perspective, Horton's scowl was an image about "values," while the angry white hands crumpling the letter were an image about "interests." Indeed, the subject of race does raise both kinds of issues, and neither racial attitudes nor racial politics can be reduced to one or the other. The succeeding sections of this chapter bring "interests" to the fore, and make clear that however often the theme of race may come together with the sex/gender theme in the politics of cultural counterrevolution, each of these themes has its own independent significance in shaping both attitudes and politics. Still, the Willie Horton and "white hands" television ads touched the same tender spot; the fear of economic competition and the fear of violent assault are twin elements of the anxieties of male rivalry.

For many in the target audiences of both ads, black manhood itself is seen as threatening. When "Crime" is depicted with a dark face, the crime that inflames those anxieties most of all is black-on-white rape. Both the law of rape and its social meaning have long been dominated by the assumed proprietary concerns of men,[30] and the law's response to interracial rape has reflected the power differentials implicit in that assumption. Black women raped by white men had no legal protection at all during slavery, had little protection during Jim Crow, and in practical effect have less protection today than white women do.[31] On the other hand, "white men used their ownership of the body of the white female as a terrain on which to lynch the black male."[32] Joel Williamson's words about the rape of white women by black men are as apt for today's New York and Los Angeles as they are for yesterday's rural South: "It was this threat that thrust deeply into the psychic core of the [white] South, searing the white soul."[33]

In the last decade we have understood the political rhetoric of race and crime as part of a larger conservative social issues agenda, but even in 1964 Sen. Barry Goldwater's presidential campaign advertised his coolness to the claims of the civil rights movement and his toughness toward crime.[34] From that day to this, the two positions have been routinely packaged together—not explicitly, but by clear implication, and often by vilifying the works of a "politicized" Supreme Court. What used to be called a southern strategy is now aimed at a nationwide audience, mainly white and mainly male. Before President Bush was nominated in 1988, Lee Atwater, who would manage his campaign, had the race/crime theme ready to go. He told a group of Atlanta Republicans: "There is a story about a fellow named Willie Horton who, for all I know, may end up being Dukakis' running mate." And one of the producers of the Horton ads said, "Willie Horton has star quality. Willie's going to be politically furloughed to terrorize again. It's a wonderful mix of liberalism and a big black rapist."[35] The power of the Horton ad and the "white hands" ad does not depend on the actual effectiveness of law in controlling Disorder in the form of crime, or Disorder in the form of black competition for jobs previously reserved to whites. The ads' success with white voters lies in the power of law as a symbol of control. However the race/crime package may be wrapped, its subtext is a promise that the candidate, unlike the opposition, will "stand up to the blacks," deploying the powers of law and government to prevent further erosion of the traditional social Order.[36]

One measure of the influence of this public relations effort is that anyone who attributes its high impact to deeply ingrained racial fears must pause to protect his flanks. Out of caution, I do so here: I do not defend the Massachusetts authorities' decision to furlough Horton from prison, nor do I minimize Horton's loathsome crimes. Religious training may teach us to feel pity for a man who responds to the anxieties of manhood by using violence to express power—but his violence still deserves severe punishment. In discussing the race/crime package as an appeal to the accustomed Order of status dominance, I am not making "order" the pivot of a play on words. Every community has a strong and entirely legitimate interest in order, in the sense of civil peace and obedience to law. It is the authors of the social issues agenda who have counted on their constituents to interpret the two senses of "order" as identical.

FORMAL RACIAL NEUTRALITY IN THE POLITICS AND LAW OF COUNTERREVOLUTION

On the subject of race the social issues agenda primarily speaks to a white audience, and says what those constituents want to hear. The message is simple: the civil rights movement long ago attained its goal of racial equality, and should stop asking for more. In this formulation "racial equality" means governmental neutrality on the subject of race, and the neutrality in question is formal. For one who accepts this premise, the principle of racial equality is not offended by the continuing harmful effects, in today's world, of the laws and private behavior that stigmatized a racial group as members of a subordinate caste. For example, racial equality has nothing to do with questions about black and white people's incomes or employment or housing or education—or, indeed, about any substantive comparisons of the lives of white and black Americans. Nor does it matter that American society is not now and never has been "color-blind."[37] The question—the only question—is whether the letter of the law establishes different rights or obligations for black and white people.

This notion of formal racial neutrality minimizes the responsibility of either governmental or nongovernmental actors to remedy the continuing effects of slavery and Jim Crow. Of course, that is precisely its political appeal to the cultural counterrevolution's constituents, who generally think the civil rights movement has already "gone far enough or gone too far" in rearranging the old racial Order,[38] and who are sure they (and not elite liberals) will have to bear the costs—at a minimum, the status costs—of any further reordering. Then who does have responsibility for eliminating the pernicious effects of racial caste from American society? For those same white constituents, the social issues agenda has a convenient answer: Once the symbols of government are made to express formal racial neutrality, no one has a legal or moral obligation to do anything further. Indeed, if anyone should undertake a race-conscious remedy to eliminate some present effect of the racial caste system, the social issues agenda promises to use the power of government to define that departure from formal neutrality as an illegal form of "reverse discrimination." The political appeal of this variation on the theme of formal racial neutrality can be seen in the "white hands" advertisement that helped reelect Senator Helms.

Even before 1980 most important civil rights cases before the Supreme Court were raising questions about the relation between formal and substantive racial equality, and about responsibilities for remedying racial inequalities. A century earlier, in the era of the *Civil Rights Cases*,[39] the Court had opted in all respects for formal racial neutrality and limited responsibility. These preferences have never been completely submerged in our constitutional law, not even while the Warren Court was giving new life to the principle of equal citizenship. Indeed, the Warren Court's earliest civil rights achievements can be seen as a redefinition of formal equality that placed officially sponsored racial segregation—even in "separate but equal" facilities—outside the constitutional pale.[40] Yet, from the 1950s to the 1970s, the need for remedying a wide variety of forms of private discrimination was also recognized: for example, by the Warren Court's decisions relaxing the "state action" barrier to the assertion of claims under the equal protection clause,[41] by the Burger Court's acceptance of group remedies,[42] and by both Courts' generous construction of federal civil rights laws.[43] These civil rights decisions nourished a countertradition of public responsibility, not just to avoid perpetuating the effects of racial caste but to take positive action to end those effects.

Against this background the period that began in 1980 has been not only the political era of the social issues agenda but also, within the Supreme Court, a time of civil rights discontinuity. Those two developments do not seem unrelated. It would be excessive to say that the Rehnquist Court has interpreted the Constitution or federal civil rights laws as if they wholly incorporated a doctrinal model of formal neutrality. Yet, such a model appears to be central in some Justices' vision of racial equality, and strongly influential for other Justices in the current majority. It does seem accurate to say that the idea of formal racial neutrality has become a homing principle for deciding civil rights cases.

What I am calling a model is a cluster of preferences.[44] First is the preference for limited governmental responsibility, in which government's only legal duty is to avoid purposeful discrimination of its own. Second, the model embodies a preference for private ordering, and a corresponding aversion to governmental interference in private decisions—in other words, a preference for civil rights deregulation. To promote this preference, the courts should hold that the Constitution imposes no limitation on private discrimination and no responsibility on government to remedy private discrimination. Furthermore, congressional remedies for private discrimination should be narrowly interpreted, absent clearly stated direction by Congress to the contrary. For example, the federal antidiscrimination laws should be read to reach only purposeful racial discrimination. Third, even when governmental or private discrimination is proved, the model embodies a preference for remedies that are individualized, in two ways:[45] (1) a remedy should benefit only those who can prove they are the direct victims of specifically identified acts of discrimination; (2) a remedy should burden only those persons who have deliberately engaged in those acts, or persons who have directly benefited by that wrongdoing. Group remedies—remedies that take race into account in allocating burdens or benefits—are strongly disfavored.

In this model of formal racial neutrality, every arguably discriminatory act is evaluated without reference to its general societal context, as if history began this morning. The presumption is that present conditions—whatever they are—represent equilibrium, or race-neutrality.[46]

That presumption stands until a specific transgression of the norm of race-neutrality is proved by a claimant who can satisfy an exacting burden of proof. Thus, every race-conscious remedy, imposed by either a legislative body or a court, violates the norm unless it is narrowly focused on correcting a previous (and particularly identified) violation. In the doctrinal model of formal neutrality, nobody—neither a private citizen nor any officer of government—is responsible to remedy the present effects of slavery and Jim Crow and the myriad deformations of our public life produced by the stigma of caste. Furthermore, an effort to remedy past societal discrimination is, under the model, a violation of the principle of race-neutrality. The legal model of formal neutrality, like the vision of racial equality outlined in the social issues agenda, is a formula for avoiding public responsibility for private discrimination.

THE PRIMACY OF PRIVATE DISCRIMINATION IN RACIAL SUBORDINATION

To see the implications of a principle of formal neutrality for race relations in America, we must begin by looking at the central role that private discrimination has played in racial subordination, from the times of slavery to the present day. I have been using the term *private discrimination* in its modern sense: racial discrimination that is not directly caused by the acts of government officials. But in the era of slavery the term had no meaning. Slavery began as the work of nongovernmental actors who used forced labor to maximize the profit on their investment in land. Governmental action, including the substantial body of law that governed slavery, was designed to protect—to legitimize, to institutionalize—private interests that the first slaveholders had created by violence. Slavery was not simply a relationship created by law; it was a social system, a culture, an amalgam of beliefs and behavior that permeated all segments of society in the slaveholding states.

The defenders of slavery did make a distinction between the public and private spheres of their society. They saw enslaved people as members of their masters' households, and argued that government had no business interfering with that private domain.[47] But "private discrimination" was not separate from the larger system of control; the slaves were properly subjected to their masters' paternalistic governance, the defenders argued, because Nature made them incapable of governing themselves. This idea of racial superiority and inferiority became a dogma as private landowners sought a justification for slavery. For the individuals who were enslaved, their bondage to private masters was their all-pervasive public status. Their membership in the slave caste indelibly stained every aspect of their lives: work, living conditions, family relations, self-image. In a society that enslaved a race, the distinction between public and private discrimination would never occur to anyone.

After Emancipation the "customs" of racial caste persisted; slavery's legal props were gone, but much of the caste system remained in place. The planters needed a labor force, and so "the dominant theme in the planters' lives became the search for a substitute for slavery."[48] In the earliest postwar days, the vagrancy laws and Black Codes served, along with a convict-lease system, to provide black workers for the plantations and other farms. A "contract lease" system held black workers on the land in an arrangement that amounted to debt peonage.[49] The law's contribution was the formally neutral enforcement of labor contracts, which typically required personal service to pay off debts. Owners would encourage workers to accept advances of money, the debts would gather interest, and the system "would hold [the workers] forever by a constantly strengthening chain."[50]

What was surprising was that some black farmers did manage to keep their heads above the waters of debt. One was Nate Shaw, who found the struggle hard: "I had men turn me down [as a sharecropper], wouldn't let me have the land I needed to work, wouldn't sell me guano, didn't want to see me with anything." Today we call similar refusals to deal—such as the refusal to rent a house to a black tenant—by the name of private discrimination. In the Reconstruction years, however, those acts had no special name. They were an undifferentiated part of a larger social system that excluded black people from equal citizenship. In ensnaring and subordinating black workers, then, "the legal net was formidable. But the new labor system . . . was more than that."[51] White supremacy again became governmental policy, but it began in private landowners' demand for a labor force, private beliefs about racial inferiority, and private fears of status displacement.

In the same post-Emancipation period, black people were subjected to a range of personal indignities that also had their origins in the slave system's assumptions about racial inferiority. Black citizens were relegated to lower-class accommodations in streetcars; if they were allowed in churches and theaters, they were routinely required to sit in the back rows; they had access only to a few hotels and restaurants that catered exclusively to black patrons. These behavioral expressions of private prejudice were underpinned by law, from common law powers over property to legislative charters for streetcar companies. The racial restrictions thus enforced by private owners were "understood rather than stated,"[52] but they were powerful customs with deep roots in slavery.

In 1867 the black editor of a New Orleans newspaper saw how these informal modes of private behavior taught lessons about the meaning of race—and thus translated readily into discrimination by governmental institutions: "For as long as [racial] distinctions will be kept on in public manners, these discriminations will react on the decisions of juries and courts, and make impartial justice a lie."[53] Later, when Jim Crow arrived, the force of law was explicitly placed behind the customs of exclusion and domination. But Jim Crow was always more than its legal framework. Like slavery, it was a comprehensive system of racial subordination in which private discrimination and the acts and policies of government officials reinforced each other.[54]

If private racial discrimination has presented a problem for our legal doctrine, one reason is the ambiguity of the categories "public" and "private." In law the label "public" carries many different meanings, the range of which is suggested by some common terms of our constitutional discourse: public figure (libel); public forum (freedom of speech in streets and parks); public purpose (economic regulation); public use (takings of property by eminent domain). A term is useful when it is adapted to its context. In the field of civil rights, the relevant context is the equal citizenship guaranteed by the Civil War Amendments and their implementing legislation. A century of legal doctrine has trained us, when we think of private discrimination, to draw an implicit distinction between governmental and nongovernmental actors. But in ordinary speech it is also common to distinguish between the public and the private in quite a different way, differentiating our shared public life from our separate private lives.

One major source of difficulty for civil rights law, both constitutional and statutory, is the tendency to assume that these two different public/private distinctions are congruent. Everyone understands that law and government are part of the community's public life. And the idea that each of us should control his or her own private life has great appeal in a society with a strong tradition of individualism. It is easy, and perhaps also morally convenient, for us to slide from those generalizations into the assumption that our public life consists entirely of dealings with government actors, and that whatever nongovernmental actors do is part of their private lives—their own business and nobody else's.

That assumption is profoundly mistaken. The behavior we call private discrimination is a spore that replicates itself in ever-widening circles. Consider the problem of housing segregation. If you are white and you have no black neighbors, it is difficult for you to know any black person well, and easy for your day-to-day assumptions about black people to be dominated by acculturated generalizations that are direct descendants of the race-based apologies for slavery—assumptions that the architects of the social issues agenda are ready to exploit.[55] In the field of housing, the result is not merely the inability of a black family to buy a particular home. The cumulative effect of this pattern—which is present in all our cities[56]—is to maintain a status difference based on race that affects the whole society. It is hard to imagine any result that would be more "public" in nature. The harm of private discrimination is not limited to its direct victims. All society suffers.

Given the continuing high levels of residential segregation, the workplace becomes the main opportunity for adults to become acquainted across the racial divisions that afflict us all. Furthermore, work in America is a major determinant of individual status. Part of the status-affecting feature of work is the income it produces and the wealth a family can accumulate. But work is also a way of expressing one's ability in ways that are visible to others. The point is not just self-expression; in this context of race relations, work ranks with schooling in educating us about people of other races and cultures.[57] In the aggregate, these employment opportunities, especially in the private sector, are crucial to the public status of historically subordinated groups. An incident of racial harassment on the job, of course, is antithetical to the integration of the workplace; multiplied by the millions, it is antithetical to the integration of American society. So it is with the separation of races in private employment—whether or not that separation results from the conscious purposes of particular employers, provable in court.

What happens in the marketplace and the workplace, then, has vital consequences for the social status, even the political status, of black people as a group, and therefore for the status of every individual black man and woman and child.[58] The history of ethnic integration in America is in great measure an economic history: as the overwhelming majority of a social group has entered the middle class, individual members of the group have come to be recognized as equal citizens.[59] The other side of this coin, both in the workplace and in the marketplace, is that the indignities imposed by private racial discrimination not only hurt people one by one but also impose a "status-harm" on a racial group, reinforcing the group's subordination.[60]

Surely this process of reinforcement is easier to understand when one is a member of the subordinated group—such as that New Orleans editor who remarked on the way private discriminatory behavior eroded the impartiality of the criminal justice system.[61] But there is more to the problem of private racial discrimination than the editor mentioned in the quoted passage. The marketplace and the workplace not only affect the sphere of public life that is governmental; they are themselves major spheres of public life. To end the effects of racial caste, it will not be enough—it has never been enough—to do away with discriminatory laws. Even without those laws, private discrimination will perpetuate the effects of racial caste. To reinforce the conventional status Order of racial groups, all that is needed from law and government is formal racial neutrality.

Few actions of government have contributed more to our society's answer to the question, How shall we think about race? than has the work of the Congress and the federal courts in developing a body of law governing racial discrimination in employment. In this field, the gravitational pull of the model of formal racial neutrality produced a seismic shift in 1989, when several decisions of the Supreme Court sharply retracted the reach of federal employment discrimination law.[62] Two of these cases vividly illustrate the current majority's preference for civil rights deregulation.[63]

The Civil Rights Act of 1866 was the Reconstruction Congress's first major effort to translate the formal equality of emancipation from slavery into the substantive equality that is the heart of equal citizenship. The act remains on the books, invigorated by decisions of the Warren and Burger Courts.[64] One section gives all persons an equal right "to make and enforce contracts" and authorizes damages for its violation. In accordance with established precedent in the lower federal courts, Brenda Patterson, a black woman, sued her employer, a credit union in Virginia, claiming damages for racial harassment.[65] The Supreme Court, by a 5–4 vote, concluded that although the 1866 act applied to some forms of employment discrimination (a race-based refusal to hire or to promote to a new position), it did not apply to racial harassment on the job. The majority said that the only federal remedies for harassment were those provided by Title VII of the Civil Rights Act of 1964, chiefly reinstatement, back pay, and an injunction against further harassment. Patterson had testified in excruciating detail about her white supervisor's differential treatment of white and black employees in workload, training, and promotion opportunities. But the hurt of racial harassment goes beyond such material concerns. She also testified that her supervisor

- criticized white employees in private (or in staff meetings) without referring to individuals, but criticized the two black employees by name in meetings;

- assigned her, but no other clerical worker, to dust and sweep;

- repeatedly suggested that a white would be able to do her job better than she could; and

- said to her on several occasions that "blacks are known to work slower than whites by nature"—once putting the same idea in these words: "Some animals [are] faster than other animals."[66]

If you were in Brenda Patterson's circumstances, would you see an injunction as an adequate remedy for these harms?

The Title VII remedies offered no compensation at all for the main harms caused by racial harassment, such as humiliation. It would take exceptional resolution for a victim of harassment to go through the ordeal of prosecuting a Title VII claim in order to make the harassing employer behave better in the future.[67] Even so, the Supreme Court declined to follow the lower court precedents construing the 1866 act to provide damages, the only commonsense remedy for the harm of harassment. Instead, the majority fell back on formal neutrality's preference for narrow construction in the service of private ordering—in this context, employer autonomy.

Ten days before the *Patterson* decision, the Court had decided *Wards Cove Packing Co. v. Atonio*,[68] the most serious setback for the civil rights cause among all the 1989 cases. Here the doctrinal story begins in 1971. That year the Burger Court recognized the inadequacy of formal neutrality as a guiding principle for defining employment discrimination under Title VII. Even absent a particularized showing of discriminatory purpose, the Court unanimously held in *Griggs v. Duke Power Co.*,[69] an employer's practice presumptively violated Title VII if it produced a disparate harmful effect on a racial group. The employer could overcome the presumption by showing the business necessity of the practice. Decisions subsequent to *Griggs* had reinforced the rule that, once the plaintiff proved a disparate impact, the employer had the burden of proving business necessity.

The *Griggs* formula responded to the idea of a broad public responsibility for ending the harmful effects of racial caste. First, it recognized that racism often lurks at the margin of consciousness, affecting behavior without ripening into anything that can be identified—even by the actor—as purpose. Second, the formula recognized the pernicious public effects of widespread racial segregation in private employment, effects that seriously impede the integration of American society. Third, by placing on employers the burden of justifying the behavior that produced those segregating effects, *Griggs* admonished employers to take responsibility for examining their practices and acting to minimize the harms of segregation.

In *Wards Cove* the employer's unskilled cannery workers were nearly all Filipinos or Alaska Natives; workers in skilled jobs, almost all of whom were better paid than cannery workers, were predominantly white. The two groups of workers were housed in separate dormitories and ate in separate dining halls. Some observers, contemplating this picture, might call it Jim Crow, Alaska style. The Supreme Court's majority, however, saw the case as an opportunity to effect a major retreat from the doctrinal scheme set out in *Griggs*.

Two changes in the Court's interpretation of Title VII were especially ominous. First, to establish a presumptive violation, it would no longer be enough for a plaintiff to show a statistical racial disparity between the employer's work force and the relevant pool of qualified persons. Now the plaintiff would have to identify a specific employment practice, and explain the mechanism by which that practice caused the disparate racial impact—a burden that would be particularly onerous when employers' hiring standards were subjective or multifactored. The *Griggs* Court had been aware that, in the area of race relations, the interplay of beliefs and behavior is often hard to detect, and yet is capable of inflicting serious group harms. In *Wards Cove* this awareness gave way to the preference for narrowly focused definitions of harm and remedy—and, not incidentally, to the preference for private ordering.

The latter preference is even more clearly visible in the Court's second major change in the *Griggs* doctrine. Even if the plaintiff could establish a presumptive violation, *Wards Cove* drastically reduced the value of that presumption by turning upside down the burden of proof on the question of business necessity. Once the employer produced some evidence of a business justification for the challenged practice, it would be up to the plaintiff to prove that the practice did not serve, "in a significant way, the legitimate employment goals of the employer." Not only was that substantive standard a far cry from "necessity"; the burden on the plaintiff to prove the required negative was heavy.

Wards Cove, then, was another disheartening illustration of the formal neutrality model's unresponsiveness to one of the most glaringly obvious facts of American life: that the system of racial caste continues to affect the members of a racial group as a group.[70] The implication of that fact for our race relations law, as I have argued elsewhere, is plain: "Either we use group remedies for past discrimination, or we give up the pretense that a remedy is what we seek."[71] But in the rhetoric of the social issues agenda, a race-conscious presumption of the *Griggs* type amounts to a racial "quota."

The effect on private discrimination of the model of formal neutrality comes into bold relief when we consider *Patterson* and *Wards Cove* together. In *Patterson* the majority relied on the availability of an unsuitable Title VII remedy to justify an ungenerous reading of the 1866 act, narrowly confining its use in employment discrimination cases. In *Wards Cove* the Court drastically limited the reach of Title VII in a type of case outside the 1866 act's scope. Both decisions, in the name of private ordering, slight the importance of the workplace in the integration of American public life. The two decisions also illuminate a larger point about the relation of formal racial neutrality to private discrimination: When judges submerge the claims of racial equality to the claims of private ordering, they reinforce the prevailing status Order.[72] For the political managers who market the social issues agenda, of course, that consequence is all to the good. Sad to say, in 1989 the Supreme Court's majority seemed to agree.

Both *Patterson* and *Wards Cove* interpreted acts of Congress, and Congress quickly responded by passing bills to restore those acts to the interpretations that had prevailed before 1989. President Bush, however, remained unmoved, and Congress could not produce the two-thirds majorities in the House and the Senate to override a veto. After two years of negotiating and vetoing and negotiating again—accompanied by muted sounds of conflict inside the White House—President Bush signed into law the Civil Rights Act of 1991.[73] The new law's main effects were to overturn several of the 1989 decisions interpreting federal civil rights laws, including *Patterson* and *Wards Cove.*[74] In chapter 7 we return to the politics of this legislation. For now it is enough to note the bearing of these developments on the question that continues to vex the nation: How shall we think about race? We have seen how the authors of the social issues agenda have offered their (mainly white) constituents two apparently discordant answers to this question. The explicit, "official" message is: *Don't* think about race; think about people as individuals. Using race to classify people, even for remedial purposes, violates the principle of formal racial neutrality. This message was the common thread in the Bush administration's arguments to the Supreme Court in the 1989 cases.[75] At the same time the tacit message of the social issues agenda—conveyed in the President's persistent use of the word "quotas" during the two years of sparring with Congress, and instantly recognizable in televised images featuring "white hands" and Willie Horton's face—is: Worry about race in your guts, and worry about it all the time. Vote for our candidates, who will protect Us from Them.

In a theoretical, intellectual sense, these two messages' attitudes toward the myth of race may seem incoherent. That sort of discrepancy, however, is of no concern to the myth makers who package the social issues agenda in thirty-second video melodramas. Ernst Cassirer, a wise European who came to our shores in search of tolerance, knew from his own painful experience that the "real substratum of myth is not a substratum of thought but of feeling. . . . [Its] coherence depends much more upon unity of feeling than upon logical rules."[76] The two seemingly disharmonious messages about race in the social issues agenda are entirely coherent at the level of feeling—and the operative feeling is fear.

GOVERNMENT, EXPRESSION, AND THE SOCIAL MEANINGS OF RACE: LABELING AND SILENCING

The means of subordination of black people in America have always included two techniques that lie in the realm of expression: labeling and silencing. Each technique has reinforced the other. From the earliest days of European and American enslavement of Africans,

racism and slavery went together as "twin aspects of a general debase-
ment" of black people.[77] By the late eighteenth century, when a growing
spirit of egalitarianism necessitated an apology for slavery, the argument was founded on a theory of the innate biological inferiority of
black men and women.[78] In this view black people as a group represented not Reason but "innocent nature"; they were called moral children who lacked the capacity for self-determination.[79] If they were to
achieve even minimally satisfactory lives, the argument concluded,
they needed the benevolent control of whites.

In the eyes of Englishmen in the era of colonization, slavery implied
something less than humanity, a status akin to that of a beast.[80] This
assumption was part of a logic that was circular; to complete the cycle of
justification, the defenders of black slavery argued that black people
were not fully human,[81] but bestial creatures "utterly devoid of reason."[82] Yet the slaveholders never truly believed the animal analogy—
as they made clear in their strict rules aimed at preventing slave uprisings. The laws forbade anyone to put slaves in possession of weapons
or to teach them to read and write. Furthermore, the laws prohibited
slaves from bringing lawsuits or testifying in court against whites—
thus implicitly recognizing the slaves' humanity.[83] But the defenders of
slavery affixed labels to the slaves that depreciated their capacity for the
reasoned deliberation of citizens, calling them carefree, prone to dis-
simulation, and promiscuous.[84]

Medieval European accounts of Africa had portrayed the men as
libidinous, and the view persisted among slavery's defenders in America; even Thomas Jefferson, who argued against slavery in the abstract
while continuing to hold slaves, was of this view.[85] The perspective was
not merely incidental to whites' perception of black people; it was fundamental, and it was closely connected with white men's sense of guilt
and self-control. From the beginnings of slavery in America, whites
associated control over black men and women with the struggle between Reason and Nature inside themselves, and with their need to
control "the blackness within."[86]

From the time of slavery to the mid-twentieth century, lynching was
the white man's ultimate ritual of control. It served not only to keep
black men in their prescribed place but to act out white men's anxieties
about themselves. The myth of the "black beast rapist,"[87] a direct out-
growth of the racial inferiority defense of slavery, provided white men

with a regular excuse for a ritual that expressed both white male power and the repression of their own tendencies toward sexual aggression. The group that performed the ritual was called, without intended irony, a lynching party. Reading a description of such a group as it goes about the grisly killing and mutilation of a black man accused of raping a white woman, you may well ask yourselves, Who are the primitives? But the members of the lynch mob had exactly the opposite view, seeing themselves as the defenders of civilization against unreasoning Nature. Here we have a textbook illustration of a larger point, equally apt across the whole range of today's cultural conflicts over status dominance: The orthodox definitions of Reason and Unreason are constructed by people with power, and serve those people's needs for reassurance about their own worth.

After slavery had been abolished and after Reconstruction had come and gone, race remained a central signifier of group status and personal identity, in the North as well as the South. Yet it was the southern system of Jim Crow that drew the color line most sharply. Black people had gained formal citizenship, and yet the whole system of expression was still rigged against them. Their own freedom of expression was severely limited, while Jim Crow gave free circulation to the messages that helped maintain their subordination.

The silencing of black people's expression ranged over the whole of public and private life. In arrant violation of the Constitution and federal laws, black citizens were effectively excluded from voting, from holding public office, and from serving on juries. Indeed, blacks were excluded from speaking with any civic authority or participating in any of the deliberations of "true" citizens. The schooling of black children was first neglected altogether and then systematically funded at inadequate levels. Segregation itself drastically limited the public occasions on which black people might communicate their views to their white cocitizens. And Jim Crow, as "a categorical barrier to social mobility,"[88] reserved to whites virtually all of a local community's positions of nongovernmental leadership.[89]

On the other side, Jim Crow was itself a stream of messages, a combined public and private exercise in the defamation of a social group. Explicit labeling was, of course, part of the system; the slaveholders' children were ready to portray inferiority and dependency as the genetic inheritance of the children of slaves.[90] But Jim Crow's most important communications about group status and personal identity were not explicit. Rather, they were contained in the thousands of insults and exclusions, big and little, that constituted the system itself.

Much of Jim Crow, in other words, was "symbolic speech,"[91] drawing the boundaries of community and placing black people outside. The relegation of black people to low-wage work, along with other tangible deprivations ranging from housing to medical care, not only worked material disadvantages, but also affixed their own implicit labels of subservience.[92] Even more vivid messages were conveyed by the proscription of interracial marriage; by the exclusion of black people from hotels and restaurants; by the segregation of the races in streetcars and ballparks; by the avoidance of interracial handshakes. Some of these rituals of social distance and one-way politeness were enforced by law; all of them had grown out of the taboos of slavery. Their repetition, day in and day out, was a course of continuing education, teaching black and white people alike that blackness was equated with dependency, and whiteness with citizenship. In a society permeated with these messages, race was the supreme marker for individual identity; to be white meant, most importantly, that you were superior because you were not black.[93]

Unhappily, themes like these have not lost their currency. Although the legal structure of Jim Crow has been dismantled, the attitudes formed in emotion-charged acculturation die hard. The longest-lasting and most damaging legacy of the system of racial caste is racism. The very word is off-putting to most whites, for it has taken on a connotation that implies the malevolence of the jackbooted skinhead. Unfortunately, the problem of racism is not so simple. The most serious problem of racism is not one of evil hearts, but of culture, of the meanings we learn to assign to our experience.[94] Necessarily, we usually assign those meanings without reflecting on what we are doing; life is too short to stop and think about everything we see and do. The unreflective meanings that most white Americans project on black Americans are the product of multiple aspects of the dominant culture.[95] Our strong individualism trains us to believe that people succeed and fail individually. Yet, without dropping a stitch, we go on from this belief to the assumption that if substantial numbers of black people do not succeed, the explanation must lie in some failing they share as a group.[96] This awkward transition from individualist to group-based assumption is eased by two emotions that also lie at the margins of consciousness. First, there is the wish to justify our own status in two contrary ways: as earned, and as the result of some innate qualities. Second, there are the fears we have already considered: the fear of violent response, and the fear of displacement from a status position that is relatively favorable. The entire process, then, is closely tied to the defense of private interests, and it is a direct descendant of the race-based apologies for slavery. The main difference is that in our time, the assignment of meaning to our experience of race often is unexpressed, even suppressed from conscious thought, and held by people who—genuinely—have the best of will. It is understandable why most of us try to suppress pain and guilt and fear. It is also understandable that the dominant culture, which includes most legislators and prosecutors and judges,[97] often hears the egalitarian claims of racial minorities as the voice of Unreason.[98]

In the Supreme Court's 1982 school censorship case, for example, black writers were a majority among the authors whose works had been removed from the library of a public high school on Long Island.[99] Some objecting parents and school board members had called the books "anti-American"; in partial proof, two board members pointed to a book mentioning that George Washington was a slaveholder. Mainly, though, they had objected to the authors' use of "filthy" language, by which they meant language with a strong sexual charge.[100] In the board's statements and in the opinions of the Justices—especially those who would have summarily dismissed the constitutional claim against the board—we can hear a persistent echo of the precept that would limit the First Amendment to the speech of Reason. Under this postulate, sexually explicit language is indecent, "low-value" speech, and just doesn't deserve much protection.

Once again the First Amendment model of civic deliberation, which inclines judges to equate the speech of the culturally dominant with the civil tones of the speech of Reason, offers nothing to shield outsiders against silencing. Reason and civility, for most whites, require expression about sexual interactions to be indirect and veiled—a style many black men and women find false.[101] Moreover, an author who seeks to portray the street life of young black men in the impoverished ghetto can avoid pungent sexual imagery only at the risk of sacrificing realistic dialogue. Perhaps, in the school library case, the association of race with the forbidden expressions of sexuality was accidental. My interpretation, however, is that it reflected generations of acculturation of white readers and listeners in a system of group subordination.

GOVERNMENT, EXPRESSION, AND THE SOCIAL MEANINGS OF RACE: THE LANGUAGES OF LIBERATION AND OF HATE

The silencing of outsiders and their exclusion from the political community go together. In the Supreme Court's infamous opinion in the *Dred Scott* case (1857) [102] Chief Justice Roger B. Taney linked civilization, citizenship, and the freedom of expression. Contrasting "this unfortunate race" with "the civilized nations of Europe," Taney concluded that black people, at the nation's founding, had been denied both the status of citizens and the constitutional freedoms of speech and assembly. A group that had been considered "an inferior class of beings," he argued, could not have been seen by the adopters of the Constitution as members of the political community. By this reasoning the imposition of civic inferiority justified itself: citizens were expected to engage in deliberative reasoning with one another, but uncivilized Nature was inconsistent with the speech of Reason. Today, too, freedom of expression is closely linked with group status, in a similar circular logic. As even Chief Justice Taney knew, however, the circle is capable of moving in the opposite direction, from the language of liberation to liberation itself. [103] Every expression of a claim to equal citizenship is, to some extent, self-validating.

Because the traditional Order's assumptions about race and status are deeply rooted in the sense of self, the personal is political, and the politics can be passionate. Correspondingly, the political is personal. The political order influences our modes of personal behavior concerning matters of race, along with our modes of thinking and even feeling about race. From either the political or the personal perspective, then, emancipation is not just something that happens in the material world; it also takes place in people's minds. Those who would end the labeling and the silencing must seek to transform the social meanings of race. Race may be a myth, as scientists have been telling us for years, but it is a myth that has powerfully shaped our social world. For our generation of Americans, no social issue is more urgent or more difficult than this: How shall we think about race?

The Supreme Court's most important contribution to the modern civil rights movement has been its reshaping of the symbols of government that express racial group status. *Brown v. Board of Education* (1954) still stands as the nation's preeminent formal declaration that the era of racial caste is over. This is not merely an after-the-fact reinterpretation; *Brown* was understood from the beginning, by friend and foe alike, for what it has proved to be: America's leading magisterial statement that we, as a people, cannot tolerate state-sponsored subordination of a racial group.[104]

Jim Crow was more than school segregation, even more than the aggregate of governmental supports for racial domination. It was an entrenched social system, a culture thoroughly imbued with norms, formal and informal, that maintained white supremacy and black subordination.[105] No one—least of all the Justices who joined in the *Brown* decision—thought Jim Crow would collapse all of a sudden, and it did not.[106] As Robert Cover reminded us, "legal interpretation is a form of bonded interpretation," requiring "many voices" to concur before even a single judge's order can translate a legal norm into actual control of a single person's behavior.[107] A large-scale social movement multiplies the cases and the judges by the thousands, and multiplies "the governed" by the millions, so that the participants in "bonded interpretation" must necessarily embrace a considerable part of the population. The Justices understood that Jim Crow would end only when large numbers of white Americans were persuaded that it should end. The *Brown* decision alone—indeed, litigation alone—could not dismantle Jim Crow, but *Brown* and its successor decisions did contribute significantly to that end.[108]

It is a measure of *Brown*'s influence that today its result has the look of inevitability.[109] The contribution of the Supreme Court to the process that ended Jim Crow is not to be found by asking whether particular actors in the civil rights movement were "inspired" by *Brown* to act as they did[110]—although it is clear that *Brown* and other NAACP litigation efforts provided critical legal and moral support for direct action such as the Montgomery bus boycott.[111] Whether or not *Brown* "inspired," undoubtedly it permeated the political atmosphere of the South. After 1954, when civil rights leaders spoke of "rights" or of "the Fourteenth Amendment" or of "the Constitution," and when civil rights demonstrators conducted boycotts or sit-ins or marches in furtherance of those claims, no listener could miss their underlying assumption: that black people's *constitutional* entitlement to equal citizenship had been established. This assumption took for granted not only *Brown* but the other decisions of the Supreme Court and lower federal courts that were relying explicitly on *Brown* as they systematically struck down all forms of state-sponsored racial segregation.[112] Indeed, it became customary to hold major civil rights marches on May 17, the anniversary of the *Brown* decision.[113] When a segregationist leader spoke of a runaway judiciary, or of states' rights, or of the assault on the southern way of life, *Brown* was there, too, as the basic subtextual reference. That implicit reference was reinforced by hundreds of "Impeach Earl Warren" billboards across the South and scores of "white citizens' councils" that targeted the NAACP—the litigation arm of the civil rights movement—and packed school board meetings to protest desegregation. The desegregation, of course, either had been ordered by judges or was being considered in response to the threat of such orders.

The Supreme Court also promoted the acculturation of Americans to the messages of the civil rights cause by validating the First Amendment claims of the NAACP (both litigators and rank-and-file members), other civil rights organizations, sit-in demonstrators, and civil rights marchers against state and local officials who were seeking to suppress the speech of freedom.[114] Some of these court victories were followed by a continuation of harassment by other means, but in the aggregate the Court's speech-protective decisions did protect speech. They also had an important by-product for the civic culture: the authoritative affirmation, to would-be civil rights speakers and to all Americans, that black voices were the voices of citizens, and were entitled to be heard.

The larger questions about *Brown* and the judiciary—the questions relevant to this book's inquiry—relate not so much to inspiration as to acculturation. Did the Supreme Court, in *Brown* and in the succeeding decade that culminated in Congress's two comprehensive civil rights acts, significantly affect the culture of our public life? Did the Court's decisions contribute importantly to black southerners' sense that they had the rights of equal citizens and were entitled to demand those rights? Did the Court's decisions weaken the authority of the laws and customs that constituted the Jim Crow culture? Did the courts' efforts to enforce the principle of antidiscrimination help acculturate black and white northerners to the status of black Americans as equal citizens? Did the judiciary, during these years, help to expand the American civic culture's definitions of the meanings of equality? For most newspaper-reading, television-viewing adults who lived through those years, the answers are not in doubt.

As my rhetorical question about the acculturation of white northerners may hint, some of the acculturating was done by southern white intransigents whose sense of self had been formed in the culture of white supremacy, and who would fight—literally, and often in view of television cameras—to retain the laws and customs that gave meaning to those identities. In Little Rock, the most famous source of this acculturation-by-television, the fight began early, and the federal courts were centrally involved at every stage. In 1955, even before the Supreme Court issued its "all deliberate speed" remedial order in *Brown*, the Little Rock school board (in a separate case) had approved a plan for gradual desegregation of the local schools, and the federal district court had approved the plan. But just before school opened in the fall of 1957 the state governor, Orval Faubus, ordered the Arkansas National Guard to keep black children out of Little Rock's Central High School. On the basis of *Brown*, the U.S. attorney general obtained an injunction against the governor, and the children entered school. A hostile crowd gathered, and the local police removed the black children. It was then that President Eisenhower, no great admirer of the *Brown* decision, was persuaded to take his first significant act supporting desegregation. He sent Army troops to Central High to protect the black children, and eight black students attended the school for the academic year.[115]

What had all this to do with the acculturation of northern whites? Alexander Bickel said it three decades ago, and I shall not try to improve on his powerful statement of the "decisive consequence" of the disturbances in Little Rock and elsewhere in the next few years:

> Compulsory segregation, like states' rights and like "The Southern Way of Life," is an abstraction and, to a good many people, a neutral or sympathetic one. These riots, which were brought instantly, dramatically, and literally home to the American people, showed what it means concretely. Here were grown men and women furiously confronting their enemy: two, three, a half dozen scrubbed, starched, scared, and incredibly brave colored children. The moral bankruptcy, the shame of the thing, was evident. . . . There was an unforgettable scene, . . . from New Orleans, of a white mother fairly foaming at the mouth with the effort to rivet her distracted little boy's attention and teach him how to hate. . . . The effect, achieved on an unprecedented number of people with unprecedented speed, must have been something like what used to happen to individuals (the young Lincoln among them) at the sight of an actual slave auction . . . . Mob action led to the mobilization of

northern opinion in support of the Court's decision [the reference is
to *Brown*; the Supreme Court had not yet heard the Little Rock
case]—not merely because the mob is disorderly, but because it
concretized the abstraction of racism.[116]

Bickel's words were presumably written in 1961. They may be jarring to
one who reads them for the first time today—not his use of "colored,"
but his reminder of how easy it was for so many white Americans in the
North and the West, as late as 1957, to be oblivious to the ugliness of
Jim Crow. After Little Rock, that ugliness was considerably harder to
ignore.[117]

Just about everyone agrees that law—for example, the Civil Rights
Act of 1964 and the Voting Rights Act of 1965—has been effective in
changing the social Order that governed race relations in the South—
and in the rest of the nation, too.[118] In his recent book Gerald Rosenberg
accepts this view, but disputes the common understanding that the
courts have played a significant part in the progress that has occurred in
the field of civil rights. He argues, to the contrary, that litigation has
been a "hollow hope," luring social reformers into squandering their
resources on "an institution that is structurally constrained from serving
their needs, providing only an illusion of change. . . . Even when major
cases are won, the achievement is often more symbolic than real."[119]
This assertion takes no account of the relation between symbol and
status—an omission all the more puzzling given the *Brown* opinion's
widely circulated (and indisputable) approval of a lower court's finding
that state-sponsored segregation burdened black pupils with a sense of
inferiority. In the attack on Jim Crow, symbolism and substance were
inextricably bound together. The central point in contention was the
status dominance of one racial group and the status subordination of
another. A generation after *Brown*, Richard Epstein concluded his attack
on laws forbidding employment discrimination with these words about
the civil rights movement: "A movement with this power and this
influence does not arise and flourish on the strength of political power
or legal coercion alone. At some level it responds to deep-seated social
conditions and powerful social symbols."[120] In the context of black
Americans' quest for authoritative public expression of their equal citizenship, nothing could be more hollow than a distinction between
what is "real" and what is merely "symbolic."

In the field of race relations as elsewhere, expression is power. Much of the strength of the civil rights movement lay in its leaders' ability to find new and dramatic modes of expression that would capture attention and win support—first among black citizens, and then in larger communities both local and national. In form, the movement's messages of liberation were addressed primarily to those who controlled most of the means of their subordination—that is, to white Americans. But the movement's leaders never forgot that those messages also promoted solidarity among black Americans. Any movement to free a group from subordination will seek to communicate a series of messages to people on the other side of the relevant cultural boundary, at the same time raising consciousness within the group. The messages, equally apt for women's liberation or gay liberation, were engendered in the modern era by the civil rights movement:

1. "Your brand of Reason entails one deplorable misconception: the myth of our inferiority."
2. "Although all our members share the burdens of the group's subordination, each of us is an individual. Don't assume that any one of us fits some stereotypical model of the group."
3. "As individuals, we share with you a great many of the same kinds of hopes and fears."
4. "We differ from you in some ways, but we are citizens. We do not have to give up being who we are in order to claim the respect, the participation, the responsibilities that come with full inclusion in the community's public life."
5. "Our views—and our points of view—deserve not just a hearing in the larger community, but that community's good-faith consideration."

The civil rights movement has communicated some of these messages effectively (numbers 1, 3, and 5). If it has been less successful in communicating the others (2 and 4), part of the reason surely lies in the reluctance of the addressees to hear messages that make them uncomfortable.[121] But another part of the reason lies in the hidden limits imposed by language. It is virtually impossible to talk, or even to think, about race relations without using words like *black* and *white*—although each of those words obscures the kaleidoscopic diversity of the flesh-and-blood people among the group implicitly represented. And once those word-labels are affixed, their historical associations with status dominance and subordination cause them to attract other labels that are hard to detach.

Given this power differential, it is not just coincidence that positive labels have tended to stick to "white" and negative ones to "black."[122] Disparaging labels are not the only harms embodied in the subordination of a racial or ethnic group, but they are among the gravest of those harms, and the most painful to endure. One response to the multifold harms of derogatory race labeling would be to enlist the power of government to suppress some forms of racist expression. The idea of applying criminal sanctions to the libel of a racial or religious group was broached in the legal literature in the 1940s,[123] and in 1952, in *Beauharnais v. Illinois*,[124] the Supreme Court upheld the constitutionality of a state "group libel" law making it a crime to distribute literature that portrayed "depravity, criminality, unchastity, or lack of virtue of a class of citizens of any race, color, creed, or religion which said publication exposes [such citizens] to contempt, derision, or obloquy." The libel before the Court was a leaflet distributed by the White Circle League, calling on whites to "stand up and fight" against the "invasion" of their neighborhoods by black residents. What did the leaflet mean to Joseph Beauharnais, a white man who lived in one of those neighborhoods? In a passage often quoted, the leaflet illustrated a general lesson about group libel: "If persuasion and the need to prevent the white race from being mongrelized by the negro will not unite us, then the aggressions, . . . rapes, robberies, knives, guns and marijuana of the negro, SURELY WILL."[125] Joseph Beauharnais was afraid. Group libel is rooted in fear.

Today the *Beauharnais* decision looks destined for explicit overruling.[126] Yet if defamatory words can hurt individuals, it seems plain—especially now that the civil rights era has heightened our awareness of the harms of stigma—that the defamation of a racial or religious group can hurt the group's members. In an era that takes *Brown v. Board of Education* for granted, it is no surprise that some writers have argued for reviving group libel laws. The writers have emphasized the harms of racist speech to individual addressees,[127] to the libeled groups,[128] and more generally to the communitarian values that are so needed, and so constantly in jeopardy, in America's racially and ethnically diverse society.[129]

The arguments for reinstituting criminal penalties for group libel, or

for making racist insults the basis for tort damages,[130] have come mainly
from the academy, and have not yet been translated into a mobilized
political movement. Within the academy itself, however, about two
hundred colleges and universities have issued regulations authorizing
discipline of students (and sometimes faculty) who engage in one or
another form of racist speech on campus. An imposing body of literature has accumulated, both supporting and attacking the constitutionality of group libel laws and campus hate-speech rules.[131]

For the near future the Supreme Court seems to have settled the main
First Amendment issue about group libel laws in its 1992 decision in the
cross-burning case of *R.A.V. v. St. Paul*.[132] The Court struck down a city
ordinance criminalizing various kinds of hate "speech" (including cross
burning, the painting of swastikas, and the like), and its opinion stated
a principle broad enough to ban group libel laws: the presumptive
invalidity of any prohibition on speech based on the ideas expressed.[133]
As the Court noted, the decision does not deny St. Paul (or the forty-six
states that had adopted similar laws) the power to punish the act of
burning of a cross on someone's lawn for purposes of intimidation. In
California, for example, prosecutors were quick to say that the laws
they typically used against such hate crimes were not affected by the
R.A.V. decision.[134] What St. Paul lost in this case—what government at
all levels lost—was a form of expression: the use of the criminal law as a
means to communicate the public's repudiation of hate speech focused
on the race, religion, or gender of its intended victims. I agree that
group libel laws are unconstitutional. Here, though, I focus not on the
problems of First Amendment doctrine raised by the several opinions in
R.A.V.[135] but on racist speech regulations as an expressive resource in a
contest over status dominance.

Group libel, like pornography, responds to a sense of inadequacy, but
the two types of hate literature are circulated differently. Where today's
pornography feeds on the felt inadequacies of its consumers, with most
distributors simply profiting from that demand and seeking to increase
it, the defamation of racial or religious groups is driven by the felt
inadequacies of its distributors. I have suggested that the suppression
of pornography would leave the sexual objectification of women largely
intact. Similarly, anxious hatemongers, thwarted in purveying their racist leaflets, can find plenty of other ways to express their fear and hate.

My point is not that some fixed quantum of racist rhetoric is "out
there" and will be expressed no matter what government may do. If a

group libel law were passed and upheld, not all self-identified racists would distribute their leaflets secretly or scrawl their hate on walls at night; no doubt the existence of the law would persuade at least some people to confine their racist expression to private conversations with listeners who were sure to be receptive. But we know from painful recent experience that there is no shortage of politicians who are willing to take up the slack, mobilizing constituents by giving a public voice to their racial fears.

These politicians do not use language that is explicitly racist, but convey their messages through code words and race-laden imagery, caricatures of enemies that tap into their listeners' phobias. It has been suggested that "Hitler's rise to political power in Germany might have been stopped if his early speeches and rallies had been suppressed."[136] Perhaps so. Yet it would have been necessary to keep Hitler from making any speeches at all—a most unlikely tactic for any but the most repressive regimes. Extremist speakers, notably including Hitler himself, know how to spread their messages of hate in indirect language that is quite beyond the law's reach. Moving closer to home, if members of the American Nazi party had actually carried out their threatened march in Skokie, Illinois, in 1978, they planned to carry signs saying, "Free Speech." But their mere presence, in uniforms or not, would have been enough to convey their taunts, insults, and defamation.[137]

Although a group libel law could not promise to prevent much racist expression, it would stand as an official expression of public values, and over the years it might succeed in injecting doses of tolerance into the body politic. Similar hopes and fears about the expressive power of law infuse all the political contests reviewed in this book, and the fears and the hopes seem as warranted here as they are in other areas of regulation. Government does teach lessons in behavior, and a time-honored method of getting its pupils' attention is the criminal law.[138] And, here as elsewhere, the muffling of public racist expression would take away some of the acculturating power of that expression—even though the private expression of racism, multiplied by the number of its practitioners, unquestionably has its own culture-shaping power.[139] Still, for those who seek to reduce the influence of racism in American life, a group libel law's possible acculturating benefit is only the starting place for discussion. Such a law would also entail costs.

Some advocates of criminalizing racist speech have proposed limiting the law to speech that vilifies members of groups that have been historically subordinated.[140] This limitation has the virtue of tailoring the restriction of speech to the harms that provoke the regulation. To uphold so clear-cut a "viewpoint discrimination" would require a drastic revision of First Amendment doctrine. The Supreme Court's majority refused to undertake such a revision in the *R.A.V.* case, and my guess is that even the Justices who thought the majority's opinion was too sweeping would vote to invalidate a "one-way" law criminalizing racist speech.[141] In any event, limiting a proposed law to the libel of subordinated groups would assure its rejection in just about any state legislature. Much more likely, then, would be a law that criminalized the libel of any racial or religious group, as did the (now repealed) Illinois law that the Supreme Court upheld by a 5–4 vote in 1952.[142] On that occasion Justice William O. Douglas, dissenting, made this gloomy prophecy: "Today a white man stands convicted for protesting in unseemly language against our decisions in validating [racially] restrictive covenants. Tomorrow a negro will be [haled] before a court for denouncing lynch law in heated terms. Farm laborers in the West who compete with field hands drifting up from Mexico; whites who feel the pressure of orientals; a minority which finds employment going to members of the dominant religious group—all of these are caught in the mesh of today's decision."[143] Justice Hugo L. Black, also dissenting, ended his opinion on the same note: "If there be minority groups who hail this holding as their victory, they might consider the possible relevancy of this ancient remark: 'Another such victory and I am undone.'"[144] No constitutional lawyer who has lived through the decades since the *Beauharnais* decision can read these warnings without recognizing their striking relevance to a wide range of cases in which members of racial minorities have invoked the First Amendment against efforts to suppress messages and methods that the dominant majority labeled as Unreason.

In the field of defamation the reckoning came in *New York Times Co. v. Sullivan*.[145] An Alabama jury in a libel case awarded half a million dollars in damages against four local black ministers and the *New York Times*, which had published an allegedly libelous advertisement over their names. In holding this award unconstitutional, the Court not only shielded minority speakers from attempts to use the threat of libel actions to silence them, but also undermined the premise of *Beauharnais* that libel was not protected speech under the First Amendment. Consider also our modern experience with laws against profanity and insults, which have been enforced lopsidedly against black speakers and other cultural outsiders who have expressed unpopular views.[146] Compare the censorship of "indecent" radio broadcasts by the Federal Communications Commission, which, in one commissioner's view, came to this: "the swear words of the lily white middle class may be broadcast, but those of the young, the poor, or the blacks may not."[147]

Similarly, film censors, right up to the 1950s, were banning films that presented sharply drawn racial conflicts, or presented a black servant as "too familiar"—even (in Memphis) a film that showed black and white children in school together. New York censors routinely banned films that treated these themes: pregnancy, venereal disease, birth control, abortion, illegitimacy, prostitution, miscegenation, and divorce—all of which would interest anyone concerned about the subordination of women.[148] Recall, too, that the methods as well as the messages of the civil rights movement challenged First Amendment orthodoxy by departing from the classical modes of civic deliberation.[149] And, finally, remember the black authors whose works were removed from the Long Island school library.[150]

Many of the potential applications of a group libel law would involve statements connected with political speech. Under today's First Amendment doctrine, for example, Joseph Beauharnais's leaflet would be constitutionally protected. In cases of racist speech at the margins of public issues, someone must make the discretionary decision whether to prosecute under the group libel statute. One of the main reasons why our constitutional doctrine is antagonistic to vagueness or overbreadth in a law restricting speech is the discretion that a vague or broad law gives to the people who apply it, from police officers and prosecutors to judges and juries. The concern is that these actors may use their discretion selectively, imposing informal censorship on messages and modes of expression that they find uncongenial. When outsiders speak, insiders often hear the tones of Unreason—and it is insiders, mostly, who administer the system that enforces the law.

The risk that a group libel law poses to minority political speech thus resembles the risk posed by an antipornography law to feminist erotic art. In each case the law's most important practical effect may be to suppress exactly the wrong communications, from the standpoint of the law's proponents. As to an antipornography law, any such prediction remains in the realm of surmise, but the experience of the civil rights movement amply justifies a prediction that a group libel law would disproportionately limit the expression—and thus the power—of racial minorities, religious minorities, and other historically subordinated groups. As these groups fight their battles at the cultural boundaries against those who would seek to maintain status dominance over them, they need a vigorous First Amendment. Justice Black spoke wisdom in 1952, and after four decades his words seem wiser still.

A public university that used the group libel model for disciplining racist speech on the campus would fall into the same traps, both constitutional and practical. But most universities that have sought to protect students against racist abuse have adopted narrower definitions of the speech that will evoke disciplinary action.[151] The University of California's regulation, for example, (i) is limited to "fighting words": face-to-face personal insults, capable of provoking immediate breaches of the peace; (ii) centers on the problem of harassment, the creation of a hostile environment that interferes with the addressee's ability to pursue his or her education; and (iii) is not limited to racial, sexual, or other viewpoint-specific harassment but applies to any harassing fighting words.[152] This regulation plainly is constitutional under any of the opinions in the *R.A.V.* case. Even a carefully drawn rule that specifies particular kinds of (racial, sexual, and so on) harassment ought to be held constitutional, although such rules do invite some of the same comments I have made about group libel laws.[153] I concede that a university bent on defending the latter kind of rule faces an uphill fight after the *R.A.V.* decision. Indeed, the *R.A.V.* majority seemed to be going out of its way to make pronouncements that would rule out some university regulations then on the books. As Justice White noted, the viewpoint discrimination ground for the majority's opinion had not been briefed by the parties, nor had it been argued orally to the Court. In a short opinion, Justice Blackmun suggested that the university rules were the majority opinion's real targets. Still, any university with a hate-speech regulation should be able to modify it into a shape that will pass the test of constitutionality.

In an article published before *R.A.V.* was decided, Robert Post, after trenchantly criticizing the criminalization of group libel as unconstitutional, cautiously endorses the validity of a campus regulation approximating the University of California model. Positing that the pursuit of truth is the central ideal of critical education, he proceeds: "The pursuit of truth requires not only an unfettered freedom of ideas, but also honesty, fidelity to reason, and respect for method and procedures.

Reason, as we have seen, carries its own special requirements of civility, which preclude coercion and abuse."[154] Even as we are admiring civility, we can also worry about the danger that may lurk in this argument. A university, of all institutions, ought to be skeptical of any process that officially defines one version of reason as authentic—what I have called Reason, with a capital R—and restricts expression that impedes Reason's flow. My own conclusion about the importance of regulating harassment of members of a university rests less on the intellectual imperatives of reason or civility than on the moral and legal imperatives of equal access to higher education. The university's most important educational responsibility in this context is not to keep discourse within the bounds of Reason, but to maintain an environment that offers all students the fullest educational opportunity possible within its resources.

The relevant First Amendment analogy would be the case law and administrative regulations governing racial and sexual harassment in the workplace, developed by the courts in enforcing federal and state employment discrimination laws—a body of law that the Supreme Court's majority explicitly distinguished from the case before it in *R.A.V.*[155] In the university as in other places where people work, a hostile environment can have exclusionary effects. It is hard to believe, for example, that the *R.A.V.* majority would invalidate a university rule forbidding teachers to insult students with personal epithets, either in the classroom or on the quad—even if the rule mentioned racial, sexual, and other kinds of epithets by way of example. It seems equally legitimate for a university to extend such a rule to students' speech on campus, thus seeking to protect the access of all its students by maintaining an atmosphere of tolerance for diverse people, ideas, and cultures. Happily, as Post says so well, such an effort will also serve larger educational purposes. An ambience of tolerance is a necessary condition for the free inquiry and expression that are the soul of a university. Even one who is skeptical about an officially defined Reason can be committed to an ideal of tolerance.

It is not paradoxical to insist on the same freedom for the lines of inquiry and the expression of ideas that challenge our cherished ideals concerning racial equality. Students and teachers must be able to discuss race and its social meanings as openly as they would discuss any other subject, and to state conclusions that other students and teachers may find hurtful—and may call intolerant or even racist. The next generation promises agony for all of us, as scholars and other citizens offer sharply differing answers to the question, How shall we think about race? No society that calls itself democratic—and certainly no university worthy of the name—can seek to avoid that pain through a strategy of suppression or evasion. One subject sure to continue producing this sort of painful debate, both in the university and elsewhere, is the topic of affirmative action.

ENACTING THE NARRATIVES OF INCLUSION

Strong opposition to affirmative action—for women as well as for the members of racial and ethnic minorities—is, logically, part of the social issues agenda. After all, the racial aspects of the agenda are centrally targeted to the anxieties of white men, anxieties that may begin in the fear of competition but do not end there. But varying forms of opposition to affirmative action—or, at least, reservations about its effects on the ways we answer the question, How shall we think about race?—have also come from quite different quarters. Some black and Latino writers, for example, are deeply skeptical about affirmative action in the academy; others generally oppose group remedies throughout the whole field of civil rights; others, who generally support race-conscious programs, have attacked some of the standard justifications for affirmative action as an unintentional—or disguised—form of derogatory labeling. Predictably, the stronger criticisms of affirmative action have been coolly received in the writings of other black and Latino intellectuals, and even more coolly in the offices of the leading civil rights organizations. If the resulting multisided debate does nothing else, it offers a pointed reminder of the diversity of views within the nation's various communities that bear racial or ethnic labels.

The labeling itself is the rub, according to Stephen Carter, a Yale law professor. To bring the point to life, he tells his own story, emphasizing his frustration at being cast in "the role of beneficiary (or suspected beneficiary)" of affirmative action in the academy.[156] As Carter sees it, a black professional today wears such dehumanizing labels as: "Do Not Assume That This Individual Is Qualified!" or "Possesses Special Perspective."[157] The first of these implicit labels is a modern version of an old canard, dating from the racist apology for slavery.[158] It is true that the professional schools are no havens, either from overt racial slurs or from the implicit labeling that never finds explicit public expression. Yet it is doubtful that "diversity" admissions are responsible for the "less qualified" label. By the time students reach professional school, after all, they are adults, and every student, black or white, has already acquired a store of attitudes from the cultures outside the school's walls, including those cultures' inheritance from the days of slavery.[159]

Carter's second point about labeling is that "diversity" admissions promote the false assumption that black people hold a particular set of beliefs.[160] As a result, he says, a black professional whose beliefs do not match this stereotypical picture tends to be dismissed as somehow not authentically black. In my own experience, some black law students have said they felt pressure to state "the" supposed "black point of view" on issues both national and local, but among the current crop of students the effects of any such pressure seem to have been consider- ably dissipated. Black students in my classes on constitutional law express an assortment of views, on race and on everything else, cover- ing a wide range—let us say, the range from Thurgood Marshall to Clarence Thomas—along with many varieties that cannot be placed on any Marshall/Thomas axis. Among professional academics, too, the label of an assumed "black point of view" is fading. Stephen Carter himself should be counted among the prominent contributors to the trend—but so should some of the black writers he seems to include as promoters of a black "party line."

Carter calls for the professional schools to abandon the "diversity" goal, returning affirmative action to its "metaphorical roots" as a means of "ensuring opportunities that might not otherwise exist for people of color to show what they can do."[161] Well, perhaps at Yale—but for a state university affirmative action program, this proposal looks like an invitation to a beheading. The universities, of course, adopted "diver- sity" admissions in response to the 1978 opinion of Justice Lewis F. Powell, who cast the decisive votes that defined the Supreme Court's two-edged decision in *Regents of University of California v. Bakke.*[162] Justice Powell concluded that the equal protection clause forbade a state uni- versity medical school to set aside a quota of its admissions for minority applicants, but permitted the school to take race into account as one admissions factor among many, for the educational purpose of diversi- fying its student body and thus exposing all students to diverse points of view.[163] The probability is slight that today's Supreme Court would uphold a state university affirmative action program based on a ground other than "diversity."[164]

The question of constitutionality aside, what difference would Stephen Carter's proposal make? In his view, the difference would lie in affirmative action's contribution to the social meanings of race. But that was precisely Justice Powell's point. He, too, was concerned with the expressive qualities of government action—concerned to avoid labeling minority admittees to professional schools as "less qualified." The clear subtext of Justice Powell's *Bakke* opinion was that he was out to save affirmative action. He plainly thought that "diversity" admissions would blur the lines of racial division by turning away from what Carter calls "the opposition of merit to [racial] preference that has brought about the pain and anger to begin with."[165] Part of Justice Powell's purpose was to show the fallacy of that supposed "opposition."[166]

Affirmative action in the universities does impose costs, including pain and anger all around. But acknowledging those costs takes us only halfway toward deciding whether the policy is justified. Elsewhere I have devoted a lot of ink to arguing the justification of affirmative action in a variety of social contexts, and I do not repeat those arguments now.[167] Here I want to keep the focus on the relation of affirmative action to the question, How shall we think about race? and to emphasize one educational advantage that went largely undiscussed at the time of my own law school's post-*Bakke* reassessment. The advantage I have in mind is not that white students learn the views of minority students or faculty members, or even that all students learn about the wide range of viewpoints within the group that wears a label such as "black" or "Latino" or "Korean American." Rather, I want to accentuate the acculturating effects of a deeper understanding that two individuals can gain about each other, an understanding that can come only from doing things together over a period of time.

This sort of acculturation is an enacted narrative.[168] In the law school context the educational benefits are possible only when the narrative is not a one-panel cartoon but a continued story. Some of that story is played out in the classroom, but most of it is told elsewhere. The story goes on, day after day, in the corridors and the library; in representing clients in clinical programs; in writing and editing law journal comments, or briefing and arguing moot court cases; over coffee, between classes; in studying for examinations; in student participation on faculty committees; in public service organizations; at afternoon colloquia and postmidnight bull sessions. It is almost impossible to work closely with another person over a space of months or years without seeing the real person emerge from behind the screen on which you have previously projected an obscuring racial label. Furthermore, once you become well acquainted with a few people who have grown up on the other side of a cultural boundary, it will be harder for you to go on seeing the boundary in the same old ways—although Brenda Patterson's experience attests that some of us resist this opportunity to get acquainted.[169] The educational advantage of a racially diverse student body, then, is not only the illumination of the curriculum by discussion from diverse perspectives. It also includes education about the meanings of race. Here, as when someone you know "comes out," expressing a gay identity, the *person* is political.[170]

This interpersonal education about race is by no means limited to people in educational institutions. It goes on in public arenas generally: the marketplace and the workplace, the arts council and the zoning board. The person becomes political when large numbers of people, two by two, do things together, live important parts of their lives in the same reality, create a common fund of unspoken assumptions that "go without saying," and so come to see each other not as abstractions but as persons. In carrying out their common tasks, in recognizing their responsibilities to each other, they enact the narratives of their common humanity and their common citizenship.[171]

Reconsider the problem of group libel. The image of "the black beast rapist" once was conveyed in explicitly racist speeches and writings and in the rituals of the lynch mob. Now the same image can be brought into our living rooms by specialists in emotional appeal. With the political air so polluted, it would be silly to argue that this kind of labeling can be answered by "more speech" in the form of specific replies. Even for an individual who is defamed, further discussion typically aggravates the harm. When a group is defamed, it is vain to hope for any simple remedy.[172] The most effective forms of "more speech" will come from the presence of increased numbers of black and Latino (Asian American, and so on) men and women, not just in the so-called opinion-making sectors of our society, but throughout the full range of tasks that people perform in all our public arenas, including private employment. This acculturating influence of genuine integration may be beyond our power to measure, but it is real.[173]

In the short run, participation is its own reward when members of racial and ethnic minorities first take their places in governmental councils, thus signaling the validation of their claims to equal citizenship. At first, these newcomers to a council are apt to find that their reasoning in the usual mode of civic debate has little influence on their fellow councilors. In fact, the very debating points that should be the most interesting—that is, the arguments that come from their own distinctive perspectives—will be the least persuasive of all. Precisely in these cases their speech is most likely to be discounted as talk outside the bounds of "normal discourse."[174] In this context the importance of "reason-giving in public debate"[175] lies not so much in any appeal to Reason as in the acculturating power of ritual behavior. Over the longer term, surely the participation of minority council members will enlarge the council's definitions of what counts as reason; the explanation, however, is not so much the cogency of their arguments as the fact of their participation. After numerous day-to-day conversations, the councilors of longer standing become acculturated to the idea that the newer councilors are capable of being full participants, whose contributions are normal and "rational."[176]

The civil rights movement prospered from the Warren Court's First Amendment decisions, not just because those decisions permitted the movements's messages to reach the public, but also because they could be understood as authoritative declarations—to black and white citizens alike—that black people's voices deserved to be heard. Manifestly, the First Amendment is not the law's only contribution to the members of subordinated groups who are seeking to participate in public life. If we add up all the ways law can be used to open the doors to that participation, we can see that law's greatest potential for reshaping the social meanings of race lies in its capacity to promote the enactment of millions of individual narratives of inclusion.

These enacted narratives have persuasive power—and, in the aggregate, political power—because they are real people's stories. Like a fable, an individual's story can dramatize a large moral by embodying it in a particular person's life. It is hard to muster up empathy for any abstraction, and especially hard when the abstraction is a subordinated group on which you have projected the frightening image of your own negative identity. If you are a white man, that image is likely to portray a number of general assumptions about black men or black women. But now you confront this live person—call her Dorothy Green—who works at the desk next to yours. Her children's pictures are on her desk. You can identify with her story: how she worked her way through school and is taking night classes to become qualified for promotion; how her daughter is a computer science sophomore at the state college, and her son, a twelfth-grader, is trying out for a scholarship in graphic arts. To know her story and her family's story is to confront a set of living examples who call your previous assumptions, and perhaps some of your fears, into question.

The most effective legislative responses to the expression that labels people as subordinate, then, are the civil rights remedies—and, yes, the affirmative action programs[177]—that bring the races together in the workplace and more generally in the public life of our communities. If yesterday much of Jim Crow was symbolic speech, so today is the integration of our public spaces—which, in some American communities, was achieved only through the intervention of law. For almost three decades black people in those communities have been routinely present in hotels and restaurants formerly limited to whites—and today their presence is not so much tolerated as taken for granted. At the same lunch counters where yesterday's sit-in demonstrators conveyed their silent messages about what might be—and ought to be—today's black and white patrons convey a message about what is. They, too, teach by their presence, by "the normative power of the factual."[178] Just by sitting there, side by side, they enact a daily parable: that the integration of our public life is the ordinary—the customary, the proper—social order.[179]

The racial integration of the workplace, however, is far from complete;[180] this sorry statistical datum comes to life in the stories about the segregation of the workers in the Wards Cove cannery and about Brenda Patterson's subjection to racial harassment. In Patterson's case the supervisor expressed his racism openly, while at the cannery racism found expression in ways that were tacit, but both stories illustrate a larger truth: the persistence in our society of widespread acculturation to social meanings of race that are direct descendants of the racist apology for slavery. Given the recurrence of stories like these in the public world of work, and given the recent and striking effectiveness of a politics of fear founded on racial polarization, it was surprising to read what Orlando Patterson, a Harvard sociologist, had to say about the Senate committee hearings that preceded the confirmation of Justice Clarence Thomas. The climactic paragraph in his *New York Times* article was this: "African Americans must now realize that these hearings were perhaps the single most important cultural development for them since the great struggles of the civil rights years. Clarence Thomas and Anita Hill suffered inhuman and undeserved pain, tragic pain, in their public ordeal, and they will never be quite the same again. Nor will we all, for what all African Americans won from their pain, 'perfected by this deed,' this ritual of inclusion, is the public cultural affirmation of what had already been politically achieved: unambiguous inclusion, unquestioned belonging. The culture of slavery is dead."[181] As that last sentence reverberates, a thought experiment comes to mind: If Orlando Patterson could meet Brenda Patterson, imagine what they would say to each other.

Still, Professor Patterson is right when he goes on to highlight the importance of the Thomas hearings in dramatizing for a huge white audience some of the social diversity within America's black population. Those hearings were, as he implies, a series of enacted narratives, and they packed a powerful punch. But they were, in the main, dramatic performances, and they did not acquaint the viewers—white or black—with the real people behind the personae we saw on our television screens. To provide a long-lasting acculturating effect, an enacted narrative must not only continue over an extended time but also be a two-way exchange rather than a one-way dramatization. To liberate a group from subordinate status requires not "more speech" but more conversation.

Conversation offers opportunities not only for conveying information or opinions to another but also for the self-reflection that can come from hearing yourself talk. Sometimes the light bulb goes on when we hear ourselves saying things we have never before articulated—and in the field of race relations *most* of what we feel lies in that shadowy zone. This sort of generative spontaneity is far less likely in a public debate on a focused issue—for example, a Senate committee hearing—than it is in a private conversation within an "unscripted relationship."[182] The hearings aside, Judge Thomas's nomination was itself a contribution to the debate over the question, How shall we think about race? Nominating him to replace Justice Marshall was, of course, a political act, and the solemn assertion that the nomination had nothing to do with race did no credit to any of the political actors who joined in that pretense. For the Bush administration, Judge Thomas was an attractive candidate chiefly because he was a black judge who had embraced the social issues agenda for race. In his previous career in the executive branch, he had opposed both group remedies for civil rights violations and race-conscious affirmative action programs. In short, he seemed committed to a definition of racial equality that begins and ends in formal racial neutrality.

Considering that a majority of the Supreme Court was already moving in that direction, Justice Thomas's appointment was unlikely to change the course of the Court's decisions about race. The political appeal lay in the expressive uses of the appointment itself. It would convey two messages to working-class whites, especially white men, who were potential recruits for the constituency for cultural counterrevolution. First, it would reaffirm the administration's opposition to "quotas." Second—and here Justice Thomas's race was crucial—it would say that one could oppose race-conscious remedies on principle, and not just out of fearful hostility to would-be black competitors. The target audience for these messages would find special appeal in a position that offered to keep black Americans from "going too far" and at the same time offered to relieve white Americans from the sense of guilt.

In the end, though, Judge Thomas became Justice Thomas by appealing, not to the white constituents of the social issues agenda, but to black people. The accusation of sexual harassment that led to the second phase of the hearings had been made by Anita Hill, an attorney and a black woman. Yet when Judge Thomas called the second phase of the hearings a "high-tech lynching," he succeeded in portraying that accusation as an attack by a group of white men against a black man, focused on the black man's sexuality. That imagery, resonating against the all-too-familiar image of "the black beast rapist," plainly touched a nerve among black Americans. As Paula Giddings said, black sexuality has long been a taboo subject in black Americans' public speech. Historically, not only were black people defined as "sexually different from whites," but "that kind of difference got people lynched; that kind of difference got women raped." Roger Wilkins summed up one reaction among black viewers of the hearings: "I thought, I don't want this guy on the Court, but I don't want him defeated for this reason."[183]

And what of Anita Hill? My colleague Kimberlé Crenshaw commented that although black viewers had a clear understanding of "lynching," they had no stories, "no historical memory" that would give Professor Hill's story a similar resonance in the community.[184] Through the medium of opinion polling, black Americans conveyed their anger to their senators. That anger, of course, had been aggravated by the 1988 presidential campaign; the irony is that its release gave a political reward to the very people who had brought the Willie Horton miniseries to the screen.

The possible answers to the question, How shall we think about race?

probably are not infinitely varied. Yet, for the foreseeable future, American law—ever linked to American politics—seems destined to go on producing answers that lead in several directions at once. In politics the polarizing potential of issues associated with race is hard to overstate, not just because race touches our emotions but also because status dominance is a zero-sum game.[185] Sadly, that polarization cannot fail to influence the development of our law of race relations, at least in the short run. In these times, then, people who would bridge this part of our "great divide"[186] must seek out opportunities—not just in legislative bodies or in courtrooms, but in the management of public and private institutions—to put people of different races into positions where they do things together. These shared endeavors, sustained over time, can engender at least some sharing of meanings. It is a long journey from any one of these interpersonal understandings to a change in the social meanings of race, but when all our individual understandings of race are added up, they *are* the social meanings of race. Even the longest journey must start from where we are.

5

Race, Gender, and Political Stagecraft: Two Revivals from Recent Seasons

During the run-up to the 1992 elections, both print and broadcast journalists reported widely on two subjects of interest to the constituency for cultural counterrevolution, both centered on law. The first concerned the armed forces and was divided in two parts: the laws and regulations excluding women from jobs bearing the "combat" label, and the regulations that purported to exclude gay men and lesbians from the services. The combat exclusion was being challenged in Congress; the antigay regulations, long under attack in the courts, were now targeted by candidate Bill Clinton, who promised to revoke them if he became President. The second subject came and went in four months' time. It was injected into the presidential campaign by Vice President Dan Quayle in a speech linking the 1992 Los Angeles riots with a "poverty of values" in the nation's inner cities. The values in question centered on sexual morality.

Each of these subjects of political discussion linked race and gender by drawing on historical antecedents. The modern forms of segregation of the services were close relatives of the racial segregation of an earlier day. Suggestions about sexual misbehavior in the ghetto combined race with gender directly, and they also recalled the image, common in seventeenth-century Europe, of the libidinous African. As these two stories unfold, we shall see that they have more in common than their ties to historical precedents.

THE MANLINESS OF WAR

In the United States as in Europe, full citizenship and eligibility for military service historically have gone hand in hand.[1] On the bright side of this linkage is the American military's advance, over the last four decades, toward racial integration and the inclusion of significant numbers of women. But the story has not been entirely happy. Not until the Korean War did black Americans begin to take their rightful place in the services. At this writing women are still excluded from most combat positions, and thus denied the opportunities that are most valuable as they seek promotion to leadership. Until 1993 the services also purported to exclude gay men and lesbians altogether. An emotionally powerful theme links these contemporary forms of segregation to the services' former practices of racial discrimination. That theme is the pursuit of manhood.

Because manhood has no existence except as it is expressed and perceived, the pursuit of manhood is an expressive undertaking, a series of dramatic performances.[2] Masculinity is traditionally defined around the idea of power; the armed forces are the nation's preeminent symbol of power; and, not incidentally, "the Marines are looking for a few good men." The symbolism is not a side effect; political theater is the main point. From the colonial era to the middle of this century, our armed forces have alternately excluded and segregated blacks in the pursuit of manhood, and this generation's forms of exclusion and segregation have also been grounded in the symbolism of masculine power. These exclusions are at war with the Fourteenth Amendment's guarantee of equal citizenship.

Black Citizenship and the Right to Fight

Citizenship is itself a form of power, and as early as the Civil War the issue of full citizenship was a subtext of the question of black participation in the armed forces. The first black volunteers for the Union Army and the militia were rebuffed. Lincoln feared that enlisting blacks would signal to the border states that he aimed to abolish slavery.[3] Furthermore, some generals "feared that the presence of black soldiers in the army would create disharmony and drive away white volunteers."[4] Working-class whites in Northern cities threatened violence to blacks who were proposing to organize military companies. To men at levels high and low in white society, so visible a symbol of black manhood suggested a new and disquieting form of rivalry, and so the Union cause had to be "a white man's war."[5]

By the end of 1862 the enlistment of black soldiers could be seen to serve a clear military need.[6] The Union had suffered serious losses in the field, white enlistments had fallen, and large numbers of slaves had begun to cross the lines seeking freedom.[7] The Emancipation Proclamation of 1863 not only provided a legal foundation for a social upheaval already begun, but converted a war to save the Union into a crusade for liberation.[8] By war's end almost two hundred thousand black men had served in the federal services, including about a quarter of the entire Navy.[9] At first used almost entirely in menial support functions, eventually black soldiers were deployed in combat, and some thirty-seven thousand were killed.[10] In 1863 black regiments showed particular heroism at Port Hudson, at Milliken's Bend, and—as the movie *Glory* dramatized—at Fort Wagner.[11]

Seventy years later, W. E. B. DuBois said it was the black man's service that enabled whites to proclaim him "a man and a brother. Nothing else made Negro citizenship conceivable, but the record of the Negro soldier as a fighter."[12] Yet, formal citizenship was one thing, brotherhood quite another. Within a generation the federal courts had largely nullified the Civil War Amendments and the Reconstruction civil rights laws, and Congress had done nothing to give them new life. Black citizens, veterans and nonveterans, learned that formal equality before the law could exist alongside the gravest sort of inequalities in fact: racial discrimination in the North and West, and Jim Crow in the South.

In 1941, when the United States entered World War II, Americans who remembered World War I might have predicted that, once again, black soldiers would be: humiliated by segregation; limited in opportunities for leadership; mainly given unskilled tasks, but eventually used in combat when the need was great; disparaged in their fighting ability by some white officers; and embittered by their experience. That is exactly what happened.

More than a million black men and about four thousand black women served in the forces during the war. Some nine hundred thousand of the men served in the Army, about three-quarters of them in jobs such as "road building, stevedoring, laundry, and fumigating."[13] Even the training of blacks for combat was exceptional; and in 1942, when someone suggested to Gen. George Marshall, the Army chief of staff, that black troops be sent to fight in North Africa, he said the commanders there would object. Blacks still had to "fight for the right to fight."[14]

Eventually the Army, which had not placed black combat troops in the line, was ordered to do so by a War Department that was reacting to political criticism.[15] In Europe, when infantrymen became scarce, the Army inserted some black platoons into larger combat units. And in the

Army Air Force the black pilots of the segregated 99th Pursuit Squadron performed well.[16] Even so, Army officials sought to minimize publicity about the achievements of black soldiers, to avoid blurring the Army's public image as the embodiment of white manhood.[17]

In 1941, before the attack on Pearl Harbor, William H. Hastie, an aide to Secretary of War Henry L. Stimson (and later the first black judge of the U.S. Court of Appeals), had written to his boss, criticizing the segregation of the Army and linking it to larger issues: "The traditional mores of the South have been widely accepted and adopted by the Army as the basis of policy and practice affecting the Negro soldier. . . . This philosophy is not working. . . . It is impossible to create a dual personality which will be on the one hand a fighting man toward the foreign enemy, and on the other, a craven who will accept treatment as less than a man at home. One hears with increasing frequency from colored soldiers the sentiment that since they have been called to fight they might just as well do their fighting here and now." General Marshall, asked to respond, had said that segregation was an established American custom, that "the level of intelligence and occupational skill of the Negro population is considerably below that of the white," and that "experiments within the Army in the solution of social problems are fraught with danger to efficiency, discipline, and morale."[18]

The connection between this assessment and the historic anxieties of white men about the rivalry of black males is not hard to see. Marshall's unstated assumptions were (i) that white soldiers would lack confidence in blacks and be hostile to them, for they defined black men in general as incompetent and cowardly; and (ii) that if black men held leadership positions, white soldiers would not accept this inversion of the historic racial definition of authority. These assumptions about the effects of integration on white attitudes proved mistaken. At the end of the war the Army surveyed white soldiers who had served in combat alongside black platoons. They admitted they were resentful at first, but three-quarters of them said "their regard for the Negro had risen" as a result of the experience.[19] The black soldiers had enacted their own narratives of inclusion. In 1948 President Harry Truman, facing an uphill fight for reelection, issued two executive orders requiring "equality of treatment and equal opportunity" in the federal civil service and in the armed services.[20] The Air Force and the Navy quickly accepted integration (on paper),[21] but much of the Army's officer corps was still "traditionally white, Southern, and deeply resistant to change."[22] Actual integration beyond the level of tokenism had to await the Korean War.[23] Even then it came about not through orders from Washington but unofficially, as Army field commanders recognized the inefficiency of segregation and quietly integrated black troops into white units.[24] By the end of 1953 the Army was 95 percent integrated,[25] and so the services have remained ever since.

Ending segregation and ending racial discrimination are not the same thing. Racial tensions ran high during the Vietnam War, especially in the Army, which had few black officers and was suffering a general decline in discipline and morale. The Defense Department reacted with serious—and successful—efforts to train service personnel in race relations matters.[26] No one today says the services are free from the effects of racism, but on this score it is hard to find any other institution in American society that has done better. Today 30 percent of the Army's enlisted personnel are black.[27] When Gen. Colin Powell became the first black officer to chair the Joint Chiefs of Staff,[28] he was no token, for black officers in the Army had become proportional to the nation's black population.[29] Reenlistment rates run higher for black soldiers than for others, and so do levels of satisfaction with service life.[30]

These data are not entirely a cause for celebration; in part they reflect the relative economic disadvantage of black workers in the civilian world. Besides, in the event of war the same figures mean that disproportionate numbers of black soldiers will be wounded and killed. The facts reflect poorly on the nation's treatment of black people generally, but they gratify those who believe that service careers should be open to all Americans. Granted, the opening of this opportunity is only part of the larger story of myriad black men and women who have claimed their places as equal citizens, but the integration of the services was an early and generative chapter in that story. Citizenship and eligibility for military service still go hand in hand.

Women and Firepower

Today, however, other kinds of segregation still plague the services. As this book goes to press, an act of Congress still disqualifies women from service on Navy "combat" ships,[31] and service regulations still exclude women from most other jobs labeled as "combat" positions. After the 1990–91 Gulf War, pressures for change mounted, and by 1993 a historic change was under way.[32] Why should women care about these restrictions? Women generally are not thirsting for the horrors of combat, and neither are most men.[33] The answer lies in the connection between the sex-integration of the services and the full recognition of women's equal citizenship.

"In the current debate, 'combat' is a synonym for 'power.' "[34] The power in issue is easily understood within the services, where the combat exclusion (1) effectively bars women from advancement to the leadership positions that really matter;[35] (2) drastically limits women's employment opportunities, and thus their access to training;[36] and (3) limits the total number of women who can be admitted to the services,[37] thus producing the usual harms of tokenism.[38] In addition, (4) women, like blacks in the two world wars, are marginalized in support roles, and (5) their low numbers subject them to increased chances of sexual harassment.[39] Within the services this stereotyping and exclusion from "the real action" is demoralizing to women: "Competing in a profession while excluded from the profession's ultimate purpose and most rigorous proving ground invites failure."[40]

Admittedly, the women's movement has made some changes in the old social Order of the services.[41] The armed forces, long some of our most influential institutions for socializing young men,[42] now are socializing young women by the hundreds of thousands. Those women and their male colleagues are becoming acculturated to the ideas that women can do the job, that women can be leaders, that women can speak with the voice of authority.[43]

Except, that is, in matters relating to combat. Every day the services have taught their members, women and men, young and old, that women do not speak with authority about the subject that is the center of the services' missions. Enlisted women are introduced to some combat skills in boot camp or basic training, but they are soon shunted off the main track, away from control over weapons. Women officers know they cannot reach high positions of command if they are excluded from the opportunities for leadership in line operations that are necessary stepping-stones to those positions.

Outside the services, the regulations excluding women from combat are influential for what they express, reinforcing a traditional view of femininity that denies women firepower. Achieving full citizenship for women in America is going to require a lot more than ending the segregation of servicewomen into "noncombat" positions, but those two goals are interrelated. Until recently women have been allowed to speak with authority only in severely limited spheres of our public life.

In a radio discussion shortly after the invasion of Panama, I heard a male retired general oppose the integration of women into jobs labeled "combat" by saying, "I have been there, and I know." The implication was, You haven't been there, and so you are not entitled to speak. Of course, he had never served in combat with combat-trained women at his side—but his view is widely shared among men. American women's voices still go largely unheard in discussions of military policy, or of the use of military force as an instrument of foreign policy.[44]

Until the 1970s, when the services were opened to substantial numbers of women, no one in government had felt any need to offer reasons for excluding women from combat positions. In two decades the defenders of the combat exclusion have worked up a set of justifications that have become a routine performance, and the challengers' responses are equally familiar. A considerable literature explores these arguments in detail.[45] Here my objective is to comment on this debate in the light of the social issues agenda and the ideology of masculinity.

First, a preliminary note: Absent an emergency compelling mobilization of forces vastly larger than we have maintained for the past twenty years, an end to the bar against women in combat positions does not necessarily imply drafting either women or men for those positions, or compelling involuntary assignment to combat units.[46] For two decades, without drafting anyone, we maintained all-volunteer forces at a level around two million members, and the end of the Cold War makes a return to the draft even more unlikely than it was a few years ago.

In contrast to women officers, most enlisted women are not particularly interested in joining the combat arms, for they are less likely to see the service as a career. But enlisted and commissioned women alike knew, even before the 1991 Gulf War, that they might be caught up in combat situations, and they were prepared to accept those risks.[47] In that war 6 percent of the forces deployed were women, and fifteen women were killed.[48] Women now serve in combat support positions that involve grave risk,[49] and—regulation or no regulation—women will be used in combat itself in case of need.[50] Here at home, women serve in missile silo firing teams.[51] And many readers will remember Capt. Linda Bray, who commanded the Military Police unit that engaged in brief combat in Panama in 1989.[52]

As these examples show, the lists of combat and noncombat positions are not exactly ordained by nature; the lists change from time to time, because they represent a compromise that has become more uneasy every year.[53] Maj. Gen. Jeanne Holm was right in saying, "If all the women were discharged tomorrow, most of the distinctions [between combat and noncombat jobs] would be abandoned the day after."[54] The Army's 1982 order adding twenty-three types of positions to the combat list was not driven by evidence that women were incapable of performing as plumbers or electricians or auto transmission mechanics or helicopter repairers. Rather it was a political choice, driven by the social issues agenda, to slow the growth of the "feminine" presence in the ranks. The expanded 1982 list underlines the central symbolic purpose of the combat exclusion, but even if the list were reduced, the symbol would retain expressive power, just by declaring with the authority of law that women are unfit to serve in "combat" positions.

In the 1990s official defenders of the combat exclusion do not talk this way—not in public, anyway—but say instead that women in combat positions will interfere with the mission of the military. These arguments present a moving target, for the defenders periodically switch from one excuse to another. They used to appeal to the biological reality that women in general are less strong than men in general, particularly in lifting capacity. Today the services make this contention infrequently, because in modern warfare most combat jobs do not require physical strength at a level that will exclude large numbers of women. The lightweight M-16 rifle exemplifies a larger development: even putting missiles to one side, combat now relies less and less on muscle power, more and more on firepower. Of course, no one should be assigned to a job requiring muscle unless he or she has the muscle to do the job; everyone accepts the justification of job-validated physical tests. If, say, a lifting test should turn out to exclude a large proportion of women, however, the chances are that the same test will exclude many men—a result that plainly is not palatable to the Army today.[55]

Before 1982 women in the field artillery were allowed to be specialists in target acquisition (target location, a "noncombat" job), but not in directing cannon fire (a "combat" job)—even though the two soldiers might be standing side by side. This distinction illustrated the general governing principle: Army women can be in positions where they will be targets, but cannot deliver violence in line-of-sight firing.[56] This principle is consistent with another male-female difference dear to the hearts of defenders of the combat exclusion: Men as a group are more inclined to be physically aggressive than are women as a group.[57] One of the defenders writes, "Man is more naturally violent than woman,"[58] giving us a textbook example of "the tyranny of averages"[59] that applies the combat exclusion to "woman" in the abstract, in total disregard of the characteristics of any particular woman. Studies of sex and aggression identify tendencies within groups; in one study, for example, 70 percent of the men and 30 percent of the women were above the group median in choosing physical aggression as a response to hypothetical conflict.[60]

If it takes high levels of physical strength and aggression to be, say, a Ranger, then the Army should not select anyone who lacks those qualifications. But neither strength nor aggressiveness has relevance for some jobs on the Army's combat list: ground surveillance radar crewman, for example, or remote sensor specialist. Sex itself should not be a disqualification.[61] If this norm has a familar look, the reason is that the constitutional guarantee of equal protection forbids government to use sex as a classification for granting or denying a benefit—including employment—unless the government offers "an exceedingly persuasive justification" showing that the sex qualification is substantially related to an important governmental interest.[62]

What function is served by the regulations that qualify for combat positions the 30 percent of men below the median in aggressiveness, and disqualify the 30 percent of women above the median? Gen. Robert H. Barrow, former commandant of the Marine Corps, provided the answer: "War is man's work. Biological convergence on the battlefield would not only be dissatisfying in terms of what women could do, but it would be an enormous psychological distraction for the male who wants to think that he's fighting for that woman somewhere behind, not up there in the same foxhole with him. It tramples the male ego. When you get right down to it, you have to protect the manliness of war."[63] After all the smoke about strength and aggressiveness, this candor is a breath of fresh air: women must be excluded from combat jobs *because they are women*. The "argument" expresses two concerns: a special regard for women who must be protected as the symbolic vessel of femininity and motherhood, and a concern about women's effects on men in combat. Let us take these in order.

The first concern is not that young women's lives are worth more than young men's lives, but that we cannot stand the thought of women's being killed or maimed or—worse?—captured and subjected to the risk of rape or other sexual assault.[64] As the Gulf War showed, women will be killed along with men in future wars, with or without the laws and regulations excluding them from jobs labeled "combat." Servicewomen are already authorized and trained to use their weapons defensively. If other uses of their weapons are seen as offensive, the main thing offended is the ideology of masculinity, the idea that Man is Woman's protector.[65]

The concern that women who are captured will be raped is well founded. Susan Brownmiller begins her study of rape with an eighty-page chapter on rape in war, including some harrowing reports of the behavior of American troops in the field.[66] The idea of Man as protector, it turns out, does not extend to protecting women who are seen as other men's women. The men who raise the question of rape in defending the combat exclusion are troubled by the idea that *our* women—I emphasize the possessive form—may be raped by men of the other side. This fear reflects a long-standing inclination to regard rape from the standpoint of the anxieties of male rivalry. From the medieval origins of rape as a property crime through the frenzy of the lynch mob to the more recent tendency to put the rape victim on trial, the focus of the criminal justice system has been to do justice to men. In view of this history it is intolerable, in considering the risk of rape in war, that men should take the decision away from women who choose to accept the risk.

The uneasiness about the effects of women on male combat troops is expressed in three ways. It is said that women will (a) cause men to divert their attention from the mission in order to provide special protection for their women comrades; (b) distract men from their jobs by creating rivalries for the women's favors; and, partly as a result, (c) undermine the "male bonding" that produces heroism and self-sacrifice. The first two arguments ignore the experience of sex-integration in other workplaces, including the police.[67] When women are tokens, they do, indeed, intensify the importance of the gender line. When women in large numbers take their places alongside men, however, they come to be accepted as coworkers, colleagues, leaders.[68] Of course, career servicemen in the combat arms have been largely insulated from this experience, but experience seems not to be the point. The Army has made elaborate studies of women's lifting ability,[69] but has not tested the effectiveness of sex-integrated combat units by actually integrating some units. No doubt the politicians fear the worst: that the units' performance would be just fine. What they say in public—echoing General Marshall's warnings about "experiments" with racial integration—is that the services should not be used as "a test tube for social experimentation" with integration of the sexes.[70]

The "distraction" argument is a relic of the conventional wisdom of the nineteenth century, and it is as phony here as in other arenas of human endeavor.[71] The related concern about sexual harassment, however, cannot be discounted in any organization that employs men to supervise women. The most serious harassment, in which sexual favors are sought from (or forced on) subordinates, is not condoned by the services, but every servicewoman knows it as a fact of service life. A more common form of sexual harassment is "testing": making a woman prove that she is up to the job. But the most persistent type of harassment of servicewomen is exemplified by the man who whistles or makes sexually charged remarks to a woman in the presence of other men. Here the woman serves as an abstraction, an object in a communication addressed to his potential male rivals and judges: "I am a real man."[72] The 1991 Tailhook incident, in which male pilots in the Navy put twenty-six women (half of them naval officers) through a gantlet of groping and other forms of sexual assault, carried this sort of ritual of group domination to an ugly extreme. It served, for the moment, to reassure some men who were nervous about female competition that they had "what it takes," and the women didn't.[73]

The Tailhook incident's immediate sequelae followed a well-worn path: scandal, cover-up, further investigations, resignations, vows to improve. The acting secretary of the Navy criticized high officers for "turn[ing] a blind or bemused eye to the crude, alcohol-inspired antics of a few idiots in our ranks," but in 1993 a Defense Department investigative report accused about 140 Navy and Marine Corps officers of sexual assaults or other misconduct.[74] Alcohol was one source of the incident, but it had another source that outlasts the hangover and is not limited to "a few idiots": male combat pilots' anxiety about what the presence of women among them will mean to their own identities and status. All these forms of harassment are more likely in conditions of tokenism[75]—but that is scarcely an argument for limiting women's duties, and thus limiting both women's numbers and women's authority.

Will men follow women combat leaders? In 1940 Secretary Stimson, who was unresponsive to Judge Hastie's calls for racial integration, wrote in his diary, "Leadership is not imbedded in the negro race yet and to try to make commissioned officers to lead men into battle— colored men—is only to work disaster to both."[76] In 1942 a board of naval officers told the secretary of the Navy that "the white man will not accept the negro in a position of authority over him."[77] These mementos of white males' struggle for manhood in earlier days have been ex-

ploded forever by the day-to-day experience of service personnel. Today, however, the same conclusions are dressed in modern uniforms
and applied to women. The very presence of women in the Naval
Academy, one critic said, was "poisoning" the preparation of men for
command. The Academy had been "objectified and neutered to the
point that it can no longer develop or measure leadership"; indeed, integration had "sterilized the whole process of combat leadership training," in major part because "woman" is less physically aggressive than
"man."[78] Why can't women lead? Because women can't fight. And why
can't women fight? Because no woman is man enough.

The "male bonding" issue goes to the heart of the combat exclusion.
The threshold question—whether men can trust women's competence
and reliability—is easily answered; as women do their jobs, they prove
themselves capable. One common retort is that we have little experience of women in combat, and so cannot know whether women will
hold up under the stresses of combat. This reply draws on the stereotype of the hysterical woman, a stereotype that is self-reinforcing. In
fact, women have performed well in combat roles from World War II to
the present, as soldiers and as guerrillas in dozens of protracted and
bloody wars around the globe.[79] Beyond the question of trust, "male
bonding" also refers to the personal bonds, often intense, formed between comrades during combat—the sort of tie that produces heroism
and self-sacrifice.[80] Any group of people will form close ties when
they feel a strong sense of mutual responsibility under conditions of
extreme stress—and that includes close nonsexual ties between men
and women.[81]

Ultimately, the argument for preserving "male bonding" by excluding women reduces to an interest in preserving male dominance and in
easing the anxieties of male rivalry. A great many men feel that their
personal worth as men is constantly being tested, and that the quest for
achievement is a way to pass the test. Men also seek reassurance of
manhood in groups, engaging in joint quests that call for the traditional
manly virtues and so express the group's power. Such a group celebrates strength and competitive achievement in ways that simultaneously dampen rivalry inside the group and heighten the inclination to
dominate outsiders. "Male bonding" offers temporary relief from the
fear of humiliation for not being man enough.

Women have been excluded from many of these quests for individual
or group power, because the presence of women has been seen as

corrupting the function of the quests as a means of proving manhood. If women are powerful, what does it mean to be a man? This question was thoughtfully posed by a young naval officer who commanded the brigade of midshipmen in 1979, when the Naval Academy graduated its first sex-integrated class:

> Historically . . . the academies and a few areas of the military—Marine Corps boot camp, airborne training—have provided a ritualistic rite of passage into manhood. It was one small area of our society that was totally male. Women now have a full range of choice, from the totally female—motherhood—to what was once the totally male— the academies, for example. Males in the society feel stripped, symbolically and actually. . . . The real question is this: Where in this country can someone go to find out if he is a man? And where can someone who knows he is a man go to celebrate his masculinity? Is that important on a societal level? I think it is.[82]

In stark form, the officer's questions put in issue the social value of the ideology of masculinity. The questions resonate against the same concerns that have made cultural counterrevolution the basis for political mobilization. The social issues agenda, replete with rhetoric evoking the ideology of masculinity, offers its constituency the hope of return to a bygone world, where men were men and women were women.

The path back to that world is blocked by the economics of the two-income family and the politics of women's condition. But even supposing the path were open to us, it would be morally and constitutionally wrong for us to go back. That world's Order identified masculinity with domination, excluding women from positions of power because those positions were reserved for those who were "man enough" to hold them. Relying on the ideology of masculinity to justify excluding women from firepower, then, is not just a harmless indulgence in nostalgia; it is a mischievous tautology, an assertion that power justifies itself. Under the American Constitution, that argument is illegitimate.[83]

The Gay Soldier in the Mirror of Mars

"Male bonding" may reassure nervous males against humiliation, but it also approaches the edge of homoerotic expression.[84] This proximity threatens the very identity that the ideology of masculinity demands. For those who want to keep the public's gaze fixed on "the manliness of war," the tensions of male bonding have seemed to demand a clear expression distancing the services from any tolerance of homosexuality. This expression was the main point of Department of Defense (DOD) policy that purported to exclude gay men and lesbians from the armed forces, and it remains central in the 1993 "don't ask, don't tell" policy.

The exclusion policy reflected both aspects of the ideology of masculinity. First, the policy was part of DOD's larger effort in the early 1980s to keep the gender line clearly marked, portraying the services as the embodiment of everything that was traditionally masculine. Second, every discharge of a gay soldier was an official degradation ceremony, an invitation to the troops—and especially to very young men—to participate in further acts of group subordination, relieving the anxieties of male rivalry through rituals of group domination.[85] The exclusion policy was, above all, political theater. Its modification could begin only after the election of a President who was not committed to the social issues agenda.

The armed forces have always included gay members. During World War II some sixteen million people served in the armed forces. The services examined about eighteen million men and rejected between four and five thousand of them on the ground of homosexuality; after induction about ten thousand, mostly men, were discharged on this ground.[86] The most conservative estimates place the number of gay servicemembers in the 1940s well up in the hundreds of thousands.[87] But if the exclusion policy failed to exclude, it did introduce the American public to the idea of personal identities centered on sexual orientation[88]—and so found a new expressive purpose that was all too attainable.

Although the Uniform Code of Military Justice (1951) made sodomy—heterosexual as well as homosexual—a crime,[89] no act of Congress has excluded gay and lesbian Americans from the armed services. The DOD, however, revamped its regulations in 1981 to exclude "persons who engage in homosexual conduct or who, by their statements, demonstrate a propensity to engage in homosexual conduct."[90] Despite this announced policy, the services continued to include large numbers of gay members.[91] Yet, somehow, the forces managed to go on fulfilling their missions—as they had in the 1940s.

The various service regulations raised a problem of definition.[92] The Army, for example, defined "a homosexual" as one "who engages in, desires to engage in, or intends to engage in homosexual acts." Discharge was mandatory for a soldier who engaged in a homosexual act, or admitted to being "a homosexual," or entered into a homosexual marriage ceremony. These grounds for dismissal came equipped with an important exception that was supposed "to permit retention only of nonhomosexual soldiers." Thus, even a homosexual act was not a ground for discharge if (i) it was a departure from the soldier's usual behavior; (ii) it was unlikely to recur; (iii) it was not accomplished by the soldier's own coercion; (iv) the soldier's retention in the Army, under the circumstances, would not harm discipline or morale; and (v) the soldier did not intend to engage in further homosexual acts. Even the soldier's statement that he was "a homosexual" was not an absolute ground for discharge, if the relevant authorities concluded that he was not; he might be trying to lie his way out of the Army.[93] So, the question was whether the soldier was or was not truly "a homosexual." The regulation's exceptions implicitly recognized a strong probability that it would be awkward to give a yes-or-no answer to the question, Is he or isn't he?—and at the same time insisted on a categorical answer.

The process centered on establishing a public sexual identity, and it offered local commanders considerable opportunity for selective enforcement. When Army authorities had evidence of a soldier's single homosexual act, the threat of discharge was a powerful incentive for the soldier to avow publicly that he was not gay.[94] The more effective he was in his job, the more likely it was that his superiors would want him to assume a heterosexual public identity. If he had conflicting feelings, they would not want to know about them. Indeed, the soldier himself might be inclined to suppress any such feelings. Military service has long been regarded as an avenue for proving manhood, and for the man who is sexually ambivalent it may seem to offer a refuge from anxiety.[95] In any case, the Army generally did not go in for wholesale purges of gay men from the ranks. It enforced its antigay regulation typically when a soldier "came out," publicly expressing a homosexual identity, or when charges of homosexual acts had to be confronted.

For women in the armed forces the story was quite different. During World War II the services displayed little concern about the presence of lesbians.[96] Those concerns came to the fore only after the services abolished their women's auxiliaries and added significant numbers of women to the regular ranks—and, more to the point, after the political climate within the Defense Department changed in 1981. After that time, in furtherance of the executive branch's social issues agenda, the Navy and Marines conducted a number of purges of lesbians. In this period women were discharged on grounds of homosexuality at a rate far exceeding the rate for men.[97]

The dynamics of these cases differed in revealing ways from the dynamics of discharges of gay men—and the main things revealed were sexual harassment and other forms of sex discrimination.[98] Given the persistence of the old canard that servicewomen are either sluts or lesbians,[99] a charge of lesbianism might follow a serviceman's rebuffed advance. Some of the most zealous investigations focused on women in jobs that are not traditionally "women's work," with the investigations driven by officers who had expressed hostility to women in their specialties. A woman's outstanding performance in these "men's jobs," far from insulating her from such an investigation, made her a prime target. The syllogism was simple: women can't do men's work; this person is doing men's work; therefore, she can't be a "real" woman.[100] The investigators were especially likely to be called in if the woman were assertive in manner, larger than average, and short-haired—the very qualities in a man that would constitute "military bearing." Dragnet investigations of groups of women—called "witch hunts" by friend and foe alike[101]—were the rule rather than the exception. Gay men, in contrast, typically were investigated and processed one by one.[102]

Lesbian baiting conveyed clear messages to all servicewomen: Stay out of men's jobs; don't be too assertive; be sure to look feminine. In sum, express your identity in ways that keep the gender line clearly marked. For both lesbians and gay men, the exclusion policy's central focus was public expression, and its central goal was to keep intact a public image of traditional masculinity for the warrior class.

If further support for these conclusions be needed, consider the flimsy excuses for the policy of discrimination. The DOD statement, after asserting that homosexuality is incompatible with military service, went on make seven more particularized assertions: "The presence of such members adversely affects the ability of the Military Services [i] to maintain discipline, good order, and morale; [ii] to foster mutual trust and confidence among servicemembers; [iii] to ensure the integrity of the system of rank and command; [iv] to facilitate assignment and worldwide deployment of servicemembers who frequently must live and work under close conditions affording minimal privacy; [v] to recruit and retain members of the Military Services; [vi] to maintain the public acceptability of military service; and [vii] to prevent breaches of security."[103]

The policy was notable for what it did not say: It did not question the capacity of gay men or lesbians to do their service jobs capably. Indeed, the records in cases of exclusion have been replete with praise from commanders and other service associates.[104] A few years ago a high naval officer confirmed as much, in a statement epitomizing much that was silly and sad in the services' exclusion policy. To get the 1990s started with a new spate of witch hunts, the admiral commanding the surface Atlantic fleet issued a message urging his officers to be vigilant in rooting out lesbian women. He pointed out that investigations might be "pursued halfheartedly" by local commanders because lesbian sailors are generally "hard-working, career-oriented, willing to put in long hours on the job and among the command's top performers."[105] Until I read the admiral's words, I had not realized that the Navy's career training included stand-up comedy.

The claim that gay Americans were security risks is the most obvious example of the circularity of the policy of exclusion. A servicemember with a gay public identity could not be blackmailed into a betrayal of trust through the threat of disclosure. As more and more men and women with homosexual orientations were "coming out," DOD itself rescinded the automatic ban on security clearances for civilians who were openly homosexual.[106] Dick Cheney, President Bush's secretary of defense, called the fear that gay employees are a security risk "a bit of an old chestnut."[107] If government lawyers continued to cling to so feeble an excuse for the military services' exclusion policy, no doubt one reason was the shortage of more persuasive arguments.

Apparently DOD forbade its officials to make any public defense of the policy statement's assertions about risks to the military mission.[108] The political utility of this "never explain" strategy may have been considerable, but it left the services' practice of discrimination resting on unsupported assertions. DOD also showed a marked reluctance to offer justifications in court, when the exclusion policy was challenged as an unconstitutional denial of equal citizenship.[109]

President Clinton took his first action concerning the DOD exclusion policy one day after a federal district court held the old policy unconstitutional.[110] In a January 1993 detente with Georgia senator Sam Nunn, the President ordered the suspension of discharge proceedings against gay and lesbian servicemembers and ordered recruiting officers to stop asking applicants whether they are gay. Further action would be delayed for six months, during which Senator Nunn would hold hearings on questions about the effects of openly gay and lesbian servicemembers on such things as recruiting, morale, discipline, and the privacy of heterosexual servicemembers. Not surprisingly, the hearings' dominant themes were variations on the assertions in DOD's exclusion policy.

The service chiefs had also expressed reluctance to end the ban, and the hearings would give them a chance to air their views in public—but they had begun a campaign of overt politicking even before the President issued his initial order. Some service leaders aided in orchestrating the early public relations blitz against the President's plan to lift the ban.[111] One method was to arrange for polls calculated to show the opposition of servicemembers.[112] Such a survey will seem an identity test for many a young male respondent; to express the "correct" attitude is to reassure his mates that he is a "real" man. So a political bonus from this tactic is that the polls themselves stir up fears and promote further expression of antigay sentiments among the troops. In contrast with the services' post-Vietnam educational programs to improve race relations, this maneuver might be called "insensitivity training."

Meanwhile, active-duty military personnel were circulating to members of Congress copies of a fifteen-minute shock video, distributed by Springs of Life Ministries of Antelope Valley, California, entitled "The Gay Agenda." The video was released just in time for use in the fall 1992 campaigns in Oregon and Colorado to repeal state laws forbidding antigay discrimination. It "depicts partly clad homosexuals writhing on floats in a parade, a physician providing graphic analysis of the asserted medical dangers of homosexual acts and children apparently crying at the sight of what are depicted as leering gays." The commandant of the Marine Corps—not the general who spoke of "the manliness of war," but a successor—distributed copies of the video to the other members of the Joint Chiefs of Staff. A former Pentagon official remarked, "The Marines are passing it out like popcorn."[113] If this is the way our "non-political" military establishment acts, imagine how a politicized one might behave.

Despite these episodes of thinly veiled insubordination, and despite the inner need of a Senate baron to teach the President a lesson about "turf,"[114] the immediate effect of the January 1993 order was to relocate the issue. It was assumed that from now on gay and lesbian Americans would be allowed to serve in the armed forces. The question for further discussion was when (and where and how) these servicemembers would be allowed to express their sexual orientation.

Within a week of his detente with the President, Senator Nunn suggested a "compromise." Recruits and servicemembers would not be asked about their sexual orientation, and could serve unless they openly stated that they were gay.[115] The President believed that if he lacked the support of the joint chiefs, Congress would convert the old DOD exclusion policy into a statute. So he accepted a "don't ask, don't tell, don't pursue" principle as the basis for a new policy adopted in July 1993.[116] Senator Nunn then introduced a bill to "clarify" the policy—in effect enacting the former DOD exclusion policy into law, with the exception that sexual orientation alone will not be a ground for discharge unless a member states that he or she "is a homosexual or bisexual."[117] The bill, pending in Congress at the time of writing, makes a series of legislative declarations about risks of harm to the military mission; these statements are modeled on the assertions in the pre-1993 exclusion regulations. The bill also tracks those regulations in allowing retention of a member who has committed homosexual acts, if the member "does not have a propensity or intent to engage on homosexual acts" and if retention is consistent with "proper discipline, good order, and morale." The bill expresses the sense of Congress that, for now, recruits should not be asked about their sexual orientation, but that the secretary of defense should feel free to reinstate that questioning in the future. (Say, in a Nunn administration?)

Under either the President's new policy or the proposed law, a servicemember's statement that he or she is gay creates a presumption that the member is engaging in homosexual conduct or has an intention or "propensity" to do so. The burden is on the member to rebut this presumption—and no one seems able to say what evidence might suffice to carry that burden. Under the President's policy local commanders are instructed not to investigate to determine sexual orientation, but to investigate when they have "credible information" that there is a basis for discipline or discharge.

So witch hunts are declared to be against official policy, but both the new presidential policy and the proposed law maintain two crucial features of DOD's former exclusion policy: they authorize discharge on the basis of public sexual identity, and they give local commanders broad discretion to decide which cases to pursue. The new policy was promptly challenged in court on First Amendment and equal protection grounds, and Senator Nunn's proposed law is equally vulnerable to constitutional attack.

Critics immediately pointed out that silencing the expression of a gay identity violates the First Amendment by prescribing "viewpoint discrimination," imposing severe sanctions on statements of homosexual orientation while allowing statements of heterosexual orientation. As chapters 3 and 7 make clear, self-identifying statements of this kind are themselves political speech, and they will often have importance in discussions of public issues. In the past government lawyers defending the DOD exclusion policy have sought to convert speech into conduct, arguing that a servicemember's acknowledgment of a gay identity amounts to a confession of a disposition to engage in sodomy, a criminal offense. But even if the courts were to accept this dubious argument, an additional First Amendment challenge should be successful. By design, both the new policy (through the accordionlike standard of "credible information") and the proposed law (incorporating the old DOD policy's exceptions) give local commanders expansive discretion to decide which statements of homosexual orientation deserve discipline or discharge, and which statements do not. Giving government officials so wide-ranging a power of target selection for penalizing speech has long been considered to present First Amendment problems of the utmost gravity.

Furthermore, it is a violation of equal protection rights to discharge a servicemember on the basis of his or her openly acknowledged homosexual orientation. The government has now dropped the pretense that homosexual orientation itself is incompatible with military service. Yet the new presidential policy authorizes discharge—and the proposed law requires it—unless the openly gay servicemember can carry an undefined burden of persuading his or her superior officers that he or she has no intention or propensity to engage in homosexual acts. In a 1980 case Judge (now Justice) Anthony Kennedy drew a careful distinction between discharges for homosexual conduct and discharges based on the status of homosexual orientation.[118] Authorizing discharge on the basis of a public sexual identity is a textbook example of discrimination on the basis of status.

At a minimum, governmental discrimination denies equal protection unless it is rationally related to a legitimate governmental purpose. Putting the "security risk" charade to one side, governmental officials have emphasized two sets of assertions to justify discharge: (i) about privacy (forced association) and (ii) about discipline, morale, and unit cohesion.

The claims about privacy allowed Senator Nunn to be photographed bending over sailors bunked in close quarters on an aircraft carrier. The political theater was effective. Yet in the barracks, in the shower room, gay and lesbian servicemembers in substantial numbers have long been present—and known to be present. If there were no threat of discharge to deter them from acknowledging their sexual orientation publicly, there would be no reason to expect an outbreak of sexual advances. Most people, whatever their sexual orientation, seek out those who will not object to their advances. Allan Bérubé has recounted how gay GIs in World War II had no difficulty in recognizing each other, and how they were able to keep sex out of the work environment, including the barracks, and generally to win the acceptance of their heterosexual comrades.[119] Today it is easier for gay servicemembers to recognize each other, as the existence of gay bars within easy distance of many military bases attests.[120] A Navy enlistee who spent four years at sea, and whose mates knew he was gay, says, "I showered with them [his heterosexual mates]. I slept with them. I ate with them. And I didn't go sashaying through the barracks."[121] The rules forbidding fraternization and harassment, along with the threat of criminal prosecution for "lewd" or "indecent" acts,[122] are one set of disincentives to unwanted sexual advances, heterosexual or homosexual. Surely, however, the major deterrents would be the high likelihood of rejection and the possibility that the rejection might be expressed physically—especially by men, who tend to be more nervous about homosexuality than are most women. In the barracks and the shower room the main thing lost, with the "don't tell" policy gone, is hypocrisy. Of course, hypocrisy has always been a central feature of an exclusion policy that did not exclude.

Declarations that the presence of openly gay or lesbian servicemembers will have harmful effects on morals and unit cohesion, and on discipline and command, rest on an unspoken premise: the hostility that many heterosexual men feel toward gay men. This hostility is left unspoken not just because it is ugly, but also because its origins lie in the nervousness about masculinity that leads many heterosexual men to define themselves by contrast with gay men. In this process, assumptions about what it means to be "a homosexual" fit the classical definition of prejudice. They have nothing to do with the qualities of any real person who is gay; rather, they are a set of abstract projections of a negative identity that must be repressed.

The attitude-based assertions that have accompanied Senator Nunn's proposed law echo the statements of service leaders in the 1940s that white troops would not accept black soldiers or follow black officers.[123] They ignore the services' own educational success; if the services can teach officers and NCOs to foster a climate of acceptance for racial and ethnic diversity, they can teach other forms of acceptance as well.[124] Such a failure of institutional memory might be tolerated. What is intolerable—what makes the recitals of Senator Nunn's proposed law unworthy of an American government—is that this is one circle that flaunts its viciousness. The U.S. government is declaring officially that the existence of prejudice against a group justifies the government in imposing its own discrimination on the group. Before 1993 government lawyers argued explicitly that "public disapproval" validated the Army's exclusion of gay and lesbian Americans. Nor did the circle end there. Through the policy of exclusion, and now through a policy of silencing, government has taught servicemembers and civilians alike that the prejudice is legitimate, and so has extended the circle to new rounds of private gay bashing—which in turn will provide new evidence of prejudice that will be offered to "justify" the silencing. The analogy to Jim Crow—and the Jim Crow Army—is depressingly clear.

As Attorney General Janet Reno strongly hinted in a memorandum to President Clinton, it would be unconstitutional for any governmental agency other than the armed services to impose a "don't tell" requirement on its gay members, enforced by explusion. Nonetheless, Reno expressed confidence that the President's new policy would survive a constitutional attack. She relied mainly on some Supreme Court decisions that abdicate judicial responsibility for bringing the Constitution to bear on the armed forces, turning upside down the old maxim that "the Constitution follows the flag." When the subject is gender, that abdication is exactly what the social issues agenda prescribes.

A few years ago I offered a detailed criticism of this notion of an across-the-board "military exception" to the Bill of Rights.[125] One aspect of that analysis is worth repeating here. No one claims that the courts have power to run the armed forces. Judicial review of the general policy excluding openly gay servicemembers would not involve the courts in supervising military administration. Rather, it would focus on the denial, to large numbers of American citizens, of full access to membership in the services. If, by some oddity, one of the services were to use a racial criterion to deny full membership, can anyone think the courts should—or would—abstain?

Those who defend the exclusion of openly gay Americans from the services seek to convert this issue of access into an issue of operational control, even a threat to the military mission. But these assertions of risk to the mission—it would be flattery to call them arguments—rest on a series of gross sociological and psychological generalizations; in any other context judges would call these "stereotypes." Consider a July 1992 letter on "homosexuality and military service" sent to all Marine generals by Gen. C. E. Mundy, Jr., the commandant of the Corps. (Yes, he is the one who distributed the attack video six months later.) Following the lead of Gen. Colin Powell, Mundy denied the analogy between antigay discrimination and racial discrimination: "Race and gender relate to *personhood* while homosexuality can, and most often, involves [sic] *behavior* . . . [which] like drug, alcohol and sexual abuse is a particular form of *conduct* which can pose a threat to the physical and moral well-being of both the individual and others."[126] Such excursions into sociological/psychological pontification would do no serious harm if generals and admirals merely said those things to each other, but these assertions are designed for communication to the lowest ranks.[127] When they are paraded in court or in the halls of Congress as "military knowledge,"[128] statements like these recall General Marshall's military knowledge about the capacities of black soldiers. Worse, they recall Gen. John DeWitt, who ran the World War II program to "relocate" Japanese Americans out of their homes and into camps. One of DeWitt's celebrated bits of military knowledge was, "The Japanese race is an enemy race."[129] General DeWitt, meet General Mundy.

The recent revival of these souvenirs of the 1940s suggests a closer look at the kinds of knowledge and professional judgment that are being invoked as the basis for legislative and judicial deference. How, for example, does an Army general become an expert on the capacity of women, or on homosexual behavior, or on the relation of traditional manhood and "male bonding" to morale, discipline, and mutual trust? The highest Army generals, with few exceptions, are graduates of the U.S. Military Academy who entered the officer corps as second lieutenants and have been consistently selected for promotion, usually in the minimum time at each grade. Typically they combine quickness of intellect with exceptional interpersonal skills—the latter referring to qualities listed in chapter 3 as political aptitude and strong personality, the traditional indicia of masculinity. It should be no surprise that officers who have an important part in selecting other officers for promotion tend to respond warmly to people who look like themselves. So, if you are a young officer who wants to get ahead, how will you behave? Of course.

The announcement that the armed forces socialize their members to institutional norms will not come as news, but the point does bear on the question of expert military judgment concerning such things as the relation of manhood and "male bonding" to morale, discipline, and mutual trust. Imagine yourself as an Army general who attended West Point before women were admitted to the Academy. In those days one of the standard techniques by which the academies introduced cadets to the officer corps was to play on young men's anxieties about masculinity in ways resembling the rites of passage administered to enlistees during basic training or boot camp. From graduation to the present you have been socialized to service norms promoting the ideology of masculinity at every turn[130]—most obviously by excluding women from the Army's central mission and by purporting to exclude lesbians and gay men altogether. By the time some judge certified you as an expert on military morale and discipline, you had spent your whole adult life immersed in a belief system that entirely excluded competing points of view on manhood and the Army's mission. The general who said, "I have been there" has never "been there" in a helicopter gunship with a woman pilot, or a tank crew that included a woman.

The ideology of masculinity is not merely a system of belief embedded in individual men's emotions, but also a self-perpetuating social force. It translates the anxieties of manhood into a set of norms that justify male dominance, and those norms in turn make the stakes higher in the pursuit of manhood. For many men who have invested their lives in a career that places so high a value on that pursuit, suggestions that seem to undermine the ideology of masculinity are deeply threatening. The emotional reaction of some men to assertive women or to men who are openly gay is not unlike the reaction of some southern whites to the black citizens who challenged Jim Crow forty years ago. When people we have subordinated and defined as the Other make a serious bid for equal treatment, they not only threaten to displace us from a power position, but threaten our very sense of self. No man, surely, has the right to be scornful of the men who feel threatened today by claims of equality for women and gay Americans, and no man has the right to cast the stone of blame. But let us not be too impressed with the idea of experts on manhood.

In any case, generals and admirals were not mainly responsible for instituting today's discriminations against women and gay Americans. By the 1970s both of those forms of segregation were crumbling. Once the principle of an all-volunteer force became national policy in 1973, the services began active recruitment of women. By the end of the decade the services were projecting a quarter of a million women members by 1985. Weapons training for women had become routine, and the Army had desegregated basic training.[131] In 1979 DOD asked Congress to repeal the laws excluding women from combat duty in the Navy and Air Force, pointing out that the combat exclusion prevented the effective use of personnel, limited opportunities for women, and limited the total number of women who could serve in the armed forces.[132] During the administrations of Presidents Ford and Carter, the Navy and the Air Force took the position that the discharge of homosexual personnel was not mandatory but a matter of local commanders' discretion—a "relaxation" that had its own problems.

Then came the Reagan administration. Rapidly, DOD reversed its position on women in combat; expanded the list of Army jobs called "combat" jobs; reinstituted separate basic training for Army women and men; instituted the "womanpause," revising downward the projected accession of women;[133] and promulgated a policy purporting to exclude gay Americans from the services. Soon the witch hunts were under way, increasing the number of discharges of gay and lesbian servicemembers throughout the 1980s. All these variations on the theme of the pursuit of manhood were attuned to the new administration's social issues agenda for gender.[134] The Burger Court's decision upholding the constitutionality of a men-only draft registration law was in harmony with the new political line.[135]

Political motivations have always driven the laws and regulations segregating the armed forces. One good indicator is that the exclusion policies are set aside whenever the occasion demands. In the Civil War, in World War II, black soldiers were first barred from combat and then put into the line when they were needed. During the Korean War, when racial segregation was impairing combat effectiveness, field commanders integrated their units. When the end of the military draft left a shortage of recruits, women were actively sought, trained with weapons, and proposed for combat eligibility. In World War II, when massive numbers were needed, induction examiners and unit commanders deliberately ignored the presence of gay men. Even during the last decade, in the midst of sporadic witch hunts, commanders tended to overlook gay and lesbian doctors; after all, service doctors are hard to retain.[136] During the Gulf War DOD suspended most of its investigations of members suspected of being "homosexuals," for they were needed for Operation Desert Storm. "Hundreds of admitted gay soldiers and reservists went off to the gulf. In some cases they were told that once the fighting was over, they would face discharge if they made it back home."[137]

A second indicator of the hand of politics is equally reliable. When a public policy is maintained even though it obviously does not achieve its stated goals, it is a fair assumption that the stated goals are not the real ones. The regulations excluding women from "combat" positions do not keep women out of harm's way, but do keep them in their place. The regulations purporting to exclude gay and lesbian Americans have never kept them out of the service, but have kept them quiet—a policy now made explicit. What exclusions like these unquestionably do accomplish is to intensify the gender line, and thus to maintain for the services a particular image: power and weapons in the hands of "real men." The central political purpose of both sets of restrictions has been to express the ideology of masculinity.

THE MORALITY OF THE POOR

The mixture of race and crime was so potent in the 1988 presidential election that the mere mention of Willie Horton's name now identifies a style of campaigning. In 1992 some promoters of the social issues agenda, looking for a way to add spice, added "family values" to the race/crime mix, this time emphasizing sexual morality and women's sexual roles. The test marketing of the new race/crime/family potion was a widely publicized speech by Vice President Dan Quayle a few weeks after the Los Angeles riots. He gave the race/crime theme a new dimension by placing much of the blame for the riots on "the breakdown of family structure, personal responsibility and social order." The Vice President chided his own baby-boomer generation for embracing a morality of "indulgence and self-gratification" that glamorized "casual sex." He said that those attitudes had caused a generic "failure" of families, and that family breakdown, in turn, was a central cause of inner-city poverty and of the Los Angeles riots in particular: "The intergenerational poverty that troubles us so much today is predominantly a poverty of values. Our inner cities are filled with children having children, with people who have not been able to take advantage of educational opportunities, with people who are dependent on drugs or the narcotic of welfare. . . . The anarchy and lack of structure in our inner cities are testament to how quickly civilization falls apart when the family foundation cracks."[138]

There was nothing new in blaming poverty on the immorality of the poor. An old Anglo-American tradition stigmatizes able-bodied paupers, separating Them from the rest of Us, the morally virtuous. In Victorian England paupers were physically separated—in the workhouse—and the separation was prescribed by law. The object of the law was not merely to get some work out of the undeserving poor; another primary purpose was to draw a line, placing the occupants of the workhouse outside the community.[139] The law's message, in other words, was not just addressed to those who were receiving state support. By reinforcing the nation's acculturation to the work ethic, the law assisted in recruiting potential workers for low-paying jobs. Whether or not we choose to describe the poor laws and their successors in the language of "social control," those laws have always had general acculturating effects, and have been so intended.[140]

Today's versions of the morality-centered attitude toward poverty assume that "many people are poor because they choose a way of life that makes them poor."[141] The immorality emphasized by Vice President Quayle, however, was not a failure to work, but "a poverty of values": the sexual immorality of single mothers and of the men who father their children. Calling marriage a moral issue, Quayle appealed for "social sanctions" to enforce the morality of marriage. "Bearing babies irresponsibly [that is, outside marriage] is, simply, wrong." Children need "both love and discipline . . . mothers and fathers"; besides, "marriage is probably the best anti-poverty program of all."[142]

Granted, two good parents generally will do better than one at raising children, and it is a truism that two incomes are better than one for keeping a family afloat.[143] But the rest of Quayle's speech should be judged as political theater. There is entertainment value in a picture of poor single mothers in the inner city taking moral instruction from J. Danforth Quayle, but of course Quayle was not speaking to them. He chose to deliver the speech at the Commonwealth Club, one of San Francisco's most elite sites, and he and his aides had taken pains to assure maximum press coverage.[144] What got the speech into the headlines was Quayle's attack on the CBS television series *Murphy Brown*. The fictional character Murphy Brown, single and pregnant, had decided to have the baby. Quayle criticized the script for "mocking the importance of fathers by bearing a child alone and calling it just another 'life style choice.'" Quayle himself had changed his text to insert these words—which he lifted, with only slight modification, from Barbara Dafoe Whitehead's op-ed piece in the *Washington Post* nine days earlier.[145]

The next day, in south-central Los Angeles, the Vice President pressed his attack on the "media elite" and "Hollywood" for glamorizing illegitimacy. (Somehow President Reagan had never gone in for bashing Hollywood.) Fresh from the Commonwealth Club and a Republican fundraiser at the Desert Horizons Country Club in Palm Springs, Quayle mustered the moral courage to say, "I wish [the media elite] were here on the streets with me today. . . . They ought to come with me out to where the real America is."[146]

Some months later, he turned away from that theme to the more congenial one of attacking Hollywood as a leading representative of what he now called the "adversary culture." As an aide made clear, the adversary culture was a new name for an old and familiar target: the cultural changes since the 1960s.[147] Murphy Brown may have been a fiction, but that made her all the more ideal as a symbol of the adversary, the Uppity Woman.

Undoubtedly the main target audience for the Vice President's message about sexual morality in the inner city were working-class white Americans. With that constituency "values" had been the Bush/Quayle ticket's salvation in 1988,[148] and four years later, with the nation's economy in serious trouble, a similar politics of division might still pay dividends.[149] To its intended white audience, the new race/crime/family mixture sends at least three implicit assurances about the application of law. The first political message is old and familiar: The people immediately responsible for the rioting are the men who committed arson and theft and violent assault. Those men are scary. (There is no need to identify the men as black and Latino; the audience saw the riots on television.) Our candidates will protect Us and keep Them under control; the opposition candidates can't be trusted to do that. The second message, a relative newcomer to the explicit rhetoric of presidential politics,[150] centers on sexual morality: The people indirectly responsible for the riots are the young single mothers who bear children outside marriage and the men who father those children but do not support them. We, the virtuous, have no responsibility for what happens to Them, the sexually irresponsible. They have been induced to abandon their moral duty by overindulgent laws—"the narcotic of welfare"—and the pushers of that drug are our political opposition. The third political message is inseparable from the second: Married mothers are morally superior to mothers who have never married and whose living groups don't really deserve the name "family."[151] Our candidates will use law and the other powers of government to discourage single motherhood and to promote the values of true "families"—that is, Our families.

The Vice President spoke in general terms and did not pause to suggest any particular changes in the law. Prominent advocates of the social issues agenda, however, have suggested amending the welfare laws (for example, denying benefits to a single mother for any child born after she is on welfare)[152] or the divorce laws (for example, denying no-fault divorce when the couple have minor children). Either type of legal change would affect real people's lives, but the primary political purpose of these proposals is to offer the expressive qualities of the enactment itself as an official definition of the moral significance of single motherhood. This latest model of symbolic politics is well designed to touch the emotions of the target audience, reinforcing their sense of identity by intensifying the line between self and the "promiscuous" negative identity they must suppress within themselves.

If the enactment of a law is a means of acculturation, it does that work within an existing cultural context. In the race/crime/family area this context includes two sets of attitudes that strongly affect the perceptions of white Americans. On the one hand, the association of race (or ethnicity) with poverty and crime affects many white citizens' views of black and Latino Americans, including those who are not poor.[153] On the other hand, the visibility of race (or ethnicity) among the urban poor affects many white citizens' perceptions of poverty—even though "fewer than 7 percent of the poor in 1980 lived in what might be called a big city ghetto."[154] In an analysis centered on presidential politics, E. J. Dionne, Jr., comments that "a majority of Americans have come to associate 'welfare recipients' with values they reject, notably single motherhood and the 'absent father' who refuses to take responsibility for his children. . . . For many Americans, welfare recipients are not part of the community they regard as their own. They are viewed as the equivalent of foreigners."[155]

This "values" formulation puts race to one side—as might be appropriate, given that welfare (Aid to Families with Dependent Children, or AFDC) benefits are received by roughly equal numbers of white and black families. Most white Americans, though, do not put race to one side; when they hear the abstraction "welfare recipient," they see a dark face. Marian Wright Edelman calls welfare "a fourth-generation code word" for race (the other three being busing, quotas, and Willie Horton).[156] It is race that heightens the perception of a "values" gap; it is race that predisposes Vice President Quayle's target audience to think of welfare as a forced donation by Our community to Them, the outsiders.[157]

Still, Dionne and others are right when they say that white working-class citizens' views of the poor are not entirely a matter of racism. Everyone in sight agrees that government should try harder to make absent fathers fulfill their responsibility to support their children—even though the effort will be futile so long as the father is unemployed. Similarly, black and white Americans generally agree in viewing the high proportion of black babies born to single mothers as social pathology. The trouble with the Vice President's speech is not that he gives voice to these widely shared evaluations, but that he says the core of the pathology is a "values" deficit. Speaking of irresponsibility, what shall we make of a high public official who lumps single mothers and violent criminals together and labels the package "anarchy"?

Even in the poorest communities, most women who choose single motherhood share the larger society's values concerning both work and families, including the preference for raising children within a stable two-parent union. First, as to the moral obligation to work: Poor women, including minority women, have always had to work, even during the years when they were stigmatized for child neglect when they did so. It was white middle-class wives and widows who were morally excused from work, with the latter group being covered by the forerunner of AFDC.[158] When AFDC was expanded in the 1960s to include black and Latina mothers who were divorced, separated, or unmarried, AFDC benefits began a long and steady decline; for some years the combined benefits of AFDC and food stamps have remained below the poverty level in every state.[159] Furthermore, most poor women, including single mothers, strongly prefer paid jobs to welfare.[160] What welfare mothers need is job training and job opportunities—and neither has been available to them in a recession economy and a political era dominated by myths about "welfare queens." Even when jobs are available, women who seek governmental support for the child care that will let them enter the job market are given a discouraging response. They are told, for example, that "most families should decide on the best mix of paid work and parenting without the distortion of government subsidies."[161] As, perhaps, middle-class families should decide whether to buy homes without the distortion of the subsidy offered by income tax deductions for mortgage interest?[162]

Now, as to the moral obligation to marry: What these welfare mothers lack is not a preference for stable marriage but a pool of sufficiently "marriageable" men.[163] Pregnancy rates of poor black teenagers have not increased much, but their marriage rate has fallen, in parallel to sharp declines in employment of young black men and in the ratio of employed black men to employed black women.[164] Real earnings for employed men, both black and white, declined by 15 percent in the decade following 1973 and still have not returned to the 1973 level.[165] Despite some writers' suggestion that welfare benefits are enticing women into becoming unwed mothers,[166] the rate of single parenthood has risen steadily while median state welfare benefits were dropping (in real terms) by 39 percent from 1970 to 1990.[167] As the number of children in female-headed households increased, the number of children in AFDC families went down.[168] William Julius Wilson and Kathryn Neckerman, summarizing a number of the most trustworthy studies, conclude that "this research indicates that welfare receipt or benefit levels have no effect on out-of-wedlock births" and have "only a modest effect on separation and divorce."[169]

Most pregnancies of poor young women are unplanned, resulting from lack of education about contraception, or contraceptive failure, or a reluctance to use contraception for fear of being labeled "bad."[170] In many such cases, of course, single parenthood is not inevitable. Diane English (producer of the *Murphy Brown* show) said, "If the Vice President thinks it's disgraceful for an unmarried woman to bear a child, and if he believes that a woman cannot adequately raise a child without a father, then he'd better make sure abortion remains safe and legal."[171] Although some young women whose pregnancies are unplanned "choose" to bear their babies in the sense that they do not seek abortions, often this "choice" (or the failure to practice contraception) is strongly influenced by other factors. As Laurie Zabin, a Johns Hopkins researcher on teen pregnancy, puts it, "As long as people don't have a vision of the future which having a baby at a very early age will jeopardize, they won't go to all the lengths necessary to prevent pregnancy."[172]

Such a teenager may see the baby not merely as someone to love but as a living credential, a symbol of her respected and responsible membership in the community.[173] From her perspective the decision to bear the child does not reject family values, but embraces them. She is most likely to see welfare benefits as temporary, a life preserver to help her reach the shore. This prediction may prove to be over-optimistic, but a majority of women who receive welfare benefits are off the rolls in a few years,[174] and a still larger majority of these young black single mothers do want to be responsible and productive.[175]

The pathology that results in increased numbers of poor black families headed by single mothers is the same pathology that has produced widespread unemployment of black men: a decline in industrial jobs of the kind that used to give poor people a start up the ladder, the persistence of serious deficiencies in the education of many inner-city children, and lingering forms of low-visibility racial discrimination in employment.[176] In turn, the young people whose uncertain futures make them skeptical about marriage are, in their own lives, creating models for their successors to emulate.[177] The public policies most likely to reduce the rates of single motherhood in the black communities will be those providing the training that offers promise for the future and the jobs that young people can fill once the training is done. It is the realistic hope of employment at a decent wage that will motivate a poor young man to stay in school, and it is the actuality of that employment that will allow him to help support a family. It is the promise of a respected alternative role that will give a poor teenager a reason to avoid single motherhood. As Dan Quayle said, marriage is a good antipoverty program for a single mother—provided, of course, that the man she marries has a job. But talking about unemployment was exactly what the Vice President did not want to do.

The "family values" challenges to welfare for single mothers have an important dimension beyond race, recognized by the authors of the social issues agenda. One of the challenges is a proposal to deny AFDC benefits altogether to single mothers, for the purpose of forcing those young women to marry, to live with parents or other relatives, or to give up their children for adoption.[178] The proposal is offered as part of a broad program of acculturation—or, more properly, reacculturation—that looks to restore the gender line to its former importance in

American society. Central to this program is the restoration of "the
father role" to its traditional place in "the family."[179] The older assumption was that a woman could not support herself or her children
without the help of a man; but the rise in women's earning power—not
unrelated to women's new ability to control their own sexual behavior
and maternity—not only calls this assumption into question for working women, but gives some hope for a nondependent future even to
women who are presently on welfare but expect that condition to
be temporary. The combination of these improved prospects for poor
women with declining prospects for poor men has its own acculturating
effects on relations between men and women, including the decision
whether to marry.[180]

When employed fathers live with their families, they do add their
incomes—a point made by the very cultural critic who proposed cutting
single mothers from the AFDC rolls.[181] But the same critic focuses on the
father as a symbol of manhood itself. Calling "the absence of a father
figure" the root cause of unwed teenage pregnancy, crime, and domestic violence, he concludes, "Linking manhood to family life has been the
ultimate challenge of human societies."[182]

Thus does the social issues agenda come full circle to manhood and its
anxieties. The critic asserts that "feminists have systematically devalued
the traditional roles of fatherhood," and so undermined "family life"—
meaning the life of a family in which women nurture and men protect
and provide. So, it is not only the absent father who earns this critic's
scorn, but "the new father," the father who is empathic or nurturing
or even—heaven help us—gentle with his children.[183] Dan Quayle's
speech echoed these views in this symmetrical passage: "Children need
both love and discipline . . . mothers and fathers." Down the "new
father" path, says the critic, lies the overturning of "traditional masculine norms within the home" and "the removal of socially defined
male and female roles from family life."[184] Love from Mom, discipline
from Dad.

If we had to encapsulate the traditional definition of masculinity in
three words, they might be "protector and provider."[185] Now that the
great majority of women—single and married, many of them mothers—are in the workforce to stay, these labels are losing some of their
power to reassure men about their identities. (Even combat pilots have
taken notice.) In an economy that has not produced jobs to keep up with
the pool of prospective workers, a lot of men, especially young men,

can become nervous about more than their flaccid incomes. Predictably, politically significant numbers of men are disposed to accept the suggestion—from Patrick Buchanan[186] and his more genteel think-tank associates—that "feminists" are the enemies who are emasculating them.[187] We have seen how these threatened men have been a prime target for the social issues agenda's messages on race; they are also among the most likely to be seduced by the promise of a cultural counterrevolution that would use the law to recreate a world in which men were men and women were women.

Vice President Quayle's San Francisco speech seemed to trap him in two related double-binds. One was quickly identified by Diane English:[188] Should an unmarried pregnant woman bear her child "irresponsibly" or have an abortion? The other has a long history in discussions of public assistance programs for mothers: Should a poor single mother sit around at home ingesting the "narcotic of welfare" or go out and get a job, abandoning her moral duty to care for her children? In logic, these are puzzlers, but in actuality both of these double-binds trap not politicians but poor women. In the moral Order of the social issues agenda, a pregnant teenager is damned if she has an abortion and damned if she has the baby; a single mother is damned if she goes to work and damned if she doesn't. Why? Because both pregnancy and motherhood make her visible as a sexual actor—and that visibility makes her politically useful in the role of enemy. In status politics, a page of anxiety is worth a volume of logic.

The Quayle speech, explicitly and by direct implication, nominates several groups as the target audience's enemies: unmarried women who are sexually active, inner-city welfare mothers, frightening young black men, and the "cultural elite" that makes up excuses for Disorder. This cast of characters, augmented by the menace of "radical feminists," follows a political libretto, voicing three of the four main themes in the social issues agenda: race, crime, and "family values," the latter being the agenda's label for the relations between men and women.[189] As to each of these themes, the social issues agenda promises to use law to discipline and control the enemy group. And in the context of the message that welfare causes riots, the agenda's various themes touch on the anxieties of manhood just as surely as they do in the context of "the manliness of war."

Both strands of the ideology of masculinity run through the social issues agenda's promise to use law to discipline the morality of the poor. First, the anxieties of male rivalry about competition and physical domination are visible in the downplaying of law as inducement (job training, jobs programs) in favor of a reliance on law as control (tougher criminal punishment). Second, the powers of law and government are invoked to further men's sense of control over women. From welfare to marriage to abortion, the social issues agenda calls for law to control women's sexual expression, and also to enforce—and, in the cultural sense, to reinforce—the power of fathers in the home. In offering to assuage the multiform anxieties of masculinity, the authors of the social issues agenda have a clear-eyed view of their task as political theater. The idea is not to achieve actual control over those who are threatening, but to create images of the power to control—images that will cause the target audience to identify with the agenda's candidates. In the politics of cultural counterrevolution, effects on real people's behavior are secondary to the symbolic promise of law.

6

The Cross and the Flag

Symbols of patriotism and of religion—specifically, the Pledge of Allegiance to the flag and prayer in the public schools—were prominently featured in Vice President Bush's 1988 presidential campaign.[1] Both themes challenged prevailing constitutional doctrine, and both emphasized the expressive uses of law and government. To the constituency for cultural counterrevolution, the flag and the emblems of religion are not only symbols of community but symbols of authority that stand for the proper Order of society. So, these two conflicts, formally separate, come together in a political environment pervaded by status politics.

THE POLITICS OF RELIGION AND THE SYMBOLS OF GOVERNMENT

The central concern of the framers of the American Constitution and the Bill of Rights was to transform a loose confederation of states into a nation.[2] Still, they deliberately discarded two unifying strategies embodied in the existing British model. The nation's head of state would not be a king but a President, and the First Amendment forbade Congress to establish an official religion. An established church for the whole nation would have been a political impossibility even in those early days, for the predominant religions differed from state to state, and in some states no single religion predominated. Furthermore, the framers had learned the clearest lesson of seventeenth-century British political history: a close alliance of church and state would destabilize the state when it confronted numerous and strong-willed religious dissenters. More than a few of the framers were descendants of colonists who had come to America to escape the persecution that was issuing from a politics of religious division.

147

In our own time one highly visible aim of religious politics is the capture of government's expressive resources. The objective is to obtain official exhibitions or pronouncements embodying the symbols of religion, from public school prayers to city-sponsored Nativity scenes to the declaration of Good Friday as a state holiday. Because religious symbolism is the central concern of proponents and opponents alike, any such dispute heightens the importance of religious division in politics.

Although the risk of religious polarization is greatest in local communities, on these subjects no clear line divides local from national politics. For nearly half a century the Supreme Court has applied the limits of the establishment clause (in terms addressed only to Congress) to state and local governments,[3] and the presidential candidates who espouse the social issues agenda have insistently portrayed official prayers in local public schools as a national political issue.

In 1943, with religion and the symbols of government centrally in mind, Justice Robert Jackson remarked: "The very purpose of the Bill of Rights was to withdraw certain subjects from public controversy."[4] In the context of the case before the Supreme Court—a school board's attempt to coerce participation in the flag salute by children whose religion forbade them to participate—there was wisdom in Jackson's words. Yet, if the words be taken to imply that the courts are capable of withdrawing the subject of religion from public controversy, they amount to wishful thinking. Religious division has played a prominent part in American politics since the colonial era, and surely it will continue to do so.

For this reason and others, the Supreme Court has balked at interpreting the establishment clause to make political divisiveness—the capacity of an issue to divide partisan politics along religious lines—into an independent ground for holding government action unconstitutional.[5] Yet, even if the concern about politicizing religion does not deserve to be translated into a bright-line judicial "test," it does deserve special weight when judges confront government expression in the form of religious symbols. The concern is not that religion and politics will intersect, but that a community's politics will be polarized around a struggle for status dominance centered on religion.

Although the concern of some Justices about political divisiveness emerged in cases of government aid to religious schools, it was in just such a case that Justice Powell commented that the risk of "deep political division along religious lines" now seemed "remote."[6] Today the risk of religious polarization does seem to have lessened in the resource-allocation context, where the issues can be seen as part of the everyday grist of the political mill: bargaining among a multitude of interests over the distribution of public resources to various uses, and thus to various groups. Issues concerning governmental deployments of the symbols of religion, however, have a greater capacity to polarize, for at least two reasons. First, unlike the typical resource-allocation questions (How much? How soon?), they are not the subject of multilateral negotiation and they do not invite compromise. Rather, they present yes/no questions that offer no middle ground. A group that has a clear-cut majority and places great importance on an issue of status dominance need not bargain with anyone about that issue; so it is with a local religious majority. When the official display of a religious symbol is the whole point of the governmental action, one group is instantly and prominently identifiable as the winner and another group as the loser—with the winner taking all.

Second, any such symbol has a diffuse meaning, and so serves as a handy referent for a whole world view and a whole cultural group. It is easy for winners and losers alike to see the symbol not only as a statement about what the town or school stands for, but also as a recognition of who counts: "This is our town"; "This is our school." So viewed, these symbols officially define the status of various religious views, and thus the status of cultural groups. If government-sponsored symbols of religion produce reactions of strong emotion, the most important reason is that they touch the sense of identity, symbolizing the status of individual citizens as members of dominant or subordinate groups. This is the stuff of "deep political division along religious lines," all right. The surest way to polarize a community and keep it polarized is to provoke an all-or-nothing struggle centered on a religious group's status dominance. In a local community this is the road to a system of de facto religious parties. In 1960 Father John Courtney Murray, S.J., calling ideological parties a "disaster," went on to explain why: "Power becomes a special kind of prize. The struggle for power is a partisan struggle for the means by which the opposing ideology may be destroyed."[7]

The people who best understand the high emotional content of these issues about official religious symbols are the politicians who feed on them. An issue concerning a symbol of religion is tailor-made for the political media consultants. Can you think of a more effective television image than the symbol itself? During the litigation over the city of Paw-tuckets's officially sponsored scene depicting the Nativity, the mayor demonstrated an alertness well attuned to the era of the "permanent campaign."[8] He held a televised press conference at crèche-side, the better to drive home his explicit message that the people who opposed the city's sponsorship of the scene wanted to "take Christ out of Christ-mas."[9] Following a line of political precedent extending back through Napoléon[10] at least to the Emperor Constantine I,[11] the mayor saw some Heaven-sent Coattails, and he grabbed them. As a means for construct-ing political enemies, then, a religious symbol is the answer to a politi-cian's prayer.

Just this sort of intensified religion-based politics is invited by the Supreme Court's recent doctrinal reformulations of the religion clauses of the First Amendment. In 1990 the Court drastically diminished the protections of the free exercise clause as a charter of religious freedom, ruling that in most cases government need not offer compelling justifi-cation for imposing generally applicable laws in ways that seriously restrict religion-based activity. Religious exemptions from such laws, in other words, are not to be constitutionally required but must be sought from legislative bodies.[12] As for the establishment clause, the formula that has purported to guide most decisions for two decades—the "Lemon test"[13]—is barely clinging to life, and may be replaced by a formula intended to be more permissive.[14] By widening the scope of legislative discretion, these Revised Versions of the religion clauses will give religious groups every reason to seek government exemption from general regulatory laws, and also to seek government support for the symbols of religion. Worse, politicians now have increased incen-tives to devise new issues that will mobilize support in majority re-ligious groups.

Ironically, the doctrinal revolution in interpreting the religion clauses has been spearheaded by Justices who also hold that race-conscious affirmative action is unconstitutional unless it is a remedy for a specific previous act of racial discrimination.[15] One reason for this antagonism to affirmative action, Justice Scalia says, is the possibility that local governments will adopt programs "clearly and directly beneficial to the dominant political group, which happens also to be the dominant ra-cial group."[16] The Justices who express the most concern about "racial spoils"[17] seem remarkably unconcerned about the politics of religious spoils. For example, in concluding that the free exercise clause does not require a religious-practice exemption from a general law, Justice Scalia goes on to say that such exemptions are constitutionally permitted and may be desirable. He acknowledges that leaving questions about religious exemptions to legislators "will place at a disadvantage those religious practices that are not widely engaged in," but concludes that any resulting preferences for large religious groups over small ones are "an inevitable consequence of democratic government."[18]

The first thing to be said about this judicial illustration of "selective indifference"[19] is that a distinction between religious politics and racial/ethnic politics would be a false one. Many of America's historic religious divisions have been ethnic and racial divisions as well.[20] If Irish immigrants and their children typically have been Catholic, Japanese immigrants and their children typically have been Buddhist. Today's immigrants include large numbers from Asia and the Middle East, most of whom are neither white nor Christian. "Today, there are more Muslims in the United States than Congregationalists, more Muslims than Episcopalians."[21] The politics of religious division will, for the foreseeable future, continue to overlap the politics of race and ethnicity.

More disturbing than this inconsistency, however, is the one glaring consistency that unites the doctrinal positions that support (1) the judicial intervention that aims to take racial spoils out of local politics, and (2) the judicial abdication that invites local politicians to mobilize constituencies with promises of religious spoils. Both positions reinforce the traditional Order of social groups in relations of dominance and subordination, just as the social issues agenda prescribes, and just as the Reagan and Bush administrations have argued in court.[22]

Justice Powell was right in suggesting that the courts have a legitimate role to play in averting long-lasting and "deep political division along religious lines." That sort of polarizing division, like the Jim Crow laws' polarization of the races, has painful and long-lasting consequences for all concerned, even when it can be contained at levels short of violence.[23] When government displays the symbols of the dominant religion, as when government displays the symbols of white supremacy, the pain is not distributed evenly. In the zero-sum game of status dominance, only the losers suffer the pain of status subordination.

Recognizing the implications of Jim Crow's lessons for the nation's treatment of religious outsiders, Justice O'Connor encapsulated her concerns in words that became famous: "The Establishment Clause prohibits government from making adherence to a religion relevant in any way to a person's standing in the political community."[24] Because the prevailing doctrinal formula seemed ill-suited to protect that interest in equal citizenship, Justice O'Connor offered a formulaic alternative that would forbid government either to endorse or to disapprove religion. In an equally celebrated passage she explained the connection between this formula and the more fundamental concern to maintain a polity that is inclusive: "Endorsement sends a message to nonadherents that they are outsiders, not full members of the political community, and an accompanying message to adherents that they are insiders, favored members of the political community. Disapproval sends the opposite message."[25]

Any generalized rule for deciding cases under the establishment clause has its problems, and this endorsement test is no exception. Commentators have pointed out that the term "endorsement" is hard to reduce to conceptual purity.[26] Although this book is filled with examples of ways in which law and other governmental behavior convey symbolic meaning along with their immediate practical effects, much of what government does is only incidentally communicative. In the era of the welfare/regulatory state, a rule invalidating all official action that in any degree symbolizes approval or disapproval of religion would immobilize government to an extent that no one would find acceptable.[27] Indeed, a rule so uncompromising would itself undermine the ideal of an inclusive polity. Justice Brennan, a staunch defender of establishment clause values, recognized that "some official governmental 'acknowledgement' is inevitable," because the alternative would be "a stilted indifference to the religious life of the people."[28]

So, every Justice who has interpreted the establishment clause accepts at least some minimal forms of "accommodation" of religion, and some would accept a great deal more.[29] It is true that no clear boundary separates the concept of endorsement from the concept of accommodation.[30] Yet each term has a different "feel," because each expresses a different general ideal. The zone where the "no endorsement" and "accommodation" principles contend is the zone where the ideals of nonestablishment and free exercise compete for judicial recognition. It is no more inconsistent to embrace a no-endorsement principle along with some principle of accommodation than it is to embrace both religion clauses of the First Amendment.[31]

For some officers of government the suggestion that we learn to live with ambivalence may be annoying. How is the trial judge—or the lawyer for the school board or city council—to know what is permissible and what is not? The only reasonable answer offers no comfort to the conceptual purist. Let us focus on the judge. She is called upon to look at the whole picture in the case before her, to compare it with the pictures the Supreme Court has accepted and rejected in its establishment clause decisions, and then to exercise judgment. I use the metaphor of pictures advisedly. Judgment, in court as elsewhere, is not so much the passive acceptance of received authority as an active process; one *draws* an analogy. No judge worthy of the title will tremble before a principle that upholds a modest accommodation of religious freedom but invalidates an undue accommodation that appears to give religion—or, more typically, one particular religion—its official approval. Given the goal of a polity in which all Americans can see themselves as full members, an emphasis on "how it looks" seems entirely appropriate. How it looks will have a great deal to do with how it feels.

If the Supreme Court were to adopt an endorsement test as an across-the-board formula for deciding any and all establishment clause cases, the definitional problems for the lower courts would be formidable.[32] Surely Justice O'Connor would agree that any such test ought to have different implications in the diverse contexts in which the clause is invoked. Consider, for example, public aid to religious schools; the exemption of religious bodies from taxation; or the delegation to a church of a veto power over liquor licensing in a neighborhood. But most of those problems dissipate when the case at hand involves an official government display of a religious symbol. Whatever else can be said about such a display, it communicates a message and is so intended. The perception of endorsement, too, is a less troubling issue in most symbol-display cases than it would be, for example, in a challenge to public financial aid to religious schools. Hardly anyone would deny that public school prayers or a city-managed Christian cross would be perceived as endorsement. A judge who is explicitly instructed by constitutional doctrine to take a non-Christian's perceptions into account should be able to understand how a government-sponsored Nativity scene carries a Christian message. If the mayor of Pawtucket could understand this without difficulty, so can the judge.

When the symbols of government are religious symbols, then, the endorsement test would be as useful as any other doctrinal formula in guiding legislators and judges to respect the commands of the establishment clause. In the near future, though, that test may or may not find majority support in the Supreme Court. So, let us step back from the details of the endorsement test and look at Justice O'Connor's concern in a wider perspective. The essence of that concern is to maintain a political community that is broadly inclusive. Although this objective is vitally important, it resists being reduced to a conceptually tidy rule of decision. Yet it deserves recognition as a part of the central meaning of the establishment clause—whatever formula the Court may adopt to explain its decisions.

Something of the sort seems to have happened in the 1992 graduation-benediction case, *Lee v. Weisman*. Writing for the majority, Justice Kennedy effectively equated the graduation prayers with classroom prayers. He emphasized that the state, by organizing the graduation ceremony to include prayers, had subjected objecting students parents to "indirect coercion" into participating in a religious exercise. Most significantly of all, he added this comment: "What to most believers may seem nothing more than a reasonable request that the nonbeliever respect their religious practices, in a school context may appear to the nonbeliever or dissenter to be an attempt to employ the machinery of the State to enforce a religious orthodoxy."[33]

"Indirect coercion," in this sense, has two crucially important elements in common with the endorsement test: a concern for the effects of a symbolic orthodoxy on a religious outsider, and a willingness to consider those effects from the outsider's point of view.[34]

Despite persistent disagreement among the Justices about the proper doctrinal explanation for establishment clause decisions, a consensus prevails as to a number of particular governmental practices. No one has ever expected the Supreme Court to stamp out every official symbol offering even marginal support to religion, or to Christianity in particular. The observance of Christmas and Thanksgiving as holidays, "In God We Trust" on the money, the addition of "under God" to the Pledge of Allegiance—all are safe, under any establishment clause formula now imaginable. One way to reconcile these instances of "de facto establishment"[35] is to call them "de minimis," the lawyer's term for a trifle.[36] Another is to say that they are of long standing, even though Christmas as a public holiday is only about a century old, and the Pledge of Allegiance was modified in 1954.[37] Still another way to uphold practices like these—and, after *Lee v. Weisman*, a strong doctrinal contender for the immediate future—is to say that the First Amendment does not forbid government to accommodate religion by symbolic displays, so long as the displays are "passive" and nonadherents are not coerced. Even an accommodation principle, however, will not be a charter for free-swinging government sponsorship of any and all symbols of religion. Officially sponsored prayers in public schools, for example, will remain unconstitutional.[38] Similarly, we can assume that the Court would invalidate the Easter season practice, abandoned by the city of Los Angeles more than two decades ago, of lighting the city hall's windows in the pattern of a Latin cross.[39]

There remain the cases in which Justices have disagreed not just about doctrinal explanations but about results. It is realistic to expect the Court to abandon the uncomfortable distinction that prevailed in the *Allegheny* case[40]—holding unconstitutional a county courthouse Nativity scene, but upholding a city-county building display of a Christmas tree and a menorah, along with a "Salute to Liberty" sign. At this writing at least four Justices seem prepared to uphold all such "passive" Christmas or Chanukah displays. I leave it to those who would applaud such a decision to draw the doctrinal distinction that differentiates a city's display of a cross at Easter time.

When he criticized Justice O'Connor's endorsement test, Justice Kennedy argued that the test, taken to an extreme, would invalidate such historically validated actions as the observance of Christmas and Thanksgiving as official holidays. In recent years this kind of appeal to history has become a standard argument for progressively enlarging governmental discretion to engage in de facto establishment. As William Van Alstyne showed nearly a decade ago, a boilerplate argument now defends each new form of governmental support for religion on the ground that it does not establish religion "any more than" the incremental establishments previously adopted by politicians and upheld by the Court.[41] In 1991 a 2–1 majority of a Ninth Circuit panel provided a textbook example of this reasoning, upholding Hawaii's declaration of Good Friday as an official state holiday.[42] For the panel majority, too, one good de facto establishment deserves another.

Good Friday, until now, has seemed the holiest of days in the Christian calendar, with its religious significance remarkably undiluted by secular errands and revelries. Now, it seems, Good Friday is to be analogized to Christmas and Thanksgiving—indeed, to Labor Day—and so transfigured into a day of shopping, family gatherings, and recreation. Pawtucket's official Nativity scene was upheld, remember, because Christmas was no longer wholly religious; in the Supreme

Court's view, the presence of reindeer, a teddy bear, and a clown in the vicinity of the crèche evidenced this partial secularization. As a mental exercise, imagine what symbols of spring would suffice to secularize a Good Friday crucifixion scene erected in front of the Hawaii state capitol next to the statue of King Kamehameha I.

This remarkable judicial transformation of Good Friday was accomplished, in part, by pointing out that the day had become a big shopping day in the islands, but the panel majority had another argument, too: Good Friday, like the crèche in Pawtucket, was surrounded by secular symbols. In the statute establishing holidays, after all, "The Friday preceding Easter Sunday, Good Friday" was one line on a list that included such holidays as the Fourth of July and Washington's Birthday.[43] Selectively deploying the Supreme Court's statements, the majority drew every possible inference that might uphold Hawaii's law on a theory of "accommodation" of religion—and ignored every possible inference that might lead in another direction.

The Hawaii case thus illustrates a familiar process: each judicial approval of a de facto establishment adds to the fund of precedents for the next extension of official support for religion. This process to date— with the semi-secularization of Good Friday an exceptionally poignant example—not only has contributed to the sense of exclusion of religious outsiders, but has watered down the symbols of Christianity. The result amply validates a fear long ago expressed by Roger Williams: Beasts from the wilderness of politics have repeatedly trampled the garden of faith. As politicians have appropriated religion to their own political uses, the jungle vines of "civil religion" have strangled more than a few varieties of the real thing.[44] Milner Ball sums it up in a paragraph: "*Lynch v. Donnelly* [upholding Pawtucket's official Nativity scene] is an offense to me as well as to those who are other than Christian believers. Normal religion's display of Jesus dolls to jolly up shoppers to spend more on Christmas presents is deeply offensive. It is blasphemous. For the Supreme Court to sanction the state's practice in giving this offense excludes me, too, as an adherent of the biblical faith."[45]

The Good Friday decision is deeply disturbing—if anything, even more than *Lynch v. Donnelly* was disturbing. Hawaii's Buddhists and Baha'is had also sought to have the state give an official status to their religious holidays, but without success.[46] Discrimination among religions has been seen as a particularly egregious form of unconstitutional establishment,[47] but the Ninth Circuit majority dismissed this argument with two remarks that responded to a different issue. First, they said that the other religions' failed efforts did not demonstrate any political divisiveness of the Good Friday holiday law. Second, they said that political divisiveness, in any case, was not an independent ground for finding an establishment clause violation.[48] These observations not only leave the issue of discrimination undiscussed; they also slight the cumulative impact of this series of legislative decisions on Hawaii citizens whose religions are non-Christian.

Even if the panel majority had addressed the Hawaii legislature's discrimination among religions, plainly they would have been content to let the politics of religion run its discriminatory course. To emphasize this point, they invoked—in this establishment clause context—the Supreme Court's 1990 opinion that gutted the free exercise clause. "The Supreme Court has recently identified as an 'unavoidable consequence of democratic government' the majority's political accommodation of its own religious practices and corresponding 'relative disadvantage [to] those religious practices that are not widely engaged in.' "[49] In this perspective Good Friday is not the only thing transformed. Discrimination in favor of a majority religion and against minority religions, until now a transgression of the establishment clause's central meaning, becomes just another fact of political life. Perhaps it is not wholly accidental that the main dissenting opinions in the Hawaii case were written by one judge who is a member of the Baha'i faith and another who is Jewish.

Political and social predictions are risky, but it is a good guess that politics will confront our courts with issues of this type at least for another generation. Once, in our "segmented society,"[50] it was possible for most Americans to live in symbolic worlds that were largely homogeneous in religion, and largely to avoid contact with people whose religious views were discordant. Today, television alone makes religious discord hard to ignore. On their living room screens fundamentalist Christians confront a veritable festival of sin, not just in the dramatic productions but in the nightly news, and Americans who support abortion rights or gay rights confront evangelists telling them they are headed for hell. Nor is it possible to suppress these antagonisms simply by switching the channel. The same growth of the welfare/regulatory state that makes it impossible for government to be neutral toward religion also makes public policy into an arena where religious antagonists inevitably confront each other.

No doubt, as several commentators have said, whatever government may do (or not do) in the way of displaying the symbols of religion, someone is apt to be unhappy.[51] An incident on my own campus is illustrative. A few years ago, at the June graduation exercises at UCLA, the invocation was given by a Buddhist priest who wore a saffron robe and chanted in Pali, a derivative of Sanskrit. Afterward, the letters of protest poured in; some were thoughtful and civil, and some were the ink-and-paper equivalent of enraged screams. Evidently the invitation to this "foreign" religionist had touched a nerve. The university explained to the letter writers that our students and their families are ethnically diverse, that the priest's part in the program recognized this diversity, and so forth.[52] We can imagine that the university's diplomatic resources would not have been tested if the invocation had been given by, say, a Presbyterian minister. Yet the reason, surely, would have been that our students who are Buddhist are used to that sort of thing, not that the Christian prayer didn't leave them and their families feeling left out.

Similarly, the Supreme Court's school prayer decisions of the 1960s left many parents, particularly fundamentalist Christians, feeling that their values had been excluded from the schools: "God has been kicked out, and Humanism enthroned."[53] In doctrinal terms, this argument equates the absence of official prayer with an establishment of "secular humanism."[54] Justice Kennedy made a similar argument in the *Allegheny* case. He charged that the Court's rulings on the Christmas and Chanukah displays required it "to act as a censor, issuing national decrees of what is orthodox and what is not. What is orthodox, in this context, means what is secular." Appealing to "our Nation's historic tradition of diversity and pluralism," Justice Kennedy would "allow communities to make reasonable judgments" about the accommodation of religion.[55]

The pluralism thus invoked is geographical, with the dominant religion differing from one locality to another. Even this geographical variety, of course, is limited to sectarian differences within Christianity. In a different usage, "pluralism" refers to the bargaining among interest groups that is often necessary in democratic politics to produce a majority position. Leaving decisions about official symbols of religion to "communities" means leaving them to politics. With negligible exceptions, local Christian majorities need not bargain at all in order to display their own religion's symbols. Consider the Pittsburgh case itself. The published judicial opinions do not explain why, in 1982, the menorah came to be displayed alongside the Christmas tree in the city-county building, but surely the explanation does not lie in the political muscle of Pittsburgh's Jews. After the crèche display was held unconstitutional, the city and county decided not to continue the menorah/Christmas tree display even though the Court had upheld it.[56] In short, neither geographical pluralism nor democratic pluralism offers protection against the exclusionary effects of officially sponsored symbols of Christianity.

We shall return to the subject of accommodation of religion in chapter 7, but as a foretaste of that discussion we can take note of one model worth study: the Equal Access Act of 1984.[57] In that act Congress assured access for student religious or political groups to "public forum" facilities in federally subsidized public high schools. Even in the absence of legislation, the First Amendment itself applies a similar equal access principle to government property that is opened up as a public forum. If an area in a city park is open to all manner of expressive displays, then a religious group has a constitutional right to display a crèche[58]—but, by the same token, the city must allow displays saluting the birthday of Josef Stalin or advocating the legalization of marijuana.

A secularized state is not the same thing as a secularized public life. A huge proportion of our public life—including expression in public and on matters of public interest—lies outside the control of government. The views of prominent religious leaders are regularly reported in the newspapers, notably during election campaigns. Not only do large numbers of American households tune in to the television evangelists; some 40 percent of the adult population attends weekly religious services.[59] Private elementary and secondary schools, most of them religious schools, are holding steady at about 12 percent of the nation's total enrollment.[60] By 1980 the sale of religious books had come to exceed 10 percent of total book sales.[61] Even a rigid constitutional rule prohibiting government from sponsoring the symbols of religion would leave open a wide array of channels for religious expression to the public, including the messages of religious proselytizing and religion-based politics: private schools and universities, direct-mail advertising, press conferences of religious leaders, religious broadcasting, religious books and magazines and newspapers.

Surely even the joyous religious message of Christmas would get across without the aid of a city-sponsored Nativity scene at the city hall. A thoughtful Catholic commentator remarked, "Accommodation is two-sided . . . . [If non-Christians should make an objection to an official Nativity scene], the Christian majority should accept it with good grace—in keeping with the season. The Nativity scene would not be lost to public view. Out of private resources it could be purchased from the local authority and erected on private property, even in some conspicuous location. To allow differences over Nativity scenes to polarize a community is to make something of a mockery of a feast that heralds peace and good will."[62] Admittedly, however, the city's sponsorship does add something to the celebration of this divine miracle. It adds a reminder, to Christians and non-Christians alike, of what majority rule means in the status politics of religious division.

"CAPTURE THE FLAG" AS A POLITICAL GAME

In 1988 Vice President Bush's political advisers made an important discovery from "focus groups" that sampled voter attitudes: Michael Dukakis would be vulnerable to an attack suggesting that he was hostile to the Pledge of Allegiance to the flag. As governor of Massachusetts, Dukakis had vetoed a bill to require public school teachers to lead their classes in daily recitations of the pledge. Some teachers had objected to the bill's compulsion on religious grounds, and Dukakis's legal advisers had counseled that the objection had a solid constitutional basis. In the Supreme Court's 1943 flag salute case[63]—a decade before Congress added the words "under God" to the pledge—the objecting schoolchildren and their parents were Jehovah's Witnesses who believed that the flag salute violated the biblical injunction against bowing down to graven images.[64] Any explanation of Dukakis's veto on this basis would come across as long-winded and pedantic, recirculating the Bush campaign's caricature of Dukakis as an intellectual who was out of touch with the people. The symbolism of the flag, on the other hand, is immediate, dramatic, packed with emotion.

Making a political issue out of a compulsory flag salute appeals to an atavism worthy of the attention of an urban anthropologist. Rituals and totems have power, and one way to protect that power from skepticism is to suggest that an enemy is undoing the good effects of the totem or the ritual.[65] At the close of his speech accepting the Republican convention's nomination, Vice President Bush led the crowd in reciting the Pledge of Allegiance, and shortly thereafter he made a videotaped visit to a flag factory. Forcing religious dissenters to lead schoolchildren in the Pledge of Allegiance may not have been the gravest question confronting the nation in 1988, but on that "issue" Governor Dukakis never regained his balance.[66]

In capturing the flag for partisan advantage, President Bush sought to match the success of Candidate Bush. After the Supreme Court's 1989 decision in *Texas v. Johnson*,[67] striking down a criminal conviction for flag burning, the President called for a constitutional amendment to overturn the decision. Now the main media event was staged at the Iwo Jima Memorial, where Marines in bronze plant the flag atop Mount Suribachi. This performance, coming on the heels of the 1988 hoopla about the flag salute, was too much for Justice Stevens—one of the *Johnson* dissenters who voted to uphold the flag burning conviction. A year later, although he was still dissenting as the Court reaffirmed *Johnson*, Stevens chided "those leaders who seem to advocate compulsory worship of the flag even by individuals whom it offends, or who seem to manipulate the symbol of national purpose into a pretext for partisan disputes about meaner ends."[68]

There is much to admire in Justice Stevens's plea for Americans to shun a politics of patriotism that constructs the opposition as unpatriotic, but for two centuries politicians have understood the power of that style of politics. The Alien and Sedition Acts of 1798 grew out of fears that aliens were involved in treason—and as the Federalists saw it, treason included the corrupting of public opinion. The Sedition Act effectively equated strong criticism of government officials with disloyalty. The antipapist fervor of colonial times reappeared in the Know-Nothing movement of the 1850s, and the notion that Catholics gave their primary loyalty to a foreign Pope served as a potent weapon against the Democratic candidate for President as late as 1928. The Red Scare of 1919–20 appealed to fears of disloyalty, mainly among aliens. After World War II the Cold War added its own anxieties about foreign infiltration of American institutions—with a major assist from ambitious politicians who turned the politics of fear to their own advantage.

The McCarthy era was a fresh memory when the question of patriotism became bound up with a number of Americans' reactions to "the movement" of the 1960s. Black citizens who opposed American involvement in the Vietnam War risked being charged with radicalism, or disloyalty, or both.[69] In fact, it was easy for politicians to characterize all protest against the war as unpatriotic, for some protesters went out of their way to invite that portrayal.[70] It was during this period that burn-ings or alterations of the American flag came into vogue. Showing disrespect and giving offense were not just by-products of these acts; among all the ideas that flag desecration symbolized, none was more salient than the spirit of cultural anarchy. Besides, trashing the flag was a good way to get a protest demonstration taped for the eleven o'clock news.

So, when Gregory Lee (Joey) Johnson burned an American flag in front of the Dallas city hall to protest the Republican convention that was about to nominate President Reagan for reelection, he was reenact-ing—or, better, acting out—a little drama from the stockpile of video memory. But 1984 was not 1969, and Johnson's conviction for violating the Texas flag desecration law did not make him a culture hero. When a 5–4 Supreme Court majority held that Johnson's conviction violated the First Amendment, the passion and anger in Chief Justice Rehnquist's dissent helped to illustrate his conclusion that most Americans have an "almost mystical reverence" for the flag. In a reflective comment on the decision, Sheldon Nahmod fittingly called the Chief Justice's opinion a portrayal of the flag as a sacred object.[71]

The first time my class in constitutional law discussed this case, a Chicano student—emphatically not a recruit for the cultural counter-revolution—described his grandfather's reaction. An Army veteran of World War II who had served in Europe, the grandfather had wept when he heard about the Court's decision. The student spoke briefly and softly; when he finished, a large classroom was engulfed by an intense silence. The decision in *Texas v. Johnson* seems incontestably correct, but the case has a dimension that cannot be captured by a cool discussion of constitutional doctrine—a dimension that resists being reduced to words, even such apt words as reverence and sacredness. With the story about his grandfather the student tapped into forms of knowledge that lie below the level of articulate Reason, and in the telling he taught an important lesson, even to his own surprised self.

The Dallas demonstrators had marched through the streets in protest against the Reagan administration and some locally based war-related industries; they called this aggregation the "Republican War Chest Tour." At oral argument to the Supreme Court, the state's lawyer con-ceded that Johnson's gesture was expressive conduct, and Justice Bren-nan's majority opinion said the message was political, expressing "dis-satisfaction with the policies of this country."[72] But what message was

Joey Johnson expressing when he soaked the flag with kerosene and set it afire, accompanied by the protesters' chant of "America, the red, white, and blue, we spit on you"? The state's lawyers argued that Texas could legitimately protect the flag as a symbol of nationhood or of national unity, and so could punish treatment of the flag that tended to "cast doubt on either the idea that nationhood or national unity are the flag's referents or that national unity actually exists."[73] Their implication was that Johnson's act communicated doubts of that kind. Chief Justice Rehnquist, on the other hand, said simply that Johnson was communicating "bitter dislike of his country," but that otherwise his flag burning was merely "the equivalent of an inarticulate grunt or roar."[74]

Speaking of doubts, I doubt that Joey Johnson would accept any judicial characterization of his message except Justice Brennan's abstract statement that it was political. When interviewed by the press, Johnson said he burned the flag as a "symbol of oppression, international murder, and plunder."[75] Yet, one need not have observed the Dallas demonstration (as the Justices had not) to know, in a general way, what Johnson's message was. Consider another protest incident in Los Angeles, early enough in the 1970s to fit into the era we call "the 1960s." A group of people who had just been admitted to the California bar trooped over to the federal building for the swearing-in ceremony that would admit them to practice in the federal district court. When the marshal told them to raise their right hands, a number of the candidates raised fists. You know how the judge reacted. He went up in smoke, as the fist clenchers had expected.

How did you know without being told that the judge would be angry? The answer is that you and the judge share a culture that has taught you a set of meanings to assign to behavior. Even at this distance in time we can understand how the medium (the fists) and the message were inseparable. We can guess that the judge saw the clenched fists as a challenge not only to the courtroom's structure of authority but also to values he considered fundamental in defining the American community, and thus his own identity. These connections linking culture and identity and passion seldom rise to the level of conscious articulation, and yet they are known to us in our fingertips. In any culture, a great many things go without saying.[76]

But what, exactly, were the fists supposed to communicate? The clenched fist was a symbol by which "the movement" protested against the Vietnam War, but it had also been used by the black power movement and by students protesting anything from the military draft to dormitory rules. The fists, as an all-purpose gesture of defiance, could easily be perceived as Chief Justice Rehnquist perceived Johnson's burning of the flag a decade later: as a deliberate expression of contempt for a political culture and a nation. Of course, even if the courtroom demonstrators' message had been explicit, the judge could not respond on the merits without stepping out of his official role. But the wordless indeterminacy of the message meant that no one could answer it. What could the judge do—point his own fist at the floor? The gesture thus carried two kinds of emotional force: it insulted the community of meaning that defined the judge's version of the nation, and it did so in a way that frustrated any attempt at a reasoned response.

So it is with the substantive meaning of flag burning. All of us understand the meaning at some level of knowing, even though we cannot articulate it with precision. At a minimum, we know Johnson ·was trying to be insulting, and he was trying to get attention. (If burning the flag had failed to attract attention, would he have tried to hold his breath until he turned blue?) But whether the insult was to the President and his supporters, or to actions of the national government, or to "the nation's values"—the latter being the solicitor general's remarkable euphemism for political orthodoxy[77]—the insult was vague rather than specific. As with the clenched fists in the courtroom, Johnson's symbolic act gained emotional force from this very indeterminacy. Yet, as Frank Michelman has reminded us, flag burners typically do not seek to insult the nation itself, or even the ideals that most people associate with the flag; rather, the paradigmatic flag burner "charges the nation with betraying its ideals as the flag burner understands them."[78] To get closer to the meaning of flag burning, we need to focus on the symbolic content that the act of burning rejects—on the potential meaning of the flag itself.

Justice Jackson was right when he said, of the flag salute, that "a person gets from a symbol the meaning he puts into it."[79] But Chief Justice Rehnquist is also right in saying that the flag is not "just simply another 'idea' or 'point of view' " but the "visible symbol embodying our Nation."[80] Most Americans get a lot of meaning from the flag, because they put a lot of meaning into it.[81] Still, as Justice Jackson implied, the meanings Americans invest in the flag are multiple. To observe that multiplicity, we need look no further than the Justices' several opinions in Johnson.

According to those opinions the flag stands for our nationhood or national unity (Brennan, paraphrasing the state's lawyers); for principles of freedom or inclusiveness (Brennan); for the nation's resiliency (Brennan); for the nation itself (Rehnquist); for something men will die for in war (Rehnquist); for "America's imagined past and present" (Rehnquist, in Sheldon Nahmod's apt paraphrase[82]); for courage, freedom, equal opportunity, religious tolerance, and "goodwill for other peoples who share our aspirations" (Stevens); and for shared beliefs in law and peace and "the freedom that sustains the human spirit" (Kennedy). So, even within the Supreme Court, the flag stands at once for freedom and for obedience to law, for war and for peace, for unity and for tolerance of difference.[83] If we look beyond this unrepresentative group of nine Americans, the meanings assigned to the flag cover an even wider range—as any veteran of the Cold War and the upheaval of the 1960s will remember.

These contrasts in symbolic meaning have a significance beyond the one Justice Jackson identified. The flag's meaning is not merely different for different viewers; it is fervently contested. For some years Americans have engaged in a political struggle over the proper meanings of the flag and, by extension, the meanings that properly define the republic for which it stands. Some contestants in this struggle over public meanings seek to preserve the dominance of traditional views about what the nation stands for, and their opponents seek to disrupt or transform those meanings.

So, the last battles of the Vietnam War are cultural and political. Does the flag stand for war or for peace? For unity or for diversity? For acceptance of existing law and custom or for the freedom to reshape those cultural patterns? Does government's legitimate authority rest on its willingness to preserve the traditional status Order of social groups? Pervading all the issues that divide the cultural counterrevolutionaries from their antagonists is the question of submission to traditional authority. In relation to this larger question, the flag and the symbols of religion come together.

SYMBOLS OF AUTHORITY AND POWER

When the American nation was founded, a very old European political tradition symbolized a country's solidarity by expressing the unity of government and religious authority.[84] In the typical arrangement the church placed the authority of religion behind the crown, and in return the crown established the church as propagator of the official religion. Not surprisingly, the church's support for "the divine right of kings" encouraged the king to be a zealous "defender of the faith." To this day, one element of the Union Jack is the Cross of Saint George.

Although the American flag displays no religious symbols, the feelings of "almost mystical reverence" that most Americans invest in the flag are feelings of the kind associated with religion. And, just as one cannot destroy the Cross by burning two pieces of wood arranged in the form of a Latin cross, "Johnson burned a 'flag,' but it was beyond his or anyone's powers to burn *the flag*."[85] As Steven Gey felicitously puts it, "The essence of the flag—which exists only in our collective minds— remains pristine and untouched."[86] The flag, as Michelman and Gey and Nahmod and others have said, is an icon, an image to be venerated, "the sacred making itself seen."[87] In spirit and in function, there is something very nearly religious about the American flag.

In a passage that speaks generally to artists' exploitations of the ambiguities of imagery, and makes no mention of religion, Gey refers to those who display or observe a flag as "communicants."[88] In its more typical modern usage, that term has a specifically religious content, referring to the persons who are entitled to receive the Holy Communion within a Christian church. The Communion symbolizes not only participation in the sacrament but also membership in the church community, and one who is excommunicated is excluded from both. Similarly, one who believes that the American flag stands for the nation is a communicant in the secular sense, either flying the flag or seeing it as a symbol of community. Undoubtedly, as the Chief Justice suggests, most Americans do think of the nation as a community, just as a Christian communicant thinks of the Church as a community. In each case the label of community membership (Christian, American) identifies a group of people who share a vocabulary, a way of translating experiences into culturally coded perceptions, a set of values, a structure of authority— in short, a world of symbols.[89] No one directly experiences a community by seeing it or touching it—not the nation, nor the church, nor a marriage, nor a business partnership. We experience the nation only through symbols; a community exists only in people's minds, as a shared symbolic world.

To say this much, however, is to recognize that others, who do not share this symbolic world, are outsiders—the very problem created by official government displays of the symbols of religion. One might think that the flag and the national anthem, unlike the divine Nativity or the Cross, symbolically embrace all Americans, and so stand outside our cultural contests over status dominance. Justice Kennedy suggested something of the sort in his concurring opinion in the *Johnson* case, calling the flag a "constant" in the midst of social conflict.[90] But American experience suggests caution about this assumption. Consider the Jehovah's Witnesses whose view of the flag as a graven image took them to the Supreme Court in the 1940s. Consider also those two black American runners at the 1968 Olympics who expressed their protest against racial discrimination by standing, during the playing of "The Star-Spangled Banner," with heads bowed and fists raised to the Mexico City sky.[91]

The cultural counterrevolutionaries tend toward orthodoxy not only in religion but also in attitudes about social relations, believing as to both that "moral authority comes from above."[92] The flag symbolizes that higher authority, and in the 1988 campaign the Pledge of Allegiance "meant unity, conformity, obedience—patriotism."[93] In contrast, the burning of an American flag signifies at least a temporary alienation from the American nation as defined by those who are "in charge," at least a temporary adoption by the flag burner of the identity of outsider. A statute designed to protect the flag from desecration will be enforced mainly against those who are attempting to convey insurgent messages that challenge the authority of the dominant social Order. Without question, as Michelman said, "the statute's *actual* impact on expression will be lopsidedly skewed along an obvious and salient partisan axis."[94]

Critics on the right have charged the Reagan and Bush administrations with deceiving their social issues constituency into accepting symbols in place of real social change. But to a political constituency defined around questions of status, in large part the symbols *are* the reality.[95] Similarly, as Jim Crow and the Nativity scene cases illustrate, the symbols of group status are especially real for the members of subordinated groups. True, Joey Johnson was not the representative of an identifiable social group that Texas had subjected to a status harm. Yet, in larger perspective, the *Johnson* case has a place in the dual contexts of the politics of cultural counterrevolution and the constitutional issues engendered by the social issues agenda. Looking at the case from these perspectives can help us to see some of the connections between membership in a community and submission to authority.

One reason why the sense of belonging is a basic human need lies in the security that comes from knowing that other members of "our" community will attach more or less the same symbolic meanings to behavior that we do. The authority of this community of meaning—this subculture—allows us to trust others in the community. It also enables us to know how to behave in ways that are acceptable to the other members of the community. A challenge to "our" culture's authority is frightening for anyone.[96] Not just for the cultural counterrevolutionaries, but for a great many Americans who otherwise reject the conservative social issues agenda, the flag and the symbols of religion are symbols of the authority that promises security.

In the eyes of many fundamentalist Protestants, of course, citizens have a duty to use the power of government to promote the symbols of God's authority. But the view that religious symbolism deserves a greater role in public schoolrooms and elsewhere in government is shared by a considerable majority of Americans, a majority far exceeding the proportion of citizens who regularly attend religious services.[97] A number of explanations for these numbers are possible. My guess is that many Americans, considering themselves vaguely Christian but not particularly religious, perceive the symbols of religion, like the flag salute, as teaching some generalized sense of "values" and "authority," and thus promoting stability.[98] (As we have seen, Americans who are not Christian tend to have doubts on both counts.) Similarly, as Joey Johnson and his chanting companions seem to have learned from video images in their 1960s childhood, nothing about the insurgent symbolism of flag burning is more threatening—and thus infuriating—than its defiance of traditional authority. In *The Wind in the Willows*, remember, Mr. Toad was fined five shillings for speeding in his motorcar, and sentenced to twenty years in prison for giving the officer cheek.

"The issue is not the issue." This mind-expanding battle cry is one of my favorite souvenirs of the 1964 "free speech movement" at the Berkeley campus of the University of California. What was at stake for "the movement" of the 1960s was not one or another public policy but the authority of an entire world view. Even then, challenging authority was an old American story, for America has always been a multicultural nation. Before the nation's founding one could have said, as Peter Clecak did in describing what he saw in 1983, that "authority in America is divided, limited, and transient."[99] From the colonial era to our own, these conditions have been a breeding ground for social conflict, and thus for political manipulation. But where cultural insurgents in the 1920s, for example, had expressed their rebellion mainly in private conduct, or in novels or low-circulation magazines, the various uprisings of the 1960s and 1970s were dramatically visible to everyone. Suddenly, images of disrespect for the symbols of traditional authority were transmitted via television to huge nationwide audiences at the speed of light. Furthermore, because "the movement" was mainly challenging the authority of the existing "structure of advantage,"[100] it threatened status positions founded on that structure.

In retrospect it now seems inevitable that the anxieties thus engendered should be mobilized into a political movement offering cultural counterrevolution, and that the means of mobilization should prominently feature the very symbols the insurgents treated irreverently.[101] The flag and the symbols of religion, after all, do cause people to associate "the nation's values" with traditional authority. Some Americans recoil from the idea that government power should be deployed to perpetuate a set of officially defined national values,[102] but for other Americans that idea—central in the social issues agenda—has a powerful attraction. Indeed, the polarization of citizens on this very question about the proper role of government is one of the defining characteristics of today's zero-sum politics of status dominance.

If authority translates into power—as we have been told repeatedly by twentieth-century practitioners of sociology and social psychology[103]—it is even more certain that the symbols of authority are perceived to symbolize power. In the case of religious symbols displayed by the government, this power relation is plain enough: non-Christians generally lack political power in local communities, and government-sponsored symbols of Christianity express not just tolerance of religion but Christian dominance. The American flag, too, is widely regarded not merely as a symbol of authority but as a symbol of power. This symbolic function of the flag was left unspoken in the *Johnson* opinions—although perhaps it was a subtext of the Chief Justice's recitation of the flag's connections with memorable moments in American military history.

Not far below the surface of the flag's symbolism of power lie the anxieties of manhood and the ideology of masculinity. We have seen how federal judges have insulated the military from constitutional review by wrapping it in the flag.[104] Of all the unhappy results of this abdication, the unhappiest of all is that the courts have helped to legitimize the national government's claim that the subordination of social groups—that is, of women, and of gay and lesbian Americans—is its own justification.[105] Thus has the moral authority of the nation been lent to further acts of domination in contexts far removed from the military—and thus has the social issues agenda fed on its own successes.

In the final chapter we look at the agenda's interactions with law in larger perspective. But, even as we consider such broader questions as the role of the courts in maintaining a national community, we must not forget how important it is for judges (and the rest of us) to pay close attention to particulars and to context. Here, as we end our exploration of the symbols of religion and of other authority, it seems apt to remind ourselves that God is in the details.

7

The Constitution of a Community of Equal Citizens

America has always been a multicultural nation, but until the middle of this century the authority of law and government—always said to rest on "the consent of the governed"—was founded on a high degree of homogeneity among those who were effective members of the polity. The moral order that made "consent" possible was in great measure the creation of smaller communities. The order was mainly enforced not by the law's coercion but by informal sanctions that sustained the norms of a locally shared culture—with the norms widely shared from one locality to another. In a famous essay David Potter pointed out that these communities were able to prevent deviation from social norms by isolating cultural "dissenters" and by excluding cultural outsiders from effective citizenship.[1] Sometimes, as in the legal framework for Jim Crow, the law explicitly forbade the outsiders to participate in the community's public life. More typically, however, law's chief contribution to the maintenance of social conformity was its embodiment of norms and values that were not only traditional but shared by all the groups that were in position to contend for political power.

In some cases—the social meanings of "woman" are illustrative—the norms thus embodied in law took for granted the exclusion of groups from public life. The laws and the informal sanctions excluding women were mutually reinforcing. The official exclusion of women from the practice of law, for example, not only grew out of the dominant view of "woman's place" but also reinforced that view, for it denied men and women alike any experience that would permit them to hear the word *lawyer* and see a mental picture of a woman. In the nineteenth century the pictures of women most familiar in the white middle class were those of wife and mother. In Myra Bradwell's case, Justice Bradley didn't merely invoke those images; he also recycled them into the cultural meanings that confined women's expectations by defining their identities.[2]

As Potter remarked, the strong role of informal sanctions in governing society had an important political by-product: public affairs could be conducted on the assumption that nothing very important would be done until the opposition could be persuaded to give at least grudging agreement. Potter showed how this version of government by "consent" had crumbled as the scale of society increased, accompanied by the growth of a national system of transportation and communications. In the great cities cultural "dissenters," previously isolated, could find each other and establish new communities of meaning founded on their own values, communities that enforced their own brands of internal conformity.[3] The "dissenting" communities also found a voice in the larger society, and many of them were able to establish competing bases of political power. These developments, Potter said, changed not only the conditions of conformity but the conditions for the legitimacy of law.

What Potter saw as a proliferation of new communities can also be seen as a series of advances by historically subordinated groups toward inclusion in an enlarged national community—a movement that continues today. The traditional values those groups reject most fervently, naturally enough, are the values that have contributed to their subordination. Naturally, too, the "dissenters" challenge the authority of laws that maintain their exclusion—precisely by expounding those values and enforcing them. Today, nearly four decades after *Brown v. Board of Education*, it is predictable that the "dissenters" will bring these challenges to court, invoking the Constitution. When they succeed in expanding the embrace of equal citizenship, they also reshape the community of meaning that defines a nation. This chapter begins with an inquiry into the proper role of our judges in this process of redefinition.

The chapter's second section turns to recent events. In 1990 the politics of cultural counterrevolution seemed an irresistible force, not only in American electoral politics but in our constitutional law. By the fall of 1992, however, much had changed. President Bush had abandoned his opposition to Congress's civil rights bill. The Supreme Court had rejected two cardinal objectives of the social issues agenda, reaffirming the core holding of *Roe v. Wade* and holding unconstitutional official prayers of benediction at a public school graduation ceremony. Finally, the agenda's "family values" theme had come to be seen as a liability to the President's campaign for reelection.

For the near future the momentum of the social issues agenda for abortion seems to have been deflected away from presidential elections and toward more localized contests. Certainly, however, the politics of cultural counterrevolution is not gone; some themes (such as the race/ crime package and the armed services' acceptance of openly gay and lesbian members) plainly have not exhausted their political appeal in national politics. The nation's experience teaches a sobering lesson: although some cultural conflicts do go away, others are more durable, and new conflicts emerge in every generation. Americans who seek intercultural community should recognize, if they want to avoid frustration and melancholy, that the path meanders, the goal is never wholly reachable, and success is measurable only in degrees. We close the chapter and the book with a look at those citizens who—despite the recent revival of the equal citizenship principle, or even because of it— feel left out. In this chapter we take stock and peer ahead.

JUDICIAL REVIEW AND THE POLITICS OF EXCLUSION

The mixture of politics with race, sex, or religion is a powerful solvent. The social issues agenda has all but dissolved the foundation for James Madison's hopes that factional domination might be eliminated from lawmaking in the national government. Even in those fields, however, Madison's concerns and his structural analysis of factional politics continue to influence our generation's judges and commentators as they think about the proper judicial role in constitutional cases. The resulting "structural" approaches to judicial review may be congenial to the authors of the social issues agenda; for groups historically excluded from full participation in American public life, however, these approaches bode ill.

A few years ago Justice Antonin Scalia quoted Madison to support his conclusion that the Supreme Court should demand more in the way of justification for a city's race-based affirmative action program than the Court had previously demanded for a similar program adopted by Congress. "The struggle for racial justice," Scalia noted, "has historically been a struggle by the national society against oppression in the individual states."[4] Surely there is wisdom in judicial deference when an act of Congress seeks to include groups long underrepresented in aspects of the community's public life as important as employment or government contracting.[5] Yet the main justification for that deference is not structural but substantive: the responsibility of Congress to enforce the Fourteenth Amendment's guarantee of equal citizenship.[6] Because today's national politics of the social issues is a series of zero-sum contests over status dominance, the structure of the national government is a weak defense against factional oppression. When judges review governmental actions in the areas of religion, gender, or race, nothing about the governmental structure justifies their taking a meekly deferential attitude toward the Congress and the President.

Coming at Madison's structural analysis from a different angle, Cass Sunstein has blended Madison's two objectives—to inhibit oppression of minority factions, and to promote legislative decisions based on deliberation about the public good—into a broader "republican" theory of judicial review under the equal protection clause.[7] At a minimum, he says, the courts should invalidate legislation that results not from public-spirited purposes but from a dominant faction's "raw power" to promote its own interests. In this view the equal protection clause requires legislators to deliberate about the public good, not just to "respond mechanically to constituent pressures."[8]

Professor Sunstein also sees the courts' intensified scrutiny of the states' asserted justifications for "discrimination against blacks, women, aliens, and illegitimates" as an inquiry into the quality of legislative deliberation. Here, too, a faction's "raw power" may be intentionally used to promote factional advantage. But, he says, factional power may also prevent or distort public-spirited deliberation in another way. Because power relations among social groups may produce stereotypical views of those who are subordinated, legislative discrimination may be the product of "ideology"—"an unthinking reflection of existing relations of power"—rather than the "reasoned analysis" that reflects disinterested deliberation about the public good. In sum, he proposes a "procedural" approach to equal protection decision making "that inspects legislation to determine whether representatives have attempted to act deliberatively" in the public interest.[9]

The equal protection clause emerged from the great national contest over slavery that culminated in civil war.[10] The legislators who adopted the Fourteenth Amendment had substantive purposes in mind, not the purpose to encourage legislators and lawyers and judges to cast their arguments in the language of disinterested, public-spirited Reason. The substantive core of the Fourteenth Amendment, and of the equal protection clause in particular, is the principle of equal citizenship. The principle originated in the purpose to recognize that the Americans once held in slavery were free citizens: respected, responsible participants in the community's public life. Their status as citizens had been vindicated not just by legislation but by force of arms. In constitutionalizing that status, the framers of the Fourteenth Amendment deliberately chose broad language linking citizenship and equality. In the past quarter-century, we have seen, the Supreme Court has given new life to that language, recognizing its force as a generalized protection against other (nonracial) forms of discrimination that stigmatize and exclude. The judiciary's central concern in interpreting the equal protection clause is not procedural but substantive, not deliberation but inclusion.[11]

An equal protection jurisprudence centered on a search for legislative deliberation will be especially unrewarding when a court considers the validity of legislative decisions in the zone where religion, sex, and politics meet. Suppose, for example, that a state legislature should forbid local school boards to provide birth control counseling for high school students. Neither the purposes nor the effects of such a law would be gender-neutral, for Margaret Sanger's 1920 comment is still true: "Birth control is woman's problem."[12] Even so, the law can be defended with "public good" reasons based on parental authority. The sponsoring legislators may say (i) that counseling a teenage girl at school may keep her parents from becoming aware that their daughter is sexually active, and thus deny them the chance to counsel her to change her ways; or (ii) that parents will be more effective counselors than a school officer, for they know their daughter's individual needs. Arguments like these may be founded on views about families and sexual behavior that have little to do with the lives of the young women who would seek counseling. But the arguments undoubtedly qualify as "reasoned analysis"; that is, they are consistent with a good-faith effort to promote the public good, as distinguished from a purpose to oppress anyone.

If we ask Professor Sunstein's next question, whether this law is an "unthinking reflection" of power—of men over women, or adults over children, or one cultural faction over another—the judge's inquiry into "reasoned analysis" confronts the problem of the zero-sum game of cultural dominance. Whose cultural values, whose perceptions of the realities of family life, are influenced by ideology? Whose are the product of Reason? It is hard enough for a judge to get at conscious legislative motives that are illicit; a search for the unconscious, ideology-based motivations that lie beneath a legislator's vote is a task no judge should be asked to perform. Each of the contending cultures, after all, sees the other as ideology-laden. As the old saying goes, "I have a social philosophy; you have political opinions; he has an ideology."[13]

The problem with a judicial inquiry focused on legislators' "reasoned analysis" is not merely theoretical; it has serious practical implications. For reasons long apparent to writers on the role of legislative motivation in equal protection doctrine, a judge who is told to focus on the question whether a law is "in fact a disguise for, or rooted in, private power"[14] will be disinclined to answer either part of that question in the affirmative if the state offers any plausible justification based on assertions about the public good.[15] Beyond the usual difficulties in assessing legislative motives, it is especially difficult for judges to see a legislative classification's roots in "ideology" when the law discriminates against a group that has, by long-established custom, been low in the political pecking order. In such a case the existing group status Order may seem part of the natural world, and thus "reason" enough to justify itself. So Justice Bradley assumed in 1873, when he wrote that "the domestic sphere" was divinely ordained as the domain of women.[16] Some "reasoned analysis" can always be found to justify a group domination that has been around for a long time. By diverting the courts away from the substantive harms of exclusion, this procedural form of judicial review will serve as a formula for upholding discrimination.[17]

If a further example be necessary, recall what the Supreme Court said in a well-known equal protection case about the need for a public-good justification for a legislative classification: "[E]very exercise of the police power must be reasonable and extend only to such laws as are enacted in good faith and for the promotion of the public good, and not for the annoyance or oppression of a particular class." Having said that, the Court went on to uphold the challenged classification, commenting that the state legislature was "at liberty to act with reference to the established usages, customs, and traditions of the people." The year was 1896, and the law thus upheld required the racial segregation of railroad cars. The established custom the Court perceived—and, by its decision, reinforced—was a social gulf separating blacks from whites.[18]

When courts review the laws that carry out the social issues agenda for religion, race, or gender, judges who limit themselves to structural or procedural approaches to judicial review will almost certainly ignore some serious denials of equal citizenship. It is substantive harm that gives any equal protection claim its power: harm to the equal citizenship values of respect, participation, and responsibility. For the judge faced with such a claim, there is no legitimate escape from inquiring into the nature and seriousness of that harm; assessing the government's asserted justifications; and weighing those substantive considerations against each other.

A relative of the various structural approaches to judicial review is the concern that Alexander Bickel called "the counter-majoritarian difficulty."[19] Ever since Bickel coined the term, its invocation has expressed an attitude, a mood of judicial deference to the products of the political process. Bickel was prepared to justify judicial review of the constitutionality of legislation, but he put judicial review on the defensive, calling it "a deviant institution in American democracy."[20] He also rounded up the most skeptical of the skeptics, from James Bradley Thayer, who worried in 1901 that common resort to judicial review tended "to dwarf the political capacity of the people, and to deaden its sense of moral responsibility," to Learned Hand, who mused in 1942 that judicial review might be unneeded in a society in which "the spirit of moderation" flourished, and useless "in a society so riven that the spirit of moderation is gone."

When legislation enacting the social issues agenda is measured against the principle of equal citizenship, the "counter-majoritarian difficulty" diminishes in gravity. To the ghost of Thayer, the principle of equal citizenship says—and our experience in the civil rights era confirms—that judicial review, focused on the values of respected participation in the community's public life, can enlarge the people's political capacity, helping to vitalize the sense of citizens' moral responsibility to each other. To the ghost of Hand, the same principle and the same experience say that judicial review can feed the spirit of moderation in a society that fits neither of his descriptions—that is, a society in which tolerance never flourishes quite enough, and yet is never so far gone that it cannot sit up and take nourishment. To the ghost of Bickel, the principle of equal citizenship says that Americans are, for all their divisions, a national community; that our individualism is matched by a sense of mutual obligation, a sense that citizenship is belonging; and that judicial review in the last half-century has served as an essential counterweight to the self-aggrandizing impulse that dominates the legislative process—in short, that "the claims of citizenship impose their own counter-majoritarian necessity."[21]

Often, when governmental acts carry out the social issues agenda, judicial review of those acts cannot be called "counter-majoritarian" in any fair sense of that expression. Consider the long-running dispute between Congress and the executive branch (under Presidents Reagan and Bush) over the 1988 "gag order" of the secretary of health and human services. The regulation forbade the employees of federally funded family planning agencies to counsel patients concerning the option of abortion. Here the courts were reviewing an administrator's statutory authority as well as the constitutionality of his action. Even the five Justices who voted to uphold the secretary's order conceded that there was considerable room for disagreement over his statutory authority. That was putting it mildly—but when majorities in both houses of Congress promptly voted to restore the original understanding, President Bush vetoed the bill, and it was impossible to muster the two-thirds votes in both houses to override the veto. It would take effrontery to describe the final legislative product as "majoritarian." Indeed, one way to tell this story is to say that when the President has a complaisant Supreme Court majority, he can effectively wrest a part of the legislative power from the Congress. To state the case more temperately, it is unpersuasive to defend the Court's submissive posture toward the President by reference to any "counter-majoritarian difficulty."

If it be argued that the "majoritarian" quality of this kind of executive branch legislation resides in the President's electoral mandate, two responses seem apt. First, we have seen how the role of the social issues in presidential politics can bring out the ugliest features of majoritarianism as a system for maintaining factional supremacy, polarizing voters in zero-sum contests over status dominance. When the zero-sum game is added to the winner-take-all feature of the Electoral College system, the combination subverts the Madisonian premise that "factions" will dampen out in the national legislative process.

In the typical two-party presidential election, the voters have an either/or choice, just as they would in voting on an initiative or referendum measure. Because these forms of direct democracy bypass the Madisonian "filtering" of the majority's will normally provided by the bargaining required to get a bill through a legislature, they carry the dangers of majoritarian tyranny that Madison cautioned us to avoid. Julian Eule has shown how legislation by initiative and referendum sharply increases the danger of factional domination, and he has argued persuasively for a strong form of judicial review of the voters' direct legislation.[22] A parallel danger lurks in presidential elections, where a long-standing and seldom-violated political tradition gives all of a state's electoral votes to the candidate who wins the largest number of voters in the state. The more an election can be made to seem a yes/no referendum on the candidates' attitudes about race, for example, the more certain it is that the racial minority's preferred candidate will lose the state's electoral votes.[23] When a President has made prominent use of the social issues agenda in gaining office, and seeks reelection via the same route, we should not be surprised if he should use his legislative capacities—both the veto power and the issuance of "interpretive" regulations—precisely for the purpose of promoting zero-sum games of status dominance in the states he sees as his electoral base.

The second response to a claim of "majoritarian" support for executive branch social issues legislation amounts to a denial. Much of the social issues agenda plainly has not represented the views of a nationwide majority. Rather, for candidates in the line reaching from Barry Goldwater to George Bush, the agenda has been targeted to the South and to swing-vote populations in the industrial North. When a President in that line has exercised legislative power to carry out one of the agenda's promises—for example, by issuing the "gag order" prohibiting abortion counseling in federally funded agencies and vetoing Congress's bill to overturn the order—the chances are excellent that the executive legislation has responded not to a national majority but to a substantial minority who are concentrated in states that are seen to be strategically vital.

I do not suggest that judges should take their cues from opinion polls on the social issues. I do suggest that judges should beware lest a phantom "counter-majoritarian difficulty" turn them away from their normal responsibility in a constitutional case: to require weighty justification for a governmental action that seriously impairs important interests. The "gag order" is an apt illustration. At stake was not only the doctors' and staffers' freedom of expression but the urgent interest of the agencies' clients in accurate—which means complete—medical advice. When government severely invades interests of such magnitude, familiar doctrine holds the action unconstitutional unless government justifies its action as necessary to achieve public purposes of great importance. Here there is no "counter-majoritarian difficulty" to divert a judge from imposing that heavy burden of justification on the government.

The zero-sum game of status dominance accentuates the tendency for partisans to characterize people on the other side of a cultural boundary as enemies. The resulting political campaigning is as unedifying as it is divisive, but it raises few constitutional problems so long as its promise of law remains only a promise. The problems arise after the election, when the "permanent campaign" translates an electoral style into a style of governing, using the power of law to express status dominance by means of stigma and exclusion. Although some politicians in the 1992 presidential campaign seemed in deadly earnest when they spoke of religious or cultural "war," the idea of cultural "enemies" of the state is itself at war with the principle of equal citizenship. Our judges have no weightier responsibility than to enforce that principle, no duty more grave than to protect against attempts by government to embody in law an Order of status dominance and subordination.

When the "family values" issues of sex and gender come to court, the constitutional claims in question may or may not be tagged with equal-protection labels. Women's claims to control their own sexual behavior and maternity, for example, may be cast in the constitutional vocabulary of privacy or autonomy. It is this vocabulary that inspires some judges and commentators to pour acid on such a claim by calling them demands for a freedom to select a "life style"[24] or for a right of "abortion consumers"[25] to gratify their consumer preferences. Yet any sensible view of the subject must recognize the centrality of controls over sexual behavior and maternity as determinants of women's place in society and in the public life of their communities—in short, of women's status as equal citizens.

The fundamentalist who links "planned parenthood, the pill . . . [and] abortion on demand" with "women's liberation"[26] agrees with the feminist who makes the same connections. But the fundamentalist, unlike the feminist, grumbles that secular humanism has taken away the "distinctive roles of male and female" and created a world in which "a woman need not honor and obey her husband." If your culture regards male power as a "family value" ordained by God, you will see nothing amiss in using the power of the state to impose that value on women, even those who disagree. Here the object of status politics includes not only the dominance of one cultural group over another, but of men over women. In these zero-sum games it is not easy to see how our courts can reach any compromise that will not deny one of the central values in contention.

The Supreme Court's opinion in *Roe v. Wade*[27] was plainly designed to give something to both sides in the controversy, but any opinion would have been doomed to fail as a compromise. The outcry against the decision would have resulted even if the Court had not dismissed the idea that a fetus could have the constitutional status of a "person."[28] In the next section we shall see how the Supreme Court in the *Casey* decision (1992) made a new attempt to reach middle ground, preserving the core of a woman's right to choose, but allowing the states to impose limits that did not "unduly burden" the right.[29] At least in rhetorical terms, this position appeared to come close to the center of gravity of public opinion on the issue.[30] Even so, the leading players in the zero-sum game, from Operation Rescue to the National Organization of Women, refused to leave the field. Any recognition of a woman's legal right to choose to have an abortion is, inescapably, the recognition of a right to terminate prenatal life. Faced with this all-or-nothing conflict at the core of the abortion issue, neither judges nor legislators can avoid taking sides.

This is not to say that there are no points of potential agreement between people in the "pro-life" and "pro-choice" camps. Nearly everyone would agree that a woman who chooses to have a baby should be protected in her decision against parents or a putative father who might try to coerce her to have an abortion. But it is hard to identify other conclusions that would find agreement across the whole cultural spectrum. No doubt the occasions for contention over abortion would be reduced if women had access to effective family planning services that allowed them to avoid unwanted pregnancies.[31] But a considerable number of Americans, on the basis of religious belief, oppose birth control by means other than abstinence and oppose even more vigorously any public endorsement of contraception. Similarly, many with "pro-choice" views would accept a system of state-financed counseling for women who want help in thinking through the abortion decision, provided (and it is a big proviso) that the counselors were nondirective.[32] But many with "pro-life" views would oppose any such counseling, precisely because it is designed to give pregnant women "an opportunity to . . . determine, for themselves, what value should be given to prenatal life"[33] rather than to submit to the teachings that the opponents hear as the Word of God.

I have argued that a woman's constitutional right to equal citizenship necessarily includes control over her own sexual expression and maternity. Others whom I respect and cherish support the power of government to prohibit abortion in order to protect prenatal life and to promote the humanity of the pregnant woman and the society. Yet, the *Casey* dissents notwithstanding, the courts cannot responsibly solve the problem of dealing with a compromise-resistant issue by the simple expedient of washing their hands and leaving abortion questions to politics. Virtually everything we know about the intersection of politics with sex and gender should make us reject this flight from judicial responsibility. The "politics of motherhood"[34] is inextricably intertwined with the question of the roles women should be allowed to play in our society.

Whatever else one can say about the politics of government regulation of abortion, it is worth remembering that the principle of equal citizenship is concerned not only with material inequalities but with stigma and stereotype. When a law significantly interferes with women's capacity for full participation in the community's public life, a court should not only consider those immediate practical consequences along with the state's interests in protecting prenatal life, but also take account of the law's expressive purposes and effects. It is intolerable for a court to pay strong deference to a legislative determination to use the law's coercion as a means of establishing a social definition of women that is itself incapacitating.

To say that a constitutional claim of equal citizenship requires a court to take into account the expressive effects of the challenged law is simply to state a corollary of a more general point: To understand the claim that a law harms a constitutionally protected interest, a court must pay attention to the environment in which the law operates. This concern for a law's context is especially important when a major feature of the relevant social landscape is the historic status subordination of a social group. Consider the initiative measure adopted by Colorado's voters in 1992, amending the state's constitution to repeal existing legal protections of gay and lesbian citizens against discrimination and to forbid the adoption of such laws and policies in the future.[35] The Colorado amendment was promptly challenged in court,[36] and its claim to constitutionality is shaky.[37] Here I do not undertake a full analysis of the amendment's validity, but use the Colorado case to illustrate how—and why—a court considering the constitutionality of this sort of law ought to take into account the law's expressive effects.

Although the Colorado amendment is decorated with buzzwords about entitlement and quotas, it is much more sweeping than a prohibition against affirmative action for gay and lesbian citizens. (Of course, no such affirmative action programs existed, except as figments in the advertising of the initiative's promoters.) The amendment forbids every governmental agency in the state to adopt or enforce any law or policy that permits a "claim of discrimination" on the basis of "homosexual, lesbian or bisexual orientation, conduct, practices or relationships."[38] Its immediate effect would be to repeal: a state statute forbidding insurance companies to discriminate on the basis of sexual orientation; broad antidiscrimination ordinances in Denver, Boulder, Aspen, and Telluride;[39] similar policies in school districts; and the governor's executive order forbidding discrimination in state employment. Plainly, however, the amendment's sponsors designed it not only to cut off one arm of the state's civil rights law but to achieve broader expressive effects.[40]

There is solid judicial precedent for considering these expressive effects. In 1967 the Supreme Court invalidated a California state constitutional amendment, similarly adopted in an initiative measure called Proposition 14.[41] That amendment effectively repealed state and local fair housing laws, and forbade the adoption of new ones. Both at the oral argument and in the Court's opinion, Proposition 14 was described as "more than a mere repeal" of laws. The Court noted that the state supreme court had (1) read Proposition 14 as if "it expressly authorized and constitutionalized the private right to discriminate on racial grounds," and (2) "assessed the ultimate impact of [Proposition 14] in California's environment and concluded that [it] would encourage and significantly involve the State in private racial discrimination contrary to the Fourteenth Amendment."[42] Two expressive aspects of Proposition 14 were thus crucial to the decision: the measure encouraged private discrimination, and it constitutionalized a right to discriminate. The state had told landowners that racial discrimination in housing was perfectly legal, and had given that discrimination a special legitimacy by enshrining it in the state's basic charter.

Both of these features are present in the Colorado case. In fact, Colorado's amendment is even more vulnerable to constitutional attack than was California's. In the California case it was necessary for the Supreme Court to look to the state court for an assessment of the race-related purpose of Proposition 14 and of the local "environment," because the amendment did not mention race at all. It merely declared (in language resonating with the Bill of Rights) a constitutional right to refuse to sell or rent real property to anyone. If the Colorado case should reach the Supreme Court, the Justices will need no such interpretive help from the state courts, for the Colorado amendment explicitly (1) singles out gay and lesbian citizens, denying government the power to protect them against discrimination, and (2) constitutionalizes the right of private individuals and companies—and, for that matter, the state itself[43]—to discriminate against citizens on the basis of their sexual orientation.

Furthermore, the Colorado amendment, unlike California's Proposition 14, is subject to constitutional attack for its effects in squelching political expression—the expression of a gay identity. Although a homosexual orientation typically is established by adolescence, for an individual the issue of public identification with homosexual orientation remains a matter of choice.[44] As we saw in chapter 3, this choice is central in the mechanism by which the *person* becomes political. Much of the recent success of the gay rights movement surely owes to the decisions of millions of Americans to acknowledge publicly their self-identification as lesbians or gay men. The 1992 amendment imposes severe new costs on Colorado residents who make such decisions. Imagine yourself as a self-identified gay or lesbian Coloradan who has not yet made that identification public. With the amendment in force, "coming out" entails greatly increased risks—of being fired from your job or evicted from your apartment—for you cannot look to an anti-discrimination law for protection against the employer or landlord who objects to your open expression of identity.

This is the essence of the First Amendment argument in the Colorado case; it has impressive credentials in Supreme Court decisions of the civil rights era protecting the right to control information about one's associations. Various state governments had tried to force disclosure of the NAACP's membership lists, with the obvious purpose of destroying the association by exposing its members to private punishment, including discharge from employment.[45] There is one difference: the Colorado antigay amendment works to silence the targeted group about their associations, while the anti-NAACP laws sought to expose the associations of the targeted group. What the two types of law have in common is the mechanism of inflicting harm. The sponsors of the Colorado amendment have mastered the segregationists' technique.

Apart from inhibiting expression, the new amendment conveys its own messages, harming the targeted group in other ways. It will not come as news to the initiative's promoters[46] that the amendment intensifies a social boundary, formally declaring the separation of a group of people from the community of citizens who are worthy of governmental protection against discrimination.[47] As the Supreme Court said in 1954 of the "detrimental effect" of the separation of black and white children in public schools, "The impact is greater when [the separation] has the sanction of the law," for the separation is usually taken to denote the inferiority of the group set apart.[48] When the law in question is adopted, not by the legislature, but by the whole electorate, the stigma is greater in two dimensions. First, the embodiment of the separation in law is communicated to everyone in the state. Second, the group thus set apart is made to understand in the most forceful way that the people of Colorado have decided that they deserve this separation from the rest of the citizenry.

This stigmatizing expression is not just an incidental feature of the new amendment. The chief objective of the sponsoring organizations is to pronounce an official anathema on homosexual orientation; the Colorado initiative is just an opening shot in what is to be a nationwide campaign. Nothing mobilizes a constituency better than an enemy on whom potential voters can project their fears. Antigay initiatives can tap a rich vein of fear—and of money—in the nineteen states and more than one hundred cities that have adopted laws forbidding discrimination on the basis of sexual orientation. Although it will often be difficult for a court to assign an invidiously discriminatory motive to a measure adopted by a statewide vote,[49] the promotion of Colorado's new amendment leaves little doubt that such a motive was at the very least "a substantial or motivating factor" in its adoption.[50] Four decades ago, when Thurgood Marshall was arguing the school segregation cases, he borrowed an old line from Chief Justice William Howard Taft. Marshall urged the Supreme Court not to ignore as Justices what they knew as men.

Questions of motive aside, a court that reviews the constitutionality of the Colorado amendment will not be doing its job unless it takes account of the amendment's harmful expressive effects: not just effects on the freedom of expression, but the stigmatizing effects of the amendment's own expression. Stigma—especially stigma propagated by government—produces harms that are both immediate and consequential. The immediate harms are psychic: insult, humiliation, indignity for the people stigmatized. But the amendment's separation of gay and lesbian Coloradans from the rest of the citizenry also expresses the legitimacy of antigay fears—and helps to translate those mental states into a wide range of privately inflicted harms, from insults to employment discrimination to physical attacks. The point is not that this legitimizing message will be persuasive to a majority of citizens,[51] but that the amendment offers reinforcement of the worst inclinations of those citizens who are just waiting to be persuaded. An example that will be familiar to many lawyer-readers is the police officer who arrested Michael Hardwick—first for carrying an open beer container from a gay bar into the street, and later, in Hardwick's own bedroom, for violating Georgia's sodomy law.[52] Gay bashing—the blood sport of choice for some nervous males among this receptive group—may be a private enterprise, but it operates with public aid.[53]

The laws of the Jim Crow era are the nation's best-known example of the official expression of stigma and its multifold evil effects. Our national experience with these laws is so familiar and so compelling that the authors of the social issues agenda have developed a rhetoric that purports to contain the idea of legally recognizable stigmatic harm within boundaries defined by official acts of racial discrimination. This strategy of doctrinal containment is conspicuous in the defense of antigay legislation, where the proponents regularly deny the analogy to racial discrimination. But—as chapter 5 made clear in the context of the segregation of the armed services—the analogy from one of these civil rights arenas to the other is chillingly close. Like the Colorado amendment, the Jim Crow laws inflicted their harms in part by silencing the target group, but also through the expressive qualities of the laws themselves, as "permissions-to-hate"[54] that legitimized private discrimination—even private violence—by people fearful for their own identities. To the black South, equal citizenship was a hope and a promise, but for many a white southerner it was a threat to a social status, an identity bound up with the idea of white supremacy. In Jim Crow, public expression and private discrimination were not separate; their interaction constituted a social system, a culture of subordination.

One of the most grievous social costs of racial subordination is that white people are kept from knowing the black people around them.[55] Of course, most white Americans are acquainted with black people, but—as Ralph Ellison said in *The Invisible Man*—knowing them requires looking behind the abstraction of blackness to find the persons. Under

Jim Crow no real opportunity existed for doing things together, for enacting the narratives of inclusion. Along with the individual tragedies portended by Colorado's new amendment comes the menace of harm to the society as a whole. Most Americans have friends and work associates who are, unknown to us, gay and lesbian. If that be so, then we do not really *know* these people, for an important part of their sense of self is hidden to us. That is a loss to us as individuals, and a loss to society as well. If we are to get beyond the fears we attach to group labels, we need to know each other, one to one, in ways that are not superficial.

The Colorado case thus illustrates several more general precepts for judicial review in the doctrinal areas touched by the social issues agenda. First, judges need to be alert to the expressive qualities of law, particularly the capacity of law's expression to inflict the direct harms of stigma and stereotype and the consequential harms that flow when official expression is translated into private hostility. Second, judges should understand that private discrimination is a public responsibility whenever it works its effects within an existing status Order of group subordination that has been promoted by law.[56]

Finally, judges should be aware of their own expressive capacities, both in deciding and in explaining their decisions. When Americans ask ourselves about the place of race, or religion, or gender in our public life, the courts (especially the Supreme Court) have affected our answers—even the answers of citizens who seldom give the judiciary a conscious thought. In the decades since *Brown v. Board of Education* American law, especially constitutional law, has taught one lesson that is vital to our sense of nationhood: No line drawn by race or religion or gender serves any legitimate function in determining who is qualified for full participation and full responsibility as a citizen—that is, in defining who is entitled to full membership in the national community.

THE ENDURING PRINCIPLE OF EQUAL CITIZENSHIP

The presidential candidates who have declared their support for the social issues agenda have been widely understood as promising to appoint Supreme Court Justices who would turn the tides of legal doctrine, and judges in the lower federal courts who would translate the revised doctrine into action. By 1992 Presidents Nixon, Reagan, and Bush had appointed seven of the nine Justices serving, and Presidents

Reagan and Bush had appointed almost three-quarters of the judges serving in the U.S. district courts and courts of appeals.[57]

A judiciary reconstituted in the image of the agenda would narrowly interpret the reach of federal civil rights laws; would be disinclined to insist on the actual integration of schools as a remedy for past segregation; would roll back the restrictions of the Bill of Rights on local law enforcement and the states' criminal processes; would uphold governmental displays of religious symbols, including official school prayers; and would uphold laws forbidding or restricting abortion. From 1980 to 1992 the White House and the Justice Department took extraordinary care to identify nominees for the federal bench who were in broad agreement with this agenda.[58] The appointments strategy had embarrassing reverberations in speeches and writings by lawyers who were "running" for federal judgeships,[59] and even in judicial opinions on the social issues blatantly advertising the authors' political suitability for elevation to the Supreme Court.[60]

In the Supreme Court itself the theme of toughness toward crime had begun to take hold in the mid-1970s, and now it is fair to say that President Nixon's "law and order" program for the federal judiciary has carried the day.[61] Among that program's most prominent triumphs are (i) a radical constriction of federal court habeas corpus remedies for state prisoners convicted or sentenced in violation of the U.S. Constitution;[62] (ii) severe limitations of the reach of the Fourth Amendment's prohibition against unreasonable searches and seizures;[63] and (iii) the definitive rejection of constitutional attacks on the death penalty, despite "the inevitability of caprice and mistake" and despite striking racial disparities in its application.[64] To the degree that any constitutional developments can be said to have a look of permanence, these changes in the field of criminal justice have that look.

During the 1980s the Court also moved toward the positions of the social issues agenda on race, on religion in government, and on abortion and other "family values" issues. With President Reagan's appointment of Justice Antonin Scalia in 1986, the movement accelerated perceptibly.[65] As the 1990s began, commentators were announcing the imminence of something like total victory for the social issues agenda within the Rehnquist Court. It is easy enough, in hindsight, to call these announcements premature, but in mid-1991 they had more than a little plausibility.

In the field of civil rights, as chapter 4 made clear, Presidents Reagan and Bush had found the Court a willing ally, particularly in its interpretations of federal civil rights legislation. In 1990 Congress had re-acted to the *Wards Cove* decision[66] by adopting a bill to restore the burden-of-proof rules that had governed "discriminatory impact" cases of employment discrimination since 1971. The same bill would have overturned several other restrictive interpretations given by the Su-preme Court to federal civil rights laws, notably including the inter-pretation in Brenda Patterson's case, discussed in chapter 4. President Bush vetoed the bill, arguing (despite the bill's explicit language to the contrary) that it would move private employers to adopt racial quotas in hiring.[67] Within the White House, political strategists had been divided over the utility of the quotas theme as a club against the Democrats in the 1992 presidential election[68]—and for the moment the show was being run by those who thought that something on the order of Senator Helms's "white hands" television ad would play well to a national audience.[69]

As with the gag rule forbidding abortion counseling, majorities in Congress could not be expanded into the two-thirds votes in both houses needed to override the veto. But, unlike those cases of executive branch legislation, this time it was the Supreme Court that had effec-tively amended the 1964 act, and the President who made the "amend-ment" stick by thwarting Congress's effort to overturn it. Late in 1991, however, the President relented, signing into law the Civil Rights Act of 1991.[70] Half a year later, within the Supreme Court, the social issues juggernaut slowed dramatically. By a 5–4 vote the Court reaffirmed the core holding of *Roe v. Wade* that a woman has the constitutional right to choose whether to have an abortion, and the same majority held uncon-stitutional an officially sponsored prayer of benediction at a public school graduation. The votes that proved crucial in applying the brakes came from three of the five Justices appointed since 1981: Sandra Day O'Connor, Anthony Kennedy, and David Souter.

Civil rights deregulation, an end to abortion rights, a revival of school prayer—the very heart of the social issues agenda, seemingly close to fulfillment, was put on hold. What happened? How can we explain the changes that deflected the executive and the Supreme Court from the paths they had been pursuing? It is still too early for a fully rounded answer, but it is not too early to think about the question. Here I offer one way to look at these remarkable events: as reflecting the centrality and the endurance of the principle of equal citizenship in American law and the American civic culture.

Let us begin with civil rights. When President Bush signed the 1991 act into law, political analysts gave much of the credit to the recent successes of David Duke and Clarence Thomas.[71] An improbable duo, to be sure—and yet these two did have something in common: Duke in campaigning for the Senate and the Louisiana governorship, Thomas in pursuing appointment to the federal bench,[72] had intoned themes closely attuned to the social issues agenda for race. Both had attacked the civil rights movement, and both had spoken the language of formal racial neutrality. After a bruising battle in the Senate, Judge Thomas had become Justice Thomas with the help of enough Democrats to make a 52–48 majority for his confirmation. A week later Duke, calling himself a Republican, had made his way into the run-off election for governor of Louisiana. A key difference between the two men was that Judge Thomas represented the Republican party's new hopes for attracting black conservatives, while Duke—a former Nazi sympathizer and Ku Klux Klan leader with a political face-lift—represented nothing but trouble. The President disavowed Duke.[73]

Orlando Patterson was half right in calling the Thomas hearings a cultural development of importance for African Americans in their quest for full inclusion in American public life,[74] but the cultural importance of the hearings was greatest of all for the relations between white women and white men.[75] Of course, the feature of the hearings that gripped the nation for several days—and the feature that gave the hearings their historical importance—was not Judge Thomas's disapproval of race-conscious remedies but the charge that, years previously, he had sexually harassed Anita Hill, an attorney under his supervision. Although Professor Hill and the other main witnesses on both sides in this second stage of the hearings were black, Judge Thomas was able to paint the proceedings as a reflection of white racism. Despite the racial currents flowing through the hearings, however, their most audible immediate effect on American society was an unprecedented national seminar on the subject of sexual harassment.

For a week or so, all over the country, men and women talked to each other—and, let us hope, listened to each other—not just in televised interviews and radio talk shows but at the dinner table, in the living room, in the bedroom. In the aggregate these myriad conversations added to our civic culture, raising consciousness not only about sexual harassment but more generally about the relations between women and men, and about the status of women in our public life. It is my belief that the hearings' acculturating effects also touched at least some of the

Justices, and I shall return to this theme in discussing the Supreme Court's 1992 abortion decision. For the moment, though, let us stay with the civil rights bill.

After some members of the Judiciary Committee ran Professor Hill through the gantlet, the opinion polls found majorities siding with Judge Thomas among respondents both male and female, both black and white. (In a poll taken a year later 48 percent said they believed Professor Hill and 34 percent said they believed Judge Thomas.[76]) The early polls evoked diverse interpretations, but one thing seems clear: behind many a respondent's crisp answer must have lurked considerable ambivalence. We know from their public statements that a number of senators, required to vote yes or no, felt a similar ambivalence. Finally, after the orgy of bloodletting came the hangover—and, as Judge Thomas said, a time for healing.

The strategists who had initially proposed the 1990 bill had not limited it to overturning the Supreme Court's 1989 civil rights decisions, all of which had been focused on racial discrimination. The sponsors had included a provision authorizing damages (not just back pay) for discrimination based on sex, religion, or disability. After the Thomas hearings a number of senators, including some Republicans who had voted to sustain the President's veto of the 1990 bill, felt the anger and revulsion of many of their women constituents against the Senate committee's treatment of Anita Hill's charges. These senators wanted to be seen as taking action against sexual harassment.

By a coincidence worthy of a Trollope novel, one of Judge Thomas's main sponsors in the Senate was John Danforth of Missouri, a Republican with a solid record of concern for healing the nation's wounds of racial division.[77] Danforth had been trying for months to work out a compromise civil rights bill, but each of his attempts had been squelched by the President—or, more accurately, by the President's chief of staff, John Sununu, and by White House counsel C. Boyden Gray, the President's friend and a principal adviser on both civil rights issues and judicial appointments. Gray, for whom "conservative" would be a conservative description, had also played a key role in the nomination of Judge Thomas for the Supreme Court.[78] The White House gave every evidence of being willing to use Danforth in the Thomas hearings, while at the same time blocking his efforts at civil rights compromise. After the hearings Republican senators rallied to Danforth in numbers strongly suggesting a veto-proof majority for his bill. When this sentiment was made known to the President, he agreed to sign the bill, with a few cosmetic amendments to lend plausibility to his claim of victory in the "quotas" battle. The Democrats, for their part, were relieved to remove the Q-word from the 1992 elections, both presidential and congressional.

Some months earlier, after the White House had rebuffed a proposal that made twenty-two concessions in order to reach a civil rights compromise, Senator Danforth said he would stop making concessions and seek the votes to override a veto. He remarked, "There's an enormous amount of political power in the race issue . . . to create a sense in people's minds that you better watch out, or blacks are going to get your job. . . . It's destructive. It's not good for the Republican Party."[79] The senator spoke truth on all three counts. His first two points are incontestable. The power of the social issues agenda for race is indeed great, and that power is indeed destructive. The interest immediately at risk was the full participation of women and racial and ethnic minorities in the employment sector of our public life, but Senator Danforth's words about the destructiveness of "the race issue" were also a warning about the larger risks in a politics of cultural counterrevolution that treats a racial minority as a threatening group of outsiders.

A year later, at the Republican national convention, Patrick Buchanan roused the audience to fervent cheering with words that illustrated Senator Danforth's point about the destructiveness of a politics of fear. Buchanan closed his speech with a military metaphor for the capture of government and the deployment of its power to impose the old status Order of cultural groups. He referred to the soldiers deployed in response to the 1992 Los Angeles riot and urged that, as those young men-at-arms had taken control of the streets, "we" must "take back our cities and take back our culture and take back our country."[80] Senator Danforth was right. In a nation of many cultures the risk in the social issues agenda for race is nothing less than the destruction of the social fabric.

Having signed the 1991 act, President Bush seems also to have heeded Senator Danforth's third point about party politics. In his 1992 campaign for reelection, although the President made some use of other social issues—particularly, in the campaign's early phases, those bearing the "family values" label—he did not play the racial card he had played in 1988.[81] For this contribution to civility and community, the nation owes a debt of thanks to John Danforth.

As the Supreme Court ended its Term in June 1992, the religion and "family values" themes of the social issues agenda were before it in two cases we have previously seen: *Lee v. Weisman*, involving officially sponsored prayers at public school graduation ceremonies, and *Planned Parenthood of Southeastern Pennsylvania v. Casey*, involving a series of state restrictions on abortion. Earlier I have shown how the constitutional rights claimed in these cases, in some ways doctrinally dissimilar, have a common tie to the larger principle of equal citizenship. Governmental religious symbols have a capacity to label nonadherents as outsiders, and a woman's right to control her own maternity is indispensable if she is to be a full participant in the public life of her community. In the years preceding these two cases, however, the Court had given strong indications that it was moving in other doctrinal directions: toward conferring its blessing on new forms of governmental religious expression, and toward nullifying the right of choice recognized in *Roe v. Wade*. The Bush administration, through the solicitor general, argued in *Weisman* and in *Casey* for those results, just as the social issues agenda prescribed. In both these areas of constitutional doctrine the Court had been closely divided,[82] and now Justice Thomas had replaced Justice Marshall.

Justice Thomas, to no one's surprise, voted in both cases with Chief Justice Rehnquist and Justice Scalia.[83] The surprise was that these Justices were writing in dissent. In *Weisman* the Court held the graduation prayer unconstitutional, and in *Casey* it reaffirmed *Roe v. Wade*'s central determination that, up to the point of fetal viability, the state cannot constitutionally deny or "unduly burden" a pregnant woman's right of choice whether to have an abortion.

In each case Justice Scalia's opinion was acidic and disdainful—and that wasn't any surprise, either, given the tone of many of his recent separate opinions. In *Weisman* (the graduation prayer case) he directed his acrimony at "the Court"—that is, at Justice Kennedy's opinion for the majority. In *Casey* (the abortion case), he focused his scorn and condescension on the three Justices (O'Connor, Kennedy, and Souter) whose votes in both cases turned the Supreme Court away from the social issues agenda and toward the values of equal citizenship.

In the abortion case the three Justices took the unusual step of writing and signing a joint opinion.[84] It is doubtful that they thought of themselves as a centrist bloc—the label affixed by the press—but even if they did, we shall need more than these two decisions before we accept the label's descriptive accuracy. Still, there is a common thread running

through these Justices' opinions in the two cases, and it deserves attention. That thread is a concern to protect a single ideal, central in our civic
culture and embodied in the Constitution by the Fourteenth Amendment: the ideal that America has only one kind of citizenship. Governmental action that treats the members of a social group as outsiders,
or otherwise denies them full inclusion in the public life of the community, violates this principle of equal citizenship and is presumptively
unconstitutional.[85]

An abiding aspiration of American public schooling is to bring together children and parents from different cultures. As Chief Justice
Warren said in the context of racial integration, public education is not
only an "instrument in awakening the child to cultural values" but "the
very foundation of good citizenship."[86] In his opinion for the Court in
the graduation prayer case, Justice Kennedy recognizes and reinforces
the tradition that extends the embrace of our public schools to all our
children, all our cultures, all our peoples. As he remarks, graduation
from high school is what my generation of students would have called a
Big Deal, for the individual graduates and for their parents. But the
graduation ceremony celebrates more than individual achievement; it
also celebrates the community of the school, the community of the
neighborhoods it serves, even—given the ubiquity of similar ceremonies in schools throughout the land—the community of the American nation. A public high school graduation ceremony is a perfect
occasion for taking notice that citizenship is belonging.

Dissenting in *Lee v. Weisman*, Justice Scalia underscores this very point
about community: "Religious men and women of almost all denominations have felt it necessary to acknowledge and beseech the blessing of
God as a people, and not just as individuals, because they believe in the
'protection of divine Providence,' as the Declaration of Independence
put it, not just for individuals but for societies."[87] Exactly so. Group
prayer cements the community of the faithful—and in so doing it
excludes nonadherents from that community. Because a "nondenomi-
national" prayer is as fictional as a unicorn, any prayer excludes not
only nonbelievers but people who are the truest of true believers—who
insist on the prayers of their ancestors and reject the watery prayers
of lowest-common-denominator "civil religion." The exclusiveness of
group prayer may be essential to the unity of the group, and certainly
that unity is a valued part of America's religious pluralism. When the
faithful pray together in church (temple, mosque, tent meeting, liv-

ing room), the exclusiveness of their fellowship works no harm to the sense of national community in a multicultural nation. Official prayer in America's public schools—the institutions that are expected to lay the foundation of our common national citizenship—is quite another matter.

This concern about the harms of exclusion is evident in Justice Kennedy's opinion for the Court in *Lee v. Weisman*. In discussing the question of coerced participation in an official religious exercise, he is careful to look at the graduation ceremony through the eyes of the "reasonable dissenter," the young graduate who is not an adherent of the religion(s) represented by the prayer of the officially chosen religious leader. The other four Justices who join Justice Kennedy's opinion also consider state-sponsored religious symbols unconstitutional, even in the absence of coercion, when "government puts its imprimatur" on religion, conveying "a message of exclusion" to nonadherents.[88] Quoting James Madison, Justice Souter elaborates on the central status harm caused by an establishment of religion: "It degrades from the equal rank of Citizen all those whose opinions in Religion do not bend to those of the Legislative authority."[89]

A similar theme echoes insistently in the joint opinion of Justices O'Connor, Kennedy, and Souter in *Casey*, the abortion case. It appears, for example, in the opinion's discussion of the doctrine of *stare decisis*— the lawyer's term for the courts' general practice of following precedent. Press accounts have suggested that this part of the opinion of the Court[90] was drafted by Justice Souter. One of its passages comes as close as any statement in any recent Supreme Court opinion to capturing the essence of the substantive concerns that lie behind the woman's right of choice. To emphasize the parallel to Justice Souter's quotation of James Madison in the graduation prayer case, I have added italics to one sentence: "[F]or two decades of economic and social developments, people have organized intimate relationships and made choices that define their views of themselves and their places in society, in reliance on the availability of abortion in the event that contraception should fail. *The ability of women to participate equally in the economic and social life of the Nation has been facilitated by their ability to control their reproductive lives.*"[91]

The essential point here is not the trifle suggested in Chief Justice Rehnquist's dissent, that "the people of this country have grown accustomed to the Roe decision over the last 19 years." Rather, the joint opinion is making a substantive point about the status of women. *Roe v. Wade* became an important precedent not with the passage of time but overnight, for it was a major acculturating event. *Roe* crystallized the awareness of a great many American women of a social fact of enormous consequence for them: that the right of "choice" is not merely a matter of concern to individual women, but is central to the social status—and thus to the sense of self—of women in general. This social fact, highlighted by the italicized sentence, can also be cast in Madisonian language: For women to assume "the equal rank of Citizen," they must control their own maternity.

In reaffirming the "essential holding" of *Roe v. Wade*, the joint opinion of the three Justices also draws an explicit connection between an individual's constitutional liberty to make "the most intimate and personal choices . . . central to personal dignity and autonomy" and the larger question of women's place in society. In a passage that may have been drafted by Justice Kennedy, the joint opinion says this:

> Our obligation is to define the liberty of all, not to mandate our own moral code. The underlying constitutional issue is whether the State can resolve these philosophical questions [about the morality of abortion] in such a definitive way that a woman lacks all choice in the matter, except perhaps in those rare circumstances in which the pregnancy is itself a danger to her own life or health, or is the result of rape or incest. . . .
>
> The mother who carries a child to full term is subject to anxieties, to physical constraints, to pain that only she must bear. That these sacrifices have from the beginning of the human race been endured by woman with a pride that ennobles her in the eyes of others and gives to the infant a bond of love cannot alone be grounds for the State to insist she make the sacrifice. Her suffering is too intimate and personal for the State to insist, without more, upon its own vision of the woman's role, however dominant that vision has been in the course of our history and our culture. The destiny of the woman must be shaped to a large extent on her own conception of her spiritual imperatives and her place in society.[92]

This concern about the relation of the abortion decision to women's social position dictates a series of particularized inquiries into the reality of women's condition in today's America. The joint opinion makes just such an inquiry in the course of invalidating the "husband notification" provision of the Pennsylvania law before the Court in *Casey*. Justice O'Connor is widely believed to have drafted this part of the opinion; certainly it follows her previous suggestion that the *Roe* "trimester" formula should be replaced by a determination whether a state law "unduly burdens" a woman's right of choice. Absent a medical emergency, the Pennsylvania law required a signed statement from a married woman that she had notified her husband of the intended procedure. Before concluding that this provision imposed a "substantial obstacle" to a woman's exercise of her right of choice (a refinement of the "undue burden" question), the opinion reviews the district court's detailed findings about the effects of requiring such a notification in the unusual case where the wife does not want to tell her husband about the abortion. Those findings concentrated on the possibility, which is considerable, that a compelled notification will lead to physical abuse of the wife (or children) by the husband. The joint opinion concludes this long analysis by commenting that, for the large number of women who face the threat of such abuse, "a spousal notice requirement enables the husband to wield an effective veto over his wife's decision" to have an abortion. After describing some of the common law's foundations for the power of men over women within marriage, the opinion concludes, "A State may not give to a man the kind of dominion over his wife that parents exercise over their children. [The Pennsylvania law] embodies a view of marriage consonant with the common-law status of married women but is repugnant to our present understanding of marriage and of the nature of rights secured by the Constitution. Women do not lose their constitutionally protected liberty when they marry."[93] In this passage, too, Justices O'Connor, Kennedy, and Souter demonstrate their awareness that the traditional status Order, in which men were seen as rightly governing women, placed great importance on the control of women's maternity.[94]

The joint opinion in *Casey* also speaks to the relation between the *Roe* precedent and the Supreme Court's own position in the American polity. This passage, part of the opinion of the Court, may have been drafted initially by Justice Souter. In it, the Court candidly discusses the political outcry against *Roe* that began in the mid-1970s and by the 1980s had generated "a national controversy." The discussion proceeds in two stages: (1) The *Roe* decision, like *Brown v. Board of Education*, called on both sides in a major national controversy "to end their national division by accepting a common mandate rooted in the Constitution." (2)

The very force of the opposition to a decision like *Brown* or *Roe* means that a decision to overrule would look like "a surrender to political pressure." Furthermore, a breach of "the promise of constancy" to the principle of *Roe* would be "a breach of faith" with Americans who expect the Court to stand by principle. In both respects, an overruling would undermine the Supreme Court's legitimacy by eroding public confidence.

This passage propelled Justice Scalia to heights of scorn that even he can rarely hope to attain. Responding as if the passage were no more than a disquisition on the relation of political controversy to overruling, he attacked both stages of the joint opinion's discussion: (1) The proper analogy for *Roe* is not *Brown* but *Dred Scott*. Like that infamous decision, *Roe* did not settle controversy but exacerbated it, making the Supreme Court itself an object of the struggle through campaigns to influence the Court's decisions and the selection of new Justices. (2) The *Casey* majority is not being "constant" to *Roe*, for it replaces *Roe*'s doctrinal formula with Justice O'Connor's "undue burden" test. Given the political campaigning on both sides of the abortion question, deciding *not* to overrule might equally be seen as bowing to political pressure. In any case, the Court must find its legitimacy not in public support but in principles of law derived from text and tradition.

Justice Scalia is a master of debate technique, and he is able to score points here (as elsewhere in his *Casey* dissent) by treating the joint opinion's central unifying theme as if it were irrelevant. In excoriating the opinion's discussion of politics and overruling, he abstracts those paragraphs from the larger argument that is their context. The several parts of the joint opinion are united by a single theme: the relation between *Roe*'s central holding and the status of women in American society. To ignore this subtext of the joint opinion's words linking politics and overruling and the Court's legitimacy is to miss the point. Pablo Casals used to say to musicians who studied with him, "Think of the music, not the notes."

Casey's theme becomes more distinct if we convert subtext into text: (1) The "national division" addressed by *Roe* was the exclusion of women from equal citizenship. *Roe* thus resembles *Brown* (and not *Dred Scott*), for it validates women's claim to inclusion. (2) The promise of *Roe* to women, then, was the option to participate fully in the community's public life. "An entire generation [of women] has come of age" understanding the centrality of that promise to their places in society and their senses of self. To them the overruling of *Roe* would be a breach of faith—especially when the overruling would be seen as a surrender to pressure from those who seek to reinstate a status Order denying women their constitutional right to full membership in the American polity.

Justice Scalia was right when he said that the national politics of abortion had affected the judicial appointments process. The White House and Justice Department had sought judicial candidates with the social issues agenda centrally in mind, and for that very reason opponents of the social issues agenda (such as civil rights groups and women's groups) had opposed some nominations (such as Judge Bork and Judge Thomas) and expressed their nervousness about others (such as Judge Kennedy and Judge Souter). To some observers the joint opinion in *Casey* has the look of a declaration of judicial independence from the appointing authority. But I am inclined to another view, founded on intuitions I have had from the beginning about each of the three authors of the joint opinion: that his or her independence could be taken for granted, and that what each needed was not more backbone, but time to settle into the daunting responsibility of interpreting a Constitution for a culturally diverse nation.[95] With hindsight, we can see a similar settling-in stage in the early careers of other Justices with diverse backgrounds and personalities. Among those who have served in the twentieth century, at least five might be mentioned: the two Justice Harlans (1877–1911 and 1955–71), and Justices Brennan, Blackmun, and Powell.

For a further example, consider Justice Kennedy. At his confirmation hearings in late 1987, some of his supporters emphasized his readiness to listen and learn. The witness who best expressed this appraisal was Susan Westerberg Prager, dean of the UCLA law school and former president of the Association of American Law Schools.[96] Dean Prager had some reservations; she said that "he is not at this point as appreciative as I might like him to be about the subtleties of discrimination in this culture, whether it relates to women, or minorities, or gays." But, she said, he is "a person who will listen, who has the capacity to be compassionate and who recognizes that his decisions affect people, not pieces of paper or theories or principles." She went on to praise Judge Kennedy's "genuine openness" and to say he was one who "is going to keep thinking over time, and reevaluating."[97] Judge Kennedy's response to a question about constitutional interpretation has relevance not only for growth in doctrine but also for growth in Justices: "To say that new gen-

erations yield new insights and new perspectives, that doesn't mean
the Constitution changes. It just means that our understanding of it
changes."[98]

Earlier I suggested that Justice Thomas's confirmation hearings, in
addition to unblocking the path to the Civil Rights Act of 1991, might
have helped turn the scale in the *Casey* case. First, as we saw, the
hearings dramatized the connections between women's power (or lack
of it) and social conceptions of women's sexuality—not just in the world
of work but across the whole range of social relations. Second, because
these issues were raised in a debate about the composition of the
Supreme Court, surely the discussion must have reinforced the awareness of some sitting Justices that the Court's *Casey* decision, whatever it
might be, would affect women's control over their own lives, and so
would contribute to the social meanings defining the status of women.
Third, a Justice who watched the Thomas hearings on television might
reasonably conclude that the Court itself, as ultimate guarantor of the
liberty of equal citizens, was under siege.

Although any claim of an abortion right ultimately presents an either/
or question, the Supreme Court's doctrinal resolution in *Casey*—recognizing a right of choice but allowing state regulations that do not impose
a "substantial obstacle" to the exercise of the right—seemingly comes
close to the center of gravity of public opinion in America's divided
public.[99] In this subject area, *Roe* seems to have had an acculturating
power of its own—not, as Justice Scalia asserted, by propagating the
view that abortion is morally neutral,[100] but by teaching women that
they are not powerless to govern their own sexual expression and
maternity. This lesson found a ready audience, because the right recognized in *Roe* touches many millions of American women's sense of who
they are and who they can hope to be.

Reflecting this growing understanding of the relation between the
power of choice and women's equal citizenship, the politics of abortion
has changed significantly. News of this change reached President Bush
about halfway through the 1992 campaign, when it became clear that
his "family values" theme, especially as articulated at the Republican
convention and in the party's platform,[101] was driving away Republican
women who were essential to his success. From that moment on, he
and Vice President Quayle invoked "family values" only in the blandest
ways.[102] The support for a formal ban on gay and lesbian members of
the armed services, along with the vote on Colorado's antigay initiative,

remind us that a considerable constituency for cultural counterrevolution still exists. Even the controversy over abortion rights will likely continue in state and local politics, and perhaps even in presidential primary elections.[103] Yet, in November presidential elections the argument for doing away with women's right of choice may well have vanished for good.

In court the abortion rights aspect of the constitutional claim to equal citizenship may, of course, be focused on the equal protection clause itself. In recent years, though, claims of reproductive freedom more often have been cast in other constitutional vocabularies, such as liberty or privacy or nonestablishment of religion. The recent leader of the resistance to claims so grounded has been Justice Scalia, whose well-developed view of these subjects centers on "text and traditional practice."[104] In this view, for example, there can be no constitutional right of choice whether to have an abortion, because abortion is not mentioned in the constitutional text and "the longstanding traditions of American society have permitted it to be legally proscribed."[105] This general doctrinal position—perhaps not coincidentally—is perfectly suited to denying the constitutional claims of people who are seeking membership in the body of equal citizens. Almost by definition, their claims to inclusion have no basis in the "longstanding traditions" that have excluded them. To the contrary, they are apt to think of those traditions as a nightmare from which they are trying to awake.

Fortunately for those Americans, the authors of the *Casey* joint opinion, speaking for the Court, explicitly reject the view that rights of liberty or privacy under the due process clauses must pass an age test in order to be vindicated.[106] Repeatedly, the joint opinion calls for sympathetic judicial attention to the claims of a social group historically excluded from shaping the very "traditions" that have accomplished the group's exclusion. As Judge Kennedy told the Senate committee in 1987, "new generations yield new insights and new perspectives."

If we ask where judges get their new perspectives on the meanings of equal citizenship,[107] the answer must lie in the same processes of acculturation that eventually led Senator Danforth to confront the White House over the issue of civil rights remedies. Those processes are as complex and wide-ranging as the whole of society; they are hard to describe, let alone analyze. It would be fatuous to offer any simple explanation for changes over the last quarter-century in Americans' diverse perceptions of race or of gender. Yet, one factor undoubtedly

contributing to those changed perceptions is the law itself, particularly
as it has been used to symbolize group status.

Another parallel between *Brown v. Board of Education* and *Roe v. Wade*,
then, is that both decisions contributed to cultural change, not just by
dissuading officers of government from unconstitutional behavior, but
by their very existence as cultural totems, as symbols of inclusion.[108] Of
course, neither decision could have had any generative effect if it had
fallen on barren ground. *Brown* and *Roe* eventually found their own potent constituencies because they resonated against the values of equality and community, two enduring themes in the American civic culture.
This development has not yet come to an end. If the adoption of the
1991 Civil Rights Act and the Supreme Court's 1992 decisions in the
Weisman and *Casey* cases reflected the civic culture's ideal of equal
citizenship, they also reinforced that ideal.

LIVING WITH PLURALIZATION AND
ITS DISCONTENTS

Even while we are taking note of the staying power of the
principle of equal citizenship, we should remember that the gender line
and the color line have staying power of their own. The political and
legal battles of the recent past have left scars and distrust all around. On
the one hand, none of the groups claiming their equal citizenship
consider those claims fully vindicated. On the other hand, the inclusion
of new groups in an increasingly pluralized polity—incomplete as it
remains—still has the capacity to mobilize a constituency around the
themes of cultural counterrevolution. Even for those who applaud the
widening of the circle of equal citizenship, this other form of alienation
should be of concern—and for reasons that are not merely strategic. On
principle, the ideal of inclusion embraces the cultural counterrevolutionaries, too.

At no time in American history has it been possible to eliminate all the
discontents produced by our cultural pluralism. Now as before, the
only realistic goal for public policy is to mitigate those discontents, or at
least to avoid aggravating them. Here, too, the expressive capacities of
law and government may serve to reduce the alienations that remain
despite—or because of—the equal citizenship principle's recent vin-
dications. Taking a last look at the social issues agenda, this section
focuses on those Americans who still feel left out, and searches for

common ground. We begin with the themes of race and crime, and conclude with the themes of religion and "family values."

Race and Crime

Law's most primitive function, and still its most vital one, is to reduce fears by bringing the organized community's power to bear on its members' aggressions. Given the persistence of race as our widest and deepest social division, it is not surprising that black and white Americans alike, when they seek protection against the aggressions they fear from the other group, continue to turn to law.

The alienation of white Americans is strongest among lower-income men who have felt threatened by the social changes of the 1960s and 1970s.[109] They express their anxieties and resentments about race most frequently in references to crime, jobs, and welfare. Black Americans, of course, have worries of their own about the same subjects, and also tend to see them as interlocked. Consider the issues connected with crime. If, somehow, our inner cities could be rid of the scourge of drugs and violent crime, no one would benefit more than the residents of those neighborhoods. Some black citizens, some of the time, may describe criminal activity as a way of "getting over" in an environment that severely limits black people's options, but even the ones who express this view tend to be ambivalent about it—for they know how costly those crimes are in their own lives.[110] So, the need to reduce violent crime is common ground for Americans of all races, and everyone can agree that effective law enforcement is essential to any crime-reduction strategy. Yet it is clear that violent crime cannot be controlled simply by building more and more prisons to house more and more young men with black and brown faces.[111] The most enduring crime control will be achieved by creating options to attract young men into lives they see as rewarding. And that leads us on—or back—to such subjects as employment and welfare.

The continued potency of racial "quotas" as a political rallying cry in the 1990s reminds us that many whites, particularly working-class white men, feel left out and resentful when employers adopt affirmative action programs. The resentment is present even when race-conscious hiring or promotion is designed to remedy the very racial discrimination that has long demonstrated to minority candidates that *they* are the ones left out. In the field of employment it seems vain, here and now, to hope that people who feel threatened—by discrimination or by its redress—

can reach common ground on the subject of race-conscious remedies. Yet structural remedies are necessary if we are ever to dismantle the structures of racial disadvantage. In chapter 4 I argued that the integration of our workforce offers our best hope for developing new attitudes toward race, based on the day-to-day experience of working together for common purposes.

Despite the disaffection of significant numbers of white men, for the moment national politics has found some common ground of its own, not about affirmative action in employment but about race-conscious remedies for past discrimination. In the 1991 act Congress and the President not only recognized the importance of those remedies but also gave new life to a political consensus about civil rights that had ruled, with little interruption, from the late 1950s to 1980. Although civil rights advocates applauded the election of President Clinton, both the President and the Supreme Court have made clear that the rhetoric of "quotas" retains power.[112] At this writing, however, the 1991 act has not been undermined by judicial interpretation. One can still hope that the Court, having liberated itself from the weight of the social issues agenda in the fields of abortion and school prayer, will heed John Danforth's wisdom in the field of civil rights.

It even seems realistic to anticipate that a majority of the Court will reject Justice Scalia's exhortations to overrule two major precedents supporting affirmative action. The first precedent is the *Bakke* case, in which five Justices agreed that a state university could take race into account as one factor in its admissions of applicants, for the educational purpose of diversifying its student body. In chapter 4 we saw how Justice Powell, who articulated this "diversity" approach, saw it as markedly less divisive than a racial quota. His political acumen has been vindicated; "diversity" may be a troubling explanation to some observers, but in political terms it has offered some of the common ground that Powell sought. It is fair to describe the "diversity" approach as part of the present civil rights consensus. Even the Reagan and Bush administrations treated Justice Powell's *Bakke* opinion as the proper standard for evaluating state university admissions.[113] The second precedent that looks more secure today than it did before the 1991 act is the *Weber* case, which upheld a private employer's voluntary affirmative action program against attack under Title VII of the 1964 act.[114]

Although a number of the Supreme Court's recent decisions on affirmative action have been restrictive, the key opinions (by Justices Powell and O'Connor) have given every evidence of an attempt to save affirmative action from death at the hands of "a politics of racial hostility."[115] The method of saving affirmative action by government agencies has been to conform it to a justification widely acceptable to white Americans: not the threatening-sounding goal of advancing the conditions of historically subordinated minority groups, but the goal of remedying identifiable acts of discrimination. The common ground here is to be found not in rhetoric but in practical results. As San Francisco has recently demonstrated in its program for government contracting, the "identifiable discrimination" formula preserves the affirmative action option for a public body that can follow the Court's blueprint for justification.[116] In other words, the Supreme Court has found a way to build the substance of substantive equality on the forms of formal neutrality. It would be surprising—and saddening—if the Court were now to make Senator Danforth fight yet another battle for civil rights restoration.

I said earlier that the most effective long-term crime control program will be the creation of jobs and the education of young people to fill them. This is a tall order, and the order will not be filled cheaply. But even the cost of an ambitious jobs program is modest when it is measured against the staggering costs, both material and human, that violent crime imposes on us all. Still, getting a majority of white Americans to make that comparison of costs may not be easy. Even at such an abstract level of social cost accounting, we may have trouble escaping the centrality of the question, How shall we think about race?

One response, borrowed from recent proposals for welfare reform, may be to try to eliminate one source of divisiveness by moving race to the margins of discussion. A national political consensus for welfare reform centers on work requirements, supplemented by such programs as job training and day care.[117] For many years most recipients of public assistance have said they would prefer employment to welfare. Backing up those statements with action, most recipients have not stayed on the welfare rolls for long periods—although some long-term recipients have taken up a disproportionate share of the funds provided.[118] The emerging political consensus will explicitly limit welfare payments to relatively short periods, emphasizing benefits that are universal rather than targeted to specific groups. Social Security is our leading example of a universal program. Proposals along these lines include such "family security" programs as health benefits, child support assurance for single parents, parental leaves, child care for working parents, and job training.[119] The political utility of a universal program is obvious: it is not limited to the poor, nor is it racially specific; rather, its constituency extends across the whole electorate. In short, a universal family security program reduces the likelihood that politics will divide along cultural boundaries, for it is unlikely to be seen by Us as a benefit targeted to Them, the "undeserving."

In addition to dampening white opposition to family security and jobs legislation, universal programs may also help to reduce black Americans' sense of distance from their white cocitizens. Two decades of success for the civil rights movement have been followed two decades of what some call consolidation—but with less charity and more accuracy should be called retrenchment. The latter period has left a great many black Americans with the feeling that the larger society has broken the promise of racial equality. If day-to-day living conditions be the test, surely this feeling is keenest among the one-third of our black cocitizens who live in poverty. But poor people rarely write for publication, and the disillusion of black Americans—including those who are poor—has found its clearest public expression in the work of writers who have indisputably "made it" in middle-class social environments.[120] One such writer is Patricia Williams: "I was raised to be acutely conscious of the likelihood that no matter what degree of professional I am, people will greet and dismiss my black femaleness as unreliable, untrustworthy, hostile, angry, powerless, irrational, and probably destitute. Futility and despair are very real parts of my response."[121]

An appreciable part of the pain is the sense of hopes betrayed.[122] The subtitle of Derrick Bell's most recent book is "The Permanence of Racism." That is the word minority writers use in describing their environment: not discrimination, but racism. The word sets most white readers on edge, for it makes them think of the people who screamed at those black schoolchildren in Little Rock in 1957, or of the young men who hounded a black teenager to his death in Howard Beach in 1986. What Bell has in mind, though, is what Williams was describing: not so much a belief as an unthinking frame of reference, in which white Americans systematically tend to undervalue the capabilities, the experiences, the opinions, the claims to justice of their black cocitizens.[123] I generalize about "white Americans" intentionally; the attitudes in question may lie at the margins of consciousness, but they are not limited to a small fraction of the population.[124] If Bell sees the movement for racial equality as an endless struggle with little hope, one reason is that today's racism only rarely comes in packages so easily identified as the Jim

Crow laws. A generation ago we could see racism as a dragon to be slain. Now we picture it as a sea of acculturated assumptions, a sea that washes up behind us, no matter where we steer the boat.[125]

If the developments recounted in this book teach any political lesson, it is this: Those who would seek the redefinition of the national community cannot afford to ignore the symbolic power of law. This acculturating function is recognized by a number of minority writers. Kimberlé Crenshaw and Patricia Williams have written compellingly of the importance of the idea of legal rights—of citizenship—to a people fighting against the labeling, the silencing, and the self-doubt that are the legacy of slavery. They recognize how much remains to be done in fulfilling the promise of civil rights, but their writings are also testaments to hope. Even for Derrick Bell, pessimism does not imply defeatism. Without expressing expectations of success, he calls for "engagement," for "commitment," for "unremitting struggle."[126] Of course, no social movement can attract large numbers of adherents without offering hope that the movement will lead to something better.[127]

It may be that "racial equality," in the sense of the full status equality of cultural groups, requires so thorough a reacculturation of a complex society that it is an unrealistic hope for the near future. Yet, racial equality is not just an abstraction; it is the aggregate of a multitude of particular manifestations, some of them quite concrete. In the parts of the world that can be seen and touched, racial equality takes a variety of forms, most of them within the reach of public policy. Even the Civil Rights Act of 1991, which mainly recaptured ground recently lost, also achieved some modest advances beyond that ground. In the cause of racial equality, the most important contribution of the 1991 act—and of law generally—lies in the realm of acculturation. Most immediately, the acculturation centered on inhabitants of the political world: the President and members of Congress taught lessons to themselves and to all of us as they reaffirmed the ideal of racial equality. In the longer term, though, the more important acculturation worked by the 1991 act will take place in the lives of individual workers of all races. The race-conscious remedies that integrate various parts of the workforce will put these Americans in positions where they will do things together, two by two, enacting their individual narratives of inclusion.

Religion and "Family Values"

If the "law and order" program of the early cultural counterrevolution has largely won the day, and if today's civil rights leaders must find their main comfort in the 1991 act's reclamation of ground lost since 1980, the outlook is different in the other fields of the social issues agenda. Religion retains its prominence in our public life, but the Supreme Court's graduation prayer decision reveals the limited ability of the agenda's promoters to deliver on their promise to restore religious symbolism to the public schools. And the social issues agenda for "woman's place," with abortion rights the central target, has been routed. Even the effort to defend the gender line against the inclusion of gay and lesbian Americans as equal citizens must seem a rear-guard action in a retreat. One result is that many Americans feel, as they did before 1980, that they have been marginalized by a secularized society.

This alienation presents a formidable challenge to the imagination of public officials: to seek ways of responding sympathetically but to stop short of official sponsorship of religion. In chapter 6 we saw how the Equal Access Act of 1984 required a federally funded public high school, outside school hours, to allow political or religious student groups the same access as other student groups to "limited open forum" facilities. Although some kinds of accommodation of the values of free exercise of religion do tend to have exclusionary effects on religious minorities,[128] the Equal Access Act does not. The crucial role of religious lobbies in getting the act passed[129] is irrelevant to its constitutionality.[130] The constitutional concern in these cases is not to squeeze religious impulses out of the legislative process, but to assure that the laws emerging from that process do not deny equal citizenship—in this setting, to assure that the state does not brand any group as outsiders.

Another accommodation of the same general type is a law simply authorizing a "moment of silence" in a public schoolroom—assuming, of course, that the teacher does not seize the moment to promote a majority religion at the psychic expense of children who are marked as religious outsiders. Here, too, the motives of many legislators might be religious, and the moment would provide a time when prayer-minded children would likely pray. But, absent harm to nonadherent children in the form of observances that convey a sense of exclusion, this sort of inclusion of the religious impulse is constitutionally acceptable. Similarly, the Constitution does not forbid public schools to teach *about* the role of religion in American public life. For example, a science unit, after presenting the views of the scientific community about human evolution, might remind the pupils that many Americans reject those views on religious grounds. The subject offers a splendid opportunity for examining the meanings of science—and the arguments for competing ways of defining what is science and what is not. Such an approach would not entirely satisfy the religious groups that sponsored the "balanced treatment" laws in the 1980s,[131] but it might give them the sense that their world view had not been excluded completely. In the midst of the clash of cultures, the equal citizenship principle should extend in all directions.[132]

Yet, even a principle of inclusion has its limits, imposed by the strong tendency of so many "family values" issues to turn into zero-sum contests over cultural dominance. No legislative agenda, no constitutional doctrine can at the same time assure women "the freedom of the city"[133] and deny them that freedom in order to keep them in domestic roles under male tutelage. Nor can the claim of gay and lesbian Americans to equal citizenship be accommodated with a legislative majority's use of law to stigmatize them. For the same reasons that issues of status dominance are resistant to legislative compromise, our courts are going to have to choose between equal citizenship and the legal regulations that deny groups of Americans full participation in our public life.[134]

Some commentators urge our judges to respond to this confrontation of values by washing their hands of the whole matter, leaving such choices to legislative majorities.[135] This prescription is not substantively neutral; it can seem neutral only to one who finds neutrality in the Supreme Court's determination in *Plessy v. Ferguson* (1896) to leave Jim Crow to politics. Nor is the principle of equal citizenship substantively neutral; its values of respect, responsibility, and participation look toward a society that embraces all Americans as full members. To put the matter negatively: No one is denied membership merely because government refuses to write his or her values into coercive law in ways that stigmatize others, or that deny them responsible participation in public life, or both. In short, equal citizenship implies tolerance.[136]

Tolerance is not just an ideal; it also has its practical uses. In *The Federalist* Madison wrote that one of the strengths of the American nation was the presence within our borders of a multiplicity of interests and religious sects.[137] The same idea has appealed to modern sociologists: the fragmentation of a social group—including a nation—may actually serve the group's cohesion, by making it possible for antagonists on one issue to be allies on another.[138] An example in our own time that Madison would have understood is the uneasy alliance between some Christian conservatives and some feminists in support of antipornography laws.[139] If tolerance for diversity has survived as a basic ideal in the American civic culture, perhaps one reason is that a multiplicity of cultures, in the long run, is a source of stability.[140]

For some Americans, however, tolerance is exactly what is wrong with a society suffering from the disease of "secular humanism." Tolerance for the open avowal of gay identity, or for young unmarried women who are sexually active, may seem a prospectus not for a society of free and equal citizens but for social dissolution—indeed, a betrayal of God's plan. If you believe in moral absolutes, then you may agree with the founder of Operation Rescue that "intolerance is a beautiful thing."[141]. When the ideal of tolerance is itself a central object of attack in the conflict of cultures, we cannot rely on that ideal to make the conflict go away.[142] In any case, a constitutional predisposition toward tolerance cannot relieve the officers of government, including judges, from making choices that are essentially moral. Francis Canavan, discussing competing views of the relation of marriage to the state, rightly comments that, whatever our officials do, "some view concerning sexual relationships gets enforced by the power of law. What is impossible is to take no view at all and call it neutrality."[143] If the principle of equal citizenship is not neutral as constitutional doctrine, neither is it morally neutral; it has become an indispensable moral grammar for America's "public language of moral purpose."[144]

When Madison assumed that the "passions" of religious and cultural division would create political factions, he based that assumption on experience. These divisions had troubled politics repeatedly throughout the colonial era, and they will continue so long as America's cultural diversity persists. For the indefinite future, then, politicians can be expected to go on mining the rich lodes of race, of religion, and of sex and gender. Inevitably, pressures will build for new laws to serve as new counters in zero-sum conflicts over cultural dominance. Two centuries ago the challenge for Madison and the other founders was to make a nation out of a loose confederation of states. In those early years the courts—especially the Marshall Court—played an indispensable unifying role. Our challenge today is to maintain a nation inclusive enough to embrace all our cultures, and again our courts have a special responsibility.

As our judges confront the political products of cultural revolution and counterrevolution, they can nourish the ideal of inclusion by making good on the Constitution's promise of equal citizenship—as the

Supreme Court did in its 1992 decisions on abortion and graduation prayers. In rising to this challenge, the courts will carry on the nation-building tradition that began in the founding generation. Any list of great early contributors to that tradition would include James Madison. But the list would also include John Marshall.

Notes

Preface

1. Richard Bond, chair of the Republican National Committee, at the party's national convention in 1992, quoted in Estrich, "Practicing Politics of Exclusion," Los Angeles Times, Aug. 23, 1992, M1, col. 1. After the election, in his last speech to the committee, Bond "offered a frank admission of mistakes and urged the party to soften its rigid opposition to abortion, gay rights and other issues dear to social conservatives." Braun, "Barbour Elected Chief of a Divided GOP," ibid., Jan. 30, 1993, A14, col. 1.
2. Among the most recent general treatments, some outstanding examples are J. Hunter, *Culture Wars: The Struggle to Define America* (1991); S. Blumenthal, *Pledging Allegiance: The Last Campaign of the Cold War* (1990); T. Edsall and M. Edsall, *Chain Reaction: The Impact of Race, Rights, and Taxes on American Politics* (1991); E. J. Dionne, Jr., *Why Americans Hate Politics* (1991); and J. Bell, *Populism and Elitism* (1992). For citations to works on the specific themes of the social issues agenda, see the notes to the appropriate chapters.
3. I am grateful for permission to reprint parts of the articles based on these three lectures: "Boundaries and Reasons: Freedom of Expression and the Subordination of Groups," 1990 University of Illinois Law Review 95 (David C. Baum Memorial Lecture on Civil Liberties and Civil Rights, March 1989); "The Pursuit of Manhood and the Desegregation of the Armed Forces," 38 *UCLA Law Review* 499 (1991) (Melville B. Nimmer Memorial Lecture, November 1990); and "Religion, Sex, and Politics: Cultural Counterrevolution in Constitutional Perspective," 24 *University of California, Davis, Law Review* 677 (1991) (Edward L. Barrett, Jr., Lecture on Constitutional Law, March 1991). In addition, I am grateful for permission to draw from these articles: "Private Discrimination and Public Responsibility," 1989 *Supreme Court Review* 1; and "The First Amendment, the Politics of Religion, and the Symbols of Government," 27 *Harvard Civil Rights–Civil Liberties Law Review* 503 (1992).
4. The reference is directed to an old friend, who will probably think this book,

213

too, is excessively optimistic. See Derrick Bell's book review "Preaching to the Choir: America As It Might Be," 37 *UCLA Law Review* 1025 (1990). Bell and I agree on one thing: optimists and pessimists alike must keep going. Of course, most laborers in this vineyard are at once optimists and pessimists. On Bell's recent writings, see chap. 7.

Chapter 1

1. On the political success of the agenda, see Glazer, "The Social Agenda," in J. Palmer, ed., *Perspectives on the Reagan Years,* at 5 (1986).
2. On the politics of nostalgia, see G. Wills, *Reagan's America: Innocents at Home* (1987).
3. J. Bruner, *Actual Minds, Possible Worlds,* chap. 7 (1986).
4. Expressive dominance, of course, can be used to maintain other forms of dominance as well. As Michael Olneck remarks, "The power to determine social definitions and interpretations, in turn, entails the power to limit the field of legitimate action and choice." Olneck, "Americanization and the Education of Immigrants, 1900–1925: An Analysis of Symbolic Action," 97 *American Journal of Education* 398, 399 (1989).
5. The point is made for somewhat younger women in W. Breines, *Young, White, and Miserable: Growing up Female in the Fifties,* 84–126 (1992).
6. 347 U.S. 483 (1954).
7. Gerald Rosenberg concludes that the *Brown* decision did not "produce . . . significant social change." See his book *The Hollow Hope: Can Courts Bring About Social Change?* 39–169 (1991). No public act, standing alone, produces significant social change. The Declaration of Independence did not produce the American Revolution; Luther's ninety-five theses did not produce the Reformation. The question is whether *Brown* contributed significantly to changes in race relations and civil rights. In chapter 4 I argue that it did.
8. Clecak, "The Movement of the 1960s and Its Cultural and Political Legacy," in S. Cohen and L. Ratner, eds., *The Development of an American Culture,* at 261, 265 (2d ed. 1983).
9. Keniston, "Heads and Seekers: Drugs on Campus, Counter-Cultures and American Society," 38 *American Scholar* 97 (1969). See also T. Roszak, *The Making of a Counter Culture: Reflections on the Technocratic Society and Its Youthful Opposition,* chap. 2 (1969).
10. D. Bell, *The Cultural Contradictions of Capitalism,* 54 (1976). See also K. Keniston, *Young Radicals: Notes on Committed Youth* (1968); M. Teodori, *The New Left: A Documentary History,* 4 (1969).
11. Like many another writer, I have taken this use of "the Other" from Simone de Beauvoir, who seems to have derived it from Sartre, who apparently took it from Heidegger. In this book I am referring mainly to men who see

women as the Other; whites (and especially white men) who see black people (and especially black men) as the Other; and people (especially men) who think of themselves as heterosexual and who see lesbians and gay men as the Other.

12. Bell, n. 10 above, at 143. See also Roszak, n. 9 above, chap. 2.

13. On Americans who reject "the supposed moral superiority of the modern," see Novak, "Pluralism in Humanistic Perspective," in W. Peterson, M. Novak, and P. Gleason, *Concepts of Ethnicity,* 27, 33 (1980).

14. Renato Rosaldo has aptly remarked that the idea of a breakdown of society's Order is particularly frightening because chaos, by definition, is undefinable and thus impossible to conceive. R. Rosaldo, *Culture and Truth,* 100 (1989).

15. See R. Wiebe, *The Segmented Society: An Introduction to the Meaning of America* (1975).

16. Mrs. Patrick Campbell, in *Bloomsbury Dictionary of Quotations,* 89 (1987).

17. Some of these citizens are securely lodged in the intelligentsia, academic and otherwise. Examples of particularly thoughtful writers who share many of these views of the social issues are Harvey Mansfield, Jr., Richard John Neuhaus, John Noonan, and Robert E. Rodes, Jr.

18. "No matter how one defines Fundamentalism, one risks joining together in Christian fellowship a lot of people who would prefer to remain apart." R. Moore, *Religious Outsiders and the Making of Americans,* 151 (1986). For example, a number of Christian fundamentalists cling to their churches' earlier pietistic traditions, believing that the church and its members should tend to their own salvation and stay out of the political realm. It is important not to equate "evangelicals" with "fundamentalists" or to equate either of these—or even "conservative Christians"—with the new Christian right. See, e.g., R. Neuhaus, *The Naked Public Square,* 40 (1984); A. Hertzke, *Representing God in Washington,* 32–36, 40–42 (1988).

19. See, e.g., K. Luker, *Abortion and the Politics of Motherhood,* 127–39, 145–46, 194–98 (1984); S. Bruce, *The Rise and Fall of the New Christian Right,* 25–49 (1988); Yinger and Cutler, "The Moral Majority Viewed Sociologically," in *New Christian Politics,* 69, 81–85 (1984).

20. See Rodes, "Greatness Thrust upon Them: Class Biases in American Law," 28 *American Journal of Jurisprudence* 1, 6–8 (1983). On abortion, see J. Noonan, *A Private Choice: Abortion in America in the Seventies,* 33–46 (1979); G. Calabresi, *Ideals, Beliefs, Attitudes, and the Law: Private Law Perspectives on a Public Law Problem,* chap. 5 (1985); Skerry, "The Class Conflict over Abortion," 52 *Public Interest* 69 (1978). Cf. Luker, n. 19 above, at 194–98.

21. This concern was not unrelated to nervousness about group status. See, e.g., S. Jeffords, *The Remasculinization of America: Gender and the Vietnam War* (1989).

22. Harvey Mansfield, Jr. has carefully recounted these concerns and preferences in his book *America's Constitutional Soul* (1991). He calls President Bush's 1988 election "another Reagan triumph" (chap. 5).

23. In referring to anxieties about status, I do not suggest that the people who are anxious are a case study in "abnormal psychology." See E. J. Dionne, Jr., *Why Americans Hate Politics*, 67 (1991). Certainly it is normal for members of a historically dominant group to view the rise of a historically subordinated group as implying a decline in their own status. This pattern has long been visible in American religious politics, from the Protestants who for many decades felt threatened by the rise of Catholic power to the citizens who today see the secularizing of government as a "cultural disestablishment of the old faith." Eastland, "In Defense of Religious America," 71 *Commentary* 6, 42 (June 1981).

24. T. Arnold, *The Symbols of Government*, 34 (1962 [1935]). I have pursued these themes in greater detail in chaps. 2, 10, and 11 of K. Karst, *Belonging to America: Equal Citizenship and the Constitution* (1989). On the Constitution as a symbol of the nation, see See R. Gabriel, *The Course of American Democratic Thought*, passim (1940); Lerner, "Constitution and Court as Symbols," 46 *Yale Law Journal* 1290 (1937).

25. See generally T. Edsall and M. Edsall, *Chain Reaction: The Impact of Race, Rights, and Taxes on American Politics*, esp. chaps. 1–3 (1991); Dionne, n. 23 above, chap. 2.

26. *Roe v. Wade*, 410 U.S. 113 (1973).

27. E.g., *Jones v. Alfred H. Mayer Co.*, 392 U.S. 409 (1968) (housing); *Griggs v. Duke Power Co.*, 401 U.S. 424 (1971) (employment).

28. E.g., *Loving v. Virginia*, 388 U.S. 1 (1967) (miscegenation).

29. E.g., *Frontiero v. Richardson*, 411 U.S. 677 (1973) (plurality opinion) ("dependents" of armed services' members); *Orr v. Orr*, 440 U.S. 268 (1979) (alimony).

30. *Engel v. Vitale*, 370 U.S. 421 (1962) (prayers); *Board of Education v. Schempp*, 374 U.S. 203 (1963) (Bible readings).

31. For citation of some of the relevant decisions and commentary, see Karst, "Boundaries and Reasons: Freedom of Expression and the Subordination of Groups," 1990 *University of Illinois Law Review* 95, 96 n.7, 98 n.9.

32. See, e.g., Judge Frank Easterbrook's dissenting opinion in *Miller v. Civil City of South Bend*, 904 F.2d 1081, 1125–26 (7th Cir. 1990), reversed, *Barnes v. Glen Theatre, Inc.*, 111 S. Ct. 2456 (1991), arguing that the First Amendment is concerned only with protecting the expression of "ideas," "thoughts," and "messages," and that the expression of "emotions" is protected only when the emotions are connected with those products of "rational human thought." (The latter concept, he assures us, includes music.) Some defenders of antipornography laws express similar views. See chap. 3 below.

33. "Common sense is not what the mind cleared of cant spontaneously apprehends; it is what the mind filled with presuppositions . . . concludes." C. Geertz, *Local Knowledge: Further Essays in Interpretive Anthropology*, 84 (1983). "Children, frequently enough women, and, depending on the society, various sorts of underclasses are regarded as less wise, in [a] 'they are emotional creatures' sort of way, than others. But . . . common sense is . . . the general property of at least, as we would put it, all solid citizens" (91).

34. See Minow, "The Supreme Court, 1986 Term—Foreword: Justice Engendered," 101 *Harvard Law Review* 10 (1987). On the language of social roles, see Peller, "The Metaphysics of American Law," 73 *California Law Review* 1151, 1274–85 (1985).

35. E. Hall, *The Silent Language*, 43 (1973).

36. R. Rorty, *Philosophy and the Mirror of Nature*, 320 (1979).

37. See J. Bruner, *Acts of Meaning*, 67–97 and passim (1990).

38. See Peller, "Reason and the Mob: The Politics of Representation," 2 *Tikkun* 28 (1987).

39. W. Jordan, *White over Black: American Attitudes toward the Negro, 1550–1812*, 40–43 (1968).

40. *The Federalist*, nos. 10 and 51 (Madison 1787–88).

41. J. Hunter, *Culture Wars: The Struggle to Define America*, 159 (1991). This is one of the general points made by E. J. Dionne, Jr., n. 23 above.

42. The Supreme Court has done something like this in the area of abortion regulation. *Planned Parenthood of Southeastern Pennsylvania v. Casey*, 112 S. Ct. 2791 (1992).

43. See generally William Safire's book *Before the Fall: An Inside View of the Pre-Watergate White House*, 307–15 (1975). The quotations from Agnew and Buchanan also appear in McElvaine, "GOP 'Values'? Read Their Lip-Service," *Los Angeles Times*, Oct. 12, 1992, B7, col. 1.

Chapter 2

1. M. Edelman, *Constructing the Political Spectacle*, 12–25 (1988).

2. I have taken the phrase "the symbols of government" from Thurman Arnold's 1935 book of that title. Arnold managed to write about current affairs in a way that continues, after half a century, not only to illuminate but to entertain.

3. S. Bruce, *The Rise and Fall of the New Christian Right*, 47 (1988).

4. Barrett, "Pulpit Politics," *Time*, Aug. 31, 1992, 34.

5. A. Hertzke, *Representing God in Washington*, 155–56 (1988). On the Christian revival as a form of dissent embracing "personal attempts to neutralize and disparage the social and cultural handicaps imposed by the structure of advantage," see P. Clecak, *America's Quest for the Ideal Self*, 141 (1983).

6. See generally J. Hall, *The Silent Language* (1973).
7. C. Geertz, *The Interpretation of Cultures*, 17 (1973). See also p. 10 (culture is an "acted document").
8. See S. Blumenthal, *The Permanent Campaign: Inside the World of Elite Political Operatives*, 4 (1980).
9. See generally Shiffrin, "Government Speech," 27 *UCLA Law Review* 565 (1980); M. Yudof, *When Governments Speak: Politics, Law and Government Expression in America* (1983).
10. *Wallace v. Jaffree*, 472 U.S. 38, 57–59 and n.45 (1985).
11. I take the term from Clifford Geertz. See his book *Negara: The Theatre State in Nineteenth-Century Bali* (1980).
12. See, e.g., E. Cassirer, *The Myth of the State* (1946). See also Weyrauch, "Law as Mask—Legal Ritual and Relevance," 66 *California Law Review* 699 (1978); Ingber, "The Interface of Myth and Practice in Law," 34 *Vanderbilt Law Review* 309 (1981).
13. Cassirer, n.12 above, at 282. On "word magic," see also E. Cassirer, *Language and Myth*, 44–62 (S. Langer trans. 1946).
14. Gargan, "Will Jesse Rise Again?" *Los Angeles Times Magazine*, Oct. 28, 1990, 18.
15. See R. Hofstadter, *The Paranoid Style in American Politics and Other Essays*, 3–141 (1965; Phoenix ed. 1979). For applications to modern politics, see Edelman, n.1 above, at 66–89; J. Hunter, *Culture Wars: The Struggle to Define America*, 144–47 (1991).
16. Molotsky, "Bush Vetoes Bill That Would Pay for Some Abortions," *New York Times*, Oct. 22, 1989, sec. 1, p. 32, col. 3.
17. In 1992 radio broadcasts I heard President Bush make this point several times. Laurence Tribe cites a 1989 nationwide poll in which 81 percent of the respondents said they would favor a woman's right to choose to have an abortion in a case of rape or incest. L. Tribe, *Abortion: A Clash of Absolutes*, 231–32 (1990). This figure necessarily includes many who would call themselves "pro-life."
18. On antipornography laws, see chap. 3; on the regulation of racist speech, see chap. 4.
19. On the role of the Constitution in the process that transferred power from local political parties to national parties, see Tushnet, "The Constitution and the Nationalization of American Politics," in B. Marshall, ed., *A Workable Government? The Constitution after Two Hundred Years*, at 144 (1987).
20. Among the main factors in that centralizing process were: the rise of national political parties (see Tushnet, n.19 above); the early steps of an infant national economy, with an occasional helping hand from the Supreme Court (see K. Karst, *Belonging to America: Equal Citizenship and the Constitution*, 177–79 [1989]); the challenge to slavery, culminating in the Civil War and Reconstruction (see Karst, *Belonging to America*, chap. 4); the growth of a

nationwide system of transportation and communication; the Supreme Court's defense of economic liberties in the name of the due process clauses; the adoption of the federal income tax; World War I; the full maturity of a national economy, made painfully apparent by a Great Depression that was nationwide; the New Deal and its constitutional ratification by the Supreme Court; World War II; the Cold War.

21. See text at n.50 below.

22. See generally T. Edsall and M. Edsall, *Chain Reaction: The Impact of Race, Rights, and Taxes on American Politics* (1991).

23. E. Jorstad, *The Politics of Moralism: The New Christian Right in American Life*, 28, 31–68 (1981). On the "electronic church" generally, see A. J. Reichley, *Religion in American Public Life*, 314–19 (1984).

24. See text at n.3 above. For other estimates of the audiences for various kinds of religious broadcasting, see Gaddy, "Some Potential Causes and Consequences of the Use of Religious Broadcasts," in D. Bromley and A. Shupe, eds., *New Christian Politics*, at 117 (1984). The number of regular viewers declined in the late 1980s.

25. See Gaddy, in *New Christian Politics*, n.24 above. For a suggestion that structural factors will cause the political influence of television evangelists to grow, see Hadden, "Televangelism and the Future of American Politics," ibid., at 151, 161–65.

26. The label "mainline" survives in an era of declining membership.

27. Lay members of these churches, including Roman Catholics, are more varied in their views. See, e.g., Chandler, "A Sexual Agenda at Churches," *Los Angeles Times*, June 6, 1991, A1, col. 1.; Ostling, "What Does God Really Think about Sex?" *Time*, June 24, 1991, 48. See also Dart, "Church for Gays Alters Mainline Religions' Views," *Los Angeles Times*, June 7, 1991, A1, col. 1. In February 1993 Cardinal Roger M. Mahony said that gay and lesbian Americans should not be excluded from the armed services, although he thought it might be proper to arrange for separate living quarters. Stammer, "Mahony Breaks Ranks to Back Gays in Military," *Los Angeles Times*, Feb. 13, 1993, A1, col. 2.

28. On direct-mail techniques by religious groups generally, see A. Hertzke, n.5 above, at 49–55, 146–60. Jorstad, n.23 above, at 69–88. On direct-mail mobilization by the new Christian right, with particular attention to PACs, see Lane, "Mobilizing Christians for Political Action: Campaigning with God on Your Side," in *New Christian Politics*, n.24 above, at 251.

29. Hertzke, n.5 above, at 53. On the use of direct-mail advertising in recent cultural conflicts, see Hunter, n.15 above, at 163–68.

30. See Houston, "Phone Frenzy in the Capitol," *Los Angeles Times*, March 16, 1993, A1, col. 1; Tumulty, "Busy Capitol Hill Phones May Not Ring of Truth," ibid., Jan. 30, 1993, A16, col. 1.

31. See Hertzke, n. 5 above, at 97.

32. Quoted in Blumenthal, n.8 above, at 226. On the direct-mail techniques of Viguerie and other operatives of the new right, see pp. 217–34.
33. Hertzke, n.5 above, at 201.
34. Prophecies of doom also abound in advertising for liberal causes. Consider the publicity campaign against Judge Robert Bork's nomination to the Supreme Court, complete with focus-group opinion sampling, media consultants, and cartoon-like television spots. See E. Bronner, *Battle for Justice: How the Bork Nomination Shook America* (1989).
35. Blumenthal, n.8 above, at 3. See also M. Wattenberg, *The Rise of Candidate Politics* (1991).
36. Blumenthal, n.8 above, at 5.
37. The role of the Supreme Court as a nationalizing agent is particularly evident in the context of constitutional limits on local control of the public schools. The Court faces these questions virtually every Term. Its present willingness to impose national constitutional norms is distinctly diminished from what it was two decades ago. The change is evident in contexts as varied as freedom of speech and of the press (compare *Tinker v. Des Moines, Ind., School Dist.*, 393 U.S. 503 [1969] with *Hazelwood School Dist. v. Kuhlmeier*, 484 U.S. 260 [1988]); public aid to religious schools (compare *Lemon v. Kurtzman*, 403 U.S. 602 [1971] with *Mueller v. Allen*, 463 U.S. 388 [1983]); and constitutional limitations on school discipline (compare *Goss v. Lopez*, 419 U.S. 565 [1975] with *New Jersey v. T.L.O.*, 469 U.S. 325 [1985]).
38. 410 U.S. 113 (1973).
39. One version of this bill was introduced as S. 158, 91st Cong., 1st Sess. (1981).
40. Hertzke, n.5 above, at 5. This figure includes all religious lobbies, including groups supporting liberal causes such as civil rights legislation, environmental protection, and the funding of day care for the children of working parents.
41. National interest groups also routinely provide funds and mobilize local constituencies to defeat local candidates. Thus "the political safeguards of federalism" are turned upside down, creating what the framers of the Constitution surely would see as a topsy-turvy political world. Cf. Wechsler, "The Political Safeguards of Federalism," 54 *Columbia Law Review* 533 (1954). Justice Powell had political developments like this in mind when he wrote his vigorous dissent in *Garcia v. San Antonio Metropolitan Transit Authority*, 469 U.S. 528, 564–67 (1985).
42. In 1990 some 39 percent of American adults identified themselves as "strong" or "weak" Democrats, and 25 percent as "strong" or "weak" Republicans. These figures excluded the 12 percent of self-styled "independent Democrats" and 12 percent of "independent Republicans"; presumably their attachments were weaker than "weak." *Statistical Abstract of the United States*, 270 (1992).

43. See generally F. Sorauf, *Money in American Elections* (1988). On the decline of parties and their share of campaign funding, see pp. 3–4, 25–28, 121–53. On PACs, see ibid., 72–120; J. Berry, *The Interest Group Society,* 117–39 (2d ed. 1989).

44. J. Berry, n.43 above, 16–43.

45. Tony Schwartz, a New York political media consultant, quoted in Blumenthal, n.8 above, at 123 (emphasis added).

46. See Berry, n.43 above, at 133–34.

47. For analyses of the electoral activities of fundamentalist Christian groups, see *New Christian Politics,* n.24 above, at 169–268; Bruce, n.3 above, at 81–90; Hertzke, n.5 above, passim.

48. The episode is discussed in chap. 7 below.

49. In some cases Congress can influence executive decisions of this kind through its control over appropriations, or through the Senate's power to confirm high-level executive appointments.

50. Moyers, "What a Real President Was Like," *Washington Post,* Nov. 13, 1988, C5.

51. The exceptions were four states that went for George Wallace, the candidate of the American Independent party.

52. Sen. Barry Goldwater's 1964 presidential campaign had used a similar strategy. On the Nixon campaign see, e.g., A. Lamis, *The Two-Party South,* 28–30 (1984).

53. See E. Carmines and J. Stimson, *Issue Evolution: Race and the Transformation of American Politics* (1989); Lamis, n.52 above, at 7–30, 210–32.

54. The Moral Majority (now rebaptized the Liberty Federation) is overwhelmingly fundamentalist and Protestant, with strong representation of Baptists, especially in the South. Hertzke, n.5 above, at 96. On the role of Protestant churches in mobilizing Southern white voters, see Guth, "The Politics of Preachers: Southern Baptist Ministers and Christian Right Activism," in *New Christian Politics,* n.24 above, at 235. On the churches' role in voter registration in 1984, see Reichley, n.23 above, at 326.

55. For demographic data from national surveys, see Younger and Cutler, "The Moral Majority Viewed Sociologically," in *New Christian Politics,* n.24 above, at 68, 81–87. See also Hertzke, n.5 above, at 143, referring to fundamentalist churches as "churches of the dispossessed." These characterizations are accurate, but it is just as true for the religious right as for the rest of American politics that political activity is correlated positively with economic class. K. Shienbaum, *Beyond the Electoral Connection: A Reassessment of the Role of Voting in Contemporary Politics,* 89 (1984). On middle-class conservative Christians, see Harper and Leicht, "Explaining the New Religious Right: Status Politics and Beyond," in *New Christian Politics,* at 101; Hertzke, n.5 above, at 35.

56. See Hill, "The South's Culture-Protestantism," 79 *Christian Century* 1094 (Sept. 12, 1962).
57. Roland, "The Ever-Vanishing South," in P. Gerster and N. Cords, eds., *Myth and Southern History,* vol. 2, at 155, 162–63 (2d ed. 1989).
58. Hertzke, n.5 above, at 33–34. One survey showed that 80 percent of "white evangelicals" (a term seemingly intended to include fundamentalists as well) voted for President Reagan in 1984. Reichley, n.23 above, at 27. Conservative strategists have also used religion and "family values" issues to attract working-class Catholics away from their historic attachments to the Democratic party. Ibid., at 299–302.
59. There are, however, counterexamples. They include the Civil Rights Restoration Act of 1987, 20 U.S.C. § 1681, adopted over President Reagan's veto; and the Civil Rights Act of 1991, signed by President Bush after a prolonged siege. The latter episode is examined in chap. 7.
60. C. Woodward, *The Burden of Southern History,* 19 (Vintage ed. 1960).
61. G. Myrdal, *An American Dilemma: The Negro Problem and Modern Democracy,* 1011 (1944). The book went to press in 1942.
62. See, e.g., Bruce, n.3 above.
63. Barrett, "Pulpit Politics," *Time,* Aug. 31, 1992, 34. In chap. 5 we return to Vice President Quayle's attack on the "cultural elite."
64. These efforts are by no means limited to the South. In California the Christian right has won majorities in about 35 (out of 58) Republican county central committees. In California they are well financed, having raised more than $1.5 million from four wealthy contributors; almost $700,000 was contributed to conservative Republican candidates in twelve Assembly districts. Lozano and Frammolino, "Christian Right Tries to Take over State GOP," *Los Angeles Times,* Oct. 18, 1992, A1, col. 3. See also Frammolino, "Ahmanson Heir Bankrolls Religious Right's Agenda," ibid., Oct. 19, 1992, A1, col. 5.
65. Eaton, " 'Purist' Right: Upward, Christian Soldiers," *Los Angeles Times,* Aug. 21, 1992, A13, col. 1; Phillips, "Pulpit Bullies," ibid., Sept. 6, 1992, M1, col. 2.
66. Federal News Service, White House Briefing, Aug. 17, 1992, Republican National Convention, remarks by Pat Buchanan, Houston Astrodome, pp. 3–4 of printout.

Chapter 3

1. *Time,* Sept. 7, 1992, 22.
2. On Aristotle's equation of mature civic identity with masculine citizenship, see J. Elshtain, *Women and War,* 54–56 (1987).
3. The extensive modern literature on this subject begins in Nancy Chodo-

row's Freudian study *The Reproduction of Mothering: Psychoanalysis and the Sociology of Gender* (1978). See also D. Dinnerstein, *The Mermaid and the Minotaur: Sexual Arrangements and Human Malaise* (1976); J. Benjamin, *The Bonds of Love: Psychoanalysis, Feminism, and the Problem of Domination* (1988).

4. I have borrowed the term *negative identity* from Erik Erikson. See his book *Toys and Reasons: Stages in the Ritualization of Experience*, 8 (1977).

5. S. de Beauvoir, *The Second Sex*, 682 (1971).

6. See M. Gerzon, *A Choice of Heroes: The Changing Faces of American Manhood*, 5 (1982). The images, of course, are socially constructed. See E. Anthony Rotundo's historical study *American Manhood: Transformations in Masculinity from the Revolution to the Modern Era* (1993).

7. Kraft, "The Iron Law of History: 'No Longing Is Completely Fulfilled': Secretary Henry," *New York Times Magazine*, Oct. 28, 1973, 21.

8. Catharine MacKinnon has expounded the other side of this unbalanced system: how men have defined women's sexuality and used the definition to maintain the gender line and the subordination of women. She is right in saying that "it is sexuality that determines gender, not the other way around." MacKinnon, "Feminism, Marxism, Method, and the State: An Agenda for Theory," in N. Keohane, M. Rosaldo, and B. Gelpi, eds., *Feminist Theory: A Critique of Ideology*, 1, 17 (1982).

9. Men's efforts to make sure that other men appreciate their masculinity are visible in a wide range of social contexts. One common method is the aggressive expression of sexuality. On peer pressure among members of athletic teams, and its occasional explosion into sexual assaults, see Toufexis, "Sex and the Sporting Life," *Time*, Aug. 6, 1990, 76. For a participant/observer's chilling analysis of the "overt images of competitive male sexuality" in modern defense intellectuals' discussion of nuclear weapons and their uses, see Cohn, "Sex and Death in the Rational World of Defense Intellectuals," 12 *Signs* 687 (1987).

10. David Leverenz's literary study *Manhood and the American Renaissance* (1989), is a perceptive essay on this theme in the work of a number of nineteenth-century American writers, particularly Emerson, Thoreau, Whitman, Melville, and Hawthorne.

11. See, e.g., A. Brittan, *Masculinity and Power* (1989); Gerzon, n.6 above.

12. See generally E. Janeway, *Man's World, Woman's Place: A Study in Social Mythology* (1971); J. Richards, *The Sceptical Feminist: A Philosophical Inquiry* (1980); MacKinnon, n.8 above; C. MacKinnon, *Feminism Unmodified: Discourses on Life and Law* (1987).

13. Jeffrey Hantover sets the success of the Boy Scouts in the context of these changes. Hantover, "The Boy Scouts and the Validation of Masculinity," 34 *Journal of Social Issues* 184 (1978).

14. I do not mean to suggest that wife beating is confined to men who are unsuccessful in the world of work. In an essay both outward-observing and introspective, Duncan Kennedy draws on recent feminist literature concerning sexual abuse and offers his own critique of that literature. "Sexual Abuse, Sexy Dressing and the Eroticization of Domination," 26 *New England Law Review* 1309 (1992).

15. See E. Fromm, *Escape from Freedom* (1941); T. Adorno, E. Frenkel-Brunswik, D. Levinson, and R. Sanford, *The Authoritarian Personality* (1950).

16. Most heterosexual men grow up associating gay men with femininity. On the inaccuracy of this "cross-gender stereotype," see Fajer, "Can Two Real Men Eat Quiche Together? Storytelling, Gender-Role Stereotypes, and Legal Protection for Lesbians and Gay Men," 46 *University of Miami Law Review* 511, 607–17 (1992).

17. For an exploration of the uses of law in this process, and for references to some of the social science literature, see K. Karst, *Belonging to America: Equal Citizenship and the Constitution,* esp. chap. 2 (1989).

18. For a list of these common negative images, and helpful discussion of their import, see Kimberlé Crenshaw's article "Race, Reform, and Retrenchment: Transformation and Legitimation in Antidiscrimination Law," 101 *Harvard Law Review* 1331, 1373 (1988).

19. J. Williamson, *The Crucible of Race: Black-White Relations in the American South since Emancipation,* 522 1984). For a fuller account of Williamson's point, see his article "How Black Was Rhett Butler?" in N. Bartley, ed., *The Evolution of Southern Culture,* at 87 (1988).

20. J. Brandeis, dissenting, in *Olmstead v. United States,* 277 U.S. 438, 485 (1928).

21. See Karst, n.17 above, at 28–42.

22. E. Goffman, *Stigma: Notes on the Management of a Spoiled Identity,* 5 (1963).

23. The "Family Issues Voting Index," a report card on legislators, is quoted in E. Jorstad, *The Politics of Moralism: The New Christian Right in American Life,* 83 (1981).

24. *Bradwell v. Illinois,* 83 U.S. 130 (1873). The Court's decision was no doubt influenced by its decision just one day earlier that eviscerated the privileges and immunities clause. *Slaughterhouse Cases,* 83 U.S. 36 (1873).

25. 83 U.S. at 139.

26. Letter of Robert Mozert, Oct. 18, 1983, quoted in Strossen, " 'Secular Humanism' and 'Scientific Creationism': Proposed Standards for Reviewing Curricular Decisions Affecting Students' Religious Freedom," 47 *Ohio State Law Journal* 333, 340 n.44 (1986). The U.S. Court of Appeals rejected the plaintiffs' challenge under the establishment clause of the First Amendment, and the Supreme Court denied review. *Mozert v. Hawkins County Public Schools,* 647 F. Supp. 1194 (E.D. Tenn. 1986) (mem.), rev'd, 827 F.2d 1058 (6th Cir. 1987), cert. denied, 484 U.S. 106 (1988). In a thought-

ful and sympathetic exploration of the claims of the plaintiffs in the *Mozert* case, Nomi Maya Stolzenberg has shown how those claims present in microcosm the fundamental dilemmas of indoctrination in schooling. When the schools are public, the dilemmas take on constitutional dimensions. Stolzenberg, " 'He Drew a Circle That Shut Me Out': Assimilation, Indoctrination, and the Paradox of a Liberal Education," 106 *Harvard Law Review* 581 (1993).

27. Although this characterization of Mary Magdalene is disputed, "the tradition of the Church has from early times identified Mary of Magdala with the woman living an immoral life in the city [Luke 7:36–50]." R. Brownrigg, *Who's Who in the New Testament*, 299 (1971).

28. E. Pagels, *Adam, Eve, and the Serpent*, esp. chaps. 5 and 6 (1988). For an exhaustive history of misogyny disseminated over two millennia by many authoritative sources of Christian doctrine, see K. Armstrong, *The Gospel According to Woman: Christianity's Creation of the Sex War in the West* (1987). See also Rev. Helen Barrett's article "Legal Homophobia and the Christian Church," 30 *Hastings Law Journal* 1019 (1979).

29. See Okin, "Women and the Making of the Sentimental Family," 11 *Philosophy and Public Affairs* 65, 87 (1982).

30. Quoted in Chandler, "The Wicked Shall not Bear Rule: The Fundamentalist Heritage of the New Christian Right," in D. Bromley and A. Shupe, eds., *New Christian Politics*, 41, 46 (1984).

31. 381 U.S. 479 (1965).

32. 410 U.S. 113 (1973).

33. See Grey, "Eros, Civilization, and the Burger Court," 43 *Law and Contemporary Problems* 83 (1980); Karst, "The Freedom of Intimate Association," 89 *Yale Law Journal* 624 (1980).

34. See, e.g., S. Griffin, *Pornography and Silence: Culture's Revenge against Nature* (1981); G. Lloyd, *The Man of Reason: "Male" and "Female" in Western Philosophy* (1984); C. Merchant, *The Death of Nature: Women, Ecology and the Scientific Revolution* (1980); H. Pitkin, *Fortune Is a Woman: Gender and Politics in the Thought of Niccolò Machiavelli* (1984); R. Sydie, *Natural Women, Cultured Men: A Feminist Perspective on Sociological Theory* (1987); Keller, "Gender and Science," 1 *Psychoanalysis and Contemporary Thought* 409 (1978).

35. See H. Hays, *The Dangerous Sex: The Myth of Feminine Evil* (1964); W. Lederer, *The Fear of Women* (1968).

36. See S. Okin, *Women in Western Political Thought*, chaps. 5–8 (1979); C. Pateman, *The Sexual Contract*, 96–102 (1988); Pateman, " 'The Disorder of Women': Woman, Love, and the Sense of Justice," 91 *Ethics* 20 (1978).

37. J. Richards, *The Sceptical Feminist: A Philosophical Inquiry*, 141 (1980); P. Wilson, *Man, the Promising Primate: The Conditions of Human Evolution*, 65 (1983).

38. See Benjamin, "Master and Slave: The Fantasy of Erotic Domination," in

A. Snitow, C. Stansell, and S. Thompson, eds., *Powers of Desire: The Politics of Sexuality*, at 280, 293 (1983). Jessica Benjamin elaborates this thesis in her book *The Bonds of Love* (1988). Of course, individual identity, by definition, implies some kind of separation from the nurturing parent—in our society, typically the mother; girls, too, must find important parts of their identities in separation. Here, however, we are concerned with acculturation to gender identity. In this aspect of identity definition, girls generally identify with their mothers—in important measure because that is what their mothers expect of them. See, e.g., Chodorow, n.3 above, at 166.

39. In these perspectives Reason itself is equated with control and with maintenance of the boundaries of the self. "Rational" calculation, in a world so largely defined by separation, tends to exclude the idea of nurturing and to treat others as instruments to be used. See Benjamin, n.3 above.

40. Note 3 above, at 108. See generally de Beauvoir, n.5 above, at xvi and passim.

41. See n.34 above.

42. Jones, "On Authority: or, Why Women Are not Entitled to Speak," in J. Pennock and J. Chapman, eds., *NOMOS XXIX: Authority Revisited*, 152 (1987); White, "Subordination, Rhetorical Survival Skills, and Sunday Shoes: Notes on the Hearing of Mrs. G.," 38 *Buffalo Law Review* 1 (1990). The men (and some women) who did speak with authority generally told women to keep their place in the domestic world. B. Ehrenreich and D. English, *For Her Own Good: 150 Years of the Experts' Advice to Women* (1978).

43. See, e.g., *United States v. Popper*, 98 Fed. 423 (N.D. Calif. 1899); see also the decisions cited in Hunter and Law, et al., "Brief Amici of Feminist Anti-Censorship Task Force," in *American Booksellers Association v. Hudnut*," 21 *University of Michigan Journal of Law Reform* 69 (1987–88). See generally L. Gordon, *Woman's Body, Woman's Right: A Social History of Birth Control in America* (1976); Wallach, "Musings on Motherhood, Marshall, Molecules: A Passage through the Heart of Maternal Darkness from God's Creation to Man's," 6 *Black Law Journal* 88, 107–17 (1978). In Nazi Germany, too, advertisements for contraceptives were prohibited as obscenity, birth control clinics were closed, and abortion was treason. B. Friedan, *The Second Stage*, 325–26 (1981).

44. See, e.g., Rabban, "The First Amendment in Its Forgotten Years," 90 *Yale Law Journal* 514, 548–49 (1981). For discussion of early twentieth-century feminist claims to sexual liberty for women, see N. Cott, *The Grounding of Modern Feminism*, 41–49, 148–52 (1987).

45. See C. MacKinnon, *Sexual Harassment of Working Women* (1979).

46. See, e.g., Elshtain, "Feminist Discourse and Its Discontents: Language, Power, and Meaning," in N. Keohane, M. Rosaldo, and B. Gelpi, eds., *Feminist Theory: A Critique of Ideology*, 13 (1982).

47. See West, "Equality Theory, Marital Rape, and the Promise of the Fourteenth Amendment," 42 *Florida Law Review* 45 (1990); Note, "To Have and to Hold: The Marital Rape Exception and the Fourteenth Amendment," 99 *Harvard Law Review* 1255 (1985).

48. *Chaplinsky v. New Hampshire*, 315 U.S. 568, 571–72 (1942).

49. *Roth v. United States*, 354 U.S. 476 (1957).

50. E.g., *Jacobellis v. Ohio*, 378 U.S. 184 (1964); *Memoirs v. Massachusetts*, 383 U.S. 413 (1966); *Stanley v. Georgia*, 394 U.S. 557 (1969).

51. *Miller v. California*, 413 U.S. 15 (1973); *Paris Adult Theatre v. Slaton*, 413 U.S. 49 (1973).

52. See the estimates in C. MacKinnon, *Feminism Unmodified*, 179, 284 n.54 (1987).

53. The President fired John Frohnmeyer in order to secure his flanks against the challenge of Patrick Buchanan in presidential primary elections in the South. In 1991 the Southern Baptist Convention had called for Frohnmeyer's dismissal. See "Southern Baptists Assail Bush for Stand on N.E.A.," *Atlanta Constitution*, June 5, 1991, B11, col. 4. Early the next year Buchanan threatened to make a campaign issue of Frohnmeyer's defense of federal funding for offensive art works. See Honan, "Arts Figures Fear for the Endowment after Frohnmeyer," *New York Times*, Feb. 24, 1992, C15, col. 5; "Mr. Bush's Artless Surrender" (editorial), ibid., Feb. 26, 1992, A20, col. 1; "John Frohnmeyer's Noisy Exit" (editorial), ibid., March 25, 1992, A22, col. 1.

54. See West, "The Feminine-Conservative Anti-Pornography Alliance and the 1986 Attorney General's Commission on Pornography Report," 1987 *American Bar Foundation Research Journal* 681.

55. For vivid confirmation of the incompatibility of the two groups on other issues, see Andrea Dworkin's book *Right-Wing Women* (1983). As I mention in the text, Dworkin is a coauthor of the model ordinance that has been proposed in most communities that have considered antipornography legislation.

56. *American Booksellers Association v. Hudnut*, 598 F. Supp. 1316 (D. Ind. 1984), affirmed, 771 F.2d 323 (7th Cir. 1985), affirmed, 475 U.S. 1001 (1986). Paul Brest's and Ann Vandenberg's account of the political battle over the model ordinance in Minneapolis is absorbing from beginning to end. It is so instructive, on so many levels of thought and feeling, that it deserves the widest possible reading. Brest and Vandenberg, "Politics, Feminism, and the Constitution: The Anti-Pornography Movement in Minneapolis," 39 *Stanford Law Review* 607 (1987).

57. MacKinnon, n.52 above, at 148, 184–86, 194. See also Sunstein, "Neutrality in Constitutional Law (with Special Reference to Pornography, Abortion, and Surrogacy)," 92 *Columbia Law Review* 1, 24–26 (1992). There

is little support in the literature for a causal connection between nonviolent pornography and physical abuse of women. See, e.g., Linz, Penrod, and Donnerstein, "The Attorney General's Commission on Pornography: The Gaps Between 'Findings' and Facts," 1987 *American Bar Foundation Research Journal* 713, 723–27; Baron, "Immoral, Inviolate or Inconclusive?" *Society*, July-August 1987, 6, 9. Even as to the effects of pornography depicting sexual violence, the evidence is mixed. Compare Linz, Penrod, and Donnerstein, above, at 716–23, with Schauer, "Causation Theory and the Causes of Sexual Violence," 1987 *American Bar Foundation Research Journal* 737, 764–67 and n.58 (citing studies). As I make clear in the text, however, there is no doubt that pornography is one contributing factor in a culture that sexualizes men's power over women. On the latter point, in addition to the works cited in the foregoing notes, see Delgado and Stefancic, "Pornography and Harm to Women: 'No Empirical Evidence'?" 53 *Ohio State Law Journal* 98 (1992).

58. MacKinnon, n.52 above, at 154, 146.

59. For Catharine MacKinnon's powerful development of these points, see her article, n.8 above, and her books *Feminism Unmodified* (1987) and *Toward a Feminist Theory of the State* (1989). On the relevance of the interrelation of "private" and governmental power in this area, see Frank Michelman's critical analysis of the Seventh Circuit's *Hudnut* opinion, "Conceptions of Democracy in American Constitutional Argument: The Case of Pornography Regulation," 56 *Tennessee Law Review* 291 (1989).

60. L. Baron and M. Straus, *Four Theories of Rape in American Society: A State-Level Analysis*, 92 (1989).

61. For teenagers, the sexual revolution has touched conduct, not just expression. Given the increase in women's average age of marriage and the lowering of the age of sexual maturity for teenage girls, "American girls and their boyfriends face over a decade of their lives when they are sexually mature and single." Luker, "Dubious Conceptions: The Controversy over Teen Pregnancy," *American Prospect*, Spring 1991, 79. The prevailing assumption among American women before the 1960s was that sex before marriage was "engagement" sex. Ibid., at 78. To put the matter conservatively, teenagers today make no such assumption. A sharp increase in teenage sex before marriage has been accompanied by a corresponding change in young people's sense of the social meaning of sex. Many teenagers who are sexually active are still living with their parents, and clearly too young to be seriously contemplating marriage. "Thus the kinds of sexuality for which they are socially eligible—sex based in pleasure, not procreation, and in short-term relationships rather than as a prelude to marriage—challenge fundamental values about sexuality held by many adults." Ibid., at 79.

62. Post, "Cultural Heterogeneity and Law: Pornography, Blasphemy, and the First Amendment," 76 *California Law Review* 297 (1988).

63. On the pervasiveness of sexism in the representations of the culture industry, see generally S. Kappeler, *The Pornography of Representation* (1986); S. Griffin, n.34 above.

64. Duggan and Snitow, "Pornography Is about Images, not Power," *Newsday*, Sept. 26, 1984.

65. See, e.g., A. Dworkin, *Pornography: Men Possessing Women* (1981); C. Mac-Kinnon, *Feminism Unmodified*, 148–50 (1987).

66. See Chesler, "Men and Pornography: Why They Use It," in L. Lederer, ed., *Take Back the Night: Women on Pornography*, 55 (1980); Lurie, "Pornography and the Dread of Women: The Male Sexual Dilemma," ibid., at 159.

67. Finley, "The Nature of Domination and the Nature of Women: Reflections on *Feminism Unmodified*" (book review), 82 *Northwestern University Law Review* 352, 367 (1988).

68. See n.9 above and associated text.

69. The viewers were all males, and the film was what was called, in the late 1940s, a stag movie. I must have been about nineteen years old.

70. See T. Beneke, *Men on Rape*, chap. 1 (1982); Griffin, n.34 above, at 2, 20.

71. The incomparable Groucho is reputed to have declined to join a country club on the ground that he would not be a member of a group that would invite someone like himself.

72. See, e.g., MacKinnon, n.52 above, at 127–33, 179–83. For one actor's story of coercion, see L. Lovelace (Marchiano) and M. McGrady, *Ordeal* (1980); L. Marchiano and M. McGrady, *Out of Bondage* (1986). No doubt the state can constitutionally punish the producers who engage in this sort of coercion, and punish at least some who force pornography on unwilling consumers. As MacKinnon says, however, it is not easy for actors to persuade law enforcement officials that they have been coerced. As to coerced performances, see the Seventh Circuit's opinion, 771 F.2d at 332.

73. Sunstein, "Pornography and the First Amendment," 1986 *Duke Law Journal* 589, 617. See also Schauer, n.57 above. Sunstein (at 604 n.94) places "visceral" speech within the First Amendment's core only to the extent that it is "directed at public affairs."

74. Sunstein, "Pornography and the First Amendment." See also Sunstein, n.57 above, at 22 (First Amendment is "a safeguard against governmental interference with rational thought").

75. Sunstein, "Pornography and the First Amendment," at 603.

76. M. Sanger, *Woman and the New Race*, 100 (1920).

77. See, e.g., J. Miller, *Toward a New Psychology of Women*, 24 (1976); Willis, "Feminism, Morality, and Pornography," in *Powers of Desire*, n.38 above, at 460.

78. Snitow, "Retrenchments v. Transformation: The Politics of the Antipornography Movement," in *Caught Looking: Feminism, Pornography and Censorship*, 10, 15 (1988).

79. Considering the clear foreseeability of this result, it seems inappropriate to argue that when government regulates pornography, it is "unlikely to be acting for constitutionally impermissible reasons or producing constitutionally troublesome harms." Sunstein, n.75 above, at 604.

80. West, n.54 above, at 693. See Susan Keller's critical exploration of the work of one such filmmaker in "Powerless to Please: Candida Royalle's Pornography for Women," 26 *New England Law Review* 1297 (1992).

81. Snitow, n.78 above, at 11, 14. See also Elshtain, n.47 above, at 135–36; K. Bumiller, *The Civil Rights Society: The Social Construction of Victims*, esp. chap. 4 (1988); Echols, "The New Feminism of Yin and Yang," in *Powers of Desire*, n.38 above, at 439.

82. West, n.54 above, at 693.

83. Note 43 above.

84. In the view of many fundamentalists, keeping sex out of sight is suited to maintaining traditional roles within the patriarchal family. The antipornography feminists, as we have seen, want to suppress images that contribute to patriarchy through the sexualization of women's subordination. One function of patriarchy, of course, is to relieve some of the anxieties of manhood. Surely it is these anxieties that produce the market for pornography; but their pervasive influence in our culture means that regulation of pornography is unlikely to achieve any significant reduction in sexist beliefs and behavior.

85. Committee headed by Dr. Mary Calderone, quoted in R. Petchesky, *Abortion and Woman's Choice: The State, Sexuality, and Reproductive Freedom*, 113 (2d ed. 1990).

86. See, e.g., D. Rhode, *Justice and Gender*, 207 (1989), and supporting citations; Sunstein, n.57 above, at 38 and his citations in n.141.

87. Petchesky, n.85 above, at 142–48.

88. Ibid., at x.

89. *Rust v. Sullivan*, 111 S. Ct. 1759 (1991).

90. The order never was enforced. President Bush ordered a "clarifying" regulation that allowed doctors, but not others, to give such advice. A group of nurses then obtained an order from a federal district court temporarily protecting their right to talk to patients about the abortion option, and the U.S. court of appeals affirmed that decision the day President Clinton was elected. Savage, " 'Gag Rule' Is Blocked by Court," *Los Angeles Times*, Nov. 4, 1992, A4, col. 4.

91. Memorandum [of the President] for the Secretary of Health and Human Services, Jan. 22, 1993, printed in 58 Federal Register 7455 (Feb. 3, 1993).

On the same day, by similar memoranda, President Clinton: reversed the ban on privately funded abortions at military hospitals; ordered reconsideration of the ban on importing RU-486 (the French "abortion pill"); and ended the moratorium on federal funding for medical research using fetal tissue.

92. *Planned Parenthood of Southeastern Pennsylvania v. Casey*, 112 S. Ct. 2791 (1992).

93. See, e.g., Graves, "Another Plan: Preparations Begin for Roe's Repeal," *Chicago Tribune*, March 29, 1992, 1.

94. Adrienne Rich spoke these words to a 1978 conference on the future of mothering. A. Rich, *On Lies, Secrets, and Silence: Selected Prose, 1966–1978*, at 261 (1979). Carol Sanger has recently explored the multifold meanings of motherhood as "a central but confusing icon within our social structure," paying special attention to legal issues and legal scholarship. Sanger, "M Is the for Many Things," 1 *Southern California Review of Law and Women's Studies* 15 (1992).

95. By identifying an alternative model of a sexual Order, I do not mean to suggest that women's claims to control over their sexuality have found complete acceptance, either in American law or in public opinion.

96. See F. Ginsburg, *Contested Lives: The Abortion Debate in an American Community*, 173–97 (1989).

97. See, e.g., Bork, "Again, a Struggle for the Soul of the Court," *New York Times*, July 8, 1992, A15, col. 2. In his dissent in *Roe v. Wade*, Justice White contributed to the same misperception when he remarked that the Court had valued "the convenience, whim, or caprice" of the pregnant woman over the fetus's potential life. 410 U.S. 113, at 221 (1973).

98. This is the argument in G. Calabresi, *Ideals, Beliefs, Attitudes, and the Law: Private Law Perspectives on a Public Law Problem*, 101–02 (1985). See also R. Posner, *Sex and Reason*, 339–40 (1991).

99. This point is systematically ignored in Judge Richard Posner's recent analysis of the constitutional law of contraception and abortion. See R. Posner, *Sex and Reason*, chap. 12 (1991). On Judge Posner's failure to take account of the realities of women's lives, see Gillian Hadfield's review "Flirting with Science: Richard Posner on the Bioeconomics of Sexual Man," 106 *Harvard Law Review* 479, 499–502, and passim (1992).

100. I set out this idea in capsule form in "The Supreme Court, 1976 Term—Foreword: Equal Citizenship under the Fourteenth Amendment," 91 *Harvard Law Review* 1, 57–58 (1977), and at greater length in "Woman's Constitution," 1984 *Duke Law Journal* 447, 472–75. See also K. Karst, n.17 above, at 119–24. Two other equality-based arguments for women's freedom of reproductive choice are then-Judge Ruth Bader Ginsburg's "Some Thoughts on Autonomy and Equality in Relation to Roe v. Wade," 63 *North*

Carolina Law Review 375, 382–83 (1985); and Sylvia Law's "Rethinking Sex and the Constitution," 132 *University of Pennsylvania Law Review* 955, 1016–28 (1984). Many of Catharine MacKinnon's earlier works made a similar case indirectly, and she stated her argument in full in "Reflections on Sex Equality under the Constitution," 100 *Yale Law Journal* 1281, 1308–23 (1991). For a short argument blending the "sex discrimination" and group subordination points, see L. Tribe, *Abortion: A Clash of Absolutes,* 105 (1990). Finally, no one's study of this subject can be complete without taking into account Reva Siegel's splendid historical/doctrinal analysis "Reasoning from the Body: A Historical Perspective on Abortion Regulation and Questions of Equal Protection," 44 *Stanford Law Review* 261 (1992).

101. See K. Luker, *Abortion and the Politics of Motherhood* (1984); F. Ginsburg, *Contested Lives: The Abortion Debate in an American Community* (1989).

102. Petchesky, n.85 above, at 209. On the potentially misleading quality of the "promiscuity" label, see ibid., at chap. 6.

103. Lacayo, "Crusading against the Pro-Choice Movement" (interview of Randall Terry), *Time,* Oct. 21, 1991, 26, 28.

104. Some writers suggest that men may favor a pro-choice policy because the availability of abortion empowers them to insist on access to women. See, e.g., MacKinnon, n.52 above, at 99 (quoting Andrea Dworkin). In public utterances on the subject of abortion, the authors of the social issues agenda do not take this line.

105. The separateness of the fetus from the pregnant woman is an imposition of a conceptual bifurcation on a biological reality that is indivisible. Christyne Neff argues that the privacy theory of *Roe v. Wade,* by pitting the artificially separated interests of the fetus against those of the woman who carries it, ignores "the physical reality of the absolute connectedness of the woman and her womb." She argues that the privacy theory should be abandoned in favor of one that emphasizes the woman's right to bodily integrity and so "reunit[es] women and their wombs." Neff, "Woman, Womb, and Bodily Integrity," 3 *Yale Journal of Law and Feminism* 327, 337, 352 (1991). Treating the fetus as separate is artificial even as a matter of the psychology of the pregnant woman. For a thoughtful account of the abortion decision as a choice made by the pregnant woman on behalf of the "dyad" of woman and fetus, a dyad closely connected in body and spirit, see Robert Goldstein's *Mother-Love and Abortion* (1986). See also Colker, "Feminism, Theology, and Abortion: Toward Love, Compassion, and Wisdom," 77 *California Law Review* 1011, 1055, 1058–59 (1989), noting the ways in which a woman who eventually chooses abortion may value fetal life.

106. B. Rothman, *The Tentative Pregnancy: Prenatal Diagnoses and the Future of Motherhood,* 114 (1986). I am indebted Rosalind Pollak Petchesky, n.85 above, at xiv, for this arresting quotation.

107. On childhood as an invention, see P. Aries, *Centuries of Childhood: A Social History of Family Life* (1962).
108. I say "theoretical availability" because the "good girl/bad girl" system of stereotypes is very much alive, inhibiting teenage girls from using forms of contraception that require disclosure to their partners. See Petchesky, n.85 above, at 226–27; Smith, "Saying No to Birth Control," *Los Angeles Times,* Jan. 6, 1993, A1, col. 1.
109. Petchesky, n.85 above, at 220.
110. "All told, more than half of all American pregnancies—3.4 million out of 6 million each year—are accidents, the result of misusing contraceptives, using unreliable contraceptives or using no contraceptives at all." Elmer-Dewitt, "Why Isn't Our Birth Control Better?" *Time,* Aug. 12, 1991, 52.
111. Petchesky, n.85 above, at 222.
112. Ibid., at 219, 227–33.
113. Ibid., at 223–23, 228–29; see also C. Stack, *All Our Kin,* chaps. 4 and 7 (1974). One reason for many black women to resist the idea that a woman's identity rests on attachment to a man is the instability of such attachments in conditions of poverty. For a fuller discussion, see chap. 5 below.
114. See Karst, "Woman's Constitution," 1984 *Duke Law Journal* 447, 473–75. See also Schnably, "Beyond Griswold: Foucauldian and Republican Approaches to Privacy," 23 *Connecticut Law Review* 861 (1991).
115. For many a teenage single mother who is black, the prospects are considerably less sanguine, as we shall see in chap. 5.
116. On the contention among wings of the Republican party for control of the party machinery in 1996—a contest that began even before the August 1992 national convention—see Decker, "Activists Moving to Forge a New Conservative Creed," *Los Angeles Times,* July 4, 1992, A1, col. 5.
117. It seems impossible to talk about this subject—even to refer to a "gay identity"—without oversimplifying. Martha Barron Barrett's splendid book *Invisible Lives: The Truth about Millions of Women-Loving Women* (1990) tells the stories of scores of individual women, and in the telling brightly illuminates what Ann Snitow, n.78 above, called "the frightening malleability of gender." For one woman's story that illustrates the point especially vividly, see Barrett's chap. 30, entitled "Labels Fall Short." For further stories, see E. Marcus, *Making History: The Struggle for Gay and Lesbian Equal Rights* (1992) (oral histories of leaders of the gay rights movement); J. Preston, *A Member of the Family* (1992) (stories of gay men's relations with their families).

    As most anthropologists know, and many lawyers could profit from learning, labels usually fall short in describing life in human societies. Yet, the alternative to shorthand references such as "homosexual orientation" or "lesbians" or "gay men" is an awkwardness of expression that would make discourse futile—at least for me. For sensitive discussions of these matters by law teachers, see Janet Halley, "The Politics of the Closet: Toward Equal Protection for Gay, Lesbian, and Bisexual Identity," 36 *UCLA Law Review* 915 (1989); Ruth Colker's brief comment "Marriage," 3 *Yale Journal of Law and Feminism* 321 (1991); and Marc Fajer's article, n.16 above. For contrasting essays on the social construction of homosexuality, see R. Mohr, *Gay Ideas* (1992). See generally D. Greenberg, *The Construction of Homosexuality* (1988).

118. Rhonda Rivera has exhaustively discussed all these issues in a series of articles: "Our Straight-Laced Judges: The Legal Position of Homosexual Persons in the United States," 30 *Hastings Law Journal* 799 (1979); "Queer Law: Sexual Orientation in the Mid-eighties," 10 *University of Dayton Law Review* 459 (1985) (pt. 1) and 11 ibid. 275 (1986) (pt. 2).

119. The majority Justices in *Bowers v. Hardwick*, 478 U.S. 186 (1986), manifest this function of the sodomy laws with chilling clarity. See Karst, n.17 above, at 201–10. The sodomy laws generally do not distinguish between heterosexual and homosexual sodomy, but in practice they have essentially no application to the former. In *Hardwick* the majority explicitly stated that it was not considering the constitutionality of Georgia's sodomy law as applied to a heterosexual couple. Criminalizing heterosexual sodomy would likely be unconstitutional under such decisions as *Griswold v. Connecticut*, 381 U.S. 479 (1965), and *Eisenstadt v. Baird*, 405 U.S. 438 (1972).

120. See Koppelman, "The Miscegenation Analogy: Sodomy Law as Sex Discrimination," 98 *Yale Law Journal* 145 (1988).

121. See, e.g., Wilkinson and White, "Constitutional Protection for Personal Life Styles," 62 *Cornell Law Review* 563, 593–96 (1977).

122. See, e.g., G. Buchanan, *Morality, Sex, and the Constitution*, 146–56 (1985). Cf. Schneider, "State-Interest Analysis in Fourteenth Amendment "Privacy" Law: An Essay on the Constitutionalization of Social Issues," 51 *Law and Contemporary Problems* 79, 100 (Winter 1988) (state's interest in avoiding a "social environment" that is "offensive").

123. In the *Hardwick* case Justice Powell, concurring in the majority's refusal to strike down the Georgia sodomy law, said that the case would be different if the state actually were to imprison someone for violating the law. 478 U.S. at 197. This comment may have been intended to soften the blow to gay rights advocates, but it made clear that the law's only effective function was to stigmatize homosexual conduct.

124. The latter is the position of Professor Buchanan, n.122 above, at chaps. 4 and 5. He sees the position as a compromise, calling it a "three-fourths loaf" proposal. Ibid., at 81–82.

125. Quoted in Jackson, "An Unenlightened Definition of Family," *Boston Globe*, June 30, 1991, 63. See Richard Mohr's discussion of the Boston proposal in

chap. 3 of *Gay Ideas* (1992). The same battle over the meaning of "the family" was at the center of a referendum to repeal a domestic partnership ordinance passed by San Francisco's Board of Supervisors. See J. Hunter, *Culture Wars: The Struggle to Define America*, 3–12 (1991).

126. On the values of intimate association, see Karst, "The Freedom of Intimate Association," 89 *Yale Law Journal* 624 (1980). Marc Fajer, n.16 above, at 550–64, writes of values of love and commitment in the context of gay and lesbian relationships.

127. For a partial catalogue of these interests, see Eskridge, "A Social Constructionist Critique of Posner's *Sex and Reason:* Steps toward a Gaylegal Agenda," 102 *Yale Law Journal* 333, 353–55 (1992). See also Symposium, "The Family in the 1990s: An Exploration of Lesbian and Gay Rights," 1 *Law and Sexuality* 1 (1991). See also Patricia Cain's article "Same-Sex Couples and the Federal Tax Laws," 1 *Law and Sexuality* 97 (1991).

128. Hicks, "New Threshold for New York Couples," *New York Times*, March 2, 1993, A1, col. 2. See also Chambers, "Tales of Two Cities: AIDS and the Recognition of Domestic Partnerships in San Francisco and New York," 2 *Law & Sexuality* 181 (1993).

129. On the failed Boston proposal, see Longcope, "Family Unit Is Expected to Be Council Topic Today," *Boston Globe*, June 26, 1991, 25. On a similar Cambridge ordinance passed in 1992, see "Cambridge Adopts 'Domestic Partner' Law," *Washington Times*, Sept. 16, 1992, A6. On gay and lesbian family structures, see Fajer, n.16 above, at 565–68. More generally, see Minow, "Redefining Families: Who's In and Who's Out?" 62 *University of Colorado Law Review* 269 (1991).

130. The "sex-as-lifestyle assumption" challenged by Fajer, n.16 above, at 558, has some basis in recent history. From around the beginning of the "gay liberation" movement in 1969 to the recognition of the AIDS epidemic in the early 1980s, as Fajer concedes, "many gay men made promiscuity and heightened awareness of their sexuality important parts of their lives." In the later 1980s the pattern of relationships among gay men began to give much more emphasis to one-to-one intimacy and long-term commitment. In addition to the sources cited by Fajer at 561–62, see F. FitzGerald, *Cities on a Hill: A Journey through Contemporary American Cultures*, 25–119 (1986).

131. Both material and psychic interests are at stake. See Eskridge, n.127 above, at 353–55; Fajer, n.16 above, at 577–84. A plurality of the Hawaii Supreme Court has held that denying marriage to same-sex couples presumptively violates the state's equal rights amendment. *Baehr v. Lewin*, 61 U.S. Law Week 2697 (1993).

132. L. Coser, *The Functions of Social Conflict*, 127 (1956). On social conflict as a law-creating unifier of opposing groups, see pp. 121–37.

133. For a review of the extensive literature linking antigay sentiments with

strong attachment to clearly marked gender differentiations, see Fajer, n.16 above, at 617–24. In the legal literature, Sylvia Law's 1988 article "Homosexuality and the Social Meaning of Gender," 1988 *Wisconsin Law Review* 187, led the way.

134. As a group, men who consider themselves heterosexual tend to feel more threatened by the idea of homosexuality than do women as a group. Furthermore, to those of either sex who feel threatened, a man's homosexual orientation seems more of a threat than does a woman's. See the works cited in Fajer, n.16 above, at 624–31.

135. On the issues raised by the visibility of gay and lesbian relationships, and the immense costs of concealment, see ibid., at 575–602.

136. Here I have drawn on J. D'Emilio, *Sexual Politics, Sexual Communities: The Making of a Homosexual Minority in the United States, 1940–1970* (1983).

137. Ibid., at 20.

138. See generally A. Bérubé, *Coming Out Under Fire: The History of Gay Men and Women in World War II* (1990).

139. D'Emilio, n.136 above, at 49–51.

140. Taylor, "Action as Expression," in *Intention and Intentionality: Essays in Honor of G. E. M. Anscombe*, 73 (1979).

141. On "camping" as a challenge to gender-role norms, see Fajer, n.16 above, at 614–15.

142. *Vallerga v. Department of Alcoholic Beverage Control*, 53 Cal. 2d 313, 1 Cal. Reptr. 494, 347 P.2d 909 (1959).

143. D'Emilio, n.136 above, at 238.

144. The recently named phenomenon of "outing"—in which one person identifies another as gay—makes clear that coming out is also something that can be *done to* an individual. In my view, each person should control his or her own public identity, and "outing" is reprehensible unless the victim has publicly expressed antigay sentiments or otherwise acted in a way that deserves the invasion of his or her privacy. For a discussion of the constitutionality of awarding tort damages for invasion of privacy in a case of "outing," see Ellwood, "Outing, Privacy, and the First Amendment," 102 *Yale Law Journal* 747 (1992).

145. See M. Price, *Shattered Mirrors: Our Search for Identity and Community in the AIDS Era* (1989).

146. On the relation between the fear of AIDS and public disapproval of gay men, see Law, n.133 above, at 195 and n.37.

147. See generally R. Shilts, *And the Band Played On: Politics, People, and the AIDS Epidemic* (1987).

148. Henry, "An Identity Forged in Flames," *Time*, Aug. 3, 1992, 36.

149. 478 U.S. 186 (1986).

150. Counsel for Georgia assured the Court at the oral argument that the state would not enforce the law against sodomy involving heterosex-

ual couples, and the Court noted expressly that such a case was not before it.

151. *New York Times,* Nov. 5, 1990, A14, col. 5.

152. I criticized the decision at some length in Karst, n.17 above, at 201–10.

153. 54 *U.S. Law Week* 3657 (1986).

154. M. Edelman, *Constructing the Political Spectacle,* 119 (1988).

155. The museum director described the jury of four women and four men as mostly composed of "working-class people who had never heard of the museum." Wilkerson, "Cincinnati Museum Quiet after Trial," *New York Times,* Oct. 7, 1990, sec. 1, p. 27, col. 1. See also Wilkerson, "Cincinnati Jury Acquits Museum in Mapplethorpe Obscenity Case," *New York Times,* Oct. 6, 1990, sec. 1, p. 1, col. 1.

156. The Supreme Court's 1977 decision holding such a law unconstitutional, *Carey v. Population Services International,* 431 U.S. 678 (1977), reflected at least some Justices' belief that the law was deterring contraceptive use without deterring teenage sex. None of them mentioned effects, if any, of the law's enforcement on attitudes concerning either sex or contraception.

157. See generally E. Durkheim, *Division of Labor in Society,* book 2, chap. 2 (G. Simpson translation 1933 [1893]). For modern defenses of the use of law to advance Christian (or Judeo-Christian) morality, see Rodes, "Sex, Law, and Liberation," 58 *Thought* 43 (March 1988); Schneider, n.122 above; and Buchanan, n.122 above. These authors' arguments are not fungible; all deserve careful reading.

158. Fajer, n.16 above, at 571–602, discusses "flaunting" and the costs of concealment of gay identity.

Chapter 4

1. In his magisterial study of the origins of white supremacy over black people, Winthrop Jordan also examines the early European attitudes toward the Indians who were here when the colonists got off the boats, and the disastrous results of those early encounters. W. Jordan, *White over Black: American Attitudes Toward the Negro, 1550–1812,* at 11–24, 91–98, and passim (1968). Jordan concluded that white attitudes toward black people were centrally driven by white people's need for self-identification. Roy Harvey Pearce had earlier argued similarly concerning white colonists' attitudes toward Indians. R. Pearce, *The Savages of America: A Study of the Indian and the Idea of Civilization* (1953). Vine Deloria has explored some of the modern consequences of these attitudes. See V. Deloria, *God Is Red* (1973) (on Indian religions and Christianity); V. Deloria and C. Lytle, *American Indians, American Justice* (1983). On modern Indian nationalism and pan-Indian movements, see V. Deloria and C. Lytle, *The Nations Within: The Past and Future of American Indian Sovereignty* (1984).

2. On nativism in American politics, see, e.g., W. Preston, *Aliens and Dissenters* (1963); L. Levy, *The Emergence of a Free Press*, 282–349 (1985) (Republican reaction to the Sedition Act, and its application to foreign-born editors); R. Billington, *The Protestant Crusade, 1800–1860: A Study of the Origins of American Nativism* (1938); A. Saxton, *The Indispensable Enemy: Labor and the Anti-Chinese Movement in California* (1971); M. Grodzins, *Americans Betrayed* (1949) (internment of Japanese Americans in World War II). For other citations see Karst, "Paths to Belonging: Cultural Identity and the Constitution," 64 *North Carolina Law Review* 303, 311–36 (1964).

3. See, e.g., T. Edsall and M. Edsall, *Chain Reaction: The Impact of Race, Rights, and Taxes on American Politics* (1991); Sears, Lau, Tyler, and Allen, "Self-Interest or Symbolic Politics in Policy Attitudes and Presidential Voting," 74 *American Political Science Review* 670 (1980). Stephen Carter, referring to the South, comments that "it is fair to say that city mayors are either black Democrats or white Republicans." S. Carter, *Reflections of an Affirmative Action Baby*, 166 (1991).

4. David Brion Davis, both quoting and paraphrasing Andrew Hacker, said, "It is not race that 'has made America its prisoner since the first chattels were landed on these shores,' but rather the ideological purposes that the idea of race has served." Davis, "The American Dilemma" (book review), *New York Review of Books*, July 16, 1992, 15.

5. See, e.g., S. Blumenthal, *Pledging Allegiance: The Last Campaign of the Cold War*, 257–66 (1991).

6. Senator Helms's campaign also ran a television commercial stating that Harvey Gantt had endorsed legislation "mandating" the presence of gay teachers in North Carolina's public schools. Thomas Byrne Edsall, after describing the "white hands" ad, called this second ad "equally effective." Edsall, "Clinton's Revolution," *New York Review of Books*, Nov. 5, 1992, at 10.

7. For a good short statement of these developments, see Levy, "Incorporation Doctrine," in L. Levy, K. Karst, and D. Mahoney, eds., *Encyclopedia of the American Constitution*, vol. 2, 970 (1986).

8. In his compelling 1984 book *Common Ground*, J. Anthony Lukas tells the story of Boston's conflict over school integration through the eyes of members of three families, one of which is a working-class white family.

9. See, e.g., E. Liebow, *Tally's Corner: A Study of Negro Streetcorner Men* (1967).

10. Clarence Page bitingly calls this process "America's War on Those Easiest to Bust for Drugs," *Chicago Tribune*, May 2, 1990, 19.

11. For analysis of those disparities, see "Developments in the Law—Race and the Criminal Process," 101 *Harvard Law Review* 1472 (1988).

12. A. Hacker, *Two Nations: Black and White, Separate, Hostile, Unequal*, 202, 206 (1992).

13. See J. Blassingame, *The Slave Community: Plantation Life in the Antebellum South*, 293–98 (rev. ed. 1979). Jacqueline Jones reports that at least one slaveholder disciplined male slaves by forcing them to do "women's work" and wear women's clothes. J. Jones, *Labor of Love, Labor of Sorrow; Black Women, Work, and the Family from Slavery to the Present*, 38 (1985).

14. On the forms of black-on-white aggression, see J. Dollard, *Caste and Class in a Southern Town*, 287–314 (Anchor ed. 1949 [1937]). On white-on-black aggression, see pp. 315–63.

15. See, e.g., A. Hacker, n.12 above, at 183.

16. See, e.g., R. Majors and J. Billson, *Cool Pose: The Dilemmas of Black Manhood in America* (1992). See also L. Bing, *Do or Die* (1991), where the anxieties of manhood come through on virtually every page.

17. Here violence is its own reward, the natural result of what Lewis Coser, interpreting and elaborating the work of Georg Simmel, called "nonrealistic conflict," in which "it is precisely in the aggressive means and not in the result that satisfaction is sought." L. Coser, *The Functions of Social Conflict*, 50–51 (1956).

18. In 1992 Ice-T (that is, Tracy Morrow, a young black singer who lives not in south-central Los Angeles but in the Hollywood Hills) released a recording called *Body Count*, including a rock (not rap) song "Cop Killer." In the declining moments of the uproar over the song, both the singer and some other observers sought to rehabilitate the message by placing it in the category of allegory. To at least some of us who were not lit. majors, the lyric sounded like advocacy. But that does not make it punishable.

    The politicians who made the most noise about "Cop Killer" had nothing to say about the same recording's other songs celebrating violence against women. See Sheila Kuehl's comment "Ice-T Critics Miss the Rapper's Real Target," *Los Angeles Times*, July 27, 1992, F3, col. 1. It does not seem merely coincidental that the chief market for lyrics of this sort is found among white teenage boys. Evidently these "rebels without a clue" think they have found a new-style ritual of group domination in which they can express some version of manhood. See Cocks, "A Nasty Jolt for the Top Pops," *Time*, July 1, 1991, 78.

19. At the singer's request, the publisher recalled copies of the *Body Count* album and rereleased it minus "Cop Killer."

20. This is the statement of a *lawyer*, mind you—one apparently unacquainted with such decisions as *Brandenburg v. Ohio*, 395 U.S. 444 (1969). The lawyer was hired by Col. Oliver North, himself no stranger to courtrooms, to represent the Freedom Alliance in protesting against Time Warner, Inc., for distributing the recording that included "Cop Killer." "North Steamed at Ice-T," *Los Angeles Times*, July 2, 1992, D1, col. 2.

21. One 53-year-old black owner of a pest control business described his

thoughts when he saw the first television images of Rodney King's beating by Los Angeles police officers: "Well, at least they *see* we're not lying to them. . . . They see that this stuff actually happens. Now the *world* sees. They always think we're making it up." Staff of the *Los Angeles Times, Understanding the Riots,* 35 (1992). For a collection of recent comments of Los Angeles residents to this effect, see Dunn and Hubler, "Unlikely Flash Point for Riots," *Los Angeles Times,* July 5, 1992, A1, col. 1.

22. After interviewing dozens of Angelenos of all races in the wake of the Los Angeles riots, a scholar suggested that whites' fears were associated with their sense of guilt and shame. Wallace, "Whites Face a New Fear: Being Judged by Color," *Los Angeles Times,* June 15, 1992, A1, col. 5.

23. In the federal civil rights damages action filed by King against the city of Los Angeles, his lawyer reported that he and the city attorney's office had agreed, after long negotiations, to a settlement for some $5.9 million. The City Council rejected that offer, and countered with its own offer of $1.75 million, which King's attorney rejected. Krilorian and Serrano, "King Rejects City's Offer of $1.75 Million," *Los Angeles Times,* Sept. 16, 1992, A1, col. 6. These negotiations took place before two of the four police officers were convicted in federal court of willful deprivation of King's constitutional rights.

24. Examples are sprinkled through John Gwaltney's 1981 book *Drylongso: A Self-Portrait of Black America* and Studs Terkel's 1992 book *Race: How Blacks and Whites Think and Feel about the American Obsession.*

25. *Report of the Independent Commission on the Los Angeles Police Department,* 67–93 (1991) (on racism and other forms of bias, highlighting male officers' selective use of excessive force). For the personal stories of some of the 44 men identified by the commission as "problem officers," see Serrano, "They Hit Me, So I Hit Back," *Los Angeles Times,* Oct. 4, 1992, A1, col. 1.

26. See, e.g., Maclin, " 'Black and Blue Encounters'—Some Preliminary Thoughts about Fourth Amendment Seizures: Should Race Matter?" 26 *Valparaiso University Law Review* 243 (1991).

27. Many black residents of south-central Los Angeles had resented a large in-migration of recent arrivals from Central America and Mexico. One result of that influx was that housing prices had risen faster for blacks than for whites in the city. A number of shops in the area are owned and managed by Korean immigrants and their families. The black community had been seething for some months about a white judge's probationary sentence for a middle-aged Korean woman shopkeeper who, after an angry exchange and brief struggle in the shop, had shot a black girl in the back. For further background, see Choi, "A Closer Look at the Conflict between the African American and the Korean American Communities in South Central Los Angeles," 1 *UCLA Asian American Pacific Islands Law Journal* 19 (1993). As

the 1992 riots developed, television depicted the deliberate targeting of shops owned by Korean immigrants and then the participation of Latinos (also, it appeared, mainly immigrants) in the looting. A majority of those arrested were Latino. With these images added to those of black rage against whites, the rioting took on the look of a war of all against all. Miles, "Blacks v. Browns," *Atlantic Monthly,* October 1992, 41. A Chicana anthropologist I know is critical of the Miles article, but she agrees—as who could not?—that serious tensions exist between the two groups.

28. The very first reported episode in south-central Los Angeles involved a 19-year-old black shoe salesman who lived in a neatly kept neighborhood, by no means destitute. He had a reputation as one "who always cautioned others about the dangers of gangbanging and counseled friends to prepare for the future." But he shared in the rage that surged through the black community, and half an hour after the verdict was announced he threw a brick at a passing pickup truck. Dunn and Hubler, n.21 above, at A18.

29. J. Tyrell, *Leoš Janáček: Kat'a Kabanova,* 163 (1982) (quoting Max Brod).

30. The medieval English law of rape unquestionably was centered on these interests. On the modern meanings of rape, see generally S. Brownmiller, *Against Our Will: Men, Women, and Rape* (1975). For a short survey of the legal questions, making clear the close connections between the status of women and the governing law, see D. Rhode, *Justice and Gender,* 244–53 and bibliography in endnotes (1989).

31. On slavery and Jim Crow, see, e.g., Wriggins, "Rape, Racism, and the Law," 6 *Harvard Women's Law Journal* 103 (1983); Hall, " 'The Mind That Burns in Each Body': Women, Rape, and Racial Violence," in A. Snitow, C. Stansell, and S. Thompson, eds., *Powers of Desire: The Politics of Sexuality,* at 328 (1983); Dollard, n.14 above, at 134–72 (chapter on "the sexual gain"). On the modern scene, see, e.g., Wriggins, cited above; S. Estrich, *Real Rape* (1987). Angela Harris discusses black women's experience of rape in "Race and Essentialism in Feminist Legal Theory," 42 *Stanford Law Review* 581, 598–601 (1990).

32. Carby, " 'On the Threshold of Woman's Era': Lynching, Empire, and Sexuality in Black Feminist Theory," in H. Gates, Jr., ed., *Race Writing, and Difference,* at 301, 309 (1986). For this quotation I am indebted to Angela Harris, n.31 above, at 600.

33. J. Williamson, *The Crucible of Race: Black-White Relations in the American South since Emancipation,* 116 (1984). On the "crime" issue as a continuation of a tradition of political rhetoric castigating sin and thrashing devils, see Gary Wills's chapter "A Theology of Willie Horton," in *Under God,* 70–75 (1990).

34. See E. Carmines and J. Stimson, *Issue Evolution: Race and the Transformation of American Politics* (1989); A. Lamis, *The Two-Party South* (1984); T. Edsall and M. Edsall, n.3 above. The one Republican candidate who did not make

use of the social issues agenda was Gerald R. Ford. See E. J. Dionne, Jr., *Why Americans Hate Politics,* 205 (1991).

35. Blumenthal, n.5 above, at 264, 265.

36. Edsall and Edsall, n.3 above, at 222–24 and passim. The absence of a Willie Horton figure in the 1992 presidential campaign should not lull anyone into believing that the race/crime package has lost its political appeal. President Bush did take a brief shot at the issue, but his handlers seem to have decided that Governor Clinton was not vulnerable. See Gerstenzang, "It's Déjà Vu as Bush Hits Taxes, Crime," *Los Angeles Times,* Sept. 29, 1992, A1, col. 6. The fears and anxieties about race that were so important in producing the earliest constituencies for cultural counterrevolution have not dissolved. See Edsall, "Clinton's Revolution," *New York Review of Books,* Nov. 5, 1992, 7, 10.

37. See Strauss, "The Myth of Colorblindness," 1986 *Supreme Court Review* 99. Neil Gotanda has demonstrated a number of pernicious effects of judicial doctrines founded on this metaphor. See his article "A Critique of 'Our Constitution Is Color-Blind,'" 41 *Stanford Law Review* 1 (1991).

38. This was the response of 66 percent of whites surveyed in a June 1991 *Los Angeles Times* poll. Richter, "Beneath the Bitterness over Race," *Los Angeles Times,* Aug. 13, 1991, A1, col. 1.

39. 109 U.S. 3 (1883).

40. See Brooks, "Racial Subordination through Formal Equal Opportunity," 25 *San Diego Law Review* 879 (1988). This point is also embodied in Roy Brooks's larger work *Rethinking the American Race Problem* (1990).

41. In the *Civil Rights Cases,* n.39 above, the Supreme Court assumed that the Fourteenth Amendment forbids only "state action" and not private racial discrimination. For a short survey, see Karst, "Private Discrimination and Public Responsibility," 1989 *Supreme Court Review* 1, 15–21. *Reitman v. Mulkey,* 387 U.S. 369 (1967), is a good example of the Warren Court's relaxation of the "state action" barrier. The most satisfying explanation for the decision would be the recognition of a state responsibility for remedying private housing discrimination. See Karst and Horowitz, "Reitman v. Mulkey: A Telophase of Substantive Equal Protection," 1967 *Supreme Court Review* 39; cf. Black, "The Supreme Court, 1966 Term—Foreword: 'State Action,' Equal Protection, and California's Proposition 14," 81 *Harvard Law Review* 69 (1967).

42. E.g., *Griggs v. Duke Power Co.,* 401 U.S. 424 (1971) (private employment discrimination); *Fullilove v. Klutznick,* 448 U.S. 448 (1980) (affirmative action in federal spending program for local government contracting).

43. E.g., *Jones v. Alfred H. Mayer Co.,* 392 U.S. 409 (1968); *Runyon v. McCrary,* 427 U.S. 160 (1976).

44. The model doesn't explain anything; models never do. I offer this one as a perspective on some civil rights issues in the political and judicial arenas, especially issues involving remedies for private racial discrimination.

45. Alan Freeman explored a number of doctrinal and practical consequences of this preference, which he called "the perpetrator perspective," in his article "Legitimizing Racial Discrimination through Antidiscrimination Law: A Critical Review of Supreme Court Doctrine," 62 *Minnesota Law Review* 1049 (1978).

46. For an excellent general discussion of the ways in which a constitutional principle of neutrality translates into support for existing distributions of power, see Sunstein, "Neutrality in Constitutional Law (with Special Reference to Pornography, Abortion, and Surogacy)," 92 *Columbia Law Review* 1, at 1–13 (1992).

47. On paternalism, see E. Genovese, *Roll, Jordan, Roll: The World the Slaves Made*, 3–7, 70–86, 123–49, and passim (Vintage ed. 1976).

48. Daniel, "The Metamorphosis of Slavery, 1865–1900," 66 *Journal of American History* 88 (1979). See also E. Foner, *Reconstruction: America's Unfinished Revolution, 1863–1877*, 128–42 (1988).

49. See L. Litwack, *Been in the Storm So Long: The Aftermath of Slavery*, 364–71, 408–20 (Vintage ed. 1980).

50. Daniel, n.48 above, at 96.

51. Ibid., at 98, 95.

52. Litwack, n.49 above, at 261–67.

53. Ibid., at 263–64. See also H. Hyman and W. Wiecek, *Equal Justice under Law: Constitutional Development, 1835–1875*, 423–26 (1982).

54. See generally C. V. Woodward, *The Strange Career of Jim Crow* (2d rev. ed. 1966); Williamson, n.33 above; Dollard, n.14 above.

55. These generalizations typically are not articulated, and often remain buried below the level of consciousness. See Lawrence, "The Ego, the Id, and Equal Protection: Reckoning with Unconscious Racism," 30 *Stanford Law Review* 317 (1987).

56. See G. Jaynes and R. Williams, eds., *A Common Destiny: Blacks and American Society*, 78–79, 89–91, 144–46 (1989); D. Massey and N. Denton, *American Apartheid: Segregation and the Making of the Underclass* (1993); Aleinikoff, "The Constitution in Context: The Continuing Significance of Racism," 63 *University of Colorado Law Review* 325, 336–38, and sources cited in nn.36–50 (1992).

57. The point is illustrated repeatedly in Studs Terkel's interviews, reported in S. Terkel, *Race: How Blacks and Whites Think and Feel about the American Obsession* (1992).

58. For two poignant personal statements by young, successful, upper-

middle-class black men, see Walton, "Willie Horton and Me," *New York Times Magazine*, Aug. 20, 1989, 52; Standard, "A Young Black Asks: Will I Be Next?" *New York Times*, Sept. 2, 1989, 13, col. 2.

59. See K. Karst, *Belonging to America: Equal Citizenship and the Constitution*, chap. 6 (1989).

60. Fiss, "Groups and the Equal Protection Clause," 5 *Philosophy and Public Affairs* 107, 157 (1976) (on "status-harm").

61. These consequences persist today. See generally Kennedy, "McCleskey v. Kemp: Race, Capital Punishment, and the Supreme Court," 101 *Harvard Law Review* 1388 (1988).

62. These decisions were widely discussed in the law journals. Part of this chapter is drawn from my 1989 *Supreme Court Review* article, n.41 above, which discusses several of the cases in greater detail than is necessary here.

63. This preference is visible across a wide range of subjects, including even school desegregation. See, e.g., *Board of Education of Oklahoma City Public Schools v. Dowell*, 498 U.S. 237 (1991); *Freeman v. Pitts*, 112 S. Ct. 1430 (1992). For a comprehensive analysis of the interests at stake, see Liebman, "Desegregating Politics: 'All-out' School Desegregation Explained," 90 *Columbia Law Review* 1463 (1990).

64. E.g., the Jones and Runyon cases cited in n.43 above.

65. *Patterson v. McLean Credit Union*, 491 U.S. 164 (1989).

66. These examples are taken from Justice Brennan's dissenting opinion in the *Patterson* case, 491 U.S. at 189.

67. An employee who had been demoted or fired would have the additional inducement of back pay.

68. 490 U.S. 642 (1989).

69. 401 U.S. 424 (1971).

70. See generally Crenshaw, "Race, Reform, and Retrenchment: Transformation and Legitimation in Antidiscrimination Law," 101 *Harvard Law Review* 1331 (1988); Fiss, n.60 above; Karst, n.59 above, at 21–27 and chap. 9.

71. Karst, n.59 above, at 151. See also Freeman, n.45 above.

72. "Almost by definition, markets incorporate the norms and practices of advantaged groups." Sunstein, "Why Markets Don't Stop Discrimination," 8 *Social Philosophy and Policy*, no. 2, 22, at 33 (Spring 1991). The point in the text is broader still, and none the worse for being obvious: Markets not only shape themselves to the preferences of those who can afford to buy, but reinforce the uneven distribution of market power. Sunstein's article illuminates a number of these larger dimensions of market behavior in the context of discrimination against subordinated groups identified by race, sex, and disability.

73. Pub. L. 102–166, 105 Stat. 1071.

74. Of course, the 1991 act came too late to give damages to Brenda Patterson. And even for future cases, the cannery workers at Wards Cove were also out of luck: in the flurry of last-minute legislative activity leading to the new law, lobbyists quietly secured a statutory exemption that covered the canneries.

75. The solicitor general, on behalf of the United States, filed briefs *amicus curiae* (friend of the Court) in several of these cases.

76. E. Cassirer, *An Essay on Man*, 81 (1944). Although this quotation is taken from a chapter on "myth and religion," in Cassirer's own terms the passage seems precisely apt for the context of advertising aimed at reinforcing America's longstanding myths about race and turning those myths to political advantage. In Cassirer's analysis one function of myth is to endow the natural world (e.g., the "nature" of black people) with dramatic qualities, infusing that world with emotion. "By these projections nature [in the mind of the perceiver] becomes the image of the social world." Ibid., at 79. In a 1945 lecture Cassirer applied his analysis to modern political myths, and particularly to the national socialism he had escaped. "Hope and fear," he said, "are perhaps the most general and deepest human emotions. . . . Myth is [historically] the first attempt to organize this feeling." "The Technique of Our Modern Political Myths," in E. Cassirer, *Symbol, Myth, and Culture*, at 242, 258 (D. Verene ed. 1979). A different version of the same paper, but with the same ending paragraphs, appears in Cassirer's last book *The Myth of the State*, 277 (1946). On the limitations of "coherence" in providing an accurate description of a cultural system, see C. Geertz, *The Interpretation of Cultures: Selected Essays*, 17–18 (1973).

77. Jordan, n.1 above, at 80. Similarly, racism played its part in the Puritans' assumption that they were bringing civilization to the "savage" Indians. Ibid., at 27.

78. Ibid., at 304–08.

79. D. B. Davis, *The Problem of Slavery in the Age of Revolution, 1770–1823*, at 46, 48, 302 (1973).

80. See Jordan, n.1 above, esp. chap. 1.

81. See G. Fredrickson, *The Black Image in the White Mind: The Debate on Afro-American Character and Destiny, 1817–1914*, at chaps. 1–3.

82. Jordan, n.1 above, at 305.

83. E. Genovese, *Roll, Jordan, Roll: The World the Slaves Made*, 25–43 (1976).

84. Davis, n.79 above, at 194.

85. Jordan, n.1 above, at 436–37.

86. Ibid,. at 40–43. On the projection of white men's desires onto blacks, and the association of self-control with the fear of slave insurrections, see pp. 150–54. On the abolitionists' view of sex and slavery, see Walters, "Control, Sexual Attitudes, Self-Mastery, and Civilization: Abolitionists and the

Erotic South," in R. Brugger, ed., *Our Selves, Our Past: Psychological Approaches to American History,* 165 (1981).
87. Williamson, n.33 above, at 115–19, 127–76.
88. Dollard, n.14 above, at 440.
89. Exceptions were confined to black leadership of segregated institutions: ministers in black churches, teachers in black schools.
90. The eugenics and Progressive movements fed each other's racism. See generally D. Kevles, *In the Name of Eugenics: Genetics and the Uses of Human Heredity* (1985); Cynkar, "Buck v. Bell: 'Felt Necessities' v. Fundamental Values?" 81 *Columbia Law Review* 1418, 1425–35 (1981). On the Progressive era, see Delgado et al., "Can Science Be Inopportune? Constitutional Validity of Governmental Restrictions on Race-IQ Research," 31 *UCLA Law Review* 128, 132–36 (1983).
91. This passage is taken from a 1989 lecture, published as Karst, "Boundaries and Reasons: Freedom of Expression and the Subordination of Groups," 1990 *University of Illinois Law Review* 95, 109–16. Around the same time Charles Lawrence was writing about the expressive aspects of the Jim Crow laws and the social practices they reinforced. See Lawrence, "If He Hollers, Let Him Go: Regulating Racist Speech on Campus," 1990 *Duke Law Journal* 431, 438–44. See also Lawrence's earlier piece " 'One More River to Cross'—Recognizing the Real Injury in Brown," in D. Bell, ed., *Shades of Brown: New Perspectives on School Desegregation,* 48, 50–54 (1980), and my discussion of Jim Crow as a culture of subordination, in Karst, n.59 above, at 64–69. Both Lawrence and I have merely annotated the gospel: Charles Black's masterful statement about Jim Crow as a status system. See Black, "The Lawfulness of the Segregation Decisions," 69 *Yale Law Journal* 421 (1960).
92. The Supreme Court saw this effect in a state law's disqualification of blacks from jury duty, held invalid in *Strauder v. West Virginia,* 100 U.S. 303 (1880). Unhappily, though, some 90 years later the Burger Court refused to see that the closing of the city swimming pool in Jackson, Mississippi, in response to a desegregation order was an implicit official expression that black people were "unfit to associate with whites." White, J., dissenting, in *Palmer v. Thompson,* 403 U.S. 217, 240–41 (1971).
93. On race as a boundary marker in the confusing context of interracial sex, see Saks, " 'The Body of an Offence': Re-Presenting Miscegenation Law," *Raritan Review,* Fall 1988, 39.
94. See Lawrence, "The Id, the Ego, and Equal Protection: Reckoning with Unconscious Racism," 39 *Stanford Law Review* 317 (1987). On the role of popular culture in subtly (and not so subtly) propagating racial and ethnic stereotypes, see Delgado and Stefancic, "Images of the Outsider in American Law and Culture: Can Free Expression Remedy Systemic Social Ills?"

77 *Cornell Law Review* 1258 (1992) (includes lists of works on ethnic depiction). For further discussion of the point in the text, and citations to other works, see Karst, n.59 above, at 21–26, 40–42, 64–69, 73–80. An especially helpful statement, with further references to the literature, is Alexander Aleinikoff's article "A Case for Race-Consciousness," 91 *Columbia Law Review* 1060, 1065–72, 1081–91, and passim (1991). A complementary article is Aleinikoff, n.56 above.

95. See Crenshaw, n.70 above, at 1373; D. Bell, *And We Are Not Saved* (1989); Crenshaw and Peller, "Reel Time/Real Justice," 70 *Denver University Law Review* 283 (1993).

96. In a 1991 poll, 56 percent of whites said that blacks were likely to be less intelligent than whites. Richter, "Beneath the Bitterness on Race," *Los Angeles Times*, Aug. 13, 1991, A1, col. 1.

97. See Martha Minow's thoughtful exposition in "The Supreme Court, 1986 Term—Foreword: Justice Engendered," 101 *Harvard Law Review* 10 (1987).

98. See, e.g., Delgado, "When a Story Is Just a Story: Does Voice Really Matter?" 76 *Virginia Law Review* 95, 103–11 (1990).

99. *Board of Education v. Pico*, 457 U.S. 853 (1982).

100. See Judge Mansfield's extracts, quoted in an appendix to Justice Powell's dissenting opinion, 457 U.S. at 897.

101. See T. Kochman, *Black and White Styles in Conflict*, 74–88 (1981). Justice Blackmun, concurring, expressed his concern about efforts to suppress not just political ideas but "social perspectives" as well. 457 U.S. at 879.

102. *Dred Scott v. Sandford*, 60 U.S. (19 Howard) 393 (1857).

103. Taney commented that recognizing even free blacks as citizens would imply that they had the right to travel freely, even into a slave state, and "would give them the full liberty of speech in public and in private upon all subjects upon which [that state's] own citizens might speak; [and freedom] to hold public meetings upon political affairs . . . ." 60 U.S. at 421. Taney's main concern, obviously, was that visiting free blacks might stir the spirit of revolt among blacks held in slavery.

104. Gerald Rosenberg, in *The Hollow Hope: Can Courts Bring about Social Change?* (1991), argues that litigation has contributed little to social reform or other forms of social change. He specifically denies that the Supreme Court's decision in *Brown v. Board of Education*, 347 U.S. 483 (1954), had much impact on either politics or public attitudes in the field of racial segregation. My different views on *Brown*'s influence on the culture of American public life are made clear in this section, both in the text and in the notes.

105. See Karst, n.59 above, chap. 5. Prof. Rosenberg, n.104 above, at 82–85, emphasizes the "social and cultural constraints" on judicial action in the desegregation field. He also identifies "social and cultural change" as a factor that tended to remove constraints on the courts: "By the late 1960s

and early 1970s there was not as large-scale or as deep-seated a social and cultural aversion to desegregation as there had been in the pre-1964 years" (p. 97). I agree with him that the 1964 Civil Rights Act accelerated this acculturation—but (as I argue below) so did the Supreme Court and the federal judges in the South who upheld the Constitution and laws of the United States between 1954 and 1970. See, e.g., J. Bass, *Unlikely Heroes: The Dramatic Story of the Southern Judges of the Fifth Circuit Who Translated the Supreme Court's Brown Decision into a Revolution for Equality* (1981).

106. I have recounted, in capsule form, the Justices' concerns about the antici-pated white southern defiance of the decision. See Karst, n.59 above, at 15–21. For the full treatment, see Richard Kluger's monumental work *Simple Justice: The History of Brown v. Board of Education and Black America's Struggle for Equality,* chap. 25 (1975). See also Bernard Schwartz's account in *Inside the Warren Court,* 448–55 (1985).

107. Cover, "Violence and the Word," 95 *Yale Law Journal* 1601, 1617, 1628 (1986).

108. Even overcoming the parts of Jim Crow that were founded on law would require more than litigation. From its founding, early in the twentieth century, the NAACP pursued a two-pronged program of law reform. It sought civil rights legislation in Congress (and in state legislatures outside the South), and at the same time called on the courts to declare unconstitu-tional the laws that were the framework for the system of racial subordina-tion. See, e.g., M. Tushnet, *The NAACP's Legal Strategy against Segregated Education, 1925–1950* (1987); G. Myrdal, *An American Dilemma: The Negro Problem and Modern Democracy,* 819–36 (1944).

109. It did not seem so early in 1954. See Karst, n.59 above, at 15, commenting on an article by Robert Leflar and Wylie Davis, "Segregation in the Public Schools—1953," 67 *Harvard Law Review* 377 (1954), which suggested and analyzed eleven different doctrinal outcomes that were possible in *Brown.*

110. This is one of the questions Rosenberg, n.104 above, asks repeatedly and answers in the negative.

111. Rosenberg, ibid., at 134–38, asserts that *Brown*—indeed, civil rights litiga-tion—had no such influence on the Montgomery boycott. The error in this conclusion is made strikingly apparent by Robert Glennon in his article "The Role of Law in the Civil Rights Movement: The Montgomery Bus Boycott, 1955–1957," 9 *Law and History Review* 60 (1991). Glennon's pain-staking historical reconstruction makes these points: (1) Rosa Parks (whose refusal to give up her bus seat to a white man caused her to be prosecuted and led to the boycott) was the secretary of the local branch of the NAACP, the main organization involved in civil rights litigation. (2) The proposal to commence a federal court action challenging the bus segregation laws first came from Robert Carter, an NAACP lawyer who helped prepare the

complaint. (3) The NAACP had decided in 1951 to challenge bus segregation in court, and in 1954, shortly after *Brown*, it had begun such an action in Columbia, S.C. The federal district judge denied relief, but the Fourth Circuit court of appeals reversed, with an opinion centrally based on *Brown*. This decision made headlines in Montgomery in July 1955, four and a half months before Rosa Parks stood her ground. (4) When Martin Luther King, Jr., and other boycott leaders were prosecuted for violating the antiboycott law, they defended by challenging racial discrimination on the basis of *Brown*. (5) In April 1956 the Supreme Court affirmed the Fourth Circuit in the Columbia, S.C., case on a jurisdictional ground; bus companies in 21 southern cities reacted by integrating their buses. On that same day the Montgomery City Lines instructed its drivers to stop segregating bus passengers. (6) In June 1956 the federal court in Montgomery struck down the bus segregation laws, citing *Brown* and the other Supreme Court decisions. Commenting on this decision, Martin Luther King said, "The battle was not yet won. We would have to walk and sacrifice for several more months, while the city appealed the case. But at least we could walk with new hope." When the city did appeal directly to the Supreme Court, NAACP lawyers represented the challenging black riders. (7) The Supreme Court affirmed in February 1957. (8) Glennon sums it up: "There is no proof that the boycott was a necessary causal condition for ending Jim Crow transit in Montgomery. . . . The modern civil rights movement employed a variety of tactics. Successful integration of Montgomery's buses came not from the boycott but from federal judicial intervention that followed from movement attorneys' actions." Ibid., at 94.

Glennon's article was not yet published when Rosenberg wrote. In asserting that litigation did not "inspire" the Montgomery boycott, Rosenberg relied heavily on generalized statements by Martin Luther King, Jr. that *Brown* "cannot explain why it happened in Montgomery," that the boycott "crisis was not produced by . . . even the Supreme Court," and that King saw litigation as no substitute for the mobilization of popular direct action. Rosenberg, n.104 above, at 137–41. Rosenberg notes (at 147–50) that the NAACP leadership and the younger leaders such as King saw each other as rivals for political and financial support. Is it not possible that King might tend to emphasize the brand of civil rights activism he was leading and to minimize the effectiveness of litigation, for which he was not trained? If he had any such inclinations, might they not even be heightened by the memory of what his movement owed to litigation in the Montgomery case? It takes nothing away from King's extraordinary leadership to say that *both* direct action and the NAACP's litigation program contributed in vital ways to the civil rights movement's success.

112. The leading Supreme Court decisions were *Mayor of Baltimore v. Dawson*,

350 U.S. 877 (1955) (public beaches); *Holmes v. Atlanta*, 350 U.S. (1955) (public golf courses); *New Orleans Park Improvement Ass'n v. Detiege*, 358 U.S. 54 (1958) (public parks); *Turner v. Memphis*, 369 U.S. 350 (1962) (restaurant in city airport). Much of the effective labor in dismantling Jim Crow's legal framework was performed by judges of the lower federal courts. This work—and its effects on local southern communities—is detailed by Jack Bass in a widely cited book that Rosenberg does not mention. Bass, n.105 above.

113. See, e.g., T. Branch, *Parting the Waters: America in the King Years, 1954–63*, 301–02, 427–28 (Touchstone ed. 1989) (Atlanta, May 17, 1960; New Orleans, May 17, 1961).

114. The indispensable (and widely cited) reference here is Harry Kalven's book *The Negro and the First Amendment* (1965). This is a major work by a major scholar at Rosenberg's university, the University of Chicago—and I found no mention of it in Rosenberg's book.

115. Rosenberg, n.104 above, repeatedly invokes the Little Rock experience as support for his view that the Supreme Court played an insignificant role in ending Jim Crow. He describes the dispatch of federal troops as evidence that court-ordered desegregation was ineffective, and says (p. 15), "Without elite support (the federal government in this case), the [Supreme] Court's orders would have been frustrated." That assessment seems valid, but it does not support Rosenberg's larger claim that the courts' influence in Little Rock (which had begun with the school board's initial effort to comply with *Brown*) was insignificant. Why did President Eisenhower send the troops? Was he not responding to a political situation in which the courts had placed him? How could he fail to support the authority of the Constitution, as interpreted by the courts? For more on that political situation, see Alexander Bickel's comment quoted in the text below.

116. A. Bickel, *The Least Dangerous Branch: The Supreme Court at the Bar of Politics*, 266–67 (1962).

117. Some white northerners, of course, sympathized with racial subordination—but not on the scale that Rosenberg suggests. He cites a 1958 poll that showed Gov. Faubus among the ten most frequently mentioned "most admired" men, and concludes that this result shows that the Supreme Court's effect on the nation's conscience was minor. A nationwide polling sample, of course, includes southern respondents, and at this time a great many white southerners could be expected to include Faubus on their lists; respondents in other regions would be far less likely to mention him, but they would also be likely to scatter their responses over other famous persons. Faubus did have an admirer here and there in the North, but outside the South he was no hero.

This single overgeneralization is trivial, but it exemplifies a distressing lack of "feel" in the parts of the Rosenberg book that discuss the effects of civil rights litigation on attitudes and opinion. The failure to deal with the point made by Bickel in the quoted passage is another example; so is the assumption (exemplified in his discussion of the Montgomery bus boycott) that a pro–civil rights action or expression has nothing to do with the courts unless it follows immediately after *Brown*, or the actor says he was "inspired" by *Brown*. Perhaps it is unfair to complain that Rosenberg doesn't give enough attention to northern whites' reactions to the video images Bickel accurately describes; Rosenberg was born in 1954, and in 1957 he may not have been a regular viewer of the Huntley-Brinkley news. In any event, the point is not that *Brown* roused the conscience of a nation, but that *Brown* and its concomitants, from the Montgomery boycott to the Little Rock mob scene, significantly promoted the acculturation of northern whites to the view that black Americans should be treated as equal citizens.

118. Rosenberg, n.104 above, chap. 2, says that these two statutes, unlike civil rights litigation, did "bring about . . . social change." By this expression he seems to mean changes in the numbers of black children in school with whites, or the numbers of black voters, or other changes similarly quantifiable.

119. Ibid., at 341. In the case of the civil rights movement, Rosenberg cites no instance in which litigation caused the diversion of resources from other reform ventures. Indeed, his essential argument is that the civil rights movement's successes were achieved through those other avenues: presidential politics, lobbying and petitioning Congress, and direct action that included bus boycotts, lunch-counter sit-ins, freedom rides, and voting rights marches. What Mark Tushnet showed in the context of university and school desegregation is true throughout the civil rights movement: litigation and political activity did not operate at cross-purposes, but complemented each other. M. Tushnet, n.108 above, passim.

120. R. Epstein, *Forbidden Grounds: The Case against Employment Discrimination Laws*, 495 (1992).

121. See, e.g., Delgado and Stefancic, n.94 above, at 1282–84.

122. See Kimberlé Crenshaw's list of negative labels, n.70 above, at 1373.

123. On criminalizing group libel, see Reisman, "Democracy and Defamation: Control of Group Libel," 42 *Columbia Law Review* 727 (1942); Lasson, "Group Libel versus Free Speech: When Big Brother Should Butt In," 23 *Duquesne Law Review* 77 (1984).

124. 343 U.S. 250 (1952).

125. 343 U.S. at 276.

126. Most observers have thought that the doctrine in *Beauharnais* could not survive such First Amendment decisions as *New York Times Co. v. Sullivan*,

376 U.S. 254 (1964), discussed in the text below; *Brandenburg v. Ohio*, 395 U.S. 444 (1969); and *Philadelphia Newspapers v. Hepps*, 475 U.S. 767 (1986). In the case involving the American Nazi party's proposed (but never performed) march in Skokie, Ill., the U.S. court of appeals concluded that *Beauharnais* had lost its vitality as a precedent. *Collin v. Smith*, 578 F.2d 1197 (7th Cir. 1978). From time to time, though, some Justices have cited *Beauharnais* with apparent approval. E.g., White, J. (writing for the Court) in *New York v. Ferber*, 458 U.S. 747, 763 (1982); Blackmun, J., in *Smith v. Collin*, 439 U.S. 916, 918–19 (1978) (dissenting from denial of a writ of certiorari that would have brought the Skokie case to the Supreme Court for decision). After *R.A.V. v. St. Paul*, 112 Sup. Ct. 2538 (1992), also discussed in the text below, a doctrinal comeback for *Beauharnais* looks impossible in the foreseeable future.

127. The most powerful statement of these harms that I know is Mari Matsuda's article "Public Response to Racist Speech: Considering the Victim's Story," 87 *Michigan Law Review* 2320, at 2326–41 (1989).

128. Compare Matsuda, n.127 above, at 2357 (laws should protect "historically oppressed groups" against messages that are "persecutorial, hateful, and degrading"), with Lasson, "Racial Defamation as Free Speech: Abusing the First Amendment," 17 *Columbia Human Rights Law Review* 11, 48 (1985) (all racial groups should be protected against group libel).

129. E.g., Arkes, "Civility and the Restriction of Speech: Rediscovering the Defamation of Groups," 1974 *Supreme Court Review* 281; Note, "A Communitarian Defense of Group Libel Laws," 101 *Harvard Law Review* 682 (1988).

130. See Delgado, "Words That Wound: A Tort Action for Racial Insults, Epithets, and Name-Calling," 17 *Harvard Civil Rights–Civil Liberties Law Review* 133 (1982). For follow-up articles, see Heins, "Banning Words: A Comment on 'Words That Wound,'" 18 ibid. 585 (1983); "Professor Delgado Replies," 18 ibid. 593 (1983).

131. Mari Matsuda's article, n.127 above, is the leading modern discussion calling for criminalizing speech that vilifies historically subordinated groups. Lawrence, n.91 above, and Delgado, "Campus Antiracism Rules: Constitutional Narratives in Collision," 85 *Northwestern University Law Review* 343 (1991), argue for the validity of campus racist speech regulations, but in terms that seem broad enough to serve as arguments in justification of group libel laws. Grey, "Civil Rights vs. Civil Liberties: The Case of Discriminatory Verbal Harassment," *Social Philosophy and Policy*, Spring 1991, 81, and Schmidt, "Freedom of Thought: A Principle in Peril," *Yale Alumni Magazine*, October 1989, 65, focus more narrowly on the campus context. See also Strossen, "Regulating Racist Speech on Campus: A Modest Proposal," 1990 *Duke Law Journal* 484, disagreeing with Lawrence's arguments.

Robert Post exhaustively appraises this literature in analyzing the First Amendment values at stake when government regulates racist speech. Post, Racist Speech, Democracy, and the First Amendment, 32 *William and Mary Law Review* 267 (1991). Post discusses both group libel laws and campus speech codes. For post-*R.A.V.* analyses, see Symposium, "Hate Speech and the First Amendment: On a Collision Course?" 37 *Villanova Law Review* 773 (1993).

132. 112 S. Ct. 2538 (1992).

133. Only five Justices joined Justice Scalia's opinion of the Court. The other four Justices concluded only that the St. Paul ordinance was unconstitutionally overbroad. The Minnesota Supreme Court had interpreted the ordinance to prohibit expression that would cause "anger, alarm, or resentment." This formulation, of course, reaches far beyond speech that is constitutionally punishable (expression that amounts to "fighting words"), criminalizing a lot of constitutionally protected expression.

134. See Warren, "Ruling Unlikely to Hinder State Prosecution Efforts," *Los Angeles Times*, June 23, 1992, A18, col. 3. *Wisconsin v. Mitchell*, 113 S.Ct. 2194 (1993), proved these prosecutors right.

135. The issues raised by the three main opinions in the case range over broad areas of First Amendment doctrine. For example: Is it useful to categorize certain kinds of speech (such as fighting words or obscenity) as unprotected by the First Amendment? Should "viewpoint discrimination" within such an unprotected category (say, a law punishing racist fighting words but not other kinds of fighting words) be evaluated under the First Amendment or the equal protection clause or both? Should it be constitutional for government agencies to enforce a law generally forbidding a type of conduct defined without reference to speech (such as an employment discrimination law) by focusing it on a particular kind of speech (such as sexual harassment on the job)? The case, in short, is a gift to law teachers who want to get their classes into animated debate.

136. Rosenfeld, "Extremist Speech and the Paradox of Tolerance" (book review), 100 *Harvard Law Review* 1457, 1474 n.41 (1987) (quoting F. Haiman).

137. See Schlag, "Freedom of Speech as Therapy" (book review), 34 *UCLA Law Review* 265, 273–74 n.23 (1986).

138. For the classic statement of the role of the criminal law in binding a community together around the values protected by the law, see Emile Durkheim's *The Division of Labor in Society*, bk. 2, chap. 2 (G. Simpson trans. 1933 [1893]).

139. Richard Delgado's comments on the cumulative harms of myriad racist expressions, n. 131 above, at 374–75, 383–84, would seem to apply to private expression as well as to expression in public.

140. See, e.g., Matsuda, n.127 above, at 2357.

141. Compare *American Booksellers Association v. Hudnut*, discussed in chap. 3, holding Indianapolis's antipornography ordinance invalid on a similar "viewpoint discrimination" ground. The First Amendment aside, a law that effectively prohibits whites but not blacks from uttering racist abuse would raise severe problems under the equal protection clause. The point would be obvious if the law were explicitly to "[make] the criminality of an act depend upon the race of the actor," as Justice Potter Stewart said in the miscegenation case *McLaughlin v. Florida*, 379 U.S. 184, 198 (1964) (concurring opinion). A similar result ought to be reached when the law's purpose and application follow the same pattern. An analogous potential for the equal protection clause was discussed in the concurring opinions in *R.A.V. v. St. Paul*, discussed above.

142. See the discussion above of *Beauharnais v. Illinois*.

143. 343 U.S. at 286.

144. 343 U.S. at 275.

145. 376 U.S. 254 (1964). In a narrative combining human drama with analytic power, Anthony Lewis tells the story of this case and its legacy to the freedom of the press. A. Lewis, *Make No Law: The Sullivan Case and the First Amendment* (1991).

146. See, e.g., *Lewis v. City of New Orleans*, 415 U.S. 130 (1974); *Gooding v. Wilson*, 405 U.S. 518 (1972).

147. Commissioner Nicholas Johnson, quoted in L. Powe, *American Broadcasting and the First Amendment*, 176 (1987). On this theme Powe's chapter 10 deserves reading in full.

148. All these examples are contained in Chief Justice Warren's dissenting opinion in the film censorship case *Times Film Co. v. Chicago*, 365 U.S. 43, 50, 69–72 (1961).

149. See, e.g., *Cox v. Louisiana*, 379 U.S. 536 (1965) (street demonstration); *Brown v. Louisiana*, 383 U.S. 131 (1966) (silent vigil in segregated library); *Garner v. Louisiana*, 368 U.S. 157, 201 (1961) (Harlan, J., concurring) (sit-in demonstration at segregated lunch counter as protected speech); *NAACP v. Claiborne Hardware Co.*, 458 U.S. 886 (1982) (statements in support of civil rights boycott).

150. *Board of Education v. Pico*, discussed above at n.99.

151. The University of Michigan's regulation, in contrast, was applied in ways that made its effective reach not only vague but extraordinarily broad. A federal district court held this how-not-to-do-it model invalid in *Doe v. University of Michigan*, 721 F. Supp. 852 (E.D. Mich. 1989).

152. Addition to sec. 51.00, on student conduct, in Policies Applying to Campus Activities, Organizations, and Students (Part A), University of California, Office of the President, Sept. 21, 1989.

153. University officials (as a group) do seem less likely than local prosecutors

(as a group) to enforce these regulations disproportionately against minority speakers. Indeed, an official of Stanford University indicated an intention to give minority speakers what amounts to an informal exemption from a campus speech code that, read literally, would apply to their racist harassment as well as anyone else's. See G. Gunther, *Constitutional Law,* 1134 (12th ed. 1991). I understand the motivation for this policy, but in a public university it would have raised severe constitutional doubts. In a private university like Stanford it is merely unwise—and, of course, politically foolish.

154. Post, n.131 above, at 324.

155. This case law is not entirely free from First Amendment problems, particularly where the harassment in question is not directed personally to individual employees. See Volokh, "Comment: Freedom of Speech and Workplace Harassment," 39 *UCLA Law Review* 1791 (1992). However, the educational responsibilities of public universities offer added justification for regulating harassment on campus, beyond the purposes that justify government in requiring employers to protect their employees from analogous harassment in the workplace.

156. The words are Carter's, and much of what I say in the opening paragraphs of this section is my reaction to his 1991 book *Reflections of an Affirmative Action Baby.* The book's title indicates the self-reflective quality of its substance and style; Carter does not conceal his inner conflicts. The words quoted in the text are at p. 3, where Carter signals an "ambivalence" that appears repeatedly in his major arguments. The conflicts not only go to the costs and benefits of affirmative action, but to broader questions as well: for example, the idea of a distinctive black American culture. On two intertwined points, Carter makes clear that he is not ambivalent. He rejects utterly the notion that there is a single, correct "black point of view," and he insists on the variety that lurks behind the group label "black Americans." Like most books worth reading, this one is valuable not so much for its policy proposals as for the questions it raises. They are all part of the larger question, How shall we think about race?

Carter's narrative style is one adopted in a number of recent writings by law academics. No sampling of this literature should omit Derrick Bell's two books *And We Are Not Saved* (1990) and *Faces at the Bottom of the Well: The Permanence of Racism* (1992), nor Patricia Williams's *The Alchemy of Race and Rights: The Diary of a Law Professor* (1991). (I return to Williams and Bell in chap. 7.) To continue the sampling, one would need to include, among others, the articles of Mari Matsuda and Richard Delgado. See Matsuda, n.127 above (racist speech); "Voices of America: Accent, Antidiscrimination Law, and a Jurisprudence for the Last Reconstruction," 100 *Yale Law Journal* 1329 (1991); and "Looking to the Bottom: Critical Legal Studies and

Reparations," 22 *Harvard Civil Rights–Civil Liberties Law Review* 323 (1987) (reparations for interned Japanese Americans). See also Delgado, n.131 above (campus speech codes); "The Imperial Scholar: Reflections on a Review of Civil Rights Literature," 132 *University of Pennsylvania Law Review* 561 (1984); "Affirmative Action as a Majoritarian Device: Or, Do You Really Want to Be a Role Model?" 89 *Michigan Law Review* 1222 (1991); and "Legal Storytelling for Oppositionists: A Plea for Narrative," 87 *Michigan Law Review* 2411 (1989). Charles Lawrence, examining his own teaching and scholarship, shows the power of subjectivity and of stories (of students, of teachers, in books) to infuse legal issues with the humanity that makes reality accessible—all in the service of what he calls "liberationist teaching." Lawrence, "The Word and the River: Pedagogy as Scholarship as Struggle," 65 *Southern California Law Review* 2231 (1992). For a nonracial analogy, see Margaret Radin's article effectively drawing on her own experience as a woman law professor: "Affirmative Action Rhetoric," 8 *Social Philosophy and Policy* 130 (1991). For contrasting overviews of this body of legal literature, see Abrams, "Hearing the Call of Stories," 79 *California Law Review* 971 (1991); and Farber and Sherry, "Telling Stories out of School: An Essay on Legal Narratives," 45 *Stanford Law Review* 807 (1993).

From Frederick Douglass to Malcolm X and beyond, this genre has long been abundant outside law school walls. Among recent narrative works offering disparate answers to the question, How shall we think about race? are Shelby Steele's *The Content of Our Character* (1990), Alice Walker's *In Search of Our Mother's Gardens* (1983), and Richard Rodríguez's *Hunger of Memory* (1981).

157. Carter, n.156 above, at 2.

158. Shelby Steele suggests that a racial preference may produce an internal label that affects the sense of self of its intended beneficiary, and he suggests a causal explanation that is more modern. A black American, he says, should "watch out that your closest friend may be your greatest enemy," for white liberals use racial preferences to "encourage us to identify with our victimization." Monroe, "Nothing Is Ever Simply Black and White" (interview), *Time*, Aug. 12, 1991, 2. Randall Kennedy argues, to the contrary, that most black beneficiaries "correctly view affirmative action as rather modest compensation for the long period of racial subordination of blacks as a group. . . . [Further, they] view claims of meritocracy with skepticism. . . . Overt exclusion of blacks from public and private institutions of education and employment was one massive affront to meritocratic pretensions." Kennedy, "Persuasion and Distrust: A Comment on the Affirmative Action Debate," 99 *Harvard Law Review* 1327, 1332 (1986).

159. This is one reason why I doubt that this sort of implicit labeling would be lessened if affirmative action were formally justified (as Carter suggests) as a way of opening up opportunities to people who had been denied them.

160. In this discussion I follow Carter's example, referring to the labeling of black people. Thus I leave to the reader the repeated translations, at once awkward and potentially misleading, that are required to make the discussion relevant to other identifications—by race, ethnicity, handicap, etc.—used in affirmative action programs.

161. Carter, n.156 above, at 84. As one who was "present at the creation" of affirmative action in the UCLA law school, I testify that Carter has correctly identified the justification that was most prominent in those early days. But any program adopted by a substantial number of people—especially a group of academics—will reflect a multitude of purposes, and affirmative action is no exception. Many objectives were mentioned in those (all-white) faculty meetings in the late 1960s: compensation for past racial injustice; providing lawyers for underrepresented black and Latino communities, or for the poor; recognition that the existing admissions system, emphasizing the ability to do well on tests, measured only a narrow band on the spectrum of abilities needed to be a good lawyer. Some of us also suggested that diversifying our classes would have educational benefits. Still, at the center of gravity of all these objectives was the one Carter mentions: providing an opportunity for legal education to people who had previously lacked that opportunity. For all these varied purposes, we adopted rough-cut racial and ethnic quotas for our entering classes—rough-cut in the sense that the numbers were not entirely rigid, and that we sought admittees who could successfully complete their studies.

162. 438 U.S. 265 (1978).

163. Universities sought to devise programs that would pass the test of the equal protection clause—that is, would satisfy Justice Powell along with the four Justices who had voted in *Bakke* to uphold even a presumptive racial quota. No doubt the multimembered faculties that adopted these programs still believed affirmative action would serve many different purposes, but we were not playing Let's Pretend. At UCLA I heard no one say, even in private, that "diversity" was a disguise for a quota; nor has our admissions system so operated. We did see, as Justice Powell did, that tokenism would not serve the educational purposes of diversity.

164. We return to the subject of affirmative action, and specifically to the *Bakke* case, in chap. 7.

165. Carter, n.156 above, at 25.

166. For a fuller discussion of the point in the text, see Karst and Horowitz, "The Bakke Opinions and Equal Protection Doctrine," 14 *Harvard Civil Rights–Civil Liberties Law Review* 7, 13–15 and passim (1979).

167. See, e.g., Karst, n.59 above, at 158–72. For specific analysis of the views of Justices Powell and O'Connor, see Karst, n.41 above, at 35–46.

168. Compare Clifford Geertz's metaphor for culture, an "acted document." C. Geertz, *The Interpretation of Cultures*, 10 (1973).

169. The public inquiry that followed the beating of Rodney King made clear
that a racially integrated police force will not necessarily be free from
racism. See n.28 above. Just as Brenda Patterson's problem lay mainly with
her supervisor, good leadership can make a difference. The Los Angeles
commission attributed much of the police department's missed opportunity in the field of race relations to insensitivity at the very top. In an
unintended self-caricature that had already become a local legend, the
police chief, questioned about the disproportionate number of black men
among those who had died from police chokeholds, had speculated that
black people might be more susceptible to chokeholds than "normal"
people. *Los Angeles Times*, May 8, 1982, pt. 2, p.1, col. 6. An instructive
counterexample, similarly indicating the importance of effective leadership, is the substantial extent to which the U.S. Army has succeeded in
carrying out racial integration. See chap. 5 below.

170. See chap. 3 above.

171. See Elshtain, "Feminist Discourse and Its Discontents: Language, Power,
and Meaning," in N. Keohane, M. Rosaldo, and B. Gelpi, eds., *Feminist
Theory: A Critique of Ideology*, at 127, 144 (1982). Indeed, it is this confluence
of two enacted narratives that makes conversation itself mutually understandable: "the act of utterance becomes intelligible by finding its place in a
narrative." A. MacIntyre, *After Virtue*, 196 (1981). Gerald López has made
this point in the context of advocacy, including legal advocacy, in "Lay
Lawyering," 32 *UCLA Law Review* 1 (1984). On the role of narratives
(novels, ethnographies, etc.) in promoting human solidarity, see R. Rorty,
Contingency, Irony, and Solidarity, 73–95, 192 (1989). See also "Symposium—
Legal Storytelling," 87 *Michigan Law Review* 2073 (1989).

172. See, e.g., Delgado and Stefancic, n.94 above, at 1277–82.

173. The argument I have made in the text is important not only for interpersonal relations but for relations among racial groups. Alan Wolfe's comment makes this larger point: "People adhere to [social] contracts when
they feel that behind them lies a society with a sense of who its members
are and why their fates are linked." Wolfe, "The New American Dilemma"
(book review), *New Republic*, April 13, 1992, 30, at 36.

174. R. Rorty, *Philosophy and the Mirror of Nature*, 320 (1979).

175. Michelman, "Political Truth and the Rule of Law," 8 *Tel Aviv University
Studies in Law* 281, 284 (1988).

176. Rorty, n.174 above, at 320.

177. Stephen Carter expressly limits his criticism of affirmative action to the
professional level, making no claim "about the propriety of affirmative
action in labor markets demanding less in the way of educational credentials." Carter, n.156 above, at 89 n.

178. G. Jellinek, *Allgemeine Staatslehre* (General theory of the state), 338 (1929).

179. See Burt, "Constitutional Law and the Teaching of the Parables," 93 *Yale Law Journal* 455 (1984).

180. See, e.g., Jaynes and Williams, n.56 above, at 294–324.

181. Patterson, "Race, Gender, and Liberal Fallacies," *New York Times*, Oct. 20, 1991, A15, col. 2.

182. Benjamin, "Master and Slave: The Fantasy of Erotic Domination," in A. Snitow and C. Stansell, eds., *Powers of Desire: The Politics of Sexuality*, 280, 293 (1983). As I suggest in chap. 7, the most important effect of the Thomas hearings on the acculturation of white Americans was that they provoked myriad private conversations between women and men about sexual harassment, the expression of sexuality, and woman-man relations generally.

183. Paula Giddings and Roger Wilkins, interviewed by Ofra Bikel for Bikel's television documentary *Public Hearing, Private Pain*, aired on *Frontline* (PBS), Oct. 13, 1992.

184. Interviewed by Ofra Bikel, n.183 above.

185. See generally Edsall and Edsall, n.3 above.

186. See S. Terkel, *The Great Divide: Second Thoughts on the American Dream* (1988).

Chapter 5

1. See, e.g., De Grazia, "Political Equality and Military Participation," 7 *Armed Forces and Society* 181 (1981); Hartsock, "Masculinity, Citizenship, and the Making of War," *Political Science* 198 (Spring 1984); Janowitz, "Military Institutions and Citizenship in Western Societies," 2 *Armed Forces and Society* 192 (1976); Segal, Kinzer, and Woelfel, "The Concept of Citizenship and Attitudes toward Women in Combat," 3 *Sex Roles* 469 (1977).

2. See chap. 3 above. On masculinity as a set of images—depictions of interests and values—in the specific context of representations of the Vietnam War, see S. Jeffords, *The Remasculinization of America: Gender and the Vietnam War* (1989).

3. See J. McPherson, *The Negro's Civil War*, chap. 2 (1965); M. Binkin and M. Eitelberg, *Blacks and the Military*, 13 (1982). Northern blacks believed that once they put on the uniform it would be hard to deny them the vote. McPherson, above.

4. Binkin and Eitelberg, n.3 above, at 13.

5. McPherson, n.3 above, at 22.

6. Even so, white officers were placed in command of black regiments, and Congress set the pay of black soldiers below that of whites. Ibid., at 174 (white officers) and chap. 14 ("the struggle for equal pay").

7. The Union Army's responses to these events were mixed. Some slaves

were sent back to their masters; others were put to work—or, as the war progressed, used as fighting troops. Ibid., at 22–23, 144–59, chaps. 11–16 passim. Congress eventually adopted acts confiscating rebel property, including slaves. It also repealed the limitation that had excluded blacks from the state-controlled militia. Ibid., at 41, 164.

8. C. Woodward, *The Burden of Southern History*, 73 (1960). For an excellent short account of the politics of race and slavery in the war years, see J. Rawley, *The Politics of Union: Northern Politics During the Civil War*, 71–88 (Bison ed. 1980).

9. M. Berry, *Military Necessity and Civil Rights Policy: Black Citizenship and the Constitution, 1861–1868*, 89 (1977). "In the last year of the war black troops made up large contingents in almost every successful battle in the Department of the South." Counting black people who served the Union forces in other capacities—as cooks and carpenters, laborers and laundresses, servants and spies—one estimate places the total number at nearly 390,000. Binkin and Eitelberg, n.3 above, at 14–15. See also R. Stillman, *Integration of the Negro in the U.S. Armed Forces*, 10 (1972). Leon Litwack eloquently summarizes the story of the "black liberators" in *Been in the Storm So Long: The Aftermath of Slavery*, 64–103 (Vintage ed. 1980).

10. McPherson, n.3 above, at 143, 158. Another estimate places the figure at 38,000. J. Foner, *Blacks and the Military in American History*, 32 (1974). The black death rate was some 35–40 percent higher than that of white troops. Compare Binkin and Eitelberg, n.3 above, at 15 (40 percent), with Foner, above, at 32 (35 percent).

11. Ibid., chap. 13. The 54th Massachusetts Regiment charged Fort Wagner, S.C., and suffered terrible losses. The heroism of the troops was widely celebrated in Northern newspapers and helped to convince Gen. U.S. Grant of the need for increased numbers of black combat soldiers. McPherson, n.3 above, at 188–92. The charge of the 54th was made on July 18, 1863, just one day after several days of antiblack rioting ended in New York.

12. W. DuBois, *Black Reconstruction in America*, 104 (1935).

13. R. Hope, *Racial Strife in the U.S. Military*, 24 (1979); R. Dalfiume, *Desegregation of the U.S. Armed Forces*, 58–63 (1969). Now it was blacks who referred, with some bitterness, to a "white man's war." Hope, above, at 112.

14. Binkin and Eitelberg, n.3 above, at 18. At the outset of the war black troops continued to suffer discrimination in the civilian communities adjoining their bases. Both at home and abroad, morale was low in black labor units, and with some frequency racial violence broke out between white and black soldiers and sailors. Dalfiume, n.13 above, at 73–74, 102; Hope, n.13 above, at 24–25.

Occasionally, proponents of a racially inclusive military force could win a small victory. In 1942 the Navy said it would no longer limit black enlistees to messmen's duties, but would allow blacks to volunteer for general service—which, in this case, meant other support duties. By the end of the war, black enlistees constituted about 4 percent of the Navy and 2.5 percent of the Marine Corps. Segregation remained the rule, however; given the problems of separation on shipboard, in 1944 the Navy established two ships with all-black crews. Soon thereafter a new secretary of the Navy ordered integration of the crews on twenty-five auxiliary ships. Binkin and Eitelberg, n.3 above, at 55–56, 101.

15. Hope, n.13 above, at 93–97.

16. Dalfiume, n.13 above, at 103; L. Nichols, *Breakthrough on the Color Front*, 45–53 (1954); Hope, n.13 above, at 25.

17. See G. Ware, *William Hastie: Grace under Pressure*, 99, 106–07, 129, 134, and chaps. 9–11 (1984).

18. The Hastie and Marshall quotations can be found in Dalfiume, n.13 above, at 61, 46–47; Hope, n.13 above, at 26; Ware, n.17 above, at 99.

19. Hope, n.13 above, at 27. On the effects of racial integration in diminishing racial prejudice, see L. Bogart, ed., *Social Research and the Desegregation of the U.S. Army*, 132–33 (1969).

20. Executive Orders 9980 and 9981, July 26, 1948. Although politics undoubtedly played an important role in the timing of these orders, President Truman had compiled a strong civil rights record during his years in the Senate, and as President he had already established the committee that eventually became the U.S. Civil Rights Commission.

21. See generally M. MacGregor, Jr., *Integration of the Armed Forces, 1940–1965*, 397–427 (U.S. Army Center of Military History 1981). The Marines had only token numbers of blacks in 1949. Ibid., at 460.

22. Broder, "Military's Unending War on Bias," *Los Angeles Times*, Sept. 20, 1989, A1, col. 1.

23. The story is told in absorbing detail by Dalfiume, n.13 above, chaps. 8 and 9.

24. MacGregor, n.21 above, at 428–59. The number of blacks in the Marines increased rapidly during the war; as in the case of Army blacks, they were integrated in response to the pressures of battle. Ibid., at 460–72.

25. See ibid., chap. 10.

26. On the creation and operations of the Defense Race Relations Institute, an ambitious training program, see Hope, n.13 above, chaps. 3–7.

27. 89 *Defense* 30 (September–October 1989).

28. See Healy, "Powell Honors Blacks Who Served," *Los Angeles Times*, Aug. 18, 1989, pt. 1, p. 4, col. 1; Seaman, "A 'Complete Soldier' Makes It," *Time*, Aug. 21, 1989, 24.

29. The other services have not done so well in commissioning black officers.

In 1989 blacks comprised 10.5 percent of the officers in the Army; 5.4 percent in the Air Force; 4.9 percent in the Marine Corps; and only 3.6 percent in the Navy. 89 *Defense* 30 (September-October 1989). See also Halloran, "Women, Blacks, Spouses Transforming the Military," *New York Times*, Aug. 25, 1986, A1, col. 3.

30. See Moskos, "Success Story: Blacks in the Army," *Atlantic*, May 1986, at 64; Moskos, "The All-Volunteer Force and the Marketplace," in E. Dorn, ed., *Who Defends America? Race, Sex, Class in the Armed Forces*, at 75, 80–83 (1989).

31. In April 1993 the Navy asked the secretary of defense to allow women to serve on certain fleet-replenishment ships and some amphibious vessels. If the secretary should approve, this action will place women on ships that enter battle alongside aircraft carriers, thus blurring still further the distinction between "combat" and "noncombat" ships. Healy, "Navy May Open More Ships to Women," *Los Angeles Times*, April 2, 1993, A1, col. 4

32. On the Gulf War, see Campbell, "Combatting the Gender Gulf," 2 *Temple Political & Civil Rights Law Review* 63 (1992); Becraft, "Women in the U.S. Armed Services: The War in the Persian Gulf," 4 *Women & Criminal Justice* 155 (1992). In 1991 Congress repealed the old statutory ban on women as combat pilots in the Navy and Air Force. In 1993 the secretary of defense ordered the services to open combat aircraft jobs to women, proposed congressional action to lift the ban on women in most combat vessels, and ordered the exploration of opportunities for women in a number of ground combat jobs, including the field artillery and combat intelligence. Healy, "Aspin Orders Wider Military Role for Women," *Los Angeles Times*, April 29, 1993, A1, col. 3.

33. Beyond this obvious reservation, some writers argue that women should be seeking to demolish "the structures of militarism." Scales, "Militarism, Male Dominance and Law: Feminist Jurisprudence as Oxymoron?" 12 *Harvard Women's Law Journal* 25, 41 (1989). See also C. Enloe, *Does Khaki Become You? The Militarization of Women's Lives* (1983); W. Chapkis, ed., *Loaded Questions: Women in the Military* (1981). On "feminism's war with war," see J. Elshtain, *Woman and War*, 231–41 (1987). Can there be a feminist argument for full inclusion of women in the central mission of an organization that is bureaucratic, hierarchical, and focused on coercion by violence? My own affirmative answer, centering on the equal citizenship principle, is spelled out in the text.

34. H. Rogan, *Mixed Company: Women in the Modern Army*, 296 (1981).

35. When the services and the Defense Department were resisting the movement in Congress to open the service academies to women, they argued with vehemence that the academies were designed to produce leaders. Leaders were, by definition, combat leaders, and women were excluded from combat. See J. Stiehm, *Bring Me Men and Women: Mandated Change at*

the U.S. Air Force Academy, 20–32 (1981); Goodman, "Women, War, and Equality: An Examination of Sex Discrimination in the Military," 5 *Women's Rights Law Reporter* 243, 254 (1979). Although a few years ago a woman, Kristin Baker, commanded the corps of cadets at West Point, nothing in the years since the academies were sex-integrated indicates any change in the services' assumption that leading a combat unit is an indispensable prerequisite for advancement to high leadership.

36. The military is well known as "a college for many of the Nation's poor" (Norman Dorsen, testifying at a 1970 congressional hearing on the Equal Rights Amendment, quoted in Goodman, n.35 above, at 244) and a major supplier of technical training and veterans' educational benefits.

37. See Korb, "The Pentagon's Perspective," in Dorn, n.30 above, at 19, 26 (1989). One reason for this effect is the services' policy of rotating personnel in and out of line operations. The Army defines combat positions by military occupational specialty (MOS), and every servicemember in a given MOS must be able to fill such a position in combat situations. Thus, if any tank mechanic can be expected to serve in combat conditions, no woman can be a tank mechanic at any time, anywhere. J. Stiehm, *Arms and the Enlisted Woman,* 147 (1989). The Navy rotates its personnel between sea and shore duty, with a general goal of three years in each position. An individual's rotation is affected by his or her specialty. If women are ineligible for any positions on combat ships, and yet are to be placed on the same six-year cycle of rotation, necessarily the total number of women in the Navy must be limited. See Stiehm, above, 267–68; Kornblum, "Women Warriors in a Men's World: The Combat Exclusion," 2 *Law and Inequality* 351 (1984).

38. The work of Rosabeth Moss Kanter is instructive on the general effects of "token women" in an organization. See R. Kanter, *Men and Women of the Corporation* (1977); Kanter, "Some Effects of Proportions on Group Life: Skewed Sex Ratios and Responses to Token Women," 82 *American Journal of Sociology* 965 (1977). On the support role of women in the services, see Kornblum, n.37 above, at 373–78.

39. See Stiehm, n.37 above, at 207, discussing a report to the Department of Defense on sexual harassment of servicewomen and noting the greater incidence of such harassment where U.S. women were few in number.

40. Goodman, n.35 above, at 255.

41. For a good overview of the connection between women's new roles in the services and changes in women's roles in society generally, see Segal and Segal, "Social Change and the Participation of Women in the American Military," 5 *Research in Social Movements and Change* 235 (1983). For thoughtful views of this social change from inside the services, see D. Schneider and C. Schneider, *Sound Off! American Military Women Speak Out* (1988).

42. In 1970, when most veterans of World War II were still alive, a presidential commission estimated that 23.7 million veterans, almost half the employed male population, had served an average of 27 months of active duty in the armed forces. Arkin and Dobrofsky, "Military Socialization and Masculinity," 34 *Journal of Social Issues* 151 (1978).

43. Many women officers and noncommissioned officers have had male subordinates who have directly or indirectly questioned their authority. The problem has been most serious where the number of women is severely limited, such as the Marine Corps, and was more prevalent in the early days of increased numbers of women in the services than it is today. As more and more women are placed in positions of authority, the more natural their authority seems. See generally Schneider and Schneider, n.41 above, at 33–79. This progression is a familiar one in civilian employment, too.

44. See Elshtain, n.33 above, at 221 (*"Who* gets to speak? *Who* listens?"); Scales, n.33 above, at 37–39.

45. For defenses of the combat exclusion, see, e.g., Webb, "Women Can't Fight," 15 *Washingtonian* 144 (November 1979); B. Mitchell, *Weak Link: The Feminization of the American Military* (1989); Kelly, "The Exclusion of Women from Combat: Withstanding the Challenge," 33 *JAG Journal* 77 (1984). For criticism of the exclusion, see, e.g., Stiehm, n.37 above, at 288–304; Goodman, n.35 above; Kornblum, n.37 above; C. Williams, *Gender Differences at Work: Women and Men in Nontraditional Occupations,* chap. 3 (1989).

46. For the contrary assumption, see Moskos, "Army Women," *Atlantic* 71, 78 (August 1990).

47. See, e.g., Schneider and Schneider, n.41 above, at 137–65; Williams, n.45 above, at 83–87; Rogan, n.34 above, at 272–302; Moskos, n.46 above, at 77–78.

48. *MacNeil/Lehrer News Hour,* PBS, Nov. 13, 1992.

49. Thousands of Army women, although banned from positions bearing the "combat" label, have been serving for some time in positions classified as those with "the highest probability of involving a soldier in direct combat." Mitchell, n.45 above, at 122, 143.

50. The Army's slogan is, "Every soldier an emergency rifleman." Tuten, "The Argument against Female Combatants," in N. Goldman, ed., *Female Soldiers—Combatants or Noncombatants?* 237, 249 (1982). The slogan omits women, but in basic training Army women are trained to shoot rifles.

51. *New York Times,* Dec. 8, 1987, pt. 1, p. 1, col. 4.

52. Of the 18,400 soldiers who participated in the Panama operation, some 800 were women, and about 150 were close to enemy fire. Moskos, n.46 above, at 72.

53. The definition of "combat" positions has changed over the years. During

the transition to the administration of President Reagan, someone in the Army Department thought the time was politically ripe for diminishing the visible presence of women in the Army. On the "womanpause" of 1981–82, see J. Holm, *Women and the Military: An Unfinished Revolution*, 380–88 (1982). In 1982, when the Army resegregated basic training, it added 23 jobs to the "combat" list, excluding women. No one familiar with American labor history will be surprised to learn that the list of new men-only specialties added the major building trades: carpenters, masons, plumbers, and electricians. The Army later reopened 13 of the occupational specialties to women. See Stiehm, n.37 above, at 54–67; Kornblum, n.37 above, at 367.

54. Holm, n.53 above, at 395.

55. The Navy and Marines do not have strength-testing programs; in these two services, if you survive the physical demands of boot camp, you're in. In 1981, the season of the "womanpause," the Air Force announced interim strength standards for a number of MOSs, but made no effort to validate the tests by reference to actual job performance. The Army's tortuous efforts to develop strength standards have been driven from the beginning by the "woman question." The problem has been to set standards that will allow small men in the Infantry but still permit a sharp line between the strength ratings of men in general and women in general. The problem is insoluble, and so the Army has used strength tests not to limit assignments but to counsel recruits. Stiehm, n.37 above, at 198–205.

56. See Goodman, n.35 above, at 259–60. See also Segal, "The Argument for Female Combatants," in Goldman, n.50 above, at 267.

57. Some of the group difference in inclination toward aggression appears to be biological, owing to the release of testosterone into male brains, and some of it owes to the ways in which boys and girls are socialized to become the men and women society expects them to be. The basic reference for the biological element in the group difference in aggression is E. Maccoby and C. Jacklin, 1 *Psychology of Sex Differences* 227–47, 360–66 (1974). See also Whiting and Pope, "A Cross-Cultural Analysis of Sex Differences in the Behavior of Children Age Three to Eleven," 91 *Journal of Social Psychology* 171 (1973). Maccoby and Jacklin agree that there is a large element of acculturation in sex-group differences in aggression. See "Sex Differences in Aggression: A Rejoinder and Reprise," 51 *Child Development* 964 (1980), responding to Tieger, "On the Biological Basis of Sex Differences in Aggression," 51 *Child Development* 943 (1980). Today part of that acculturation is the combat exclusion itself.

58. Webb, n.45 above, at 148. James Webb, a Marine officer who fought in Vietnam, later became President Reagan's secretary of the Navy. In case you were wondering, he explains why nature has made "man" aggressive:

"Man must be more aggressive in order to perpetuate the human race. Women don't rape men, and it has nothing to do, obviously, with socially induced differences." Ibid., at 147–48.

59. Treadwell, "Biologic Influences on Masculinity," in H. Brod, ed., *The Making of Masculinities*, at 259, 278–81 (1987).

60. Reinish and Sanders, "A Test of Sex Differences in Aggressive Response to Hypothetical Conflict Situations," 50 *Journal of Personality and Social Psychology* 5 (1985). In combat itself, "man" as the eager aggressor appears to be the exception and not the norm. Only about 15 percent of American riflemen in combat in World War II actually fired their weapons at enemy soldiers. S. L. A. Marshall, *Men against Fire*, 77–78 (1947). In Vietnam, the main victims of fragging—deliberate "friendly" fire—were officers seen by their men as too aggressive.

61. A related argument in defense of the combat exclusion is that pregnancy disables women. Under present regulations, pregnant servicewomen are not sent overseas. The time lost from duty by women is approximately the same as the time lost from duty by men. The difference is that women take more time off for medical reasons, while men miss duty more often for reasons of discipline, alcoholism, and the like. "When I point this out, people tend to dismiss it by saying, 'Well, we can't count that because boys will be boys.'" Korb, n.37 above, at 19, 25. See also Stiehm, n.37 above, at 210–13.

62. *Mississippi University for Women v. Hogan*, 458 U.S. 718, 724 (1982).

63. Quoted in Wright, "The Marine Corps Faces the Future," *New York Times Magazine*, June 20, 1982, 74. General Barrow was fond of saying that "while he wanted his men to be men, he wanted his women to be women." Holm, n.53 above, at 273. So it is that the basic training manual for Women Marines—as they are officially called, to distinguish them from men, who are called Marines—requires recruits to wear makeup, with lipstick and eye shadow the allowable minimum. Women recruits also take classes on makeup, hair care, poise, and etiquette. Williams, n.45 above, at 63 (1989).

64. A derivative worry is that the anticipation of "women coming home in body bags" will weaken "the national resolve," making decisionmakers less willing to deploy troops. This was the view of the Senate Armed Services Committee that rejected registering women for a military draft. The committee's report is quoted by Wendy Webster Williams in her perceptive analysis of *Rostker v. Goldberg*, 453 U.S. 57 (1981), "The Equality Crisis: Some Reflections on Culture, Courts, and Feminism," 7 *Women's Rights Law Reporter* 175, 183 (1982).

65. Judith Stiehm asks, "Is it possible that the aversion of men to the suffering of women is actually based on their feeling that when a woman suffers it is because men have failed to protect that woman? Is the pain they feel *for*

women, or is it the pain of their own failure?" Stiehm, "Women and the Combat Exemption," 10 *Parameters: Journal of the U.S. Army War College* 51, 53 (June 1980). See also Stiehm, n.37 above, at 288–301; J. Stiehm, *Bring Me Men and Women: Change at the U.S. Air Force Academy* (1981), at 224–27.

66. S. Brownmiller, *Against Our Will: Men, Women, and Rape*, 31–113 (1975).

67. Women police officers now routinely face the risks, physical challenges, and cooperative responsibilities of patrol duty, and routinely they perform well. See, e.g., P. Horne, *Women in Law Enforcement* (1980); H. Rogan, n.34 above, at 297–98; P. Bloch and D. Anderson, *Policewomen on Patrol: Final Report* (1974). As more and more women take on these duties, their status in the eyes of male officers progresses—from ornaments to tokens to valued coworkers. In the 1980s women went from 2.4 to 12.2 percent of the Los Angeles force; they are projected to go to 20 percent before the 1990s end. Katz, "L.A. Police United in Attitude, Survey Says," *Los Angeles Times*, Sept. 2, 1990, B1, col. 5, at B6.

68. Studies suggest that the critical mass of women is about one-quarter, if they are not to be singled out in mixed groups. See Thomas and Prather, "Integration of Females into a Previously All-Male Institution," in *Proceedings of the Fifth Symposium on Psychology in the Air Force*, at 100–101 (U.S. Air Force Academy, Department of Behavioral Sciences and Leadership 1976). See also Webber, "Perceptions and Behaviors in Mixed-Sex Work Teams," 15 *Industrial Relations* 121 (1976); Ruble and Higgins, "Effects of Group Sex Composition on Self-Presentation and Sex Typing," 32 *Journal of Social Issues* 125 (1976).

As one would expect, it is the long-term work relationship under conditions in which women are present in more than token numbers that is most likely to produce these changes in men's attitudes toward women coworkers and women supervisors. For validation of this generalization in the military services, see, e.g., Schneider and Schneider, n.41 above, at 42–60; Moskos, n.46 above, at 74.

69. Stiehm, n.37 above, at 134–54.

70. Webb, n.45 above, at 147. The Senate committee that recommended in 1981 against registering women for the draft said that sex-integrated combat units would be "an experiment to be conducted in war with unknown risk." Williams, n.45 above, at 183.

71. It was said that women must be kept out of public roles, especially those with decisionmaking powers; their presence in, say, the legislature, might distract men from exercising the Reason that should guide their deliberations. See Okin, "Women and the Making of the Sentimental Family," 11 *Philosophy and Public Affairs* 65, 87 (1982).

72. In a two-year Defense Department survey of 20,000 servicewomen, 64 percent of the women said they had experienced some form of sexual

harassment during the previous year. In civilian employment, where women are a far greater proportion of the work force, the comparable figure runs from 30 to 40 percent. Schmitt, "2 Out of 3 Women in Military Study Report Sexual Harassment Incidents," *New York Times,* Sept. 12, 1990, A12, col. 1.

73. In 1991 in Las Vegas, the Tailhook Association (named for the hook that catches a plane as it lands on an aircraft carrier) held its annual convention of Navy pilots. By tradition the convention allows junior officers to ask questions of the most senior flying officers. When a woman lieutenant asked the nine male admirals on the stage how long it would be before women would fly combat missions, "scores of male fliers took to their feet with a rising tide of hisses, jeers and catcalls." Healy and Bornmeier, "For Women in the Navy, Rough Waters Run Deep," *Los Angeles Times,* June 28, 1992, A1, col. 5. A few hours later, in the hotel corridor, came the group sexual assault. Kempster, "What Really Happened at Tailhook Convention," ibid., April 24, 1993, A1, col. 5.

74. Broder and Abrahamson, "Navy to Undergo Training to End Sex Harassment," *Los Angeles Times,* July 4, 1992, A1, col. 2 ("alcohol-inspired antics"); Healy, "140 Officers Faulted in Tailhook Sex Scandal," ibid., April 24, 1993, A1, col. 4 (DOD report).

75. See also Stiehm, n.37 above, at 16–19, 150–53. For women's responses to sexual harassment, and confirmation that tokenism exacerbates the problem, see Schneider and Schneider, n.41 above, at 42–49.

76. Quoted in Dalfiume, n.14 above, at 57.

77. Quoted in ibid., at 55. Similar sentiments were expressed by a number of white soldiers, both officers and enlisted men, during the Korean War. L. Bogart, n.19 above, at 154–55. But a "large proportion of the white soldiers express[ed] a willingness to accept Negroes in positions of authority." Ibid., at 155. See also ibid., at 139, 155–59 (white attitudes toward black leaders); 159–62 (black attitudes toward white and black leaders).

78. Webb, n.45 above, at 273, 146, 147.

79. Women fought with the French Resistance; with the Italian and Yugoslav partisans; in the Polish uprising; and in the Soviet Union's Red Army. In the years since then, American women have come under enemy fire as support troops in the Gulf War, as and Army nurses in Korea and Vietnam. See generally S. Saywell, *Women in War* (1986).

80. For the argument that women in combat will impair male bonding and thus combat effectiveness, see, e.g., Gabriel, "Women in Combat? Two Views," *Army Magazine* 44 (March 1980); Tuten, n.50 above, at 251–52. See, e.g., S. Stouffer et al., *The American Soldier,* 98–100 (1949); M. Gerzon, *A Choice of Heroes: The Changing Faces of American Manhood,* 54–57 (1982). On representations of battlefield male bonding—with both explicit and im-

plicit exclusion of women—as a temporary solution to rivalry among male (racial) groups, see Jeffords, n.2 above, at 54–62.

81. See Devilbiss, "Gender Integration and Unit Deployment: A Study of GI Jo," 11 *Armed Forces and Society* 523, 540–44 (1985). Capt. Carol Barkalow, who served in the 1991 Gulf War with a combat support unit, writes: "In the desert, I witnessed the same type of relationships forming between men and women as traditionally occur among men—mutual respect and caring [born] of enduring similar dangers and hardships. My division ended up 50 kilometers west of Basra, Iraq. At one point, I lived in a tent with six men and another woman. There were no problems." Barkalow, "Let Women in the Military 'Be All That We Can Be,'" *Los Angeles Times,* July 28, 1991, M2, col. 4.

82. Quoted in Webb, n.45 above, at 280.

83. The Supreme Court forcefully made this point in the context of sex-stereotyping in *Mississippi University for Women v. Hogan,* 458 U.S. 718 (1982).

84. See W. Menninger, *Psychiatry in a Troubled World,* 56–68, 269 (1948).

85. A number of studies confirm what common experience suggests: that the strong rejection of homosexuality is correlated positively with endorsement of traditional sex-role stereotypes. See, e.g., Krulewitz and Nash, "Effects of Sex Role Attitudes and Similarity on Men's Rejection of Male Homosexuals," 38 *Journal of Personality and Social Psychology* 67 (1980); Dunbar, Brown, and Amoroso, "Some Correlates of Attitudes toward Homosexuality," 89 *Journal of Social Psychology* 271 (1973); MacDonald, Huggins, Young, and Swanson, "Attitudes toward Homosexuality: Preservation of Sex Morality or the Double Standard?" 40 *Journal of Consulting and Clinical Psychology* 161 (1972).

86. Ibid., at 33, 201.

87. Such estimates are notoriously hard to validate, for they raise the definitional problem that confounds analysis of this whole subject: What determines who is "a homosexual"? Allan Bérubé uses the population percentages suggested by the Kinsey Institute's wartime surveys, and estimates the number of male homosexual service members during World War II to be "at least 650,000 and as many as 1.6 million." A. Bérubé, *Coming Out Under Fire: The History of Gay Men and Women in World War II,* 3 (1990).

88. See, e.g., Bérubé, n.87 above, at 21, 24.

89. 10 U.S.C. §925 (1992).

90. 32 C.F.R. pt. 41, app. A, pt. 1.H. The final version of the policy was issued in 1981. Previous regulations allowed commanders to make exceptions to the general rule requiring the discharge of homosexual servicemembers, retaining gay and lesbian members who were of special value to the services. In *Matlovich v. Secretary of the Air Force,* 591 F.2d 852 (D.C. Cir. 1978),

implemented in 23 *Fair Employment Practice Cases* (BNA) 1251 (D.D.C. 1980), the District of Columbia Circuit held that the Air Force could not discharge a gay airman unless it clearly articulated standards for applying the exception. The regulation discussed here was the Reagan Defense Department's response. Instead of removing the bar to gay members of the services, DOD eliminated the commanders' authority to make exceptions.

91. This assumption is hard to prove, given the historically strong incentives for gay and lesbian servicemembers to hide their sexual orientation. See generally Gross, "For Gay Soldiers, Furtive Lives of Despair," *New York Times*, April 10, 1990, A1, col. 2. A 1988 report of the Defense Personnel Security Research and Education Center to the Defense Department made the assumption that gay men and lesbians comprised 3 to 10 percent of servicemembers—which, given some two million men and women in uniform, translates to a range of 60,000 to 200,000 persons who were theoretically subject to discharge. T. Sarbin and K. Karols, "Nonconforming Sexual Orientations and Military Suitability," 22 (December 1988). This study, which the Defense Department did not even acknowledge until it was leaked to members of Congress, also called for a thorough reexamination of the DOD's exclusion policy.

One trouble with playing this numbers game is that the aggregate statistics may obscure the faces of real people. In a tour de force of modern journalism, Randy Shilts has brought to the foreground the personal stories of more than a thousand gay and lesbian veterans and servicemembers. His book *Conduct Unbecoming: Gays and Lesbians in the U.S. Military* (1993) culminates five years of interviews and painstaking analysis of official records. Behind every case name in my footnotes is a story recounted by Shilts. For anyone who wants to understand this subject, *Conduct Unbecoming* is an indispensable text.

92. The individual services had their own regulations, which tracked the DOD policy in all matters relevant here.

93. Army Regulation 635–200, quoted in *Watkins v. United States Army*, 875 F.2d 699, 713 n.5 (9th Cir. 1989) (en banc) (Norris, J., concurring). A similar Navy regulation, adopted in 1978, was involved in *Dronenburg v. Zech*, 741 F.2d 1388 (D.C. Cir 1984).

94. See Halley, "The Politics of the Closet: Towards Equal Protection for Gay, Lesbian, and Bisexual Identity," 36 *UCLA Law Review* 915, 951–53 (1989).

95. A military psychiatrist analyzed the cases of eleven transsexuals in the military—men who were requesting cross-gender hormones, or sex-reassignment surgery, or both. He reported one "striking similarity" in nearly all the cases: "They joined the service, in their words, 'to become a real man.'" For these men, joining the service was a last-ditch "flight into hypermasculinity" that failed to end their gender-dysphoria. Brown,

"Transsexuals in the Military: Flight into Hypermasculinity," 17 *Archives of Sexual Behavior* 527, 529 (1988).

96. Bérubé, n.87 above, at 28.

97. The statistics are collected in Sarbin and Karols, n.90 above, Appendix B. See also Benecke and Dodge, "Recent Developments—Military Women in Nontraditional Job Fields: Casualties of the Armed Forces' War on Homosexuals," 13 *Harvard Women's Law Journal* 215, 222 (1990); K. Bourdonnay, R. Johnson, J. Schuman, and B. Wilson, "Fighting Back: Lesbian and Gay Draft," *Military and Veterans Issues* 5–6 (1985).

98. Here I have drawn on Michelle Benecke's and Kirstin Dodge's thoughtful analysis of the services' bout of lesbian bashing in the 1980s, n.97 above. See also Stiehm, n.37 above, at 128–32.

99. See Treadwell, n.59 above, at 191–218. On the persistence of the canard, see Stiehm, n.37 above, at 25–26.

100. See Benecke and Dodge, n.97 above, at 237–38. In the services as elsewhere, men as a group have tended to be more nervous about homosexuality than are women as a group. See, e.g., Moskos, n.46 above, at 74. As we saw in chap. 3, historically both men and women have been more tolerant of lesbian relationships than of male homosexual relationships. Given this pattern, the focus of Navy and Marine investigators on lesbians might seem odd. But the investigations, usually instigated by men and primarily conducted by men, are understandable as means to keep the gender line from becoming blurred.

101. The label is soundly grounded in history; the "witch hunts" of centuries past were often directed at departure from conventional sexual norms. See, e.g., C. Merchant, *The Death of Nature*, 127–48 (1980). See the bibliography in A. Evans, *Witchcraft and the Gay Counterculture*, 171–76 (1978).

102. A deviation from this pattern was the 1990 investigation into a "ring" of eighteen male noncommissioned officers at Carswell Air Force Base in Texas. See Weisberg, "Gays in Arms," *New Republic*, Feb. 19, 1990, 20.

103. Note 90 above.

104. To cite just one live example, consider the case of Sgt. Perry Watkins. While the Army Department's lawyers were litigating to throw him out of the Army for being gay, Sergeant Watkins was given extraordinarily high ratings for job performance and professionalism (85 out of 85 possible points) and was recommended for promotion. His immediate superior officer said, in the course of an extremely laudatory evaluation, "SSG Watkins is without exception, one of the finest Personnel Action Center Supervisors I have encountered. . . . I would gladly welcome another opportunity to serve with him, and firmly believe that he will be an asset to any unit to which he is assigned." *Watkins v. United States Army*, 875 F.2d 699, 703–04 (9th Cir. 1989) (en banc).

105. Gross, "Navy Is Urged to Root out Lesbians Despite Abilities," *New York Times*, Sept. 2, 1990, pt. 1, p. 9, col. 5.

106. The DOD has, however, subjected gay applicants for security clearances to "expanded investigations" that were not mandated for other applicants. This discrimination was upheld in *High Tech Gays v. Defense Industrial Security Clearance Office*, 895 F.2d 563 (9th Cir. 1990), and the Ninth Circuit refused to hear the case en banc. Judge William Canby, dissenting from the latter order, argued forcefully for a standard of judicial review that is more demanding than the panel's limp-wrist, "rational basis" review, and he demolished the argument that the exclusion of persons who were openly homosexual was founded on their conduct. His remark applied with equal force to the exclusion of lesbians and gay men from the armed forces: "The Department of Defense is discriminating against homosexuals for what they *are*, not what they do." 909 F.2d 375, at 380 (emphasis in original).

   The National Security Agency has stopped denying homosexual persons security clearances for access to "sensitive compartmented information," a very high classification. Sarbin and Karols, n.93 above, at 5. On security clearances, see generally "Developments in the Law—Sexual Orientation and the Law," 102 *Harvard Law Review* 1508, 1556 (1989).

107. Lancaster, "Defense Study: Gays Pose No Greater Security Risk; Military's Ban on Homosexuals Unaffected," *Washington Post*, Oct. 10, 1991, A20; Gibbs, "Marching out of the Closet," *Time*, Aug. 19, 1991, 14, at 15.

108. Weisberg, n.102 above, at 21.

109. E.g., *Pruitt v. Cheney*, 963 F.2d 1160 (1991), cert. denied, 113 S. Ct. 655 (1992). General criticisms of the exclusion policy are stated succinctly by Richard Mohr in *Gays/Justice: A Study of Ethics, Society, and Law*, 194–99 (1988). For more elaborate critiques, centered on the unconstitutionality of the policy, see Judge William Norris's opinion for a Ninth Circuit panel that held the Army's regulations unconstitutional, *Watkins v. United States Army*, 847 F.2d 1329 (9th Cir. 1988), aff'd en banc on other grounds, 875 F.2d 699 (1989); and his concurring opinion in the en banc proceeding, 875 F.2d at 711. Similar arguments are made in Bourdonnay et al., n.98 above, chap. 1; Harris, "Permitting Prejudice to Govern: Equal Protection, Military Deference, and the Exclusion of Lesbians and Gay Men from the Military," 17 *New York University Review of Law and Social Change* 171 (1989–1990); "Developments in the Law—Sexual Orientation," 102 *Harvard Law Review* 1508, 1559–62 (1989); Note, "Homosexuals in the Military: They Would Rather Fight than Switch," 18 *John Marshall Law Review* 937 (1985); and Weisberg, n.102 above.

110. *Meinhold v. United States Department of Defense*, 808 F. Supp. 1455 (C.D. Calif. 1993).

111. On the telephone campaign, see Tumulty, "Busy Capitol Phones May Not Ring of Truth," *Los Angeles Times*, Jan. 30, 1992, A16, col. 1. Now that the anti-abortion movement has proved a failure in presidential politics, Randall Terry, the leader of Operation Rescue, has begun to defend the exclusion of gay and lesbian Americans from the services. See Lauter, "Clinton Strikes Deal with Military on Gays," ibid., Jan. 29, 1993, A1, col.6, at A20. This shift of attention recalls the charity that switches its target from one disease to another rather than stop soliciting contributions.

112. The first polls to be released were preliminary surveys of Air Force and Army personnel. The Army then set about preparing "a new, more detailed round of polls," and the Marine Corps followed suit. Meanwhile, the Navy "adamantly refused to use polls or to establish a planning group to draw up contingency plans for any change in policy, believing that such planning would undercut its opposition to lifting the ban, Pentagon officials said." Healy, "Military Using Polls in Debate over Gays," *Los Angeles Times*, Feb. 7, 1993, A19, col. 1. The *Times* took its own poll in shopping centers and residential neighborhoods, and the title of its story tells the result. Healy, "74% of Military Enlistees Oppose Lifting Gay Ban," ibid., Feb. 28, 1993, A1, col. 2.

113. Pine, "Issue Explodes into an All-out Lobbying War," *Los Angeles Times*, Jan. 28, 1993, A1, col. 6. The doctor who appears in the video, who once led the Santa Cruz, Calif., chapter of the John Birch Society, ran for Congress in 1988 on the Republican ticket. His videotaped recital of exotic sex practices is based on a sample of 41 gay men in a study by a researcher who was dropped from membership by the American Psychological Association and censured by the American Sociological Association for consistently misrepresenting research. Colker, "Statistics in 'Gay Agenda' Questioned," ibid., Feb. 22, 1993, A16, col. 1. In February 1993 the video was shown on Rev. Pat Robertson's *700 Club* television program, and by then more than 25,000 copies had been distributed by Springs of Life Ministries. Colker, "Anti-Gay Video Highlights Church's Agenda," ibid., Feb. 22, 1993, A1, col. 3.

114. A "former senior defense official" (i.e., not a Clinton appointee) said that Senator Nunn "sees this in part as a *mano-a-mano* test of manhood about who runs defense policy." Lauter, "Clash with Nunn Becomes Test of Power for Clinton," *Los Angeles Times*, Jan. 28, 1993, A1, col. 5. It is hard to think of a more appropriate political arena for playing manhood games.

115. Healy and Tumulty, "Aides Say Clinton to End Prosecution of Military's Gays," *Los Angeles Times*, Jan. 28, 1993, A1, col. 5. When military leaders opposed the racial integration of the services in 1948, somehow no one suggested that black soldiers be made to wear white masks.

116 Memorandum of Secretary of Defense Les Aspin to Secretaries of the Army, Navy, and Air Force and Chairman, Joint Chiefs of Staff, "Policy on Homo- sexual Conduct in the Armed Forces," July 19, 1993.

117. Senate Bill 1298, § 546 (103d Cong., 1st Sess., 1993).

118. *Beller v. Middendorf,* 632 F.2d 788 (9th Cir. 1980).

119. Bérubé, n.87 above, chap. 4; ibid., at 40, 52, and passim. The acceptance disappeared when gay soldiers were imprisoned for homosexual acts. Ibid., chap. 8. The obvious difference is that a coworker is seen as a whole person, while a prisoner is seen as an abstraction, "a homosexual."

120. See Boxall, "Gays Relate War Stories of Shadow Life in Military," *Los Angeles Times,* Feb. 7, 1993, A1, col. 5, at A8.

121. Ibid.

122. Punishable under Article 134 of the Uniform Code of Military Justice, 10 U.S.C. §934, authoritatively interpreted by the military justice system to forbid "lewd and lascivious" acts and "indecent assault."

123. The "discipline and command" reference may also have reflected a fear that gay officers and NCOs would impose their attentions on subordi- nates, or would form attachments that might lead to favoritism or other- wise blur the lines of authority. The same arguments have been offered as reasons for drastically limiting the number of women in the services. E.g., Webb, n.45 above, at 275; Mitchell, n.45 above, at 189–92. Homosexual attachments are no more likely than heterosexual attachments to interfere with command relations, and the obvious nondiscriminatory response to such cases is to apply the services' existing rules against sexual harassment and fraternization. For half a century the services have included large numbers of gay members; it is ludicrous to suggest that their presence during all these years has undermined the system of command.

124. Here, too, lessons can be learned from the experience of police depart- ments. Not only are more and more officers openly acknowledging their gay and lesbian identity, but departments from New York to San Diego are engaged in vigorous public campaigns to attract gay and lesbian recruits. California's Commission on Peace Officer Standards and Training, which certifies police officers, recently reported on a statewide study. One of the commission's conclusions bears specifically on the question whether gay soldiers are to be trusted in the pressures of combat: "The stiff upper lip macho mentality characteristic of the average police officer collapses under too much stress." Serrano, "Gay Police Leave the Shadows," *Los Angeles Times,* Sept. 3, 1990, A1, col. 1, at A26. The police chief of Portland, Oregon, has remarked on the similarity between questions asked about gay servicemembers and questions asked about gay officers: "Can they share a locker room? Can you count on them under fire?" His answer to

both questions is yes. See Balzar, "Why Does America Fear Gays?" ibid., Feb. 4, 1993, A1, col. 1, at A14.

125. Karst, "The Pursuit of Manhood and the Desegregation of the Armed Forces," 38 *UCLA Law Review* 499, 563–81 (1991).

126. Memorandum for Active and Reserve General Officers, dated July 21, 1992, and signed by Gen. C. E. Mundy, Jr., commandant of the Marine Corps. Enclosure (1) is entitled "CMC Comments on the DOD Policy Regarding Homosexuality"; the quoted material is on p. 1 (italics in original). The best response to the claim that antigay discrimination by the services differs from racial discrimination is William Eskridge's article "Race and Sexual Orientation in the Military: Ending the Apartheid of the Closet," 2 *Reconstruction* 52 (no. 2, 1993).

127. In an interview a black sailor said, "Being gay is a lifestyle. Being black is no lifestyle. It's what we are. There's a difference." Martinez and Perry, "Where Military People Gather, There's Only One Topic Debated," *Los Angeles Times*, Jan. 28, 1993, A16.

128. This is the term used by a panel of the U.S. Court of Appeals to describe the assertions in the DOD's former exclusion regulation. See *benShalom v. Marsh*, 881 F.2d 454, 461 (7th Cir. 1989), certiorari denied, 110 S. Ct. 1296 (1990).

129. J. tenBroek, E. Barnhart, and F. Matson, *Prejudice, War, and the Constitution: Causes and Consequences of the Evacuations of the Japanese Americans in World War II*, 110 (1970).

130. For a capsule exposition of the normative system that equates competence in combat with "aggressive masculinity" in the traditional mode, see Hirschhorn, "The Separate Community: Military Uniqueness and Servicemen's Constitutional Rights," 62 *North Carolina Law Review* 177, 222 (1984).

131. See Holm, n.53 above, at 258–59, 273–74, and chaps. 18 and 19 generally.

132. It was the leadership of the relevant congressional committees that scuttled DOD's proposal to repeal the laws barring women from combat positions—albeit with an assist from some generals and admirals who differed with their immediate civilian superiors. See Holm, n.53 above, at 337–45. See also Williams, n.45 above, at 54–55.

133. See Stiehm, n.37 above, at 47–67; J. Holm, n.53 above, at 380–88. See generally n.53 above.

134. See generally Eisenstein, "The Sexual Politics of the New Right: Understanding the 'Crisis of Liberalism' for the 1980s," in N. Keohane, M. Rosaldo, and B. Gelpi, eds., *Feminist Theory: A Critique of Ideology*, at 77 (1982).

135. For another revealing example of the role of politicians in policing the

gender line in the services, see Wendy Webster Williams's discussion of Congress's 1981 decision to limit draft registration to men, n.64 above, at 183–85 and passim.

136. Gross, n.91 above, at A10.

137. Gibbs, n.107 above, at 15. See also Shilts, "Military Again Targets Gays in Wake of War," *San Francisco Chronicle*, Aug. 5, 1991, A1, col. 1.

138. Quoted in Rosenthal, "After the Riots; Quayle Says Riots Sprang from Lack of Family Values," *New York Times*, May 20, 1992, A1, col. 6; and "After the Riots; Excerpts from Vice President's Speech on Cities and Poverty," ibid., at A20, col. 1. Quayle's remark about drugs left out one important point: white high schoolers are twice as likely as black high schoolers to use cocaine. "Studies Deflate Myth of Blacks and Drugs," *Chicago Tribune*, May 14, 1992, 2, col. C.

139. A large and well-crafted literature documents this point, from Victorian England to present-day America. See generally G. Himmelfarb, *The Idea of Poverty: England in the Early Industrial Age* (1984); J. Handler, *Reforming the Poor*, 8 (1972).

140. F. Piven and R. Cloward, *Regulating the Poor: The Functions of Social Welfare* (1971). For a short critique of the rhetoric of "social control" and the anti-coercion sentiment behind the rhetoric, see Schwartz, "The Moral Environment of the Poor," *Public Interest*, 21, 29–32 (Spring 1991).

141. J. Handler and Y. Hasenfeld, *The Moral Construction of Poverty: Welfare Reform in America*, 10 (1991), characterizing C. Murray, *Losing Ground: American Social Policy, 1950–1980* (1984) and L. Mead, *Beyond Entitlement: The Social Obligations of Citizenship* (1986).

142. Note 138 above.

143. See generally D. Ellwood, *Poor Support: Poverty in the American Family* (1988).

144. Rosenthal, "Campaign: The Politics of Morality," *New York Times*, May 22, 1992, A19, col. 1.

145. See Whitehead, "What Is Murphy Brown Saying? For Starters, That Unwed Motherhood Is a Glamorous Option," *Washington Post*, May 10, 1992, C5. Whitehead is a research associate at the Institute for American Values, described briefly in n.179 below. After the election, Whitehead returned to the fray in "Dan Quayle Was Right," *Atlantic Monthly*, April 1993, 47. The thesis of the article is more restrained than its provocative title might suggest. Whitehead argues for 21 pages that children tend to do best in two-parent families where both parents are the children's natural parents. Quayle's thesis was far more sweeping, as I show in the text.

146. Wines, "Views on Single Motherhood Are Multiple at White House," *New York Times*, May 21, 1992, A1, col. 3.

147. Broder, "Quayle Decries Hollywood for 'Adversary Culture,'" *Los An-*

geles Times, Sept. 3, 1992, A24, col. 2 (quoting Quayle spokesman David Beckwith). See also M. Medved, *Hollywood v. America*, 95–157 (1992).

148. See E. J. Dionne, Jr., *Why Americans Hate Politics*, 300–316 (1991); T. Edsall and M. Edsall, *Chain Reaction: The Impact of Race, Rights, and Taxes on American Politics*, chap. 9 (1991); S. Blumenthal, *Pledging Allegiance: The Last Campaign of the Cold War* (1991).

149. In a tough editorial, the *Los Angeles Times* said this: "By raising the issue of 'family values,' the vice president has attempted to punt the presidential campaign away from the economy, which clearly has not improved fast enough to assure a November win, to the culture." "Political Value in the Values Debate," *Los Angeles Times*, June 16, 1992, B6, col. 1.

150. The idea of a "culture of poverty," defined to a considerable extent by the immoral behavior of the "underclass," is not new. See, e.g., K. Auletta, *The Underclass*, 27–29 (1982). On the "culture of poverty" thesis and related explanations of intergenerational poverty, and the role of such theories as "a conservative rationalization for cutting welfare," see M. Katz, *The Undeserving Poor: From the War on Poverty to the War on Welfare*, 9–52 (1989).

151. This implication quickly drew fire from single mothers both black and white. See, e.g., Suro, "For Women, Varied Reasons for Single Motherhood," *New York Times*, May 26, 1992, A12, col. 1.

152. New Jersey adopted such a law in 1991. On a related proposal in Wisconsin, see Prud'homme, "Learn, Work and Wed," *Time*, Aug. 19, 1991, 18. In 1992 the voters of California narrowly defeated a similar initiative measure.

153. For two poignant personal statements by young, successful, upper-middle-class black men, see Walton, "Willie Horton and Me," *New York Times Magazine*, Aug. 20, 1989, 52, and Standard, "A Young Black Man Asks: Will I Be Next?" *New York Times*, Sept. 2, 1989, 11, col. 2.

154. Ellwood, n.143 above, at 193 (italics in original omitted here).

155. Dionne, n.148 above, at 136.

156. Toner, "Rethinking Welfare," *New York Times*, July 5, 1992, A1, col. 2, at A27.

157. Three weeks after his "Murphy Brown" speech, the Vice President spoke to a Southern Baptist convention in Indianapolis, again attacking "the cultural elite." Afterward, to a reporter, he said, "Us versus them, and I'm on the 'us' side." Gerstenzang, "Quayle Attacks 'Cultural Elite' on Moral Values," *Los Angeles Times*, June 10, 1992, A1, col. 4.

158. Handler and Hasenfeld, n.141 above, at 25.

159. A. Leyser, A. Blong, and J. Riggs, *Beyond the Myths: The Families Helped by AFDC*, 3 (1985).

160. See, e.g., L. Goodwin, *Causes and Cures of Welfare: New Evidence on the Social Psychology of the Poor* (1983); L. Goodwin, *Do the Poor Want to Work? A Social-Psychological Study of Work Orientations* (1972).

161. Samuelson, "Political Child Abuse," *Newsweek*, Feb. 3, 1992, 42.

162. On the nation's long history of subsidizing middle-class families, see Coontz, "A Nation of Welfare Families," *Harper's*, October 1992, 13.

163. Middle-class single mothers agree. A survey of the 1,600 members of a group called Single Mothers by Choice showed that "98% would have preferred to raise their children in a good marriage. 'You have to note the word *good*,'" the group's president said. "Between 1980 and 1989, the birth rate for single white women between the ages of 30 and 34 rose 93%, and it rose 91% for those [aged] 35 to 39." One single mother put it this way: "My motivation for having a child ironically is that I am traditional. Home and family life are more important to me than a career." Smith, "Taking the Solo Road to Motherhood," *Los Angeles Times*, June 12, 1992, A1, col. 1.

164. See Wilson and Neckerman, "Poverty and Family Structure: The Widening Gap between Evidence and Public Policy Issues," in S. Danziger and D. Weinberg, eds., *Fighting Poverty: What Works and What Doesn't*, 232 (1986); *Losing Generations: Adolescents in High-Risk Settings*, chaps. 2 and 3 (Comm'n on Behavioral and Soc. Sci. and Education, Nat'l Research Council, 1993). Duncan and Hoffman, "Teenage Underclass Behavior and Subsequent Poverty: Have the Rules Changed?" in C. Jencks and P. Peterson, eds., *The Urban Underclass*, 155 (1991).

165. D. Jaynes and R. Williams, eds., *A Common Destiny: Blacks and American Society*, 534 and chap. 6 (1989). Marriage rates have also fallen among employed black women, presumably for similar reasons. While average wage differentials between employed black and white men have remained high, average wage levels for employed black women have come far closer to average wages for white women. During the same time paid employment of black women has risen. Thus, as poor black women have had progressively fewer chances to find marriage partners who can help provide for their families, employed black women have become less dependent upon men for support.

166. E.g., Murray, n.141 above.

167. Handler and Hasenfeld, n.141 above, at 122.

168. Katz, n.150 above, at 220.

169. Wilson and Neckerman, n.164 above, at 81.

170. See K. Luker, *Taking Chances: Abortion and the Decision Not to Contracept*, 124–27 (1974); R. Petchesky, *Abortion and Woman's Choice*, chaps. 5 and 6 (2d ed. 1990).

171. Rosenthal, n.138 above.

172. Quoted in Luker, "Dubious Conceptions: The Controversy over Teenage Pregnancy," *American Prospect* 73, 77, 81–82 (Spring 1991).

173. C. Williams, *Black Teenage Mothers: Pregnancy and Child Rearing from Their*

Perspective, 83–101 (1991). See also Anderson, "Neighborhood Effects on Teenage Pregnancy," in Jencks and Peterson, n.164 above, 375.

174. Katz, n.150 above, at 220–21. It remains true that teenage mothers, once on welfare, are more likely to remain dependent on it than are women who become mothers later. This result seems partly explained by disproportionate numbers of very young mothers who come from the most disadvantaged backgrounds. Luker, n.172 above, at 80–81.

175. See Williams, n.173 above. There is no strong correlation between black teenage childbirth and transmission of poverty to the next generation. A twenty-year study of poor (and mostly black) children of teenage mothers in Baltimore showed that two-thirds of the children either had completed high school, or had obtained a general education diploma, or were about to do so. Furstenberg, Hughes, and Brooks-Gunn, "The Next Generation: The Children of Teenage Mothers Grow Up," in M. Rosenheim and M. Testa, eds., *Early Parenthood and Coming of Age in the 1990s,* at 113 (1992).

176. See generally Gibbs, "The Social Context of Teenage Pregnancy and Parenting in the Black Community: Implications for Public Policy," in M. Rosenheim and M. Testa, eds., *Early Parenting and Coming of Age in the 1990s,* at 71 (1992). On discrimination, see Kirschenman and Neckerman, " 'We'd Love to Hire Them, But . . .': The Meaning of Race for Employers," in Jencks and Peterson, n.164 above, 203.

177. Mare and Winship, "Socioeconomic Change and the Decline of Marriage for Blacks and Whites," in Jencks and Peterson, n.164 above, 175.

178. The proposal of David Blankenhorn, head of the New York–based Institute for American Values, described in n.179 below.

179. This is the heart of the program of the Institute for American Values, a self-described culture factory focused on "family values" of the kind offered by the social issues agenda to the constituency for cultural counterrevolution. The institute has succeeded famously in disseminating its messages through government commissions, interviews, and op-ed pieces. For example, it has sponsored a Council on Families in America, chaired by Louis Sullivan, President Bush's secretary of health and human services, to consider the problems of families headed by single mothers. If you are hoping the council will concern itself with the devastating effects of unemployment and deficient education on marriage and family relationships, don't bet on it. One of the institute's most effective publicists provided Vice President Quayle with his lines on Murphy Brown. See n.145 above and accompanying text.

180. Jencks, "Is the American Underclass Growing?" in Jencks and Peterson, n.164 above, 28, 90.

181. Of course, the typical gay or lesbian couple raising children also has two incomes to support the family, but this advantage is not emphasized by the Institute for the American Family.

182. David Blankenhorn, quoted in Smith, "Single Mothers Apt to Be Poorest: Married Couples with Children Fare Better, Census Shows," *Los Angeles Times* (Orange County ed.), May 18, 1992, B1, col. 3.

183. David Blankenhorn, paraphrased by Mona Charen, in "Let Fathers Play Dad Once Again," *Atlanta Constitution*, March 26, 1992, A17.

184. David Blankenhorn (one more time), quoted by William Raspberry in "Fathers: The New, the Old, and the Unnecessary," *Chicago Tribune*, Jan. 30, 1992, C23. See also Charen, n.189 above. Blankenhorn has said elsewhere that he is "not in favor of going back to the 1950s family, predicated on separate-sphere family roles, with the woman playing the role of lifelong homemaker. Roles can, and should shift." Quoted in Klein, "Whose Values?" *Newsweek*, June 8, 1992, 19, 22. Presumably it is all right for a man to wash the dishes, so long as he does not nurture the kids.

185. Susan Faludi unearthed the datum that the Yankelovich Monitor survey, for two decades, has asked its respondents to define masculinity. Here is Faludi's statement of the results: "For twenty years, the leading definition, by a huge margin, has never changed. It isn't being a leader, athlete, lothario, decision maker, or even being 'born male.' It is simply this: being a 'good provider for his family.'" S. Faludi, *Backlash: The Undeclared War against American Women*, 65 (1991).

186. See chap. 2 above.

187. Susan Faludi, n.185 above, at 59–70, lays out what political operatives would call "the demographics" of the antifeminist revolt, and places the revolt in a succession of such "crises of masculinity" in American history. Faludi's book deserves a wide reading, but I think she has been much too hard on the writers she calls "neofeminists," including Betty Friedan and Carol Gilligan. If nurturance and a concern for family are valuable traits in men—and they are—those traits are also valuable in women. It may be that women's "different voice" (a group tendency, not a universal) is in considerable part the result of generations of subordination. It is nonetheless a voice that deserves a hearing, and a voice worth cultivating in both women and men. I have pursued this theme in my article "Woman's Constitution," 1984 *Duke Law Journal* 447.

188. See text at n.171 above.

189. The agenda's other category, religion in public life, is at least suggested by the addition of a "cultural elite" to the enemies list; in the eyes of many an apostle of cultural counterrevolution, that elite's cardinal sin is secularism.

Chapter 6

1. See generally S. Blumenthal, *Pledging Allegiance: The Last Campaign of the Cold War* (1990).
2. On the constitutive purposes and functions of the Bill of Rights, see Amar, "The Bill of Rights as a Constitution," 100 *Yale Law Journal* 1131 (1991).
3. *Everson v. Board of Education*, 330 U.S. 1 (1947).
4. *West Virginia State Board of Education v. Barnette*, 319 U.S. 624, 638 (1943).
5. Another name for political controversy is democratic decision making; it would not do to allow the opponents of every governmental action bearing on religion to secure a judicial veto simply by raising the decibel level. Furthermore, a number of commentators have remarked that such factors as race, ethnicity, and socioeconomic class have comparably divisive effects on politics. For these and other criticisms of "political divisiveness" as an establishment clause "test," see Gaffney, "Political Divisiveness along Religious Lines: The Entanglement of the Court in Sloppy History and Bad Public Policy," 24 *St. Louis University Law Journal* 205 (1980); Choper, "The Religion Clauses of the First Amendment: Reconciling the Conflict," 41 *University of Pittsburgh Law Review* 673 (1980); M. Smith, "The Special Place of Religion in the Constitution," 1983 *Supreme Court Review* 83, 94–100. See also S. Smith, "Symbols, Perceptions, and Doctrinal Illusions: Establishment Neutrality and the 'No Endorsement' Test," 86 *Michigan Law Review* 266, 304–05 (1987).
6. *Wolman v. Walter*, 433 U.S. 229, 263 (1977) (Powell, J., concurring in part and dissenting in part).
7. J. Murray, *We Hold These Truths: Catholic Reflections on the American Proposition*, 73 (1960). In Murray's perspective, the religion clauses of the Constitution were not "articles of faith" but "articles of peace in a pluralist society." Ibid., at 78.
8. S. Blumenthal, *The Permanent Campaign: Inside the World of Elite Political Operatives* (1980).
9. *Donnelly v. Lynch*, 525 F. Supp. 1150, 1158–59 (D.R.I. 1981), reversed, *Lynch v. Donnelly*, 465 U.S. 668 (1984).
10. "The appeal of religion for Napoléon was largely political: 'In religion,' he said, 'I do not see the mystery of the Incarnation but the mystery of the social order.'" E. Kennedy, *A Cultural History of the French Revolution*, 377 (1989).
11. In the year 312, just before a crucial battle for imperial control over Italy, Constantine purportedly saw a blazing cross in the sky and said, "In this sign I shall conquer." Conquer he did, and he consolidated the Christian church into a single establishment. Eventually—the time-ordering sug-

gests something about his priorities—he converted to Christianity. In *Friedman v. Board of County Commissioners*, 781 F.2d 777 (10th Cir. 1985) (en banc), certiorari denied, 476 U.S. 1169 (1986), a federal court of appeals held unconstitutional a New Mexico county's official seal of a gold Latin cross surrounded by rays of light and the motto "Con Esta Vencemos" (With This [Cross] We Conquer); the Supreme Court denied review. Seven years later another court of appeals held unconstitutional city seals that prominently included the Latin cross and other religious symbols, and the Supreme Court again denied review. *City of Rolling Meadows v. Kuhn*, 927 F.2d 1401 (7th Cir. 1991), certiorari denied, 112 S. Ct. 3025 (1992); *City of Zion v. Harris*, 927 F.2d 1401 (7th Cir. 1991), certiorari denied, 112 S. Ct. 3054 (1992).

12. *Employment Division v. Smith*, 494 U.S. 872 (1990). See Michael McConnell's trenchant criticism "Free Exercise Revisionism and the Smith Decision," 57 *University of Chicago Law Review* 1109 (1990).

13. Named after *Lemon v. Kurtzman*, 403 U.S. 602 (1971), this formula holds governmental action invalid if it (a) is adopted with a purpose to aid religion, (b) has the primary effect of aiding religion, or (c) unduly entangles government with religion or religious institutions. In practice this "test" has not decided cases but rationalized decisions.

14. In *Lee v. Weisman*, 112 S. Ct. 2649 (1992), a 5–4 majority of the Supreme Court held unconstitutional officially sponsored prayers of benediction in public school graduation ceremonies. The Court did not find it necessary to "revisit the difficult questions dividing us in recent cases"—that is, questions about the *Lemon* formula's current status—no doubt because the majority included Justices with a range of views about that formula. Justice Blackmun, for example, supports its continuation; Justice O'Connor supports its modification; and Justice Kennedy, who wrote for the Court in *Lee v. Weisman*, supports outright abandonment of *Lemon*'s precedent. The leading doctrinal candidate to replace the *Lemon* formula prominently features an element called "coercion." I discuss this element below, and return to *Lee v. Weisman*'s larger significance in chap. 7.

15. See chap. 4 above.

16. *Richmond v. J. A. Croson Co.*, 488 U.S. 469, 524 (1989) (Scalia, J., concurring).

17. The term is William Van Alstyne's, in "Rites of Passage: Race, the Supreme Court, and the Constitution," 46 *University of Chicago Law Review* 775, 809 (1979).

18. *Employment Division v. Smith*, 494 U.S. 872, 890 (1990) (opinion of the Court by Scalia, J.).

19. I borrow the term from Paul Brest, in "The Supreme Court, 1975 Term—

Foreword: In Defense of the Antidiscrimination Principle," 90 *Harvard Law Review* 1, 14 (1976).

20. See Karst, "Paths to Belonging: The Constitution and Cultural Identity," 64 *North Carolina Law Review* 303 (1986).

21. Eck, "True Liberty Cherishes Difference," *Los Angeles Times*, July 5, 1992, M5, col. 2.

22. Presidents Reagan and Bush have called for a constitutional amendment that would authorize "voluntary" prayer in public schools, and in *Lee v. Weisman* (discussed above) the solicitor general, on behalf of the United States as a friend of the Court, urged the Court to uphold prayers of benediction at public school graduation ceremonies. 60 *United States Law Week* 3351 (1991). On race (especially affirmative action), see Charles Fried's memoir of his tenure as solicitor general during President Reagan's second term. C. Fried, *Order and Law: Arguing the Reagan Revolution—A Firsthand Account*, 89–131 (1991).

23. On the bloody side of deep and prolonged religious division in America, see R. Hofstadter and M. Wallace, eds., *American Violence: A Documentary History*, 87–338 (1971).

24. *Lynch v. Donnelly*, 465 U.S. 668, 687 (1984) (O'Connor, J., concurring).

25. Ibid., at 687–88. As Arnold Loewy observed, this formulation resonates with notions of "a badge of inferiority" now well understood in the law of race relations. Loewy, "Rethinking Government Neutrality towards Religion under the Establishment Clause: The Untapped Potential of Justice O'Connor's Insight," 64 *North Carolina Law Review* 1049, 1051 (1986). See also Conkle, "Toward a General Theory of the Establishment Clause," 82 *Northwestern University Law Review* 1113, 1164–82 (1988).

26. See Steven Smith's comprehensive critical analysis, n.5 above. One may sympathize with Justice O'Connor's larger concerns and yet have some reservations about her endorsement test. See Marshall, "'We Know It When We See It': The Supreme Court and Establishment," 59 *Southern California Law Review* 495, 533–37 (1986); Tushnet, "The Constitution of Religion," 18 *Connecticut Law Review* 701, 711–12 (1986).

27. "The Christian Scientists, for example, have serious and sincere objections to the use of their tax funds to support government hospitals and government funding of medical care; the Quakers oppose military funding; Catholics oppose funding of abortions; fundamentalists oppose the teaching of evolution. No case law supports their 'right' to enjoin such programs or a right to refund to a pro rata share of their tax dollars." Shiffrin, "Government Speech," 27 *UCLA Law Review* 565, 593 (1980).

28. *Lynch v. Donnelly*, 465 U.S. 668, 714 (1984) (Brennan, J., dissenting).

29. See McConnell, "Accommodation of Religion," 1985 *Supreme Court Review*

1; Tushnet, "The Emerging Principle of Accommodation of Religion (Dubitante)," 76 *Georgetown Law Journal* 1691 (1988); Lupu, "Reconstructing the Establishment Clause: The Case against Discretionary Accommodation of Religion," 140 *University of Pennsylvania Law Review* 555 (1991).

30. See S. Smith, n.5 above, at 279–82.

31. See Johnson, "Concepts and Compromise in First Amendment Religious Doctrine," 72 *California Law Review* 817 (1984).

32. Steven Smith carefully states these problems in his article, n.5 above. For my response to Smith, published just before the Supreme Court decided *Lee v. Weisman*, n.14 above, see Karst, "The First Amendment, the Politics of Religion, and the Symbols of Government," 27 *Harvard Civil Rights–Civil Liberties Law Review* 503 (1992). Much of this chapter's first section is drawn from that article.

33. 112 S. Ct. at 2658.

34. Justice Scalia, dissenting in *Lee v. Weisman*, mounted a scathing attack on Justice Kennedy's notion of indirect coercion, deriding it as pop psychology and insisting that real coercion was limited to such things as punishment for nonattendance at church, or taxes on nonadherents to support an established church. These kinds of coercion, he said, were unconstitutional because they were the kinds of coercion known to the framers of the First Amendment. Thus, presumably, they lack the requisite "deep foundations in the historic practices of our people" to immunize them from constitutional attack. I discuss this sort of invocation of history in chap. 7.

35. The term is Mark DeWolfe Howe's, in *The Garden and the Wilderness: Religion and Government in American Constitutional History*, 11 (1965).

36. Variations on this approach would be to say that an expression or motto has lost much of its original religious significance, or to call it "ceremonial deism." The Seventh Circuit recently referred to such expressions in Supreme Court opinions when it upheld the reference to God in schoolroom recitations of the Pledge of Allegiance. *Sherman v. Community Consolidated School District 21 of Wheeling Township*, 980 F.2d 437 (7th Cir. 1992).

37. 68 Stat. 249 (1954).

38. Justice Kennedy signaled this result in *County of Allegheny v. American Civil Liberties Union, Greater Pittsburgh Chapter*, 492 U.S. 573, 661 n.1 (1989) (Kennedy, J., concurring in part and dissenting in part), and virtually carved it in stone in *Lee v. Weisman*, discussed above. Even Justice Scalia, dissenting in the latter case, hinted his agreement that classroom prayers were unconstitutional.

39. For a more modern example, see *ACLU v. City of St. Charles*, 794 F.2d 265 (7th Cir.), certiorari denied, 479 U.S. 961 (1986). Cf. *Hewitt v. Joyner*, 940 F.2d 1561 (9th Cir. 1991), holding that the California state constitution forbids a county's ownership and maintenance of a public park exclusively

containing immovable religious statuary depicting scenes from the New Testament.

40. Note 38 above.

41. Van Alstyne, "Trends in the Supreme Court: Mr. Jefferson's Crumbling Wall—A Comment on Lynch v. Donnelly," 1984 *Duke Law Journal* 770, 782–87.

42. *Cammack v. Waihee*, 932 F.2d 765 (9th Cir.) (2–1 decision), rehearing en banc denied, 944 F.2d 466 (1991). The Supreme Court declined to hear the case, 112 S. Ct. 3027 (1992). Judge Stephen Reinhardt wrote the main opinion dissenting from the denial of a rehearing en banc. The vote of the entire circuit on this issue is not reported; the six judges who noted their dissent did not include Judge Dorothy Nelson, the dissenting member of the panel.

43. Here is a sampling of the panel majority's further observations: (a) Hawaii's Good Friday state holiday was of such long standing that it could not be perceived as endorsing Christianity. 932 F.2d at 782 and n.19. (The law is fifty years old—and thus one of the youngest "long-standing" official government symbols of religion yet to receive judicial approval.) (b) Even if one purpose of the legislature were to promote Christianity, a secular purpose—any secular purpose, "primary" or not—would get a governmental action past the first requirement of the *Lemon* test. Hawaii's secular purpose was to establish a spring holiday. 932 F.2d at 773–77. (c) If the Sunday Closing Laws were constitutional, then the Good Friday holiday must be, too, for the Sunday laws were originally adopted (in the colonial era) to get people to attend church, and the Good Friday holiday lets people do whatever they like. 932 F.2d at 777–79.

44. On the transformation of Chanukah to make it more Christmaslike, see Cobin, "Crèches, Christmas Trees and Menorahs: Weeds Growing in Roger Williams' Garden," 1990 *Wisconsin Law Review* 1597, 1609–10. Professor Cobin sketches Williams's writings in ibid., at 1598–1601. Similar points had been made in briefer compass by Van Alstyne, n.41 above, at 785–87.

45. Ball, "Normal Religion in America," 4 *Notre Dame Journal of Law, Ethics, and Public Policy* 397, 416 (1990).

46. 932 F.2d at 781.

47. *Larson v. Valente*, 456 U.S. 228 (1982). Daniel Conkle has shown how a "principle of religious equality" has found acceptance across the whole spectrum of Justices and commentators. Conkle, "Different Religions, Different Politics: Evaluating the Role of Competing Religious Traditions in American Politics and Law," 10 *Journal of Law and Religion* 1 (forthcoming 1993).

48. 932 F.2d at 781.

49. 932 F.2d at 776, quoting from *Employment Division v. Smith*, n.12 above, 494 U.S. at 872.

50. See R. Wiebe, *The Segmented Society* (1975).

51. See, e.g., Johnson, n.31 above, passim; Smith, n.5 above, at 309–16.

52. I have the story from Vice Chancellor Alan F. Charles, who drew the duty of replying to these letters.

53. See chap. 3 above.

54. This is the view of one federal district judge in Alabama. See *Smith v. Board of School Commissioners*, 655 F. Supp. 939 (S.D. Ala.), reversed, 827 F.2d 684 (11th Cir. 1987).

55. *County of Allegheny v. American Civil Liberties Union, Greater Pittsburgh Chapter*, 492 U.S. 573, 677–79 (1989).

56. See "Officials Opt Not to Set up Creche in Secular Display," *Los Angeles Times*, Nov. 26, 1989, A28.

57. 20 United States Code §§4071–74 (1988), upheld in *Board of Education v. Mergens*, 496 U.S. 226 (1990).

58. The Supreme Court, citing freedom of speech, has held that if a public school allows after-hours access to its facilities for "social, civic, and recreational" purposes, it must allow access to a film series on Christian family values. *Lamb's Chapel v. Center Moriches Union Free School District*, 61 U.S. Law Week 4549 (1993).

59. G. Gallup, *The Gallup Poll: Public Opinion 1989*, 204 (1990).

60. For historical figures, see *Statistical Abstract of the United States*, 128–65 (1990). Of some 28,000 private schools in the United States, about 23,000 (82 percent) are religious schools. P. Benson, *Private Schools in the United States: A Statistical Profile, with Comparisons to Public Schools*, 15 (1991).

61. Dessauer, "Book-Buying Patterns in the '70s Showed Real Gains—Mostly through Retailers," 221 *Publishers Weekly* 37–39 (1981), cited in R. Wuthnow, *The Restructuring of American Religion: Society and Faith since World War II*, 164 (1988).

62. R. McBrien, *Caesar's Coin: Religion and Politics in America*, 182 (1987) (paragraphing omitted).

63. Discussed at page 148 above.

64. Exodus 20:4–5.

65. See M. Douglas, *Purity and Danger*, 174 (1966).

66. On the use of the flag in this campaign, see S. Blumenthal, n.1 above, at 262–64, 292.

67. 491 U.S. 397 (1989).

68. *United States v. Eichman*, 497 U.S. 310, at 323 (1990).

69. Martin Luther King, Jr., was the subject of surveillance and harassment by the FBI under the directorship of J. Edgar Hoover, in part because of his opposition to American involvement in the Vietnam War. For a detailed

account, see D. Garrow, *The FBI and Martin Luther King, Jr.: From "Solo" to Memphis* (1981). See also *Bond v. Floyd*, 385 U.S. 116 (Georgia legislature's effort to refuse to seat a black legislator for his statement of sympathy for draft resisters).

70. For example, the demonstrators who waved the flag of the People's Republic of Vietnam and chanted the praises of Ho Chi Minh, that nation's leader.

71. Nahmod, "The Sacred Flag and the First Amendment," 66 *Indiana Law Journal* 511 (1991). For those who would think seriously about the flag cases, this article is indispensable reading.

72. 491 U.S. at 411.

73. This is Justice Brennan's paraphrase of the Texas lawyers' argument. 491 U.S. at 413.

74. 491 U.S. at 432.

75. Grogan, Demaret, and Stewart, "Unimpressed by the Freedom to Burn Old Glory, Joey Johnson Still Wants a Revolution," *People*, July 10, 1989, 99. For the quotation and citation I am indebted to Robert Justin Goldstein, "The Great 1989–1990 Flag Flap: An Historical, Political, and Legal Analysis," 45 *University of Miami Law Review* 19, 32 (1990).

76. See E. Hall, *The Silent Language* (1973); A. Montagu and F. Matson, *The Human Connection* (1979).

77. Brief for the United States at 40, *United States v. Eichman*, 496 U.S. 310 (1990).

78. Michelman, "Saving Old Glory: On Constitutional Iconography," 42 *Stanford Law Review* 1337, 1362 (1990). Neither Michelman's reference to paradigmatic "flag burners" nor mine should be taken as an assertion that a lot of Americans are taking to the streets to burn flags. Much of the political energy devoted to the subject in 1989–90 surely derived from the success of Vice President Bush with the flag salute "issue" in the 1988 campaign. But there just aren't very many flag burners out there, and the ones who followed Joey Johnson's example in the fall of 1989 burned their flags for no other reason than to test the constitutionality of the flag protection statute adopted by a timid Congress following the *Johnson* case. See Goldstein, n.75 above, at 30, 91.

79. *West Virginia State Board of Education v. Barnette*, 319 U.S. 624, 632 (1943).

80. 491 U.S. at 429.

81. Feelings are crucial to an understanding of the flag cases, and I ought to acknowledge my own. For years I tended to associate flag waving with chauvinism. In the early 1960s, however, my wife and children and I lived for a year in Latin America, immersed in political cultures differing markedly from our own. Since then I have been more receptive to patriotic displays. Undoubtedly, the flag can lend itself to deplorable uses: cloaking

evil conduct of public officials, or (as in 1988) diverting some voters from other issues. In Joey Johnson's case, though, my sympathies (like Justice Brennan's, apparently) are with the man who gathered the remains of the burned flag and buried them respectfully in his back yard. Of course, the core values of the First Amendment do—and should—protect people like Johnson. See S. Shiffrin, *The First Amendment, Democracy, and Romance* (1990).

82. Nahmod, n.71 above, at 530.
83. A previous Supreme Court said that the flag symbolized not only freedom but "government resting on the consent of the governed; liberty regulated by law; the protection of the weak against the strong; security against the exercise of arbitrary power; and absolute safety for free institutions against foreign aggression." *Halter v. Nebraska*, 205 U.S. 34, 43 (1907). The Court upheld a law forbidding use of the flag for commercial purposes—in the case at hand, on a beer bottle.
84. In the fourth century Constantine I established Christianity as the official religion of the Roman Empire. See n.11 above.
85. Michelman, n.78 above, at 1346 (emphasis in original).
86. Gey, "This Is Not a Flag: The Aesthetics of Flag Burning," 1990 *Wisconsin Law Review* 1549, 1589. Gey's illuminating discussion deserves a full reading.
87. Nahmod, n.71 above, at 530. More generally, see ibid., at 525–31 and passim.
88. Gey, n.86 above, at 530.
89. K. Karst, *Belonging to America: Equal Citizenship and the Constitution*, 176 (1989), following a path long ago cleared and marked by George Herbert Mead. See his *Mind, Self, and Society*, at 142–44 and passim (1934).
90. 491 U.S. at 421. So did Chief Justice Rehnquist, when he commented that the flag stood for no particular political party or political philosophy. 491 U.S. at 429. As Justice Stevens strongly hinted, that view may not be shared by the authors of the social issues agenda. See the text at n.71 above.
91. On the reluctance of some black Americans to join in singing the national anthem, see, e.g., J. Gwaltney, *Drylongso: A Portrait of Black America*, 5, 19 (1981).
92. J. Hunter, *Culture Wars: The Struggle to Define America*, 44 (1991).
93. Blumenthal, n.1 above, at 263.
94. Michelman, n.78 above, at 1353 (emphasis in original).
95. The constituency cares little whether Joey Johnson goes to jail; the important thing is that the President recognize the constituency's sentiments (and authority) by making his pilgrimage to the Iwo Jima Memorial. On the other side, too, the question for civil libertarians is not so much Joey

Johnson's future as it is the future of the First Amendment. (Still, whatever you think of Johnson's behavior, surely his sentence—a one-year prison term and a $2,000 fine—was excessive.) The long-term concern is that the Supreme Court could not write a principled opinion allowing Texas to jail Johnson without, at the same time, inviting other serious incursions on the freedom of expression. For the doctrinal argument, which seems to me unanswerable, see the articles of Michelman, Nahmod, Gey, and Goldstein cited above.

96. Introducing an article that explores, in interesting ways, the relations between the rule of law and authoritarianism, Lynne Henderson has expressed some reservations about the "posited human 'need' for authority." Henderson, "Authoritarianism and the Rule of Law," 66 *Indiana Law Journal* 379, 386–90 (1991). My own sense of the matter is that the posited need is real, growing out of the need to belong. The authority of culture is part of the paradox of community that has been celebrated (and lamented) by numerous law academics over the past two decades.

97. In a 1991 nationwide poll of 500 adults, 78 percent of those who were willing to express a view favored "allowing children to say prayers in public schools." Gibbs, "America's Holy War," *Time*, Dec. 9, 1991, 61, 64. That question was inartistically drawn, for children have always had the right to say prayers; the question for government is whether the prayers should be officially sponsored. Even so, other polls confirm that a majority would approve official school prayers, and in this same poll 67 percent favored displaying such symbols as a Nativity scene or a menorah on government property.

98. On the perception of the Pledge of Allegiance as a symbol of teaching children "values," see E. J. Dionne, Jr., *Why Americans Hate Politics*, 314–15 (1991).

99. P. Clecak, *America's Quest for the Ideal Self*, 287 (1983).

100. Ibid., at 279–80 and passim.

101. In his opinion for the Court in *Johnson*, Justice Brennan said, "We can imagine no more appropriate response to burning a flag than waving one's own." 491 U.S. at 420.

102. See text at n.77 above.

103. The father of it all was Max Weber, whose discussions of the subject of authority are so scattered (and penetrable only with difficulty) that it is now customary to refer to secondary sources rather than to the master. For a more accessible (and more useful) statement, see Anthony Kronman's book *Max Weber*, chaps. 3 and 4 (1983). See also T. Adorno, E. Frenkel-Brunswik, D. Levinson, and R. Sanford, *The Authoritarian Personality* (1950); R. Sennett, *Authority* (1981).

104. See chap. 5, n.109, above and accompanying text.

105. One of the more egregious of such cases is *benShalom v. Marsh*, 881 F.2d 454 (7th Cir. 1988), certiorari denied, 110 S. Ct. 1296 (1990). I have discussed this decision in my article "The Pursuit of Manhood and the Desegregation of the Armed Forces," 38 *UCLA Law Review* 499, 563–74 (1991).

Chapter 7

1. D. Potter, "Social Cohesion and the Crisis of Law," in *History and American Society,* at 390 (D. Fehrenbacher ed. 1973).
2. See chap. 3 above.
3. Compare the discussion of the origins of the gay liberation movement in chap. 3 above.
4. *City of Richmond v. J. A. Croson Co.*, 488 U.S. 469, 522 (1989) (Scalia, J., concurring). Justice O'Connor wrote the principal opinion in the case, and took an even more generous view of Congress's power to enforce the Fourteenth Amendment. 488 U.S. at 486–93. Justice Kennedy dissociated himself from this view. 488 U.S. at 518.
5. Justice Scalia's deference to Congress knows bounds. He was in dissent when a 5–4 Court upheld an affirmative action plan, approved by Congress, to govern the transfer of broadcast licenses. See *Metro Broadcasting, Inc. v. FCC*, 110 S. Ct. 2997 (1990).
6. Justice Scalia noted this responsibility.
7. Sunstein, "Interest Groups in American Public Law," 38 *Stanford Law Review* 29, 48–64, 68–85 (1985). Despite the disagreements I express here, I greatly admire Prof. Sunstein's illumination of the subject of rationality review. See also Sunstein, "Naked Preferences and the Constitution," 84 *Columbia Law Review* 1689 (1984); and Sunstein, "Beyond the Republican Revival," 97 *Yale Law Journal* 1539 (1988).
8. Sunstein, "Interest Groups," n.7 above, at 50–51.
9. Ibid., at 56–59. Although Sunstein starts his discussion of "ideology"-based legislative classifications by linking racial discrimination with the other forms, he does not explicitly say that judicial review in race cases is explainable as a search for "reasoned analysis." He quotes that expression from the Supreme Court's opinion in the sex discrimination case *Mississippi University for Women v. Hogan*, 458 U.S. 718, 726 (1982).
10. See, e.g., H. Hyman and W. Wiecek, *Equal Justice under Law: Constitutional Development, 1835–1875* (1982); W. Wiecek, *The Sources of Antislavery Constitutionalism in America, 1760–1848* (1977); J. tenBroek, *Equal under Law* (1965). The line reaching from the Fourteenth Amendment back to *Dred Scott v. Sandford*, 60 U.S. (19 How.) 393 (1857), is also traced in K. Karst, *Belonging to America: Equal Citizenship and the Constitution,* chap. 4 (1989).
11. Sunstein is obviously right in saying that government must offer a legiti-

mate purpose for treating anyone unequally, that some kinds of inequalities require more justification than others, and that an ideology of group subordination is not a legitimate justification. These points are common ground for nearly all commentators on the equal protection clause. But where he sees judicial review under the clause as focused on the procedural question "whether representatives have attempted to act deliberatively" ("Interest Groups," n.7 above, at 59), I see the heart of the clause as a cluster of substantive values, and judicial review in these cases as centered on those values.

12. M. Sanger, *Woman and the New Race*, 100 (1920). There is no good reason why high school boys should not also seek birth control counseling. In referring to girls as the counselors' likely clients, I recognize that teenage boys, like their male elders, generally do not assume the responsibilities that should accompany sexual activity. That is exactly what Sanger was saying, and in the last seven decades male responsibility in this area has progressed remarkably little. The text references also assume that parents are generally more fearful about their daughters' sexual activity than they are about their sons'—an assumption closely related to the fears of female sexuality that drive so many public policies in this whole area.

13. C. Geertz, *The Interpretation of Cultures*, 194 (1973). Sunstein, "Interest Groups," n.7 above, at 77–85, recognizes problems of this type. He does not pretend that his procedural principle of judicial review presently adds much disinterested deliberation in our legislatures, nor does he argue that the principle will seriously limit legislators' real power. He does suggest that genuine legislative deliberation might increase if the courts would take more seriously their utterances about rationality review and "reasoned analysis." See also ibid., at 69–73.

14. Ibid., at 58.

15. On the myriad difficulties presented by inquiries into illicit legislative motives, see, e.g., Lawrence, "The Id, The Ego, and Equal Protection: Reckoning with Unconscious Racism," 30 *Stanford Law Review* 317 (1987); Karst, "The Costs of Motive-Centered Inquiry," 15 *San Diego Law Review* 1163 (1978); Karst, n.10 above, at 151–58.

Sunstein, "Interest Groups," n.7 above, at 57–59, recognizes that legislators often engage in deliberation, enact laws, and then offer public-spirited justifications founded on values that are themselves "the product of private power." Legislative classifications should be held invalid, he says, when they are "inevitably the product of power even if there has been actual discussion of their costs and benefits." As he remarks, this concession "makes the distinction between 'procedural' review [a search for deliberative reason] and 'substantive' review quite thin." Ibid., at 58 n.121. That assessment is persuasive and would seem to undermine the thesis that legislative deliberation about the public good is the central requirement of equal protection jurisprudence.

Similarly, Sunstein says that the search for legislative deliberation is irrelevant in cases involving "fundamental rights." Ibid., at 80 n.218. Here, too, distinctions are thin. Consider the case of birth control counseling discussed in the text. Does the challenged law raise an equal protection issue, so that the judge should uphold it if some "reasoned analysis" supports the law? Or is access to birth control counseling a "fundamental right"? Would a wise judge *begin* to think about this case by asking these questions?

16. *Bradwell v. Illinois*, 83 U.S. 130, 139 (1873) (concurring opinion).
17. Carl Schneider has said that when a state legislature is considering a law that would "impinge on a fundamental right" such as sexual privacy, it is entitled to make use of "a theory of human nature" when the theory "has been substantially relied on in the past" and "has substantial intellectual antecedents." Schneider, "State-Interest Analysis in Fourteenth Amendment 'Privacy' Law: An Essay on the Constitutionalization of Social Issues," 51 *Law and Contemporary Problems* 79, 102 (Winter 1988). Under this standard Justice Bradley's theory of women's "nature" surely would qualify. To move to our own time, the theories that homosexual orientation is sinful or the manifestation of mental disease have been widely relied on, with intellectual antecedents galore. This approach, too, is a formula for upholding any discrimination that is long-standing and pervasive.
18. *Plessy v. Ferguson*, 163 U.S. 537, 550 (1986). *Plessy* was effectively (though not explicitly) overruled in *Gayle v. Browder*, 352 U.S. 903 (1956), the Montgomery case that held the segregation of municipal buses unconstitutional.
19. A. Bickel, *The Least Dangerous Branch: The Supreme Court at the Bar of Politics,* 16–23 (1962).
20. Ibid., at 18.
21. Karst, n.10 above, at 228. See also ibid., at chap. 12 passim. Ronald Dworkin made a similar point, centered on liberty rather than equality, in more theoretical terms: "America's principal contribution to political theory is a conception of democracy according to which the protection of individual rights is a precondition, not a compromise, of that form of government." Dworkin, "The Reagan Revolution and the Supreme Court" (book review), *New York Review of Books,* July 18, 1991, 23.
22. Eule, "Judicial Review of Direct Democracy," 99 *Yale Law Journal* 1503 (1990). Judge Hans Linde approaches the problem from another doctrinal angle in "When Initiative Lawmaking Is Not 'Republican Government': The Campaign against Homosexuality," 72 *Oregon Law Review* 19 (1993).
23. A thought experiment will help to make this point. Contrast the likelihood

that minority interests will be taken seriously when (a) a legislature considers an affirmative action plan for hiring by public contractors as a remedy for demonstrable past racial discrimination, or (b) a similar issue is put to all the state's voters in a yes/no initiative or referendum.

24. Bork, "Again, a Struggle for the Soul of the Court," *New York Times*, July 8, 1992, A15, col. 2.

25. Scalia, J., dissenting, in *Planned Parenthood of Southeastern Pennsylvania v. Casey*, 112 S. Ct. 2791, 2882 (1992). Cf. White, J., dissenting, in *Roe v. Wade* and *Doe v. Bolton*, 410 U.S. at 221 (1973) (referring to woman's right to have an abortion for a variety of reasons "or for no reason at all," on the basis of "convenience, whim or caprice").

26. See chap. 3 above.

27. 410 U.S. 113 (1973).

28. Cf. G. Calabresi, *Ideals, Beliefs, Attitudes, and the Law: Private Law Perspectives on a Public Law Problem*, chap. 5 (1985), arguing that the uproar might have been diminished if the Court had recognized a constitutional status for fetal life, but nonetheless placed its decision on an equal protection ground. My own view is that the uproar resulted not from the opinion in *Roe* but from the result.

29. *Planned Parenthood of Southeastern Pennsylvania v. Casey*, n.25 above, discussed below.

30. See E. J. Dionne, Jr., *Why Americans Hate Politics*, 341–43 (1991).

31. See L. Tribe, *Abortion: The Clash of Absolutes*, 212–20, 228 (1990).

32. This is the proposal of Ruth Colker in her insightful article "Abortion and Dialogue," 63 *Tulane Law Review* 1363, 1393–1403 (1989).

33. Ibid., at 1396.

34. See K. Luker, *Abortion and the Politics of Motherhood* (1984).

35. The amendment passed by a 53–47 percent margin. Building on this success, the Christian Coalition and the other national organizations that sponsored the amendment are promoting similar measures in a number of other states.

36. In *Evans v. Romer*, 62 U.S. Law Week 2052 (1992), the Colorado Supreme Court held the new amendment unconstitutional, relying on the *Hunter* and *Seattle* cases, n.37 below, to find a violation of the equal protection clause of the Fourteenth Amendment.

37. The plaintiffs' two central claims are that the amendment denies the equal protection of the laws and, by effectively penalizing expressive conduct, violates the First Amendment.

One equal protection argument that I do not detail in the text is founded on *Hunter v. Erickson*, 393 U.S. 385 (1969), holding unconstitutional an amendment to Akron's city charter that required a popular referendum on any ordinance regulating real estate transactions on the basis of race. In parallel to the Colorado amendment, Akron's was adopted after the city council had adopted an ordinance forbidding racial discrimination in the sale or lease of real property. In Akron as in Colorado, the electorate had impeded the political process for enacting laws prohibiting discrimination against an identified group; "the reality is that the law's impact falls on the minority." 393 U.S. at 391. Colorado's amendment is a stronger case for judicial intervention than was Akron's, on two grounds. First, the Colorado amendment does not merely impede antidiscrimination legislation, but altogether forbids it. Second, the amendment to the Akron charter was adopted by that city's voters; under the Colorado amendment, voters in cities with antidiscrimination policies were overridden by the vote of people outside those cities. A parallel case is *Washington v. Seattle School District No. 1*, 458 U.S. 457 (1982), in which the Court, citing *Hunter v. Erickson*, invalidated (as unconstitutional racial discrimination) a state initiative law that overrode the Seattle school district's desegregation plan. The Seattle case is ably analyzed in Eule, n.22 above, at 1562–67.

38. The text of the amendment reads: "Neither the State of Colorado, through any of its branches or departments, nor any of its agencies, political subdivisions, municipalities or school districts, shall enact, adopt or enforce any statute, regulation, ordinance or policy whereby homosexual, lesbian or bisexual orientation, conduct, practices or relationships shall constitute or otherwise be the basis of, or entitle any person or class of persons to have or claim any minority status, quota preferences, protected status or claim of discrimination. This Section of the Constitution shall be self-executing." It is not clear whether the reference to "protected status" would forbid a city to adopt a "domestic partnership" ordinance extending to gay and lesbian couples.

39. Telluride adopted its ordinance after the state court issued the preliminary injunction against enforcement of the new amendment.

40. The initiative campaign had its own expressive objectives that reached beyond the immediate issue: to mobilize a constituency in support of a broad range of measures supported by the Christian Coalition and its allies.

41. *Reitman v. Mulkey*, 387 U.S. 369 (1967).

42. 387 U.S. at 376.

43. California's Proposition 14 had contained an exception for state-owned property. The Fourteenth Amendment surely would not have allowed the state to refuse to rent housing to black applicants—and, besides, the real estate lobbyists who promoted Proposition 14 had no interest in protecting the state's right to discriminate. Colorado's new amendment forbids even antidiscrimination laws addressed to government itself. The amendment allows a school board or the state police or any other agency to set employ-

ment qualifications that reject gay or lesbian applicants—until the courts hold that those qualifications violate the equal protection clause of the Fourteenth Amendment.

44. See Halley, "The Politics of the Closet: Toward Equal Protection for Gay, Lesbian, and Bisexual Identity," 36 *UCLA Law Review* 946–63 (1989). Halley provides a helpful critical review of the literature about homosexual orientation at pp. 915, 933–46. See generally R. Green, *Sexual Science and the Law*, 62–86 (1992); Herek, "Myths about Sexual Orientation: A Lawyer's Guide to Social Science Research," 1 *Law and Sexuality* 133, 148–52 (1991).

45. E.g., *NAACP v. Alabama*, 357 U.S. 449 (1958); *Bates v. Little Rock*, 361 U.S. 516 (1960); *Shelton v. Tucker*, 364 U.S. 479 (1960); *Gibson v. Florida Legislative Investigation Committee*, 372 U.S. 539 (1963).

46. The most prominent sponsor of the initiative measure was the local chapter of Rev. Pat Robertson's Christian Coalition. During the campaign the sponsoring groups ordered some 4,000 copies of the attack video "The Gay Agenda" (described in chap. 5 above) for distribution in Colorado. Colker, "Anti-Gay Video Highlights Church's Agenda," *Los Angeles Times*, Feb. 22, 1993, A1, col. 3. Local chapters of the Christian Coalition have been gathering signatures for petitions to place similar initiatives on the ballots in other states.

47. A group called Colorado for Family Values issued a publication warning "authentic minorities" against laws that provide "special rights for gays." *Evans v. Romer*, n.36 above, Brief in Support of Plaintiffs' Motion for Preliminary Injunction, p. 5.

48. *Brown v. Board of Education*, 347 U.S. 483, 494 (1954) (quoting the three-judge district court in the Topeka case).

49. See Eule, n.22 above, at 1551–68.

50. The quotation is from *Mt. Healthy City Board of Education v. Doyle*, 429 U.S. 274, 287 (1977). Some of the promotional advertising for the Colorado initiative is summarized in the plaintiffs' brief in *Evans v. Romer*, n.36 above, at 4–9. Some Coloradans apparently voted for the amendment on the theory that the existing antidiscrimination laws would bring civil rights remedies on the order of "quotas." See Carroll, "Coloradans on the Gay Amendment," *Wall Street Journal*, Dec. 15, 1992, 18, col. 4. The authors of the initiative crafted its wording with just such voters in mind.

51. Judge Richard Posner notes that public opinion polls in the three years following the Supreme Court's decision in *Bowers v. Hardwick*, 478 U.S. 186 (1986) (upholding Georgia's sodomy law), showed a decline in the number of Americans who thought homosexual relations among consenting adults should be criminalized. He draws from these data the conclusion that the decision did not "legitimate the policy embodied in the statute in the public's eye." R. Posner, *Sex and Reason*, 347 n.56 (1991). What I am arguing

in the text is that in thinking about such questions it helps to disaggregate "the public." Even as tolerance is generally rising, the law, including constitutional law, ought not to lend legitimacy to the bigotry of any segment of the population—especially a segment with a demonstrated inclination toward violence.

52. For a fuller telling of Hardwick's story, see Karst, n.10 above, at 201–10.

53. Kendall Thomas has analyzed the connections between the sodomy laws' identification of homosexual sex with evil and "private"—that is, nongovernmental—violence against gay men. See his article "Beyond the Privacy Principle," 92 *Columbia Law Review* 1431, 1436–41, 1461–70, 1481–85, and passim (1992). Some 40 percent of the incidents of antigay violence and harassment reported in Denver in 1992 came after the passage of the Colorado amendment in November. Boxall, "Survey Shows 4% Rise in Anti-Gay Violence, Harassment in U.S.," *Los Angeles Times*, March 11, 1993, B1, col. 2.

54. C. V. Woodward, *The Strange Career of Jim Crow*, 81 (2d ed. 1966).

55. The barrier to knowledge works in both directions, but those who suffer from a system of dominance usually know a good deal more about people in the dominant group—because they need to know more.

56. Here, too, the analogy to racial discrimination is apt. See chap. 4 above.

57. See Gottschall, "Reagan's Appointments to the U.S. Courts of Appeals," in S. Goldstein and A. Sarat, eds., *American Court Systems*, 405 (1989); Goldman, "Reagan's Judicial Legacy: Completing the Puzzle and Summing Up," 72 *Judicature* 318 (1989); Goldman, "The Bush Imprint on the Judiciary: Carrying on a Tradition," 74 *Judicature* 294 (1991).

58. This concern was present from the beginning of the Reagan administration, but came into high visibility during President Reagan's second term, when Attorney General Edwin Meese III became "the key figure" in the selection process. See Goldman, "Reagan and Meese Remake the Judiciary," in Goldstein and Sarat, n.57 above, 307.

59. Such a campaign need not be subtle to achieve its aim. A good illustration for this proposition would be the collected speeches and articles of Clarence Thomas before he was appointed to the U.S. Court of Appeals for the District of Columbia Circuit. See, e.g., Thomas, "Civil Rights as a Principle versus Civil Rights as an Interest," in D. Boaz ed., *Assessing the Reagan Years*, at 391 (Cato Institute 1988); Thomas, "Why Black Americans Should Look to Conservative Policies," The Heritage Lectures, no. 119 (speech to Heritage Foundation, 1987); Thomas, speech to luncheon meeting of Business Law Section, American Bar Association (1987); Thomas, "The Higher Law Background of the Privileges or Immunities Clause of the Fourteenth Amendment," 12 *Harvard Journal of Law and Public Policy* 63 (Winter 1987). When Judge Thomas was nominated to the Supreme Court, the NAACP

Legal Defense and Educational Fund, Inc., issued a report, *An Analysis of the Views of Judge Clarence Thomas* (1991). At p. 2 the report comments, "Beginning in late 1986, Judge Thomas' writings and speeches underwent a sharp transformation . . . [with] an outburst of denunciations of both the Supreme Court and its civil rights decisions."

60. After giving the matter more reflection than it was worth, I have decided not to name names. Instead, I repeat what a schoolteacher of mine used to say half a century ago when she wanted to avoid singling out particular children for shame: You know who you are.

61. Larry Simon has provided a capsule synopsis of the Rehnquist Court's decisions completing the Nixon "strict construction" program in the field of "law and order. Simon, "Rehnquist Court," L. Levy, K. Karst, and J. West, eds., *Encyclopedia of the American Constitution*, Supplement I, at 428 (1992).

62. A sampling of the decisions that culminated these developments would have to include *Teague v. Lane*, 489 U.S. 288 (1989); *Coleman v. Thompson*, 112 S. Ct. 2546 (1991); *McCleskey v. Zant*, 111 S. Ct. 1454 (1991); and *Keeney v. Tamayo-Reyes*, 112 S. Ct. 1715 (1991).

63. See generally Arenella, "Fourth Amendment," in Levy, Karst, and West, n. 61 above, 223.

64. See C. Black, *Capital Punishment: The Inevitability of Caprice and Mistake* (2d ed. 1981). In the main racial disparity case, one study presented to the Court showed that a black defendant who killed a white victim was four times more likely to receive a death sentence than was a defendant of either race who killed a black victim. *McCleskey v. Kemp*, 481 U.S. 279 (1987). See generally Kennedy, "McCleskey v. Kemp: Race, Capital Punishment, and the Supreme Court," 101 *Harvard Law Review* 1388 (1988); Burt, "Disorder in the Court: The Death Penalty and the Constitution," 85 *Michigan Law Review* 1741 (1987).

65. For a thorough (and thoroughly readable) account, see D. Savage, *Turning Right: The Making of the Rehnquist Court* (1992).

66. See chap. 4 above.

67. A White House aide told Elizabeth Drew that the vetoes were consciously designed to keep the "quotas" issue alive. Drew, "Letter from Washington," *New Yorker*, June 17, 1991, 102, 105. We saw in chap. 4 how *Wards Cove* dealt a devastating blow to plaintiffs in employment discrimination suits. See also Karst, "Private Discrimination and Public Responsibility: Patterson in Context," 1989 *Supreme Court Review* 1. The sponsors of the 1990 bill, responding to the Bush administration's use of the term *quotas* as a hammer, had included a provision that nothing in the law "shall be construed to require or encourage quotas."

68. After the November 1990 election, William Bennett, the chair apparent of

the Republican National Committee, had made a major speech blasting the idea of race-conscious remedies for past discrimination. Bennett, who had campaigned actively for Sen. Helms's reelection, had been a longtime foe of affirmative action. See W. Bennett and T. Eastland, *Counting by Race* (1979). His speech seemed to signal that the 1992 campaign would feature an aggressive use of the rhetoric of "quotas." Shortly afterward, however, Bennett withdrew from consideration for the post, and political commentators reported that White House strategists were divided over the question whether the party should push the race button again in 1992. See Barrett, "Testing the Waters on Race," *Time*, Dec. 24, 1990, 21. See also Eaton, "House Panel Backs New Rights Bill Opposed by Bush; Showdown Seen," *Los Angeles Times*, March 13, 1991, A4, col. 1.

69. The ad is described in chap. 4 above.

70. Public Law 102–166, 105 Stat. 1071. Among other effects, the act overturned the *Wards Cove* decision and codified the *Griggs* test; it also overturned the *Patterson* decision by providing damages under the Civil Rights Act of 1866 for racial harassment. (Both these decisions are discussed in chap. 4 above.)

71. Lauter, "Rush of Events Broke Rights Bill Impasse," *Los Angeles Times*, Oct. 26, 1991, A1, col. 6.

72. See n.59 above.

73. In the November election Duke lost the governorship, but he carried 55 percent of the white vote.

74. See chap. 4 above. I say half right, because the hearings made nothing at all of Anita Hill's blackness. In one perspective—I believe it to be Prof. Patterson's—this factor evidences the integration of black professionals with white professionals. In another perspective it evidences the ascendance of the symbolism of "woman" over the symbolism of "black," thus reinforcing a common tendency to ignore the consequences for a black woman of the dual stereotypes of race and sex—consequences that seem dramatically evident in Hill's story. Kimberlé Crenshaw has analyzed this larger issue in her article "Demarginalizing the Intersection of Race and Sex: A Black Feminist Critique of Antidiscrimination Doctrine, Feminist Theory and Antiracist Politics," 1989 *University of Chicago Legal Forum* 139. She applies her analysis to the Hill-Thomas confrontation, and specifically criticizes another portion of Patterson's comment on those hearings, in "Race, Gender, and Sexual Harassment," 65 *Southern California Law Review* 1459 (1992).

75. See the symposium "Gender, Race, and the Politics of Supreme Court Appointments: The Import of the Anita Hill/Clarence Thomas Hearings," 65 *Southern California Law Review* 1279 (1992). Among black Americans the hearings were chiefly an occasion for severe pain. The Hill-Thomas con-

frontation opened old wounds for both black women and black men, wounds that had their origins in racism. Toni Morrison has edited an excellent series of reflective essays by black writers, written after the dust had settled, *Race-ing Justice, En-gendering Power* (1992). Brief comments from black writers across a wide political spectrum, written around the time of the hearings, are collected in R. Chrisman and R. Allen, eds., *Court of Appeal* (1992).

76. "The Legacy of Anita Hill" (editorial), *Los Angeles Times*, Oct. 10, 1992, B7, col. 3.

77. Many years earlier, when Danforth was attorney general of Missouri, one of his assistants was the young Clarence Thomas, just out of law school. In the 1960s Danforth had served with Martin Luther King, Jr., on the board of trustees of Morehouse College. Just a few days before the nomination of Judge Thomas to the Supreme Court, Danforth had spoken in the Senate to defend race-conscious remedies of the kind Thomas had strenuously opposed. See Grove, "John Danforth's Noble Challenge," *Washington Post*, Oct. 7, 1991, D1; Clymer, "Washington at Work: Senator Faces a War on Two Fronts," *New York Times*, July 7, 1991, sec. 1, pt. 1, p. 12.

78. See T. Phelps and H. Winternitz, *Capitol Games: Clarence Thomas, Anita Hill, and the Story of a Supreme Court Nomination* (1992). Gray almost managed to derail the compromise embodied in the 1991 Civil Rights Act on the very day the act was signed. See Sedler, "Employment Equality, Affirmative Action, and the Constitutional Political Consensus" (book review), 90 *Michigan Law Review* 1315, 1335–36 (1992); Rosenthal, "Reaffirming Commitment, Bush Signs Rights Bill," *New York Times*, Nov. 22, 1991, A1.

79. Eaton, "Sununu Blocking Rights Accord, GOP Senator Charges," *Los Angeles Times*, June 28, 1991, A30, col. 1.

80. CNN Transcripts, Aug. 17, 1992. For other excerpts from Buchanan's speech, see chap. 2 above.

81. Some of his supporters were less restrained. At the Republican convention Dan Lungren, California's attorney general, went to some length to revive memories of Willie Horton and to call the Democrats soft on crime. At that time Vice President Quayle had only recently launched the trial balloon for a campaign proposition that welfare and sexual immorality in the inner cities were responsible for the 1992 riots in Los Angeles and elsewhere. As we saw in chap. 5, the balloon crashed.

82. Most notably, in *Webster v. Reproductive Health Services*, 492 U.S. 490 (1989), four Justices had strongly indicated that they would vote to overrule *Roe v. Wade*.

83. At his confirmation hearings Judge Thomas would express no views on the abortion question—indeed, he said he could not remember discussing *Roe v. Wade* seriously with anyone or expressing an opinion about the

decision. T. Phelps and H. Winternitz, n.38 above, at 179–80, 191–95. *Roe* had been decided while Clarence Thomas was a law student at Yale; he must have been the only person at the law school who did not discuss the case. It seems unlikely that his statements were taken at face value by many of the fifty-two senators who voted for his confirmation, let alone the forty-eight who voted against it.

84. It is generally understood that parts of the joint opinion were initially drafted separately in the three Justices' chambers; on opinion day, each of the three read a part of the opinion. Justices Blackmun and Stevens joined in several of the parts, and the concurrence of five Justices made those parts "the opinion of the Court."

85. For a capsule statement, see Karst, "The Supreme Court, 1976 Term— Foreword: Equal Citizenship under the Fourteenth Amendment," 91 *Harvard Law Review* 1, 5–11 (1977). For a longer treatment, see K. Karst, *Belonging to America: Equal Citizenship and the Constitution* (1989).

86. *Brown v. Board of Education,* 347 U.S. 483, 493 (1954).

87. 112 S. Ct. at 2686.

88. Justice Blackmun, concurring, joined by Justices Stevens and O'Connor, 112 S. Ct. at 2665.

89. J. Madison, "Memorial and Remonstrance against Religious Assessments" (1785), in 5 *The Founders' Constitution* 82, at 83 (P. Kurland and R. Lerner eds. 1987), quoted at 112 S. Ct. at 2674.

90. Justices Blackmun and Stevens joined in this section of the joint opinion.

91. 112 S. Ct. at 2809.

92. 112 S. Ct. at 2807.

93. 112 S. Ct. at 2831 (paragraphing omitted).

94. The Court upheld against a "facial attack" (a challenge to the law itself, in advance of any application) the part of the Pennsylvania law that imposed a 24-hour waiting period on a woman seeking abortion. For poor women, or rural women, this requirement may be quite onerous. It is important, however, to note the limited nature of the Court's holding on this issue. As the joint opinion makes clear, even in the *Casey* case itself the challenging parties can still offer evidence that the 24-hour wait requirement, as the opinion said in discussing the husband notice provision, is "likely to prevent a significant number of women from obtaining an abortion." If such a finding should be made, then we can expect the Court to hold the law invalid.

95. I relegate to this note the impressionistic bases for these intuitions. As for Justices O'Connor and Kennedy, I am closely acquainted with some people who have known them well, and conversations with them gave me some clear impressions of their character. Justice O'Connor's body of Supreme Court opinions are themselves good sources for forming intu-

itions, and before Judge Kennedy was nominated I had read a number of his opinions in the court of appeals on subjects in my field of constitutional law. As for Justice Souter, my belief came from two sources: first, anecdotal evidence from one who was for a time an insider at the New Hampshire Supreme Court and who saw the respect universally given to Judge Souter as an honest and careful judge; second, some of Judge Souter's responses to questions at his confirmation hearings. When he spoke movingly about his predecessor, Justice Brennan, either he was utterly sincere or he was an actor of exceptional talent. I discounted the "actor" hypothesis as improbable.

96. Dean Prager was a student in my last torts course more than twenty years ago, and she has been my colleague and good friend for more than three-quarters of the years since then. She is a first-rate judge of people.

97. These quotations appear in part in *Nomination of Anthony M. Kennedy to Be an Associate Justice of the United States Supreme Court*, [Senate] Executive Report 100–13, 100th Cong., 2d sess. (1988), at pp. 38, 2, and 39, respectively. The added words that fill out my rendering of Dean Prager's statements are taken from a videotape of the hearings before the Judiciary Committee. In response to a question about Judge Kennedy's likely treatment of women's issues, Dean Prager said she thought he was "a person who has a deep respect for the advancement of the law in these areas," and that she did not "think we're going to see any backtracking [from] where we are." This quotation is taken from the same videotape.

98. Ibid., at 8.

99. Before *Casey* was decided, E. J. Dionne, Jr., suggested that a consensus had formed among large numbers of Americans about abortion, and that the consensus was ambivalent. Americans seem to believe that a woman should have the right of choice, but they also believe: (a) that a million and a half abortions a year are too many; (b) that government ought to be able to insist on a short "think-it-over" waiting period; (c) that teenagers should be required to get their parents' permission—and so forth. Dionne, n.30 above, at 341–42.

100. In his view *Roe* "created a vast new class of abortion consumers and abortion proponents," partly by leading people to think, "If the Constitution guarantees abortion, how can it be bad?" *Casey* dissent, 112 S. Ct. at 2882. Of course the Constitution guarantees choice, not abortion.

101. See Kevin Phillips, "Pulpit Bullies: When the Big Tent Becomes a Revival Meeting," *Los Angeles Times*, Sept. 6, 1992, M1, col. 3.

102. The curtain rang down on the harsher uses of "family values" in a single week in early September. Gerstenzang, "Bush Retreats on 'Family Values' Issue, Asks Tolerance," *Los Angeles Times*, Sept. 12, 1992, A1, col. 5; Broder, "Quayle Tries to Distance Ticket from Anti-Gay Views," ibid., Sept. 9,

1992, A1, col. 5; Broder, "Quayle Appears to Soften His Stand on Abortion Ban," ibid., Sept. 14, 1992, A12, col. 1.

103. See the insightful analysis of Rachael Pine and Sylvia Law, "Envisioning a Future for Reproductive Liberty: Strategies for Making the Rights Real," 27 *Harvard Civil Rights–Civil Liberties Law Review* 407 (1992). With President Clinton's election Congress is considering, at this writing, a freedom-of-choice bill that would short-circuit at least some local political activity relating to abortion rights. For analysis of the legislative choices facing Congress, and the constitutionality of alternative approaches to such a law, see Lupu, "Statues Revolving in Constitutional Law Orbits," 79 *Virginia Law Review* 1, 37–52 (1993).

104. This is the language of his *Casey* dissent, 112 S. Ct. at 2884. See also his account of the general tradition of prayer at public ceremonies in his dissent in *Lee v. Weisman*, 112 S. Ct. at 2679–81.

105. *Casey* dissent, 112 S. Ct. at 2874. In a footnote, Justice Scalia distinguishes the "longstanding tradition" of laws forbidding interracial marriage, on the ground that the equal protection clause of the Fourteenth Amendment "explicitly establishes racial equality as a constitutional value." Ibid., at n.1. The clause, of course, does no such thing; what it says is that no state shall "deny to any person within its jurisdiction the equal protection of the laws." Now, "any person" is pretty broad, and yet surely the clause would not give a seven-year-old boy the right to marry his sister. Nor, when the clause became law in 1868, would the Supreme Court have interpreted it to protect an interracial marriage. A century would pass before the marriage of Mildred Jeter and Richard Loving came before the Court, and only then did the Court declare that a state could not constitutionally forbid an interracial marriage. See *Loving v. Virginia*, 388 U.S. 1 (1967). Are we supposed to believe that the highly uninformative text of the equal protection clause came to the Court in 1967 unencumbered by a traditional interpretation?

    For a telling critique of Justice Scalia's restricted view of constitutional liberty, see West, "The Ideal of Liberty: A Comment on Michael H. v. Gerald D.," 139 *University of Pennsylvania Law Review* 1373 (1991).

106. 112 S. Ct. at 2804–08.

107. Charles Fairman, discussing the framing and adoption of the Fourteenth Amendment, made a comment that resonates with Justice Kennedy's reference to "new perspectives." The notion of the privileges of citizenship, Fairman said, "is not static. As the nation experiences change—in its transportation, commerce and industry—in its political practices—in the way in which people live and work and move about—in the expectations they entertain about the quality of American life—surely the privilege of membership in this national community must broaden to include what has

become essential under prevailing circumstances." C. Fairman, *Reconstruction and Reunion, 1864–88,* pt. 1, at 1388 (1971), vol. 6 of P. Freund, ed., *History of the Supreme Court of the United States.*

108. Gerald Rosenberg has no use for this proposition, as applied either to *Brown* or to *Roe*. On *Roe*, see G. Rosenberg, *The Hollow Hope: Can Courts Bring about Social Change?* 173–425 (1991). In the text and notes of chap. 4 above, I dispute his view of *Brown* at some length. As to abortion rights, the Supreme Court did not take the leadership role. Without question, though, the Court's recognition in *Roe* of the constitutional status of a woman's right to reproductive choice gave the politics of abortion rights a symbolic core. The social issues agenda for abortion was effective only up to the point when that constitutional right seemed seriously endangered— and then the abortion issue became a liability for President Bush.

109. See generally T. Edsall and M. Edsall, *Chain Reaction: The Impact of Race, Rights, and Taxes on American Politics* (1991).

110. See Regina Austin's instructive analysis of this ambivalence in her article " 'The Black Community,' Its Lawbreakers, and a Politics of Identification," 65 *Southern California Law Review* 1769 (1992). Large numbers of black Americans believe (or at least suspect) that the plague of drugs is part of a white conspiracy to pacify young black men, or to keep them occupied in a civil war, or to provide a justification for locking them in prisons.

111. Joan Petersilia, former president of the American Society of Criminology, has offered a powerful capsule statement of the reasons why. Her main points are these: Criminal careers usually start around age 14, increase until the early 20s, and decline until around age 30. The average age of arrest in California is 17; the average age of first commitment is 26. Juveniles are not imprisoned; young first offenders are imprisoned only rarely; thus, prison terms generally are imposed when criminal activity is decreasing. More than half of all violent crimes are committed by offenders who are under the influence of alcohol or drugs, and so are unlikely to give much thought to the cost of potential imprisonment. One study suggests that prison (as opposed to probation) may even increase postrelease crime. Finally, "some crime—for example, car theft, fencing stolen property and distributing illegal drugs—does appear organized along the lines of a labor market. In these instances, an arrest and a prison sentence create a vacancy. Typically, however, that vacancy is quickly filled. As a result, crime in the community continues unabated." Petersilia, "Building More Jail Cells Will Not Make Us Safer," *Los Angeles Times,* Oct. 4, 1992, M6, col. 1. Petersilia's conclusion is not that we should stop imprisoning "the truly violent," but that we cannot afford to omit programs to alter the economic conditions that lead so many energetic young men to believe that crime is the only game in town.

112. When Lani Guinier's opponents pinned the "quotos" label on her, the President withdrew her nomination for head of the Justice Department's civil rights division. Lauter, "Clinton Withdraws Guinier as Nominee for Civil Rights Job," *Los Angeles Times*, June 4, 1993, A1, col. 5. Soon a 5–4 Supreme Court majority invalidated a group remedy for a voting rights violation, calling the remedy "racial gerrymandering." *Shaw v. Reno*, 61 U.S. Law Week 4818 (1993).

113. For example, in a 1992 "compliance review" of admissions policies of the law school of the University of California, Berkeley, the U.S. Education Department's Office of Civil Rights treated Justice Powell's *Bakke* opinion as authoritative, and criticized the school for its asserted failure to abide by that opinion. Letter of Gary D. Jackson, Regional Civil Rights Director, Region X, Office of Civil Rights, U.S. Department of Education, to Chancellor Chang-Lin Tien, dated Sept. 25, 1992.

114. *United Steelworkers v. Weber*, 443 U.S. 193 (1979). Justice Scalia explicitly called on the Court to overrule *Weber* in his opinion in *Johnson v. Transportation Agency*, 480 U.S. 616, 657 (1987) (dissenting opinion). Before he became a judge, Prof. Scalia scorned both the *Weber* decision and the racial-diversity aspect of the *Bakke* decision in his comment "The Disease As Cure," 1979 *Washington University Law Quarterly* 147.

115. Justice O'Connor, in *Richmond v. J. A. Croson Co.*, 488 U.S. 469, 493 (1989). A similar concern for appearances is central in Justice O'Connor's opinion for the Court in *Shaw v. Reno*, n.112 above.

116. I have traced this history, and the important roles played by Justices Powell and O'Connor, in my article "Private Discrimination and Public Responsibility: Patterson in Context," 1989 *Supreme Court Review* 1, 35–51. The text reference is to *Richmond v. J. A. Croson Co.*, n.5 above, in which the Court struck down Richmond's set-aside of 30 percent of city building contracts for minority-owned businesses. In her opinion for the Court, Justice O'Connor provided a how-to-do-it manual for a city that wants to justify such a set-aside as a remedy for past discrimination. The city and county of San Francisco followed these instructions, and their minority business set-aside has been provisionally upheld by the U.S. district court and the U.S. court of appeals. The courts held that the challenging building contractors had not shown a sufficient likelihood of success to justify a preliminary injunction against the affirmative action program. *Associated General Contractors of California v. Coalition for Economic Equity*, 950 F.2d. 1401 (9th Cir. 1991). See Equal Rights Advocates and the San Francisco Lawyers' Committee for Urban Affairs, "The Affirmative Action Handbook: How to Start and Defend Affirmative Action Programs," 3 *Yale Journal of Law and Liberation* 1 (1992).

117. See generally J. Handler and Y. Hasenfeld, *The Moral Construction of Pov-*

erty: Welfare Reform in America, 201–41 (1991). See also D. Ellwood, *Poor Support: Poverty in the American Family* (1988).

118. About one-quarter of the women who receive AFDC benefits have received them for ten years or more; these beneficiaries use almost two-thirds of AFDC funds. Ellwood, n.117 above, at 148.

119. For a persuasive defense of this strategy, see Theda Skocpol's article "Sustainable Social Policy: Fighting Poverty without Poverty Programs," *American Prospect,* Summer 1990, 58. A more elaborate version of this article appears in C. Jencks and P. Peterson, eds., *The Urban Underclass* (1991).

120. For recent personal accounts across a considerable range of economic conditions, see S. Terkel, *Race: How Blacks and Whites Think and Feel about the American Obsession* (1992); N. Lemann, *The Promised Land: The Great Black Migration and How It Changed America* (1991). E. Anderson, *Streetwise: Race, Class, and Change in an Urban Community* (1992); J. Jones, *The Dispossessed: America's Underclasses from the Civil War to the Present* (1992). For a vivid rendering of the feelings of black people of the working class, see J. Gwaltney, *Drylongso: A Self-Portrait of Black America* (1980).

121. P. Williams, *The Alchemy of Race and Rights: The Diary of a Law Professor,* 147 (1991).

122. I have already discussed Stephen Carter's views on the effects of affirmative action on black professionals. For a different perspective, emphasizing the extreme difficulty (or impossibility) of eradicating racism, see Derrick Bell's two powerful works *And We Are Not Saved: The Elusive Quest for Racial Justice* (1987) and *Faces at the Bottom of the Well: The Persistence of Racism* (1992). Bell disagrees with Carter on the subject of affirmative action, but agrees that black professionals feel the effects of racism in their own careers and more generally in their lives.

123. Derrick Bell has recently written, for example, of "the rules of racial standing," under which white listeners discount the testimony of black Americans about their own condition—unless the testimony says what the listeners want to hear. Bell, *Faces,* n.122 above, at 109–26. Some years ago Richard Delgado made an analogous point about legal scholarship in his article "The Imperial Scholar: Reflections on a Review of Civil Rights Literature," 132 *University of Pennsylvania Law Review* 561 (1984). Returning to the subject eight years later, he finds some improvement but no sweeping transformation. Delgado, "The Imperial Scholar Revisited: How to Marginalize Outsider Writing Ten Years Later," 140 *University of Pennsylvania Law Review* 1349 (1992).

124. See Charles Lawrence's article "The Id, the Ego, and Equal Protection: Reckoning with Unconscious Racism," 39 *Stanford Law Review* 317 (1987). On the larger social effects of unconscious racism, see Alexander Al-

einikoff's discussion in "A Case for Race-Consciousness," 91 *Columbia Law Review* 1060 (1991).

125. I have lifted this metaphor from Simón Bolívar, who said (of another America) in 1830, "America is ungovernable. Those who have served the revolution [against Spain] have plowed the sea." H. Herring, *A History of Latin America*, 286 (2d ed. 1961).

126. Bell, *Faces*, n.122 above, at 198–200. See also Bell, "Racism Is Here to Stay: Now What?" 35 *Howard Law Journal* 79 (1991).

127. Charles Lawrence, taking as a starting point W. E. B. DuBois's famous discussion of the "twoness of the American Negro," has recently offered a moving account of the crucial—and demanding—role of legal scholars "who experience the duality of belonging and not belonging." Lawrence, "The Word and the River: Pedagogy as Scholarship as Struggle," 65 *Southern California Law Review* 2231 (1992), at 2275. These scholars have accepted the demanding task of acting as cultural and institutional translators, all the while seeking fundamental changes in the institutions and the cultures they inhabit. Lawrence makes vivid the pains of this venture and the pains of the duality itself, but his fundamental message—to my mind, indispensable—is one of hope. Ibid., at 2291–98.

128. E.g., the "released time" program upheld in *Zorach v. Clauson*, 343 U.S. 306 (1952). The *Zorach* opinion is the paradigm expression of a broad view of the establishment clause's receptivity to governmental "accommodation" of religion.

129. A. Hertzke, *Representing God in Washington*, 161–98 (1988), ably analyzes the act's path through the Congress.

130. See Leedes, "Taking the Bible Seriously," 1987 *American Bar Foundation Research Journal* 311. See also K. Greenawalt, *Religious Convictions and Political Choice* (1988).

131. The Supreme Court held Louisiana's law invalid in *Edwards v. Aguillard*, 482 U.S. 578 (1987). This decision may not be the last word on the subject. See Phillip Johnson's critique of a more recent decision of a U.S. court of appeals in a case involving the University of Alabama's restrictions on the activities of a creationist professor, both in class and out. Johnson, "The Creationist and the Sociobiologist: Two Stories about Illiberal Education," 80 *California Law Review* 1071, 1073–80 (1992). The case is *Bishop v. Aronov*, 926 F.2d 1066 (11th Cir. 1991), certiorari denied, 112 S. Ct. 3026 (1992).

132. A considerably more controversial proposal for accommodation would provide state funding for education through a voucher system that would extend to parents of children in religious schools as well as parents of children in public schools and secular private schools. The Constitution aside, there are reasons for skepticism about the wisdom of such a program, reasons centering on its foreseeable effects on the education of poor

children. And, even after *Zobrest v. Catalina Foothills School District*, 113
S.Ct. 2462 (1993), doubts remain as to the program's constitutionality. See
generally Sugarman, "New Perspectives on 'Aid' to Private School Users,"
in E. West, ed., *Nonpublic School Aid: The Law, Economics, and Politics of
American Education*, at 64 (1976). For a recent argument in favor of a
voucher system, agnostic on the inclusion of religious schools, see
J. Chubb and T. Moe, *Politics, Markets, and America's Schools* (1990).

133. M. Walzer, *Spheres of Justice: A Defense of Pluralism and Equality*, 240 (1983).
134. Carl Schneider, writing of the clash of cultures in the area of sexual
morality, says that one "advantage of a political, as opposed to a judicial,
solution to the conflict over what sort of society we are to be is that it can
give people some sense of control over their environments and their lives."
Schneider, "State-Interest Analysis in Fourteenth Amendment 'Privacy"
Law: An Essay on the Constitutionalization of Social Issues," 51 *Law and
Contemporary Problems* 79, at 117 (Winter 1988). The "people" in this statement are those who can command a legislative majority, writing their
views of sexual morality into coercive laws forbidding or severely restricting birth control, abortion, homosexual sex, and the like. It is not easy to
understand how these laws will enhance the sense of control for the gay
and lesbian Americans and the sexually active women whose environments and lives are the objects of the laws' coercion.
135. E.g., R. Bork, *The Tempting of America* (1989).
136. On tolerance and constitutional equality, see generally Karst, n.10 above,
at 97, 183–84, 207–08.
137. *The Federalist*, no. 51 (Madison 1788). See the discussion of Madison above.
138. See, e.g., L. Coser, *The Functions of Social Conflict*, 139–49 (1956).
139. See West, "The Feminist-Conservative Anti-Pornography Alliance and the
1986 Attorney General's Commission on Pornography Report," 1987 *American Bar Foundation Research Journal* 681. See chap. 3 above.
140. On the American civic culture, see Karst, "Paths to Belonging: The Constitution and Cultural Identity," 64 *North Carolina Law Review* 303, 367–68
(1986).
141. Randall Terry, quoted in Savage, "Abortion Foes Target Doctors for Harassment," *Los Angeles Times*, March 14, 1993, A1, col. 2. Two weeks later
Terry deplored the murder of a doctor outside a Pensacola birth control
clinic.
142. Maya Stolzenberg demonstrates that the "liberal" jurisprudence reflected
in the *Mozert* decision (outlined in chap. 3 at n.26) produces its own brand
of official indoctrination: the use of public schools to inculcate children
with an ideology of tolerance. This ideology is seen as harmful by parents
who believe that they and their children face eternal damnation if the children read books positively portraying "humanist" or "feminist" values. As

Stolzenberg also shows, no magic formula can resolve such a conflict in values, given a system of compulsory and largely public schooling. Stolzenberg, " 'He Drew a Circle That Shut Me Out': Assimilation, Indoctrination, and the Paradox of a Liberal Education," 106 *Harvard Law Review* 581 (1993). For contrasting views on the free exercise claim in *Mozert*, see Breyer, "Cinderella, the Horse God and the Wizard of Oz: Mozert v. Hawkins County Public Schools," 20 *Journal of Law and Education* 63 (1991) (arguing, contrary to *Mozert*, for a free exercise right of parents to choose to have their children excused from public school "indoctrination" in secularism); and Sullivan, "Religion and Liberal Democracy," 59 *University of Chicago Law Review* 195, 220 (1992) (*Mozert* was correctly decided).

To put it another way, the "paradox of pluralism" is that it is impossible to accord equal respect and validity for all positions when one of the positions thus respected and validated is an absolutism that brooks no contradiction. See Ladd, "Politics and Religion in America: The Enigma of Pluralism," in J. Pennock and J.Chapman, eds, *NOMOS XXX: Religion, Morality, and the Law,* at 263, 277–78 (1988).

143. Canavan, "The Pluralist Game," 44 *Law and Contemporary Problems* 23, 36 (1981).
144. R. Neuhaus, *The Naked Public Square,* 197 (1984).

Index

Cheney, Dick, 128
Chodorow, Nancy, 223n
Christian Coalition, 29, 294–95n
Christian fundamentalists. *See* Evangelical
and fundamentalist Christians
Christian holidays, 148, 150, 154–60
Christians. *See* Evangelical and fundamentalist Christians
Christmas, 148, 150, 154, 155, 159–60
Christopher Commission, 72
Citizenship. *See* Equal citizenship
Civil Rights Act of *1866*, 81, 82, 84
Civil Rights Act of *1964*, 27, 65–66, 68, 82–84, 94
Civil Rights Act of *1991*, 85, 172, 189–92, 200, 204, 207, 208
Civil rights movement: and blacks, 4–5; expressive methods of, 11, 91–92; Goldwater on, 73; messages of liberation in, 95–96; and Nixon, 1, 27; retrenchment in, 206; and social issues agenda, 74–75; and Supreme Court, 9, 10, 75–76, 94–95, 107, 188–92; and working-class white men, 7
Civil War, 113–14, 135
Clecak, Peter, 168
Clinton, Bill: and abortion, 29, 51, 231n, 302n; Buchanan on, 29; and gays and lesbians in military, 112, 129–31; and racial "quotas," 304n; significance of election of, 204
Clinton, Hillary, 29–30
Cold War, 161, 165
Colker, Ruth, 293n
Colorado, constitutional amendment on sexual orientation, 66, 182–87, 200
Colorado for Family Values, 295n
Columbus, Ohio, busing in, 69
Combat exclusion, for women in military, 112, 116–24, 136, 137
Common Cause, 22
Communications media. *See* Media; Television
Community, membership in, 167–68
Congress: on abortion, 178; and affirmative action, 173–74; and civil rights legis-

lation, 68, 189; dispersal of power in, 25; and presidential veto, 26; and racial discrimination in employment, 81, 84–85; Senate confirmation hearing of Clarence Thomas, 108–10, 190–91; and social issues agenda, 24–26; and student religious or political groups in public high schools, 159
Conkle, Daniel, 285n
Constantine I, 281n
Contraception. *See* Birth control
Contract lease system, 78
Coser, Lewis, 239n
"Counter-majoritarian difficulty," 177–80
Court cases. *See* Supreme Court; and names of specific cases
Crenshaw, Kimberlé, 110, 207, 224n, 251n, 298n
Crime: current anxieties and resentments on, 203–07; Goldwater on, 73; interracial crime, 70–71; and race, 68–74, 137, 203–07
Criminal justice: current anxieties and resentments on, 203–207; and law and order theme, 71; and Nixon, 27, 188; Supreme Court on, 8, 21, 27, 68, 188
Cultural counterrevolution: constituency for, 1–2, 7–8, 16, 21–23, 202–11; as contest for influence over dominance of expression, 3; and formal racial neutrality, 74–77; and social issues agenda, 1–2, 16; and Supreme Court, 8, 9, 21, 187–89, 193–202, 209. *See also* Family values; Social issues agenda; and other issues
Cultural pluralism. *See* Pluralism
Culture, definition of, 17

D'Emilio, John, 236n
Danforth, John, 191–92, 201, 204, 205, 299n
Davis, David Brion, 237n
De Beauvoir, Simone, 32, 214n
Defense Department, 116, 122, 125–29, 131–32, 136
Delgado, Richard, 253n, 255–56n, 305n